Gender at Work

Howard Giles
General Editor

Vol. 18

The Language as Social Action series
is part of the Peter Lang Media and Communication list.
Every volume is peer reviewed and meets
the highest quality standards for content and production.

PETER LANG
New York • Bern • Frankfurt • Berlin
Brussels • Vienna • Oxford • Warsaw

Melanie C. Steffens & Ma. Àngels Viladot

Gender at Work

A Social Psychological Perspective

PETER LANG
New York • Bern • Frankfurt • Berlin
Brussels • Vienna • Oxford • Warsaw

Library of Congress Cataloging-in-Publication Data

Steffens, Melanie C.
Gender at work: a social psychological perspective / Melanie C. Steffens, Ma. Àngels Viladot.
pages cm. — (Language as social action; vol. 18)
Includes bibliographical references and index.
1. Sex role in the work environment. 2. Sex discrimination in employment.
3. Sexism. 4. Women—Employment. I. Viladot, Maria Angels. II. Title.
HD6060.6.S74   306.3'615—dc23   2015009644
ISBN 978-1-4331-2204-0 (hardcover)
ISBN 978-1-4331-2203-3 (paperback)
ISBN 978-1-4539-1534-9 (e-book)
ISSN 1529-2436

Bibliographic information published by **Die Deutsche Nationalbibliothek**.
Die Deutsche Nationalbibliothek lists this publication in the "Deutsche
Nationalbibliografie"; detailed bibliographic data are available
on the Internet at http://dnb.d-nb.de/.

Cover art by Lorraine Hurley

The paper in this book meets the guidelines for permanence and durability
of the Committee on Production Guidelines for Book Longevity
of the Council of Library Resources.

© 2015 Peter Lang Publishing, Inc., New York
29 Broadway, 18th floor, New York, NY 10006
www.peterlang.com

All rights reserved.
Reprint or reproduction, even partially, in all forms such as microfilm,
xerography, microfiche, microcard, and offset strictly prohibited.

Printed in the United States of America

CONTENTS

Preface   vii
Introduction   1

Part I: Stereotypes, Attitudes, and Social Roles   11
Chapter 1.   Gender Stereotypes   13
Chapter 2.   Implicit Cognition   23
Chapter 3.   Effects of Stereotypes on Judging Others   33
Chapter 4.   Effects of Stereotypes on One's Own Behavior   53
Chapter 5.   Gender Attitudes   63
Chapter 6.   Gender Differences   71
Chapter 7.   Social Role Theory   93
Chapter 8.   Maintaining Social Hierarchies   105
Chapter 9.   Career Choice   113
Chapter 10.   The Role of Organizational Cultures   123
Chapter 11.   Role Models   133
Chapter 12.   Parenthood and Work-related Impressions   137
Chapter 13.   Conclusions   145

Part II: Social Identities, Communication, and Gender ... 155
Chapter 14. Social Identity Perspective ... 157
Chapter 15. Identity Management Strategies ... 165
Chapter 16. Discrimination and Self-discrimination of Women at Work ... 179
Chapter 17. Conservatives Versus Liberals ... 191
Chapter 18. Interactions Between Gender and Power: Sexual Harassment ... 195
Chapter 19. Communication Accommodation Theory and Intergender Boundaries ... 203
Chapter 20. Intergroup Contact, Gender, and Leadership ... 215
Chapter 21. Leadership and Gender Identity in Organizations ... 223
Chapter 22. Conclusions ... 235

Epilogue ... 241
References ... 247
Index ... 289
Author Index ... 299

PREFACE

In numbers greater than ever before, women today are working in business and industry, law and medicine, academics and government, no longer only as support staff for male executives but as managers and executives in their own right. With some regularity, newspaper articles and television programs profile women who have "made it," doing extraordinarily well in fields that were previously lacking any high-level female representation. Yet while the increases in women's professional attainments are measurable, they are only partial. The 2014 Forbes' list of "The world's most powerful people" was proclaimed notable because for the first time, two women were listed among the top 10 (German Chancellor Angela Merkel and U.S. Federal Reserve Chair Janet Yellen). But at the same time, only 7 women were included in the next 90 rungs on the ladder of those deemed powerful. Glass ceilings, glass cliffs (Ryan & Haslam, 2005), and labyrinths (Eagly & Carli, 2007) remain, posing challenges to women who want to attain equity in their careers and their lives.

In the words of Virginia Valian (1997), "Why so slow?" Why, after four to five decades of discussion and debate, assessment and appraisal, do the statistics still show that gender equity is far from a reality in organizations throughout the world? So often, the first answers to this question focus on women themselves. What are they doing wrong? What could they do differently?

Why don't they do what men do? In her best-selling book on women in business, for example, Sheryl Sandberg (2013) advised women to "lean in" and tried, using personal anecdotes as well as social science data, to encourage women to develop their "will to lead."

But as social psychologists Melanie Steffens and Ma. Àngels Viladot well know, a full explanation of women's progress, or the lack thereof, requires an understanding of the cognitive biases and the interpersonal processes that operate in any organizational setting. The first choice of a social psychologist is typically to look to the situation for factors that influence behavior—in this case, the behavior of women and men in the organization and behavior toward women and men in these settings. And that is exactly what social scientists have been doing for nearly half a century.

In the early 1970s, investigators began to show that the simple act of attaching a woman's name versus a man's name to a work product will lead to different evaluations, typically enhancing the evaluation of a man relative to that of a woman. Similarly, my colleagues and I showed that explanations for a successful outcome also varied, attributed by observers to skill if done by a man and to luck if done by a woman. This finding, which has been replicated with depressing regularity over the years (though with "extra effort" sometimes accorded to women rather than simply "dumb luck"), has become so commonplace as to emerge in the popular press as general knowledge, needing no scientific stamp of validity. Hundreds of other significant findings have emerged in subsequent decades to identify the conditions and factors that encourage and perpetuate unequal opportunity and uneven progress toward equity in the workplace. Researchers in these fields are not typically content, however, to simply document the contributing factors. Rather than viewing these conditions as invariant and inalterable, the social psychological perspective assumes that situations can change and, when they do, behavior will change as well. Thus, the intellectual agenda is to articulate the conditions that are likely to lead to one outcome over another and to show how change is possible.

It is this belief in the possibility of change that underlies the efforts that Melanie Steffens and Ma. Àngels Viladot have undertaken here. As representatives of an army of social scientists who have been studying gender for nearly half a century, Steffens and Viladot have culled the literature in social psychology, communication, and other related fields to present an up-to-date summary of just what we do know about gender as it influences activities in the work setting. When are outcomes for women and men most likely to be different? How does discrimination operate and when is it most likely to occur? How do these processes operate within the individual, among people, and between groups defined on the basis of their gender composition? These are the kinds of questions that Steffens and Viladot address in this volume.

The book is not merely a summary of the science, however. Throughout the book, Steffens and Viladot provide thoughtful evaluation and integration of the relevant evidence, offering interpretations and drawing conclusions. More importantly, and perhaps more uniquely, their intended audience is not limited to their academic compatriots. A major goal of *Gender at Work* is to encourage change in the workplace by giving nonacademic readers a clearer understanding of how gender operates and how constraining and discriminatory situations might be changed. Thus, in addition to summary, Steffens and Viladot also offer some advice to those who may want to create more equitable working climates for women and men alike.

It is the authors' hope, and my hope as well, that this book will be widely read and taken to head and heart. For those readers who are in a position to enact change in organizations, the information and insights that this book provides can help to increase the opportunities available to all workers and to more rapidly progress toward a truly equitable work setting.

Kay Deaux

New York

INTRODUCTION

What is the current state of affairs?

Women's roles in many societies have changed dramatically over the last hundred years. In little more than a century, women have gained the rights to obtaining an education, to voting, to running for public office via election, and choosing to work without their father's or husband's consent. In short, gender equality in the eyes of the law has mostly been obtained. In hindsight, some of the dates at which equal rights for women were acquired appear out of sync. As one example from the realm of sports, the Austrian soccer association prohibited women's teams in 1957 and did not officially recognize them until 1982 (from Wikipedia). Of course, there are also many countries in the world today where women still do not possess the same rights as men.

In many countries, women have caught up with men in education (United Nations Development Program Human Development Report, 2014). In fact, they now even outnumber male students in some countries (e.g., U.S. Department of Education, 2000). Equal education, it should seem, is an ideal precondition for gaining equality at work. Alas, such equality is nowhere in sight. The United Nations' Gender Inequality Index reflects inequality in men's and women's achievement in health, empowerment, and the labor market. As one figure reported there, the share of women's seats in government is below 50% in all major countries and a low 21% on average in the world. Women also still trail behind men with respect to participation in the labor force. Women's participation has increased from 43% to 59% between 1970 and 2004 in the United States, whereas participation among men decreased from 80% to 73% (U.S. Department of Labor, 2005).

The difference between women's and men's career success is all the more visible when it comes to more prestigious, higher paying jobs. Men still earn significantly more than women (Blau & Kahn, 2000; Kulich, Trojanowski, Ryan, Haslam, & Renneboog, 2011) and are more likely to be promoted (Blau & DeVaro, 2007), even when factors as important as experience or qualifications are similar (Hoyt, 2010). This bias, far from being a problem unique to executive positions, seems to operate at all levels of the organizational hierarchy (Eagly & Carli, 2004, 2007). Although women in the United States account for about half of the labor force, less than 15% of executive management positions in the Fortune 500 list in 2013 were held by women, a number that has remained flat in the last decade (Mulligan-Ferry, Bartkiewicz, Soares, Singh, & Winkleman, 2014). In Germany, an increase in women taking over leadership positions was reported, from 10% in 1996 to 21% in 2004 (German Federal Office of Statistics, 2006). But in top management and in boards of directors, percentages are only around 10% (see van Quaquebeke & Schmerling, 2010).

In academia, women also have less access to careers and lower chances to achieve the highest positions. The recent "She Figures Report 2012—Gender in Research and Innovation" from the European Commission provides the following evidence. In 2010, the proportion of female students (55%) and graduates (59%) exceeded that of male students, but men outnumbered women among PhD students and graduates (the proportion of female students was 49% and that of PhD graduates was 46%). Furthermore, women represented only 44% of lower level academic staff, 37% of intermediate level and 20% of highest level staff. The underrepresentation of women is even more striking in the fields of science and engineering. The proportion of women increased from just 31% of the student population at the first level to 38% of PhD students and 35% of PhD graduates, but it stood at 32% of lower level positions, 23% and just 11% at intermediate and highest level positions, respectively.

Women also earn considerably less money than men. In no country in the world do women earn more than about 80% of what men earn (for a review, see Lips, 2013). This is even the case after important predictors of income, such as education and specialization, are taken into account. For example, women in medicine, engineering, and management earn substantially less than their male colleagues with equal qualifications. Female faculty earn more than $3,000 less per year than their male colleagues after adjusting for discipline, rank, and years of service, both in female- and male-dominated disciplines.

Why this book?

Given women's equal or even better education, the question of course is this: Why? Why does women's education pay off less than men's, on average? Why do men with better final grades later earn more, but this relation is absent for women (e.g., Evers & Sieverding, 2014)? When all factors that should explain career success are taken into account, why are women still less successful than men (Abele, 2000)? The answers to these questions are not simple or straightforward. In fact, our senses may be bombarded with daily answers from TV, newsprint, popular books, and many other sources.

Strikingly, "authors who write about the engaging gender questions of the day often fail to ground their answers in psychological research. Why?" (Eagly & Wood, 2013, p. 340). Similarly, the debate surrounding the small number of women in science has been described as "often superficial and unsupported by scientific evidence. Why was this the case?" (Williams & Ceci, 2007, p. 9). In our view, the answers social-psychological research provides are often not easily accessible to a more general audience of nonpsychologists because the findings of original research studies are scattered over many specialized scientific journals; the texts are typically not available to the public (for free). Even if they are, the writing may appear inaccessible to nonexperts. With this book, we hope to make that research more accessible to an academic audience interested in this issue. We believe the presented research is of great interest to a large audience, and a book that reviews the evidence in an accessible way can have a big impact on people's thinking and decision making in this central area of sustained injustice.

Social-psychological research, broadly defined, provides many excellent answers to questions concerning gender at work. Many of the work contexts we are interested in for these purposes are domains (e.g., engineering) and positions (e.g., leadership elite) that are marked by women's underrepresentation. Instead of speculating about women's and men's different career motivations, we turn to the scientific evidence. Instead of wondering whether women are still discriminated, we look at the host of studies testing this. Instead of believing that gender differences in ability explain differences in men's and women's career trajectories, we review the evidence in this domain. In short, there is hardly any question that one needs to speculate about. Answers have already been provided by research from social psychology and related fields including, but not limited to, cognitive psychology, economics, and sociology. Admittedly, each of the thousands of studies that have been conducted typically looks only at one small aspect. Studies provide scientifically grounded responses concerning one of the pieces in the puzzle at a time. So what is still needed is an integration and weighting of the evidence—something we undertake throughout the book and particularly toward the end of each section where we draw conclusions.

Does gender play a role at work at all?

In principle, there is no reason why the relationship between a supervisor and a subordinate, or between colleagues at work, or between a buyer and a seller, should have anything to do with their genders. If you go to the market to buy fruit and cheese, it should be completely irrelevant whether it is a man or a woman you buy them from or even whether the person's gender is indeterminable. These relationships are task-centered because they are focused on the products and services that are developed or sold. However, there is consensus among researchers that gender roles spill over to the workplace (see Eagly & Karau, 2002). This means that male supervisors can be perceived differently from female supervisors, and male and female employees doing similar things may be perceived differently. In turn, they may be treated differently, including rewards and punishments. To illustrate, take the following recent quotation about a German minister (taken from the German weekly newspaper *Die Zeit*, 32, 2014, p. 55): "If she seeks dialogue, she is interpreted to be a weak leader. If she does not, she is accused of ruling too much." Would a male minister be the object of the same criticism? We can only speculate about the answer. As another illustration, take the following reflections on dress codes for in Europe female top politicians: "… they are asked to modify their outfit in order to adapt to male discretion. If they do not, they are sanctioned for dressing in a too striking way…. But if they appear very masculine they are also sanctioned. So women face a dilemma on how to dress" (Gallego, 2014,

El País, p. 85). Often, someone's gender does not have a big influence on what that person does and how he or she behaves in a certain job. We will see in this book that behavior is often tied to social roles: Ministers need to make informed decisions, and so they do, whether they are male or female, dressed colorfully or in a black suit. But how is their behavior interpreted? What do we think about it? There is a thin line between being perceived as "a weak leader" and "ruling too much," dressing "not discrete enough" or "too masculine." People's perceptions concerning this may differ depending, among other things, on the actor's gender. Of course, this is primarily a social-psychological perspective: How do people's interpretations of others' behavior depend on the social groups they belong to? Therefore, we as social psychologists set out to provide comprehensive responses in the text that follows.

In fact, gender plays such a big role at work that many talk about *gender segregation* (see Pratto, Stallworth, Sidanius, & Siers, 1997): There are women's jobs such as hairdresser and nurse and men's jobs such as carpenter and scientist. Also within the same firms, men and women typically split up, for example, into bosses and secretaries. Even within the same professions, men and women may end up in different specializations, such as male managers who are responsible for the products and female managers who are responsible for personnel. It is hard to imagine where gender does not play a role at work. The aim of this book is to shed light on all the different ways that work-related perceptions, attributions, outcomes, and the like differ for women and men. Do gender stereotypes lead to discrimination of women? Do men and women behave differently because of these stereotypes? How do communication processes at work differ between women and men? Do traditional social roles of mothers and fathers influence careers in different ways? These are examples of the many questions that we turn to in the text that follows.

Our perspective

If men are interested in different careers than women, why should anyone care? We want to be clear from the beginning about one thing that we are not interested in: There is no need to obtain equal numbers of men and women in each and every profession. If male doctors are more interested in specializing in surgery and female doctors prefer specializing in pediatrics, why object to this? There is no reason to interfere with choices if more men than women are interested in engineering and more women than men in veterinary medicine. But as we will see, matters are not that simple. Fairness enters into the equation. There are systematic forces in our cultures that (given equal talent, interest, etc.) encourage members of one gender, while deterring the other, to carry out certain behaviors, to develop certain skills, and to choose certain jobs. This is all the more so if these jobs systematically differ in prestige, power, and income. We describe the state of knowledge regarding strong forces working against equal opportunities for all. Readers can then form their own opinions on this basis.

The literature available on gender-related issues concerning work is huge. Out of necessity, we focus on some studies while omitting others that are also important. We devote more space to some topics than others based on our evaluation of their importance and on the available literature. We also take a specific perspective. It is not our intention to portray women as poor, helpless victims and men as bad perpetrators. However, current gender relations must be understood in the context of a historically patriarchal culture characterized by power hierarchies. We will see that this past still has a potent influence on young men's and women's chances in life. (Though young women often disagree at this point, we hope that some of their thinking has changed by the time they read our conclusions.) Similarly, to avoid portraying victims and perpetrators, we try not to ask biased questions. As we will see in the chapter on communication, one example of such bias is if gender differences concerning work-related aspects are explained with a focus on women. Instead, one could focus on men or on both (Hegarty, Lemieux, & McWueen, 2010; Hegarty & Pratto, 2001, 2004). We will also see that there are few if any cases where research questions boil down to differences in women's and men's traits (such as an individual being too emotional or too dominant to reach some goal). Instead, the interpretation and interaction of self and other in a social system structured by gender stereotypes, traditional power hierarchies, and group identities are often key.

Most of the literature we cite is from the United States because the majority of the research on the topic has been conducted there. In addition, we provide a European perspective wherever possible, including research conducted in Spain, Germany, the United Kingdom, and other countries. Still, our approach is restricted to Western cultures and to the groups that have been studied. Only recently, psychology has started to pay attention to intersections of social identities (see Cole, 2009; Shields, 2008): People belong to several social categories at once. For example, they are not only women, but they may also be Black, working class, or lesbian. Traditionally, research pertaining to women has overlooked those minorities. We include research on these subcategories of women but must concede that there is far too little literature to arrive at a full picture of the situation of those groups.

How large are gender differences?

If you were to divide a large group of people into two groups for some analysis, which groups would you select? Much of the older literature on the social and cognitive psychology of gender has focused on the development of a catalog of gender differences, be they real, perceived, or suspected. In general, this research has yielded inconsistent results. As you may imagine, gender is one of the preferred ways of splitting a group into two. Gender differences are often stressed while similarities are not (Unger, 1979). However, variations within each gender group are typically much larger than between-gender differences (e.g., Fiske, 2010; Reilly & Neumann, 2013). For example, the difference between the women with the lowest and the highest verbal ability scores is much larger than the difference between the average woman and the average man.

What would you discover if you divided people into four groups, by gender and occupation? You would probably find that those in the same occupation, whether male or female, are more similar, psychologically, to each other than to the other groups. For example, male and female entrepreneurs were found to be more similar to each other than to nonentrepreneurs (see Johnson & Powell, 1994; Powell & Ansic, 1997). In another study, male and female graduates of medicine differed neither in typically male traits such as independence and self-confidence nor in typically female traits such as being gentle and understanding of others (Evers & Sieverding, 2014). In other words, knowing about a person, whether he or she is an entrepreneur, a medical doctor, a kindergarten teacher, or a carpenter, gives us much more work-related information on what the person is like than knowing whether he or she is male or female. As another example, risk propensity in Finnish business owners differed much more from U.S. business owners than the men and women in each country differed from each other (Hyrsky & Tuunanen, 1999). In that case, being Finnish or American was much more informative for knowing something about their willingness to take risks than being male or female. In spite of this, there are a lot of attempts to explain gender differences in risk propensity and few attempts to explain intercultural differences. The take-home message is that gender differences in work-relevant traits, attitudes, and behaviors are generally overestimated. We would be well served in approaching men and women in the same profession with the general idea that they are very similar to each other, not different.

Terminology and overview

Throughout this volume, we use the terms *gender differences*, *gender groups*, *gender stereotypes*, and the like to take into account that gender expressions are influenced by the individuals, groups, and societies surrounding us (i.e., gender categories are socially constructed, as we explain in the section on stereotypes). Using a term such as *sex differences* implies that sex categories are a biological given. In recent years, philosophical and sociological analyses have yielded that this is not the case; the commonly practiced "sex assignment treatment" of intersexual infants immediately after birth is a case in point (see Gregor, 2014): Biology is adapted to fit the culture. There is no biological antecedent that exists outside of cultural practices. Therefore, we decided not to refer to sex differences, for example, but to consider the cultural aspect throughout by speaking about gender. Using this language, we keep in mind that "science is a dynamic process, and the certainty of yesterday can easily be replaced by ambiguity today, or vice versa" (Deaux, 1993, p. 125).

The same is, of course, true for all of our elaborations here. It is possible that factors that have been overlooked up to this point will be considered crucial in 10 years and that other factors will play a less prominent role by then. This is also the case because societies are changing. Thus, some things that we discuss today as restricting women's and men's opportunities may, 30 years from now, appear as anachronistic as the late official recognition of women's soccer in Austria.

How is the present text organized? It may not be an overgeneralization to state that social psychology is a perspective that focuses on the social situation—we as social psychologists do not regard people as fixed, with certain traits and behaviors that result from these. Rather, the social situation in which people find themselves plays a predominant role in explaining their behavior. A group of male teenagers may behave very differently than each of them would on their own. A woman is perceived and acts differently if she is the only woman in government rather than one among many. In the first part of the book, written by Melanie Steffens, we regard *Gender at Work* as based on stereotypes, attitudes, and social roles. After we review gender-specific theories, we apply more general social-psychological theories to our topic. Subsequently, beginning with Chapter 9, we focus on various applied questions. At the end of Part I, we draw a first set of conclusions and recommendations. As mentioned, most of these research perspectives originated in the United States.

Taking a social identity and communication perspective, in the second part of the book, Ma. Àngels Viladot goes much more into the details of situations in which men and women interact, carrying even further the situational account. The social identity perspective also adds a more European stance to the topic. Again, these general theories are applied to the context of gender at work and then conclusions are presented. The epilogue draws these two parts together. Generally, the theories we present are complementary rather than contradictory, each of them adding pieces to the puzzle of why men's and women's careers are so different.

Finally, before we start, we need to thank many people who supported the making of this book. We are indebted to Howie Giles for his quick and enthusiastic support during the whole project and to Mary Savigar from Peter Lang for her professional guidance. We are delighted to have won Irena D. Ebert for writing parts of the chapters on gender stereotypes, implicit cognition, and gender attitudes, and Kay Deaux for writing the preface. Finally, we thank our first readers for their most helpful comments that made us notice where our writing was less easy to understand than we thought—Jordi Aymerich, Lorraine Hurley, Nadine Knab, Clara Montagut, Iris Paschedag, and Gloria Rubiol.

PART I: STEREOTYPES, ATTITUDES, AND SOCIAL ROLES

The first eight chapters provide various theoretical perspectives relevant to *Gender at Work*. To better understand men's and women's different careers, we start with explaining gender stereotypes in Chapter 1. As we will review, such stereotypes may not only affect how we perceive and evaluate others' behavior, but their effect on how we see ourselves may be even more profound. Also, gender stereotypes are insidious because they comprise not only aspects that people are aware of but also more automatic ("unconscious") ones that are hard to avoid.

We then turn to gender attitudes—evaluations of men and women and of their roles in society ("sexism"). Gender stereotypes suggest that, on average, men and women differ a lot, psychologically. Our chapter on gender differences takes a close look at the evidence concerning this question. In the final theory section, we review theories that focus on gender roles, gender hierarchies, and how they are maintained.

· 1 ·

GENDER STEREOTYPES

"Women are interested in people and men in things."
"Men and women have different leadership styles."
"Men are better at math than women, and women have higher verbal abilities than men."
"Given the same objective information, people will form a better impression of a man's than a woman's work-related skills."

These quotes are just a few of the gender-related myths *or* scientifically corroborated facts that may be of relevance in many work contexts. But which are the myths and which are the facts? The responses to this question follow in this and subsequent chapters.

Imagine you are communicating over the Internet with a person and you do not know whether you are writing to a man or a woman. Will you find out? Does it matter at all? One of the major ways to categorize people in our culture is by gender. If your communication partner likes to watch soccer, drink beer, and marvel at cars, you may be inclined to think it is a man. However, if the person possesses 30 pairs of shoes and talks for hours on the phone, this rather seems to be a woman. These are only a few gender clichés among many others that promptly come to mind. We all have ideas about what is typically female and typically male. How helpful is this gender knowledge? Is it useful? Or will it turn out to be deceptive and potentially bias perception and action?

Definition of stereotypes and related constructs

If our feeling, thinking, and behavior toward another person is influenced by a social category this person belongs to, we deal with *prejudice, stereotypes,* and *discrimination*. Social psychologists distinguish these interrelated concepts from each other. According to a classical model, prejudice, stereotypes, and discrimination correspond to three components of *attitudes* (e.g., Katz & Stotland, 1959). An attitude can be defined as an evaluation of people, objects, or ideas (see Olson & Zanna, 1993). The first, *affective component*, refers to the feelings and emotions that are associated with the attitude object. For example, if you like risk taking, you will experience thrill and joy when engaging in some risky choice during gambling. The *cognitive component* includes a person's thoughts and beliefs associated with the attitude object. For example, when gambling, you try to evaluate the options and their associated chances of winning and losing. The behavioral component encompasses how a person acts with respect to the attitude object. For instance, if you like risk taking, you will choose more risky options than a person who is risk averse. We chose the example of risk taking because there has been much debate about gender differences in risk propensity that we review in Chapter 6 on gender differences.

When the attitude object is a social category, the three attitude components are prejudice, stereotypes, and discrimination. Prejudice is related to the affective reaction toward a person based on his or her group membership, whereas stereotypes and discrimination are the cognitive and behavioral responses, respectively (see Eagly & Mladinic, 1989). Stereotypes can be defined as assumptions concerning the traits and behaviors of members of social groups (Kite, Deaux, & Haynes, 2008). Stereotypes operate as generalizations or rules of thumb, ascribing all members of a given group identical characteristics, neglecting variations within the group. These characteristics include many attributes, such as physical features (e.g., men are taller than women), personality traits (e.g., men are aggressive; women are anxious), skills (e.g., girls are good at language; boys are good at math), preferences (e.g., men are interested in sports; women are interested in fashion), and everyday behaviors: Who puts flowers on their desk, wraps presents carefully, repairs the drain, and puts the meat on the grill (Athenstaedt, 2003)? These examples show that stereotypic contents are not confined to negative characteristics but comprise positive aspects as well. Gender stereotypes also comprise aspects of jobs (Deaux & Lewis, 1984). In fact, gender stereotypes are so deeply ingrained in our culture that there are even typical female and male food items, drinks, colors, sports, cars, shapes, and so on (see Gal & Wilkie, 2010). Cultural stereotypes are socially shared and widely approved convictions (Schneider, 2004). For instance, many people agree that men in general are more independent, competitive, and self-assured than women. In contrast, women are perceived as more understanding, caring, and aware of others' feelings than men. Stereotypes even transgress cultural boundaries. Williams and Best (1990) investigated gender stereotypes in a large-scale multination study comprising 25 countries in North and South America, Europe, Africa, and Asia. The authors used a list comprising 300 personality traits and asked participants to rate whether each adjective was more characteristic of men than women, of women than men, or none of these. This classic study demonstrated a high cross-cultural consistency in gender stereotypes.

How accurate are stereotypes? The impressive consensus on gender beliefs within societies and across different nations hints at two important aspects of stereotypes: First, consensus suggests that stereotypes could comprise valid information about social groups. Second, it indicates that there are certain functions and mechanisms that explain the pervasiveness of stereotypes. The question of the accuracy of stereotypes has long been debated among scientists. According to the first theories brought forward, stereotypes may possess a "kernel of truth" (see Prothro & Melikian, 1955) but depict differences among social groups in an exaggerated way (Allport, 1954). This view was questioned by a meta-analysis that examined the accuracy of gender stereotypes (Swim, 1994). Meta-analyses are quantitative analyses that determine the average finding of many studies on the same topic. This meta-analysis showed that participants were more likely to be accurate or even underestimate differences between women and men than overestimate them. In other words, participants' estimates about the size of gender differences were not larger than the respective gender differences that had been discovered by research. Thus, stereotypes were not exaggerations of gender differences. However, one should be cautious before leaping to conclusions. First, the fact that stereotypes may accurately depict group differences does not necessarily mean that the perceived differences are caused by biological differences among the groups (we elaborate on this in Chapter 6 on gender differences). Moreover, stereotypes can never be as accurate as the consideration of individual group members. That is, when people's characteristics are inferred based on their group memberships, individuating information falls by the wayside, thus forfeiting accuracy. For example, when we expect someone to be caring and warm simply because she is a woman, we may be terribly wrong.

Because stereotypes neglect individuating information, out-groups (i.e., groups one does not belong to) are typically perceived as more homogeneous than they actually are, a phenomenon termed *out-group homogeneity* (e.g., Ostrom & Sedikides, 1992). For example, Whites perceive Asians as relatively similar to each other, whereas Asians perceive Whites as relatively similar to each other. If you are not German and you meet a German, you expect the person to be organized, energetic, and responsible, and you tend to forget that there are Germans who are unorganized, lazy, and irresponsible. We see out-groups as more homogeneous than they are, and this is one reason for prejudice and discrimination (e.g., Brauer & Er-rafiy, 2011).

Much evidence is in line with the "kernel of truth" theory of stereotypes. Still, there are other theories about stereotype formation. An interesting theory claims that stereotypes can be completely wrong because they are based on misperceptions and thus appear to come from thin air (Hamilton & Gifford, 1976). More concretely, group stereotypes can emerge from so-called illusory correlations. An illusion is created that two things are related even if they are not. If two infrequent events that grab our attention come together, we tend to associate them with each other and remember them particularly well. (They stand out as *salient* because they are infrequent and/or negative.) Our attention is grabbed in particular when minority members perform negative behaviors. Whereas later research has challenged Hamilton and Gifford's (1976) original explanation, the phenomenon they have shown has firmly been established: If you learn many positive and a few negative things about members of a small and a large group, you form an impression of the small group as more negative than the large group. For example, you meet several male CEOs and have rather pleasant encounters with them, and then you meet one female CEO and dislike her. You may jump to the conclusion that female CEOs are dislikable. Then, you may meet a dislikable male CEO, but this encounter is not memorable; similarly, you meet a few likable female CEOs, but you quickly forget these latter encounters because they do not fit well into the cognitive categories that you have already formed. But the next dislikable female CEO that you meet grabs your attention again, reminds you of that first unpleasant woman, and thus firmly establishes your stereotype: Female CEOs are bitches. This is called the illusory-correlation account of stereotypes: You associate some infrequent trait or behavior with a minority, and once this stereotype is formed, it appears to be corroborated whenever you encounter confirming evidence. As another case in point, take the stereotype that all gay men are effeminate and all lesbians are masculine (e.g., Kite & Whitley, 1996). Every time you meet a feminine lesbian and a masculine gay man, their sexual orientation goes unnoticed. Instead, every time you meet a feminine man or a masculine woman, you think they must be gay and thus affirm your stereotype.

Taken together, there is both evidence that stereotypes contain some truth and that they may be at times unfounded. In any case, they are robust against change due to a cognitive process that is mentioned here (i.e., you remember what meets your expectations) and additional processes that are explained later.

Functions of stereotypes

One of the two major functions of stereotypes is *cognitive simplification*, also referred to as the "law of least effort" (Allport, 1954; for a fine-grained taxonomy on the functions of stereotypes, see Eckes, 2008). In our daily life, we are continually confronted with a vast amount of information that often needs to be processed and evaluated within milliseconds. If there were no organizing principles assisting us to structure an otherwise overly complex world, our cognitive systems would be rapidly overcharged. Thus, stereotypes help us navigate through a complex social environment (Hamilton & Sherman, 1994). They provide an energy-saving method for handling complex social information. In that sense, the activation and use of stereotypes are functional. Conversely, stereotypes may be considered dysfunctional because of the overgeneralization they imply (Gollwitzer & Schaal, 1998).

The second major function of stereotypes is *rationalization* (Allport, 1954). That is, stereotypes enable perceivers to justify the existing structures within a given social system (Hoffman & Hurst, 1990; Jost & Banaji, 1994; Sidanius & Pratto, 1999). For instance, if men are ascribed higher leadership qualities than women, and women are ascribed superior social skills than men, this can legitimize a situation that allows men professional positions high in status and assigns women to those roles that require warmth-related characteristics. The latter are naturally located on lower levels within the social hierarchy. We more fully discuss this function of stereotypes in Chapter 8 on maintaining social hierarchies.

These two functions of stereotypes correspond to the distinction between *descriptive* and *prescriptive* stereotypes (for a review, see Heilman,

2012). Descriptive stereotypes serve the need for cognitive simplification in describing what members of social groups typically are like. For example, a descriptive stereotype many Europeans hold is that Americans are outgoing. Importantly, such stereotypes affect information processing (see Heilman & Parks-Stamm, 2007): We interpret others' traits and behaviors differently, depending on the stereotypes of the groups they belong to (this is elaborated in Chapter 3). In contrast, prescriptive stereotypes serve to justify existing social structures by establishing normative expectations of what members of groups should be like. Applied to gender stereotypes, descriptive gender stereotypes designate what women and men *are* like (e.g., men are taller than women), whereas prescriptive stereotypes designate how they *should be* and how they *should not be* (Prentice & Carranza, 2002). For example, men should stand on their own feet, but for women, it is acceptable if they do not. Women should be considerate toward others, but men do not need to. Men are allowed to be aggressive at times, but women should not be. Women are allowed to be weak sometimes, but men should not be. Accordingly, if stereotype-based expectations are violated, perceivers' reactions substantially differ dependent on whether the stereotype was descriptive or prescriptive. If a descriptive stereotype is violated, people react with surprise. If a prescriptive stereotype is violated, however, disapproval and derogation follow. As is discussed later, both descriptive and prescriptive gender stereotypes promote gender bias that severely obstructs women's way to the top in regard to occupational achievement (Heilman, 2012).

The primacy of gender categorization

As a precondition of developing and applying stereotypes, we must categorize others into meaningful social entities. At the base of social categorization are characteristics that operate as organizing principles, such as age, race, or occupation. If we do not put someone into a given "box," our associated stereotypes cannot come into play. Which of the numerous means to put people into a box do we use? Among the possible characteristics that can be used to categorize people, gender is often said to be the most fundamental and salient social category (Fiske, Haslam, & Fiske, 1991; Kurzban, Tooby, & Cosmides, 2001; Stangor, Lynch, Duan, & Glass, 1992). Many languages mirror that large role ascribed to gender. We do not address people by saying "old and young" or "Blacks and Whites," but we do say "ladies and gentlemen."

That gender is the fundamental social category people use was intriguingly demonstrated in the "Who said what?" paradigm. This paradigm assesses which characteristics people use to categorize others. First, participants watch a "discussion" by different people, varying by gender and race. One by one, a face is presented on the computer monitor along with a written sentence of what this person says. Subsequently, participants are asked to remember who said what, that is, they are presented with the statements from the discussion and must assign each statement to the person who made it. The underlying assumption is that people more strongly confuse discussants they put into the same category. Hence, if someone uses the category gender more than the category race, more within-gender errors than within-race errors should occur. In other words, what one woman said is falsely believed to have come from another woman more often than statements from one White person are falsely assigned to another White person. Exactly this pattern was observed, thus pointing to the primacy of the category gender (Stangor et al., 1992). However, a study from our laboratory demonstrated that categorization also depends on the way in which information is presented in an experiment (Rakić, 2008). In one condition, we did not present the statements in written form, but they were spoken either with an Italian accent or in standard German. We reasoned that speaking with or without an accent would elicit categorization by ethnicity. As expected, in the condition in which statements were presented in written form ("control condition" in our case), Stangor and colleagues' (1992) pattern of findings was replicated: We found a primacy of gender categorization. However, when statements were spoken with or without an accent, there was as much ethnicity categorization as gender categorization. To illustrate, people mixed up one woman speaking with an accent with another woman speaking with an accent but not with another woman speaking without an accent. Thus, gender is a very important social category, but it is not always more important than all other social categories. How important a category is depends on the context, including the topic about which people speak (Klauer, Ehrenberg, & Wegener, 2003).

As stated, categorization is the first step, and the activation of respective stereotypes is the next: We can only apply gender stereotypes to a given woman if we are aware that she is a woman (e.g., we cannot apply gender stereotypes in an electronic message to J. Smith who could be male or female). So what are the contents of gender stereotypes that may be activated after gender categorization has taken place?

Contents of gender stereotypes

Gender stereotypes are defined as cognitive structures that comprise socially shared knowledge about the characteristic features of women and men (Ashmore & Del Boca, 1979), including physical characteristics, personality traits, preferences and interests, jobs, and social roles. On a very general level, gender stereotypes can be depicted by two fundamental dimensions (see Deaux & LaFrance, 1998, for a review). These have been referred to as *communion (communality)/expressiveness/warmth* versus *agency/instrumentality/competence* (Bakan, 1966; Fiske, Cuddy, Glick, & Xu, 2002). Blatantly, they can also be regarded as interpersonal versus task orientation (Sidanius, Pratto, & Bobo, 1994). *Communion* and *agency* are the concepts most frequently used in contemporary social psychology, but for ease of understanding, we will speak of warmth and assertiveness/competence. Warmth reflects a concern for one's connection with other people and comprises characteristics that are perceived as typically female (e.g., kind and nurturing). Assertiveness/competence comprise characteristics that are perceived as typically male (e.g., competitive, individualistic, self-promoting, task-oriented; Diekman & Eagly, 2000; Eagly & Steffen, 1984). Concerning our topic of gender at work, the association of men and competence is particularly troubling. In other words, in the absence of additional information, men are thought to be more competent than women: "Women are expected to be less competent than men and their contributions are expected to be less valuable" (Wharton, 2008, p. 57). We return to the consequences of this stereotype later. Perceptions of assertiveness/competence and warmth are tied to high and low status roles, respectively (e.g., Eagly & Steffen, 1984; Hoffman & Hurst, 1990). Thus, as we elaborate in later chapters, they justify inequalities such as men's overrepresentation in upper management and women's responsibility for domestic tasks.

A more general model that is closely related to the distinction introduced earlier is the *stereotype content model* (Fiske et al., 2002). According to that model, stereotypes of social groups vary along two core dimensions, *warmth* and *competence*. Women and men, given their traditional social roles as breadwinners versus homemakers, are two exemplary groups to which these stereotypes have been applied: Men are characterized as high in competence but low in warmth, whereas women are characterized as high in warmth but low in competence. Fiske and colleagues (2002) argued that in interpersonal and intergroup situations, people are primarily interested in other people's goals or *intent* (positive or negative) that could affect the self or the in-group (i.e., the group one belongs to), as well as the counterpart's *capability* to pursue those goals. These characteristics correspond to perceptions of warmth and competence: Positive goals relate to warmth; high capability relates to competence. If you are meeting people for the first time, you should be most interested in knowing these two things about them: Are they well-meaning or do they harbor negative intentions? And if their intentions are negative, are they capable of pursuing them? With respect to gender, the authors found that given the traditional distribution of women into the role of the homemaker and men into the role of the breadwinner, women are generally seen as high in warmth but low in competence, whereas men are generally seen as high in competence but low in warmth.

Gender subtypes

In spite of such generality of gender stereotypes, one should note that the groups of men and women form very general categories. Theoretically, each gender stereotype refers to approximately half of the world's population, and certainly, drawing on knowledge based on such global categories often proves insufficient (Kite et al., 2008). This is one reason why, next to overall gender stereotypes, there are more specific male and female subtypes. In other words, not every woman (man) is assumed to be like the typical woman (man), but there are other types as well. For example, the businesswoman is thought to be very different from the typical woman—higher in assertiveness and lower in warmth. Similarly, the softie differs from the typical man. Research has identified an impressive 200 gender-associated subtypes, substantiating people's inclination to form highly specific categories (Vonk & Ashmore, 2003).

Importantly, if female and male subtypes do exist, overall gender stereotypes can be maintained more easily. Because stereotypes are rules of thumb, subtype exemplars are perceived as exceptions to the rule. That is, allocating counterstereotypical women to certain subtypes leaves the conception intact of what a typical woman is like. This also means that people's tendency to form and apply subtypes of women and men makes it hard to modify overall gender stereotypes, thereby preventing a change in thinking. A critical mass of women who deviate from traditional role behavior would be necessary to cause a fundamental rethinking of women and their allocated position within society. For example, if you get to know several women who are unlike the traditional female (homemaker) stereotype, the option of categorizing them into a subtype (e.g., businesswomen) provides you with the opportunity to leave your stereotype unchanged.

In addition to different gender subtypes, it should be noted that the contents of gender stereotypes also depend on other social categories, such as ethnicity, that intersect with gender. For example, the expected female stereotype was applied to White women, whereas Black women were believed to be more hostile and superstitious (Landrine, 1985). Blacks in general are perceived as masculine, whereas the stereotype of Asian women and men is more related to femininity than that of Whites (e.g., Galinsky, Hall, & Cuddy, 2013). Taken together, different subtypes of women and men play a crucial role in understanding how gender-related stereotypes affect daily life, including career-critical situations.

Research on the stereotype content model revealed a *paternalistic stereotype* of women who abide in traditionally female domains (e.g., female homemakers). These women are stereotypically perceived as particularly high in warmth but low in competence, thus resembling the overall stereotype of women. However, clearly diverging conceptions emerged for the female subtypes of businesswomen, feminists, and lesbians. The *envious stereotype* applied to them was characterized by ascriptions of low warmth and high competence, thus resembling the overall stereotype of men. We come back to the consequences of such stereotypes later.

Summary

To sum up, gender is one of the most fundamental social categories, determining our perception of a person: We cannot help but sort people into categories of men and women. Researchers agree that gender stereotypes comprise two general dimensions: Men are seen as high in assertiveness and competence, and women are seen as high in warmth. Stereotypes in general are inevitable; they help humans to quickly grasp situations and react. But stereotypes also help us to rationalize the status quo, and they also have a prescriptive component, implying what women and men should and should not do. Because the distinction between men and women is so crude, gender subtypes play an important role in addition to these very general stereotypes: We hold very different expectations concerning a female homemaker and a businesswoman, for example. As we will see in the next chapter, these stereotypes may influence our perception and behavior even if we have no intention of stereotyping and are unaware that we are stereotyping.

· 2 ·

IMPLICIT COGNITION

Imagine you are part of a job search committee and you are reviewing applications. Out of 10 applicants, only 1 woman has applied for the job. She seems less qualified to you than the best of the men. How do you know whether she is truly less qualified or if knowing her gender influenced your impression? Over the last few decades, social psychology has witnessed a tremendous interest in so-called implicit cognition (e.g., Greenwald & Banaji, 1995). *Implicit stereotypes* are beliefs of social groups that are triggered automatically by the mere presence of the stereotyped object, often without a person's awareness or control (see Bargh, 1994). For example, if a personnel manager encounters a newly employed female executive in the company, he or she may spontaneously lower his or her performance expectations of the female employee compared to her male colleagues because the manager *implicitly* ascribes a lack of management skills to women (see Heilman, 2012). This example points to the importance of assessing people's implicit beliefs in addition to their explicit opinions. Explicit opinions are typically assessed with self-reports. That is, people are asked in a transparent way to provide their opinion on the topics of interest. There are two main reasons for the use of implicit measures. First, other than explicit measures, they do not rely on participants' willingness to report private knowledge (Greenwald et al., 2002). This property is essential whenever socially delicate topics are addressed. In such situations, people typically prefer not to disclose their personal beliefs, due to social desirability concerns. Gender stereotypes are particularly prone to intentional distortion. Returning to the earlier example, driven by impression management concerns, the personnel manager may have explicitly attested women leadership qualities that are equal to men, while secretly denying them the aptitude for successfully filling an upper management position. Second, implicit measures do not rely on participants' ability to report their inner beliefs accurately. In fact, people's ability to introspect is very limited (i.e., their ability to self-observe inner processes; Nisbett & Wilson, 1977): Often, people do not know any better than observers why they did something.

Researchers assume that both social desirability and lack of introspection ability can be overcome by measuring implicit cognition (e.g., Devine, 1989; Fazio, Sanbonmatsu, Powell, & Kardes, 1986). Gender stereotypes can be automatically activated (Banaji & Hardin, 1996) and applied to both men and women. Here is an illustration: Stereotypical male or female terms were activated in people's minds by asking them to work on an apparently unrelated task (Banaji, Hardin, & Rothman, 1993). Specifically, they were asked to form sentences from words that either described neutral behaviors (e.g., "R read book by the" should become "R read the book", eliminating one word, here: "by"), or aggressive behaviors ("M at shouts others of"), or dependent behaviors ("P alone cannot manage a"). They were then asked to judge a female or male target. When female stereotypes were activated ("dependent"), the female target was judged as more dependent than the male target. When male stereotypes were activated ("aggressive"), the male target was judged as more aggressive than the female target. Thus, it could be that a personnel manager implicitly ascribes more competence to his or her male employees without being aware of it. As we will see later, a single piece of information can be sufficient for activating stereotypes, for example, a perfume, a picture, or a word.

Regarding topics that are prone to social desirability concerns, implicit measures are better predictors of behavior than explicit measures (Greenwald, Poehlman, Uhlmann, & Banaji, 2009). Let's apply this to our example: Even if he or she states the contrary, the personnel manager's implicit stereotype of women as lacking leadership skills may finally influence his behavior (e.g., thwarting the pending promotion of his or her female subordinate).

People's implicit thoughts can be assessed using various measures (for a review, see De Houwer, Teige-Mocigemba, Spruyt, & Moors, 2009). One of the most prominent methods is the *implicit association test* that measures reaction times while people are sorting words (this test can be taken at http://www.projectimplicit.net/). Other measures (called priming) often rely on reaction times as well. These measures are based on the fact that connections among concepts in our brains can be revealed by measuring reaction times. For example, people can decide faster that "robin" is a word after having seen "bird" than after having seen an unrelated word or no word (Neely, 1976). Conversely, researchers deduce that concepts fit together well for an individual if the person can react faster when the concepts are paired than in a comparison condition. For example, if someone can react faster when math-related words are paired with male rather than female names, it appears that math is more connected for that individual with men than women, and he or she seems to hold an implicit math-male stereotype (e.g., Nosek, Banaji, & Greenwald, 2002b).

With regard to gender stereotypes, many studies that used explicit measures found that women showed more egalitarian beliefs and attitudes than men. However, when implicit measures were used, this gender difference disappeared and equally biased perceptions were found among women and men (e.g., Rudman & Kilianski, 2000). For example, an implicit test assessed whether participants associated career more with men than women and family more with women than men (Nosek, Banaji, & Greenwald, 2002a). A traditional men-career/women-family stereotype emerged for both men and women. However, when assessing participants' explicit stereotypes by using self-reports, women's stereotypes were substantially reduced whereas men's were not. This pattern of findings demonstrates that implicit measures contribute in a unique way to the examination of gender beliefs.

Implicit gender stereotypes

Research on implicit gender stereotypes shows that traditional beliefs of women and men prevail. Considering the two basic dimensions of stereotype content, warmth and competence, according to many studies, warmth is still ascribed to women more than men, whereas assertiveness/competence is ascribed to men more than women (Rudman & Glick, 2001; Rudman & Kilianski, 2000; Steffens, Schult, & Ebert, 2009). A study conducted with German managers qualified this overall pattern: Whereas male managers showed an implicit men-assertiveness/women-warmth stereotype, female managers did not

(Steffens & Mehl, 2003). A possible explanation for this divergence could be that perceptions of the groups we belong to can be informed by perceptions of ourselves (see Greenwald et al., 2002). More concretely, since assertiveness is deemed necessary for successful leadership, a leadership position should go along with a self-image marked by assertiveness, and this could counteract female managers' gender stereotypes (see Alicke, Dunning, & Krueger, 2005).

Also, when varying the stereotype dimensions under investigation, traditional implicit gender beliefs were obtained. For example, an implicit association of women with *warmth* and men with *potency* was found (Rudman, Greenwald, & McGhee, 2001). Similarly, women were more related with *warmth* and men with *power* (Rudman & Goodwin, 2004). Analogously, research addressing more specific implicit gender stereotypes (i.e., gender-specific skills, gender roles) revealed traditional gender beliefs. As mentioned earlier, when measuring the strength of association between academic domains (math/arts) and gender, both male and female U.S. students implicitly ascribed math to men and arts to women (Nosek et al., 2002b). Similarly, German university students revealed an implicit math-male stereotype (Steffens & Jelenec, 2011). However, departing from generally ascribing math to men and language to women, the researchers found a language-female stereotype only for women; men showed an implicit language-*male* stereotype, too. That is, implicit ability stereotypes were self-serving for men but not for women: The men thought their group was good at both math and language. Traditional gender perceptions also pertain to gender roles: men's and women's roles in society. For example, when presented with the concepts career/family and men/women, both men and women implicitly linked career to men and family to women (Devos, Blanco, Rico, & Dunn, 2008; Nosek et al., 2002a). Similarly, there are stronger implicit associations of women and domestic-related words on the one hand and men and career-related words on the other (Rudman & Kilianski, 2000).

Although much research has thus corroborated traditional implicit gender beliefs, some findings point to a departure from traditional gender perceptions. For example, Richeson and Ambady (2001) found associations of own gender and competence for both men and women. While the authors argued that this pattern may reflect the fact that their female participants were "highly motivated, competent women attending an exclusive, competitive university" (p. 504), research conducted in Germany indicated that implicit associations of own gender and competence are not confined to a specific type of sample. A series of studies in Germany consistently found that different groups of participants (students, managers, professionals of various backgrounds) held implicit associations of own gender and competence (Ebert, Steffens, & Kroth, 2014; see Chapter 7). It thus appears that the traditional gender stereotype that associates men with competence is eroding.

Malleability of implicit gender stereotypes

Stereotypes have a wide scope. They affect how we perceive the world around us and determine social interactions and can decide whether we succeed or fail in the face of a challenge. As mentioned earlier, implicit stereotypes are particularly powerful predictors of discriminatory behavior. Considering the insidious effects of implicit gender stereotypes, there is tremendous interest in examining their malleability and developing efficient intervention strategies. How can implicit gender stereotypes be changed (see Blair, 2002)?

Under certain circumstances, strategies can be used to suppress the automatic activation of stereotypical gender beliefs (i.e., prevent automatic stereotyping). *Implementation intentions* can prevent stereotype activation (Gollwitzer & Schaal, 1998). More specifically, in one condition of Gollwitzer and Schaal's (1998) study (i.e., goal-intention condition), male participants were asked to judge two female targets in a fair and nonstereotypical manner. In a second condition (i.e., implementation-intention condition), the men were additionally asked to tell themselves the following: "Whenever I see Ina (Bea), I will ignore her gender." Merely asking participants to behave in a fair and nonstereotypical manner did not suffice to suppress automatic stereotype activation. However, additionally asking them to form an implementation intention ("Whenever I see Ina [Bea], I will ignore her gender") counteracted implicit gender beliefs. It must be noted, however, that this effect was obtained only under certain conditions. First, participants were highly motivated to behave in a fair and nonstereotypical manner. Second, the suppression of automatic stereotype activation was specific to the target person (i.e., it was effective in the case of Ina but not for Bea). In spite of these limitations, this study can inspire the development of practical interventions in several ways. First, inducing the motivation to appear in a nonprejudiced way can be a fruitful avenue for counteracting harmful effects of disadvantageous gender beliefs (see also Heilman, 2012). For employers, this could mean to explicitly declare impartiality and fair-mindedness as primary business goals and develop concrete codes of practice that are communicated throughout all company levels.

Social factors also influence implicit stereotypes (Sechrist & Stangor, 2001). If people believed that few rather than many of their peers agreed with their stereotypes, they showed significantly lower levels of implicit stereotypes.

Second, the study by Gollwitzer and Schaal (1998) demonstrated that detracting people's attention from the category gender can curb the automatic activation of gender beliefs. The study suggests that this can be obtained by forming implementation intentions. For example, prior to a job interview with a female candidate applying for a leadership position, a personnel manager could actively form an implementation intention such as, "When talking to Mrs. X, I will concentrate on her accomplishments and her performance during the interview, not on her gender," thus escaping the pitfalls of automatic stereotype activation. In addition, the female candidate herself can counteract the activation of unfavorable implicit gender beliefs. In one interesting study, participants were exposed to a Chinese woman (Macrae, Bodenhausen, & Milne, 1995). In one condition, the Chinese woman was shown putting on makeup. In another condition, she was shown using chopsticks. Subsequently, implicit stereotypes of both Chinese and women were measured. Compared to a control condition, participants who had seen the Chinese woman putting on makeup exhibited stronger stereotypic beliefs of women, whereas those who had seen the Chinese woman using chopsticks exhibited stronger stereotypic beliefs of Chinese. Thus, a single gender-specific cue sufficed for activating implicit gender beliefs. Likewise, drawing the attentional focus to gender-irrelevant information about a person can prevent the activation of implicit gender stereotypes. Gender-specific cues can be very important for career advancement (Sczesny & Stahlberg, 2002). Considering possible effects of applicants' perfumes (feminine vs. masculine), Sczesney and Stahlberg (2002) asked their participants to assume the role of a manager who had to evaluate a candidate applying for a junior manager position. Applicants wearing a masculine perfume were employed with a higher degree of certainty than applicants wearing a feminine perfume. Importantly, this was the case both for male and female applicants. This research implies that to a certain extent, women themselves can counteract the activation of their gender category by avoiding strong gender-typical cues or behaviors.

Under which conditions do strategies to modify people's underlying beliefs operate effectively? Important boundary conditions are *cognitive constraints* (Blair & Banaji, 1996). In our daily life, we often need to form an impression of a given counterpart within milliseconds. That is, we must quickly judge what a person is like without drawing on the cognitive resources that would be necessary for reaching a well-considered decision. Many studies have shown that stereotypes are more likely to operate when time is limited (e.g., Bodenhausen, 1990; Gilbert & Hixon, 1991). Therefore, strategies that do not rely on the availability of cognitive resources should be most effective. Stereotype strategies can effectively counteract implicit gender beliefs even if cognitive constraints are high (Blair & Banaji, 1996). The authors asked participants to either expect stereotypical or counterstereotypical information. For example, participants were first shown a typically masculine word (e.g., ambitious). In the stereotype-congruent strategy condition, participants should expect a male name to follow (e.g., Brian); in the counterstereotype strategy condition, participants should expect a female name (e.g., Betty). Even if cognitive resources were highly limited, automatic stereotypes were effectively mitigated. This finding is particularly promising with regard to adverse effects of gender beliefs in daily life. Even if people must form impressions in a minimum of time, gender bias can be counteracted by using counterstereotype strategies (see also Kawakami, Dovidio, Moll, Hermsen, & Russin, 2000; Kawakami, Dovidio, & van Kamp, 2005).

Another effective technique for counteracting implicit stereotypic beliefs is the use of mental imagery (Blair, Ma, & Lenton, 2001). In one study, participants were given a few minutes to form a mental image of a strong woman. Whereas participants in a control condition held an implicit gender stereotype of women as weak and men as strong, participants who had imagined a strong woman no longer exhibited an implicit men-strong/women-weak stereotype. The mere power of imagination can suffice to counteract implicit gender beliefs. Thus, specific imagery exercises could be implemented within diversity training. To help prevent severe consequences at the workplace, participants would learn to reduce their underlying gender beliefs they might not even be aware of.

A further and particularly worthwhile avenue for mitigating career-limiting implicit gender beliefs is the presence of counterstereotypic female role models (Dasgupta & Asgari, 2004). In a laboratory study, female participants were exposed to either biographical information of several famous female leaders (experimental condition) or flowers (control condition). Subsequently, implicit gender beliefs were assessed with respect to the two concepts, leader versus supporter. Participants who had previously seen female leaders were significantly faster at associating women with leadership than those who had previously seen the control examples. Moreover, they were faster at associating women with leadership and men with supporter.

For control participants, there was a tendency to react in the opposite way (i.e., associating women with supporter and men with leadership). That is, exposing women to counterstereotypic role models (successful female leaders) led to a reversal of traditional implicit gender beliefs. Since the automatic ascription of the stereotype concepts leader and supporter should have a strong impact on hirability judgments for a wide range of professions, these findings are particularly consequential for the workplace. More than that, Dasgupta and Asgari (2004) found that the less pronounced implicit stereotypes were, the more participants believed that the famous women's success could be attained by other women, including themselves. Although the causal link underlying this relationship was not examined in this study, this finding further demonstrates that implicit stereotypes are highly relevant for career-related psychological variables (such as the confidence to succeed). A subsequent study was conducted in a natural environment over a time span of one year. Implicit gender stereotypes of female students attending a women's college versus a coeducational college were assessed. In their first semester, women at both colleges showed similar implicit gender beliefs (ascribing supporter to women and leader to men). However, one year later, implicit stereotypes had completely disappeared for the women at the women's college but they remained strong for the women at the coed college. A higher proportion of female faculty in the women's college as compared to the coed college accounted for this difference in implicit gender beliefs. That is, the higher the proportion of female faculty, the smaller was the magnitude of an implicit women-supporter/men-leader stereotype. These findings are highly interesting when evaluating the importance of counterstereotypic female role models in professional domains. They suggest that the presence of successful female leaders in work contexts reduces unfavorable implicit gender beliefs, thus paving the way for the next generation. Two factors should be noted, however. First, it appears crucial to establish a critical mass of female leaders to alter people's underlying belief systems. With a small proportion of women in top positions, they will still be perceived as "exceptions to the rule" (i.e., have the status of tokens), and as those, they will be subtyped as a specific group of women that is not representative for the general group of women as a whole. Second, it appears crucial that the counterstereotypic role models do not impose a threat to those women who have not yet achieved similar accomplishments (see Chapter 11 on role models).

Summary

Taken together, research on implicit social cognition rests on two assumptions: People are not willing to tell us their stereotypes and prejudice, and even if they were, they could not. This is because many of these cognitions are learned so early on and deeply engrained into our thinking that we cannot even voice them. Reaction time measures have been developed, validated, and used in hundreds of studies for measuring implicit social cognition. These demonstrate that many gendered associations are automatic. For example, math, physics, power, and career are more associated with men, and arts, languages, warmth, and family are more associated with women. Both men and women hold most of these associations. Still, such implicit stereotypes are malleable. For example, long-term exposure to female leaders and changes in the task distribution between men and women in society should eventually lead to changes in such stereotypes.

· 3 ·

EFFECTS OF STEREOTYPES ON JUDGING OTHERS

A recent commercial showed men and women in different situations at work—during a meeting, giving a presentation, alone in the office at night. It suggests that a male leader is perceived as the boss, while a female leader seems bossy; where he appears persuasive, she appears pushy; and when working long hours, he appears dedicated, whereas she appears selfish (thanks to Laurie Rudman for pointing this out to us). The message is this: If women and men do the same, others (i.e., perceivers) interpret their behavior very differently. The gender stereotypes we introduced earlier would thus have profound consequences for how we "see" individual women and men. Whether this is the case is not a trivial question. For instance, it could be that we hold the stereotype that more men than women are natural leaders, but the moment we see a woman leading, we simply note that she is an exception and perceive her identically to her male colleagues. Alternatively, as the commercial suggests, gender stereotypes may influence how we perceive and judge individual women and men. In the following, we devote much space to this question, because hundreds of studies have tested it and provide more nuanced responses than a simple "yes" or "no." We ask the questions: Are individual women and men described in gender-stereotypical terms? If women and men act similarly, are they still perceived to differ?

Research findings suggest that the answer is yes. Evidence that others are described in gender-typed ways comes from many studies. For example, one study analyzed obituaries published between 1974 and 1998 in different newspapers (Rodler, Kirchler, & Hölzl, 2001). How deceased leaders were described in the 1970s depended on their gender. Whereas men were always described in terms of assertiveness and competence (i.e., agency, e.g., professional, expert, experienced), women were described predominantly as venerable in the 1970s and only later as more agentic (e.g., work-oriented, committed). Descriptions of women changed more over the years, but men gained in warmth and person-oriented leadership style in the descriptions of the 1990s as well. We discuss such changes in more detail in Chapter 7 on social role theory.

These and similar studies cannot tell if differences in the descriptions are due to "true" gender differences or only to gender stereotypes. It could be that female leaders are less assertive than their male colleagues; alternatively, it is possible that impressions of them are colored by gender stereotypes or even that obituary writers believe it to be in their best interest to be described in these terms. It is even possible that changes in descriptions are caused by a growing awareness of obituary writers not to portray female leaders in gender-stereotypical terms.

Often, the effects of gender stereotypes found in respective studies are rather small. In other words, men appear only a little less warm and/or a little more assertive and task-oriented than women. There has been some ongoing debate in social psychology about the practical significance of small differences (i.e., small effects) in the evaluations of women and men. A first point to be made is that a small disadvantage (e.g., worse evaluation of a female than male manager because of gender stereotypes), when applied repeatedly at every level in a hierarchy, can have a big cumulative effect, with many more men than women reaching the very top of the hierarchy. "A little bias hurt women a lot" (Martell, Lane, & Emrich, 1996, p. 158). As Martell, Emrich, and Robison-Cox (2012) elaborated, if women receive somewhat worse evaluations than men ("small gender differences"), men get promoted faster. The resulting early career success, short time in rank, and velocity of moving up the organizational hierarchy all contribute to determining future promotions to the men's advantage, whereas loss of competition creates a disadvantage for the women. Consequently, the small difference present at first is soon exacerbated.

Well-meaning observers may tell the woman not to make a mountain out of a molehill. What they do not understand is what the notion of the accumulation of advantage encapsulates. Mountains are molehills, piled one on top of the other. (Valian, 2007, p. 35)

In sum, one needs to keep in mind that small differences can have huge effects. Thus, when determining the influence of gender stereotypes on impressions of women and men, the questions are these: Are judgments of individuals colored by gender stereotypes? And if so, how important is this factor in relation to other factors such as individual qualifications, choices, and gender roles?

How can researchers determine whether gender stereotypes influence judgments of men and women? Nearly 50 years ago, Goldberg (1968) introduced an important method that has since been used in thousands of studies. The quality of identical texts was to be rated. Whereas half of the study participants were led to believe John McKay had written the text, the other half believed it had been Joan McKay (for example). The answer to the question of whether stereotypes influence judgments appeared simple and straightforward: Female college students rated the quality of texts and the competence of the author higher for men. Not even in stereotypically female domains such as dietetics was this trend reversed. Thus, Goldberg introduced a method that can be used to determine the influence of a target's gender on impression formation. We can use all kinds of written materials such as reports, résumés, job applications, and supervisors' performance evaluations. Later research qualified his conclusion. First, while planning a study, it is important to note that there are stereotypes associated with first names (Kasof, 1993). For example, Germans perceive a person named Katharina or Alexander to be considerably more intelligent than Heike or Mike (Rudolph, Böhm, & Lummer, 2007). So researchers need to select comparable names in terms of perceived age, intelligence, and attractiveness to find true gender effects—a comparison of Katharina and Mike, or of Alexander and Heike, for example, would not be telling. From a practical point of view, it is important to keep in mind that we all should be careful not to be prejudiced against a person because of his or her name.

Several meta-analyses have been conducted to determine the average effect of target gender on various ratings (e.g., competence, hirability, promotability, social skills). An early meta-analysis on 123 separate studies concluded that the majority of studies found no effect of target gender on evaluations, and on average, gender explained less than 1% of the variance in ratings

(Swim, Borgida, Maruyama, & Myers, 1989). In other words, on average, ratings depended much more on factors other than gender (i.e., there was a small effect). At the same time, effect sizes of the gender effect varied. The meta-analysis could not determine why. This means that women were evaluated worse than men in some studies (and men worse than women in a few other studies), for unknown reasons.

Many recent studies found no difference in competence impressions of (childless) women and men with equal qualifications (e.g., Cuddy, Fiske, & Glick, 2004; Fuegen, Biernat, Haines, & Deaux, 2004; Heilman & Okimoto, 2008; Rudman & Glick, 1999, 2001; Steffens & Mehl, 2003; Steffens et al., 2009). However, some interactions with other factors were found. For example, female humanities professors appeared less competent than male science professors, and a African American Black female professor was rated lower than any other combination of ethnicity and gender (Bavishi, Madera, & Hebl, 2010). To evaluate under which conditions biases emerge, we first introduce some more specific models based on gender stereotypes.

Perceived fit between person and job

A model that constitutes a milestone in the analysis of the role of gender in workplace discrimination is the *lack of fit model* (Heilman, 1983). On a general level, it brings into focus that stereotypes do not pertain solely to social groups but also to nonliving entities such as professions or jobs (e.g., Kunda & Thagard, 1996). The stereotypes or presumed requirements of a given position can fit well with those of a given individual or social group, or not. If you believe the chief of police needs to be tall, strong, and have a loud voice, most women probably would not fit. If you believe the job requires, above all, intelligence and social skills, a female candidate could appear much better. What is deemed necessary for a given job is not objective and fixed; for example, traditionally, managers were required to have only stereotypically male (leadership) traits, whereas in the past few decades, stereotypically female interpersonal skills have additionally been required (see Eagly & Karau, 2002; Rudman & Glick, 1999). Later, the lack of fit model was extended into role congruity theory that explains more generally prejudice against women as leaders (Eagly & Karau, 2002).

The lack of fit model postulates that descriptive gender stereotypes may lower women's chances whenever women are believed to fit certain jobs less well than men. Likewise, descriptive gender stereotypes lower men's chances to be hired for jobs believed to require typically female traits. Unfortunately, the jobs high in prestige, power, and income have historically been men's jobs and are believed to require typically male traits. As a side note, as the aforementioned example of management indicates, the stereotype of a job may also change. Stereotypes of some traditionally male jobs that now attract a majority of women, such as veterinary medicine, should eventually change. Until a job stereotype has changed, everything else being equal, a female applicant should appear less suited than a male applicant for a position stereotyped as male, including traditionally male domains such as information technology.

A case in point is the "think manager–think male" phenomenon (e.g., Schein, Mueller, & Jacobson, 1989). Trait ratings of successful middle managers are more similar to ratings of men in general than they are to ratings of women in general. In other words, managers are seen as more similar to men than to women. When people imagine a manager, they most often think of a man. Many studies have replicated this finding, both in the United States and other countries (Schein, 2001). In the United States, however, this image of middle management is changing. As newer studies have shown, female managers and business students no longer see managers as more similar to men than to women, whereas their male colleagues still do (Schein, 2001). Similarly, in other countries, the image of leadership is becoming less traditional (Sczesny, 2003; Sczesny, Bosak, Neff, & Schyns, 2004). In Sweden, the image of typical leaders is that they are team-oriented, they motivate subordinates, and they search for a consensus—in other words, more similar to the female than male stereotype (see Mölders & van Quaquebeke, 2011). As we discussed earlier, implicit stereotypes are malleable: After being exposed to female leaders, the association between men and leadership is reduced (Dasgupta & Asgari, 2004), particularly for female participants (van Quaquebeke & Schmerling, 2010). This indicates that the image of leadership as male will be reduced the more female leaders there are. A large improvement in women's status can go a long way. The studies indicating that the image of leadership is becoming less traditional illustrate this.

There is consensus among researchers that the match between the masculine and feminine features needed on the job and an individual's gender influences opportunities (Eagly & Karau, 2002; Heilman & Parks-Stamm, 2007; Isaac, Lee, & Carnes, 2009). As reported in a meta-analysis, the 8 experiments using female-typed jobs found that women were, on average, selected with a higher probability than men, whereas the 13 experiments using male-typed jobs, on average, found a promale bias in selection; the 4 studies with male-typed jobs that included a compensation measure also found a promale bias (Davison & Burke, 2000). For example, participants would be asked, "Which salary would you offer the candidate if initial salaries are typically between $30,000 and $50,000?" Participants selected higher salaries for men than women applying for male-typed jobs. That meta-analysis tested these relations, including original studies conducted between 1977 and 1994. Perceived lack of fit has "consequences for hiring, starting salaries and job placement decisions as well as for opportunities for skill development, pay raises and promotions" (Heilman, 2012, p. 117). Given male-typed jobs, the majority of studies included in a more recent review also found that men were evaluated more positively than women (Isaac et al., 2009). Similarly, participants who perceived a blue-collar job as masculine showed a hiring bias against female applicants (Güngör & Biernat, 2009).

The lack of fit model also implies that the perceived femininity of a given woman affects how well she is perceived to fit a given position. Studies investigating several different features have corroborated this (for reviews, see Eagly & Karau, 2002; Heilman & Parks-Stamm, 2007). For example, employment decisions were less favorable for physically attractive or pregnant women, whose femininity is more obvious. Feminine dress (see Eagly & Karau, 2002), high-pitched voice (Ko, Judd, & Stapel, 2009), or, as mentioned, flowery perfume (Sczesny & Stahlberg, 2002), may also lower competence or hirability impressions. Notably, the latter aspects do so for both women and men. For instance, men with a high-pitched voice would also appear less competent and hirable than men with a low-pitched voice. Motherhood also is a potentially dangerous status concerning women's perceived lack of fit (discussed more in Chapter 12). Extending these findings, recent experiments from our laboratory showed that the mere fact that a woman indicated being involved in a lesbian, as opposed to a heterosexual, relationship, shielded her from negative impressions concerning her task competence, because a lesbian was assumed to possess the required masculinity (Niedlich, Steffens, Krause, Settke, & Ebert, 2014).

In addition to stereotypes of jobs, an important factor determining whether gender biases impression formation is this: How much information about an individual do raters possess? Imagine you were to make a best guess about which of two people is more dominant, and you knew nothing about them except that their names are John and Jane. This situation is very different from one in which you know that John is a nurse and Jane leads the Brazil group of an international enterprise. Your guesses may differ, accordingly, being more based on gender stereotypes in the first case. Several social-psychological models specify how impressions are formed from different sources of information (Brewer, 1988; Fiske & Neuberg, 1990; Kunda & Thagard, 1996).

Several seminal studies have demonstrated that stereotypes, similar to other rules of thumb, have their largest effects when little information about individuals is present (i.e., little individuating information). *Individuating information* is any other information about an individual, for example, appearance, behavior, or personality (Kunda & Thagard, 1996). Individuating information such as hobbies, even if totally unrelated to job-related skills (Glick, Zion, & Nelson, 1988), or including a "minimal amount of subjectively diagnostic target case information" (Locksley, Borgida, Brekke, & Hepburn, 1980, p. 821), may eliminate effects of gender stereotypes on impression formation (see also Pratto & Bargh, 1991). Deaux and Lewis (1984) investigated the perceived relations between gender and gender-related components such as role behaviors (e.g., head of household vs. takes care of children), traits, occupations, and physical characteristics (e.g., tall, broad-shouldered vs. soft voice, graceful). Given any additional component information, gender never explained a large part of the impressions formed. In contrast, each of those components affected impressions concerning each other component, as well as gender and even sexual orientation (e.g., the probability that a man with feminine physical characteristics was estimated to be homosexual was .58). Thus, people readily generalize from one component to the other, and information on gender played a smaller role in impression formation than such gender-related components. Physical characteristics played a particularly large role. In line with the conclusion from the previous studies, individuating information determines impression formation more than gender does.

An explanation for the large influence of behavior information is that behavior is seen as more predictive of a person's traits than are group stereotypes (Kunda & Thagard, 1996). However, if the information presented about an individual is ambiguous, stereotypes continue to color impressions (Kunda & Thagard, 1996). For example, if you hear that Peter is vain, you may imagine him obsessed with the look of his muscles, whereas if Petra is known to be vain, this interpretation is less likely (see Dunning & Sherman, 1997). Interestingly, these findings indicate that you may interpret differently the same information that you receive about an individual, depending on the social group to which he or she belongs (e.g., whether the person is male or female). It is thus important to note that we should not jump to conclusions when forming impressions of others—our first impressions could be based on a misinterpretation of ambiguous information.

Davison and Burke (2000) found no strong support for the prediction that more information goes along with less discrimination, in the more than 40 studies included in their meta-analysis (i.e., the effect of amount of information was not statistically significant). However, when interpreting this lack of effect, one needs to consider that few studies ask that ratings be made on the basis of only receiving names of applicants. Thus, in almost every study, several pieces of individuating information were included.

One central piece of individuating information is this: How much evidence of the individual's abilities is available and is it unambiguous? Rosette and colleagues (2010) recently demonstrated that female leaders who have made it to the top because of their abilities may even appear *more* capable than men in comparable positions. It appears that people think like this: If she has come so far in spite of the disadvantages women face, she must indeed be exceptionally qualified (for more examples on such contrast effects, see Eagly & Karau, 2002; Kunda & Thagard, 1996). Other studies also reported that women without children appeared more competent than men without children (Correll, Benard, & Paik, 2007; Cuddy et al., 2004): Adopting a (counterstereotypic) role in spite of major obstacles—such as a woman in a male-typed job—increases perceptions of competence and related traits such as assertiveness and decisiveness (Baron, Markman, & Hirsa, 2001).

Stereotypes of career women and backlash effects

Taken together, the delineated arguments imply that there may be a lack of fit between how the typical woman is perceived and how most leadership positions or jobs in traditionally male domains are perceived. Only if clear evidence is present that an individual woman does not fit the stereotype of the typical woman will she be perceived to fit the job as well as a typical man. But do we think of typical women when reviewing applications, for instance, for management positions? In many of the career-related situations that we focus on here, it is unlikely that the stereotype of the typical woman is evoked at all. Businesswomen are perceived as being very different from the typical woman but similar to typical men and to managers (see Eckes, 1994, 1997, and subtyping in Chapter 1). As one example, if you know that a woman has worked as the CEO of a large business, you do not imagine a traditional woman; you imagine a very different subtype: a businesswoman. If businesswomen are not ascribed the typically female features of being warm, but lacking assertiveness, should we assume that there is no discrimination against them? Several research findings speak against this (see Heilman & Parks-Stamm, 2007). Here we return to prescriptive stereotypes: Which traits and behaviors *should* women possess, and which are they *not allowed* to possess? Businesswomen may be punished for violating prescriptive behavior standards for women: Behaviors indicating dominance and self-assertion may be considered more inappropriate if carried out by a woman than by a man. If a woman behaves in such gender-inappropriate ways, she may be disliked by others and thus risks social sanctions (for a review, see Heilman & Parks-Stamm, 2007). For instance, in organizations where male norms have been established, leadership roles may require that you present your ideas as if they were the *ne plus ultra*. At the same time, this violates the female modesty prescription (see Mölders & van Quaquebeke, 2011). In organizational contexts, men use male-associated impression management tactics such as self-promotion and self-enhancement more than women do (Guadagno & Cialdini, 2007).

As Rudman (1998) found, women who self-promoted were indeed judged as more competent than more modest women, but they were also disliked. Men behaving in the same manner did not consistently suffer these negative consequences. Further studies tested what happens if job descriptions include typically female social skills. After reading job descriptions, participants saw a videotape of an applicant and then rated the individual on several measures. As that study showed, if social skills were included in a job description, men behaving in assertive ways, but not women, were given the benefit of the doubt that they possessed the necessary social skills (Rudman & Glick, 1999, 2001). Consequently, men were judged more hirable than women only in this condition. This pattern of findings is quite ironic: Only if typically female strengths (i.e., social skills) were part and parcel of the job description did participants discriminate against women. Rudman called this a *backlash effect*. Both men and women who self-presented as warm were judged low in hirability because they appeared to lack the required competence. So women were in a no-win situation.

When interpreting these findings, two caveats need to be mentioned. First, videos of men and women cannot be equal in every respect but gender. In other words, it cannot be excluded that the women appeared less likable for reasons other than gender. For example, slight differences in facial expression and tone of voice can influence how a message comes across. In our own research conducted in Germany, *both* men and women were punished for behaving overly assertive and dominant when job descriptions included social skills (Steffens et al., 2009). However, at the same time, we had adapted targets' self-portrayal because their behavior as scripted by Rudman and Glick (1999, 2001) appeared too extreme in the German cultural context. We deemed their degree of assertiveness and dominance totally inappropriate in a job interview in our culture. A second caveat is that only some researchers concluded that self-promotion is associated with career success (Guadagno & Cialdini, 2007). Others hold that the relationship is more differentiated (Blickle, Schneider, Perrewé, Blass, & Ferris, 2008). Specifically, during personnel selection, self-promotion enhances success because little objective information on an individual's performance is available. Therefore, those who self-promote appear more competent. In contrast, in the presence of much information obtained on the job, self-promotion does not signal competence but instead a lack of modesty. Whenever modest subordinates are liked more than less humble ones, the initial success of self-promotion (i.e., getting hired) may ultimately turn into a disadvantage (i.e., not being promoted).

Similar findings to those of Rudman and Glick (1999, 2001) were reported in a more recent study relying on written materials (Rudman, Moss-Racusin, Phelan, & Nauts, 2012). Thus, idiosyncrasies of people (e.g., shown in videos) cannot be the basis for the obtained backlash effect. Participants were asked to rate English professors with high credentials who had applied for a professorship at an Ivy League university. Women who were described as "brutally honest" literary critics were judged as less likable and less hirable than comparable men. No gender difference in ratings emerged in the absence of such a description. Also, when women were clearly successful in male-typed jobs, they were rated as more hostile and were disliked (Heilman, Wallen, Fuchs, & Tamkins, 2004). In turn, more likable targets were recommended for higher salaries and career opportunities. More generally, if people dislike someone, this negatively affects performance ratings and other behavior that is relevant for career success (for a review, see Heilman & Parks-Stamm, 2007): Social networks play an important role in promotion.

These studies indicate that women may be punished for behaviors that are not in line with female gender stereotypes. Imagine the boss is shouting and throwing a book at the wall. Would it make a difference for the interpretation of this behavior whether the boss is male or female? According to a recent study in the United States, it would. Brescoll and Uhlmann (2008) found that expressing anger is interpreted differently when reported by a man than by a woman. The male targets were ascribed a higher status and appeared more competent than the female targets when expressing anger due to a work-related incident. The interpretations for their getting angry differed: If a man got angry, the reason must have been his coworkers or other circumstances; if a woman got angry, it was interpreted as a flaw in her personality. But this finding should be extended to other contexts to be sure that the findings generalize beyond the specific conditions present in the aforementioned research. For example, it has been suggested that behavior needs to appear extreme to produce a different impression of women and men (Eagly & Karau, 2002).

Taken together, we conclude from these studies that there are conditions under which men may get away with negative behaviors proscribed for women (see Rudman et al., 2012). We think that one reason for this can be conceived of as benevolent sexism against men (discussed in Chapter 5). If perceivers see a man boasting in inappropriate ways or more generally misbehaving in a "typically male" fashion at work, they may secretly roll their eyes and think that the poor lad does not know any better, despite his general competence. In contrast, women should know better than that. In other words, in a patronizing way, social deficits are forgiven for the group that is somewhat socially deficient in perceivers' eyes (men) but not for the socially skilled group (women). Alternatively, these double standards applied to men's and women's dominance were interpreted as indicating that certain behaviors are appropriate only for the high-status group (men) but proscribed for the low-status group (women).

There are also pieces of information that are more easily forgiven for women than men, for instance, discontinuity in employment (Smith, Tabak, Showail, Parks, & Kleist, 2005). And we wonder whether there are behaviors that are proscribed for men but that women could show without being damaged as much. If these behaviors were typically female but inappropriate in the job context, we think they would damage both women and men (e.g., a leader certainly should not burst into tears). But it is conceivable that a woman may use gender-typical means to accomplish something that is out of reach for a man. Up to now, we do not know of respective findings. Using "feminine charm," a combination of friendliness and flirtation, in negotiations may lead to positive impressions and liking of female negotiators (particularly by men); at the same time, it may have economic costs in that women using their charm may obtain worse economic deals than women focused on economic outcomes (Kray, Locke, & Van Zant, 2012). Thus, charm does not seem to do the trick (see also Guadagno & Cialdini, 2007).

Can women do anything to avoid the trap of either being judged not competent enough for the job or not nice enough for a woman? Convergent findings indicate that they can if they go the extra mile to prove their warmth in addition to their competence (Rudman & Glick, 2001; for a review, see Heilman & Parks-Stamm, 2007). For example, a letter of application that first draws attention to one's stellar performance and then adds evidence that one is a true team player who has an open ear for subordinates' problems may suffice to convey both competence and warmth.

Although some researchers go as far as stating that success in a male domain (still) violates prescriptive stereotypes of women (e.g., Heilman & Parks-Stamm, 2007), in our view, recent evidence paints a less pessimistic picture. As we stated earlier, top women leaders were rated higher in competence than comparable men, and they were also rated higher in warmth (Rosette & Tost, 2010). In our own research, women were considered comparably competent and hirable as men even if job descriptions were male-typed (Steffens et al., 2009). In that research, women were also regarded comparably warm as men or slightly more so. We believe these findings are best explained by taking into account changes in descriptive and prescriptive gender stereotypes. As fewer people believe that women are less competent than men (e.g., Foschi, 2000), and as more people give women the same latitude for dominance and bossiness that they give men, prescriptive gender stereotypes will play a diminishing role in explaining the scarcity of women in top positions. It is our interpretation of the literature that a gender bias in hirability judgments remains in the presence of individuating information if jobs are strongly gender stereotypical. But for less gender-typed jobs, if no extreme behavior is displayed, the effects of gender on judgments may be small or nonexistent. In addition, in Chapter 8 on maintaining social hierarchies, we will see that individual differences between perceivers influence findings.

Field studies

Landy (2008) harshly criticized laboratory research with undergraduate students for being too artificial to discover anything of relevance for "real world, work-related decision making" (p. 382). For example, receiving information about an unknown person is much different from evaluating a subordinate one has known for years. It is true that basic processes discovered in laboratory research cannot be generalized to be playing a role in different contexts, under different circumstances (see Tetlock, Mitchell, & Murray, 2008). However, there are many reasons why Landy's critique is overstretched. For example, when reviewing applications, human resources managers *do* receive information about strangers. And many studies demonstrate their findings based both on student *and* on manager samples (e.g., Heilman & Okimoto, 2008; Steffens & Mehl, 2003). Further, as research shows, if initial impressions are colored by stereotypes, people often do not adjust their impressions enough after this initial "anchor" and seek confirmatory information (Maynard & Brooks, 2008); stereotyped individuals may also tend to confirm stereotypes through their behavior (Wessel & Ryan, 2008; also discussed in Chapter 4). For these and many other reasons, stereotypes may still color judgments when more information about a person is available (see also Hanges & Ziegert, 2008; Heilman & Eagly, 2008; O'Leary & Turillo, 2008). Moreover, people in powerful positions, particularly, tend to use rules of thumb, such as stereotypes, when forming impressions of others (see Ashburn-Nardo, 2008; Eagly & Karau, 2002). Finally, less artificial studies in real-world settings must not be overlooked when presenting a full picture of the literature (Ashburn-Nardo, 2008; Heilman & Eagly, 2008). We present some of these in the following section.

A famous analysis of postdoctoral fellowships granted by the Swedish Medical Research Council in 1995 (20 out of 114 applicants) yielded that female applicants needed more high-quality publications to be judged as scientifically competent as men (Wennerås & Wold, 1997). Specifically, the women needed three extra papers published in the very top journals (*Nature* or *Science*) to appear as competent as men. These effects are so striking that replications in other countries, fields, and years would be very informative. Ceci, Williams, and Barnett (2009) criticized the small sample of that study. Only four women were given a grant, and findings could be due to factors other than gender (such as field of expertise). To illustrate, in psychology, so-called journal impact factors as well as the number of citations are used as important indicators of research quality. Articles published in high-impact journals that receive many citations appear to be of particularly high quality. Both impact factors and citation numbers are typically higher in neuropsychology than in other fields. If the proportion of women differs across fields, then differences between fields could appear as if there were gender biases. If the proportion of women were higher in neuropsychology than in other fields, and if neuropsychologists needed a higher impact factor and more citations to be as successful with their grants as other psychologists, we would consider this as perfectly reasonable and fair. But it would appear to be a gender bias if field of expertise was disregarded.

There is converging evidence from other studies. When (gender-) blind auditions were introduced, more female players were hired by major symphony orchestras (see Heilman & Eagly, 2008; Reskin & Bielby, 2005). This appears to indicate that gender stereotypes reduced women's chances before blind audition was introduced. But other explanations are possible for such nonexperimental findings. Blind auditions are not introduced by chance, but this happens in a particular social context, for example, a growing awareness that some social groups may be privileged over others. Thus, one can never be sure whether this awareness or (any of) the antibias measures that were consequently introduced produced the effect.

A recent study showed a strong gender bias against female applicants by science faculty (Moss-Racusin, Dovidio, Brescoll, Graham, & Handelsman, 2012). Professors were asked to give feedback on the application of a science student who applied for a lab manager position. Given a male rather than a female name, the applicant appeared more competent, hirable, and deserving of mentoring but less likable. All of these effects were large and independent of faculty gender. The higher the professors scored on a measure of subtle bias against women (i.e., modern sexism, discussed in Chapter 5), the lower they rated the woman's competence and hirability. Clearly, double standards were at work in this study. To avoid overinterpretation, we want to point out, however, that offering a student honest feedback is not exactly the same as actually hiring him or her. It cannot be totally excluded that women got harsher feedback than men because professors liked them more. In spite of this potential limitation, such studies point at large biases operating "in the real world."

The most recent meta-analysis shed light on the effect of target gender on performance evaluations in 60 field studies (Roth, Purvis, & Bobko, 2012). Note that the included studies did *not* use experiments, as introduced earlier, to determine the influence of gender stereotypes with everything else being equal, but actual differences between male and female employees could be present. The strength of the study is its applied setting. In line with the idea that gender stereotypes are used to "fill in the blanks" if there is a lack of information (Heilman, 2012), no gender bias on *job-performance ratings* was found. On the contrary, women's performance was rated a bit higher on average than men's. In contrast, in *promotability* ratings, where the predicted (i.e., unknown) level of performance plays a crucial role, men were rated higher than women. Taken together, when unambiguous information was available (i.e., performance), gender stereotypes did not influence judgments, but in more ambiguous situations (i.e., How do you expect this person to perform given new challenges?), a gender bias appeared (see also Pratto & Bargh, 1991). To us, it appears particularly noteworthy that the same set of studies found better performance of women than men, and at the same time, men were rated more promotable than women.

Unambiguous evidence along these lines was provided in a classic experiment that varied the time point at which ratings were made (Martell, 1996). It is realistic to assume that supervisors sometimes need to rate performance several days after it has actually occurred. Participants received identical descriptions of "effective" behaviors a police officer had performed during the last few days. When ratings were given immediately afterward, as many "effective" behaviors were assigned to officer Jane as to officer John. When ratings were delayed by five days, John was given the benefit of the doubt too often: When people did not remember whether a behavior had occurred, they assumed that he had done it. Such a liberal bias did not occur for Jane. In other words, a male police officer was held to a lower standard than a female: If one did not know whether he was capable of accomplishing a certain task, one still assumed that he was, presumably due to gender stereotypes.

Shifting standards and attributions

There are several theoretical models and empirical findings on different standards applied to different social groups (for reviews, see Biernat, 2003; Foschi, 2000). Briefly, "a (high-status) man has to do less than a (low-status) woman to prove his ability, and he is allowed more latitude (more demonstrations of low ability) than a woman before lack of ability is inferred" (Biernat & Kobrynowicz, 1997, p. 546). To put it blatantly, a woman has to do more to appear as competent as a man. At the same time, a single mistake will hurt impressions of her more than of him (Brescoll, Dawson, & Uhlmann, 2010). The most elaborate model is the *shifting standards model* (e.g., Biernat & Kobrynowicz, 1997). According to this model, stereotypes serve as group-level standards against which an individual's performance is assessed. If you subscribe to a stereotype that men are better leaders than women, and you are to judge an individual, your standard for evaluating the woman's performance will be lower than that for men. Consequently, she would receive a higher rating for the same performance. If both do reasonably well, you may be more positively surprised in the case of the woman than of the man. To illustrate, take an example of a male math teacher who praises the new girl in class for some trivial computation that she solved correctly. This will probably not make her happy but inform her of his low expectations and thus of his negative stereotype (see Biernat, 2003, for other examples). Another illustration is that a woman will be considered very tall if her objective height is lower than a very tall man's: "Tall for a woman" is less than "tall for a man." Subjective language is slippery, and the objective meaning of a given concept differs, depending on the context. Let us illustrate this idea with an extreme example: I think my dog is very intelligent, but when saying this, I mean something very different than when I judge a human as very intelligent. I am applying different standards.

What effects on judgments of individuals can these shifting standards have? As already mentioned, members of negatively stereotyped groups may receive more positive reviews for the same performance. For the purpose of taking a closer look, we need to distinguish between minimum standards and high standards (Biernat & Kobrynowicz, 1997). Minimum standards are those required for surpassing a low threshold. Here, stereotypes are directly used to form expectations of group members. If you have low expectations concerning women's competence, a woman may pass a minimum threshold more easily than a man because you hold his social group to higher standards. For example, a female but not a male applicant with one relevant internship may appear worthy of a job interview. However, as stated earlier, "given low expectations, one seems to require more evidence to be certain that an individual possesses an unexpected attribute" (Biernat, 2003, p. 1023). Thus, members of negatively stereotyped groups need to be better than those of positively stereotyped groups before the same level of competence is inferred with certainty. As reviewed by Biernat (2003), one implication of minimum standards is that women may be more likely to be short-listed than men for masculine jobs. Ironically, the implication of high standards is that they will be less likely to actually be hired. This insidious mechanism must be very frustrating for the involved women.

The shifting standards model can also explain why women's performance evaluations can be better than men's, and at the same time, men are rated higher in promotability (Roth et al., 2012). If a gender stereotype is operating that women are less competent than men, the women easily receive (subjective) praise. But when it comes to more objective ratings, such as income or promotion, shifting standards disappear and men are once again a step ahead.

A larger theoretical framework for explaining what is happening when judgments of stereotyped group members are made are biases in so-called *causal attributions*: biases that occur when we try to explain why something happened. Imagine the best soccer team that you know has won the championship. What do you think about why this happened? Now imagine instead that a team you always thought was mediocre won the championship. What types of explanations can you come up with for why the team won? Maybe, if your explanations (i.e., causal attributions) are in line with existing research findings, in the first case, you are convinced that the team won because it played better than any other team. In the second case, you will find other reasons: Team members were lucky; they put in a lot of effort; and so on. And what if they played horribly (both teams)? Then it could be that you think the wonderful team was out of luck, and the mediocre team was simply as bad as you thought.

This example illustrates how causal attributions may depend on people's expectations, including causal attributions for other people's behaviors and achievements. Outcomes that match expectations are attributed to the person, and those inconsistent with expectations are attributed to the situation (see Deaux & Major, 1987). This is one mechanism that can explain why stereotypes are resistant to change: If you do not observe a difference in behavior expected on the basis of your stereotypes, the explanations you find for this behavior can nevertheless perpetuate those stereotypes.

What do we know about gender-related expectations? We know that assertiveness and competence are part of the traditional male stereotype. So the expectation people would start out with is that males act competently. In contrast, it is not part of the traditional female stereotype to be competent with regard to certain tasks. Everything else being equal, then, if the woman and the man show equally good performance, could it still be that attributions differ? Traditional research found evidence for this subtle mechanism. Men's success was attributed more to ability whereas women's success was attributed to the situation or to effort (i.e., a less stable factor), and this difference was even augmented if targets were attractive (see Deaux & Major, 1987). As this implies, attractiveness may be a double-edged sword for women at work. In fact, even though there is often a bias in favor of attractive people, they may also be discriminated against by same-gender raters. In particular, this happens if the raters themselves are average looking (Agthe, Spörrle, & Maner, 2010).

As meta-analyzed by Swim and Sanna (1996), in a paper tellingly titled, "He's Skilled, She's Lucky," when successful on masculine tasks, more skill was attributed to men than women and more effort to women than men. For failures, it was reversed: With regard to men more than women, people thought they did not try hard or were out of luck. With regard to women as compared to men, people thought the task was too difficult for them. It is important to note that the reverse was found for feminine tasks: In the presence of success, men had a more difficult time than women in being regarded as skillful. Two caveats are in order when interpreting the scope of these findings. First, the original studies were done at least 20 years ago, and in parallel with the changing stereotypes we have described, such effects may grow smaller over time. Second, as the authors stressed, all effect sizes are small, implying that "gender has little impact on the attributions given for his or her performance" (pp. 514–515).

A final factor that has an influence on the emergence of gender biases is this: A rater's time and high motivation to make accurate judgments diminishes the use of gender stereotypes and thus improves judgments. For example, accountability has a positive influence on accuracy and diminishes the use of stereotypes (Heilman & Parks-Stamm, 2007).

Summary

What can we conclude about the effects of stereotypes on judgments of others? In the laboratory, hundreds of experiments have tested if, when, and why stereotypes influence judgments of individual women and men. These experiments have been complemented by field studies that test the identified effects "in the real world." Often, effects of target gender are rather small, but small effects, occurring repeatedly, can have huge consequences. More importantly, there is no general effect such that women will always appear less competent than men. But there are conditions that make biases more likely. Biases appear if judgments are made quickly and if little diagnostic information on an individual is available. Biases also result if an ambiguous piece of information activates negative stereotypes pertaining to one, but not another, individual's group membership. Finally, biases are likely if there is a perceived lack of fit between job features and the stereotyped group. Under these conditions, biases may operate against members of negatively stereotyped groups, for example, women applying for leadership positions. Additionally, due to prescriptive stereotypes, negative behaviors such as acting too dominantly or aggressively may be held against women but be more forgiven in men. Women in leadership positions walk a fine line because they have to demonstrate at the same time that they can fulfill the role of a leader but also are as nice as a woman should be.

At the beginning of this chapter, we asked whether group stereotypes still operate if we receive information about an individual that contradicts the negative stereotype. Research on social cognition demonstrates the many ways in which the stereotype biases perception and attribution. For members of negatively stereotyped groups, more information is required until the same level of competence is inferred as for members of positively stereotyped groups. There appears to be something to the proverb that a woman needs to work twice as hard as a man to be perceived similarly competent.

· 4 ·
EFFECTS OF STEREOTYPES ON ONE'S OWN BEHAVIOR

Even if we acknowledge that our impressions of others can be biased by stereotypes, it may be harder to accept that our own interests, choices, and behaviors depend on those very stereotypes. However, they clearly do. In our societies in which gender is one of the most pervasive social categories into which people are "sorted" quite automatically (see the section on gender categorization in Chapter 1), children start at an early age to use this category as an organizing principle for experiences and perceptions (see Deaux & Major, 1987). In particular, in situations in which one gender is a minority, this category becomes very accessible (i.e., salient). People also differ in their readiness to use gender as an organizing theme for perception and action (see the concept gender schema in Part II of this book). For example, implicit gender stereotypes of science and humanities were related to women's career plans, particularly when women were highly gender identified (Lane, Goh, & Driver-Linn, 2012). The stronger their stereotypes that science is male and humanities are female, the more likely they indicated a preference for majoring in humanities and not in science.

An important topic in this context is domain-specific achievement-related behavior. It is assumed "that the conscious and non-conscious choices people make about how to spend their time and effort lead, over time, to marked differences between groups and individuals in life-long achievement-related patterns" and "... that these choices are heavily influenced by socialization pressures and cultural norms" (Eccles, 2005, p. 10). Among these pressures and norms are gender role stereotypes, cultural stereotypes of jobs and school subjects, and gender roles (Eccles, 2005). School, in general, is associated more with "female" than with "male" (Heyder & Kessels, 2013). More specifically, students are confronted with math-gender stereotypes at various occasions, for example, stereotypic beliefs expressed by teachers or parents (Jacobs & Eccles, 1992). Both parents and teachers influence children's math attitudes and achievement, perpetuating gender stereotypes (see Gunderson, Ramirez, Levine, & Beilock, 2012). The media also tend to portray men and women, girls and boys, in stereotypical ways (Leaper & Friedman, 2007). In turn, different ability self-concepts are established that mirror cultural stereotypes. Ability self-concepts in math are one factor explaining the math gender gap (Eccles, 1994). These self-concepts exert an influence on math achievement (Marsh & Yeung, 1997), having a greater impact on course selections than math grades (Köller, Daniels, Schnabel, & Baumert, 2000).

Gender differences in ability self-concepts emerge as early as Grades 3 or 4 (Marsh, 1989). Implicit gender stereotypes linking math with boys are observed from second grade on (Cvencek, Meltzoff, & Greenwald, 2011). Boys have more positive math self-concepts than girls, and girls show more favorable self-concepts related to language skills (Steffens, Jelenec, & Noack, 2010). Notably, these differences in self-concepts are found in the presence of better German grades for girls than for boys but no gender difference in math grades. As other research has shown, boys' higher math self-concepts relative to girls' are particularly pronounced in adolescence (see Hyde, Lindberg, Linn, Ellis, & Williams, 2008). In other words, the hard numbers (i.e., grades) seem to suggest that girls are as good at math as boys. The girls (and boys) themselves do not buy into this.

More generally, female and male participants explain their own success at a given task differently, depending on the gender typicality of the task (for a review, see Deaux, 1984). If a task is perceived to be typically male rather than female, female participants expect lower performance than if the same task is introduced as typically female. Success in the allegedly male task is then attributed to luck or effort more than success in the same task perceived as typically female, where success is explained more with ability. As readers may have noticed, there are strong parallels between actors and observers regarding these causal attributions: If a task is gender-atypical, both actors and observers attribute success to more fleeting factors such as luck or effort than if a task is gender-typical. Women in science, technology, engineering, and math (henceforth, STEM) fields believe they need to devote more effort to their studies than their peers. The more effort women (but not men) thought they needed to devote to succeed, the less they felt they belonged to the field, and in turn, the less motivated they were (Smith, Karyn, Hawthorne, & Hodges, 2012). It appears that attribution to effort is likely in counterstereotypical domains and eventually undermines motivation to pursue these domains.

As other research has shown, girls held stronger implicit gender stereotypes than boys with regard to physics, and girls also held more negative implicit attitudes toward physics (Kessels, Rau, & Hannover, 2006). Moreover, women's implicit attitudes toward math were more negative after they were subtly reminded of gender as compared to a control condition (Steele & Ambady, 2006). In a prospective study, stronger implicit math-gender stereotypes predicted worse math performance and lower interest in math-related careers in female college students (Kiefer & Sekaquaptewa, 2007). Taken together, all of these findings demonstrate unambiguously that cultural conceptions of what are girls' domains play an important role in determining individuals' decisions about what to excel at, and even implicit associations contribute to this. I remember a (male) math teacher pleading that I should not waste my talent and I should take advanced math courses. But my gut feelings were not in line with his reasoning—I did not feel I belonged there.

Precarious manhood

Although we tend to talk more about women than men in this book, this section is an exception. As we will see, demonstrations that men's behavior is influenced by gender stereotypes are striking. "Boys don't cry!" is an easy way to illustrate the restrictions that gender stereotypes pose upon men. During the last decade, several interesting studies have demonstrated that men, mostly (college) students, are much affected by these restrictions in various ways (for a review, see Bosson & Vandello, 2011). According to this perspective, "being a real man" is a status that one must earn and then repeatedly demonstrate to keep. Earning a man's status is reminiscent of tribal rituals during the transitions from boyhood to manhood: Men are not born; they are made. Historically, men are the high-status group as compared to women, so this worth and status need to be proven. If there is doubt concerning a specific man's manhood, one way to prove he is a "real" man is via toughness, risky physical behavior, and aggression. If this sounds to you like a crude idea from times long past, consider how many men you know today who would wear something feminine in public (e.g., pink with a flower pattern). What man would "dare" buy a pair of pants from the women's rack if they fit him better than those made for men? Who would not mind being the only heterosexual person in a gay bar (see Hegarty, Pratto, & Lemieux, 2004) or even being mistaken as gay?

Research has tried to pinpoint the consequences of gender-atypical behavior and achievement. Imagine you were taking part in a psychological study. At some point, you are asked to respond to a series of difficult, forced-choice, trivia questions (Rudman & Fairchild, 2004). Some of the questions appear typically feminine (e.g., Which company invented hair color?), others masculine (e.g., Who were the first people to use flamethrowers in battle?). After you finish the test, you learn that among all participants, you actually won the other-gender knowledge test. Then you are asked to decide whether you want your results to be published and also whether you would worry about what others think of you. And then you rate your interest in several occupations and sports (e.g., military officer, fashion model). As the experimenter enters the room, he asks you which test you won. An experiment by Rudman and Fairchild (2004) showed that alleged winners of the other-gender knowledge test wanted their success to be published less often than those of the same-gender knowledge test. They were even more reluctant the more they feared what others would think of them. These participants also reported afterward more interest in the gender-typical occupations and sports. Most strikingly, several of the participants actually lied to the experimenter by saying they won the own-gender knowledge test—again, because they feared what others would think. Although this study was not conducted to test theorizing on precarious manhood, these findings are well in line with those ideas.

These and similar findings extend the research on differences in explaining success in gender-typical and atypical tasks (introduced earlier). There, it appeared to be based on descriptive gender stereotypes that attributions for success differed ("Was it luck or ability?"). Now we see the prescriptive element involved: It appears that women and men fear social punishment for gender-atypical behavior. That could be a good reason for claiming luck instead of ability in the case of gender-atypical success. Complementing these findings, men's self-esteem is increased after they learned that they performed poorly on a task at which women do better than men (e.g., Reinhard, Stahlberg, & Messner, 2009): Failures can make you feel good!

Other research was designed specifically to test whether manhood is precarious. As its findings showed, using implicit tests, after being informed of scoring toward the "feminine end" and similar to average women, men felt anxious and upset (Vandello, Bosson, Cohen, Burnaford, & Weaver, 2008). Moreover, they thought of physical aggression more than participants in the control condition. In another study, participants all performed the same manual task (braiding). The task was called "hairstyling" in one condition and "rope reinforcing" in the other, and the context was changed accordingly (Bosson, Prewitt-Freilino, & Taylor, 2005). Men doing the hairstyling task reported more self-conscious discomfort than those reinforcing the rope, unless they were allowed to publicly state their heterosexuality in advance (i.e., affirming their masculinity). As compared to rope reinforcing, after hair braiding, men chose to hit a punching ball as their next task (instead of solving puzzles), and they hit a pad harder than those in the control condition. After being given such a chance to displaying physical aggression, men, after hair braiding, felt less anxious than those who had no chance to display aggression (see Bosson & Vandello, 2011). It appears that displaying aggression may be an effective mechanism to reduce the anxiety that is provoked by a threat to a man's masculinity. After a masculinity threat, men behaved more aggressively against a gay, but not a heterosexual, interaction partner (Talley & Bettencourt, 2008). Aggression was measured as the intensity of noise blasts delivered to an alleged partner if they made errors during a learning task. Other findings also suggest that one reason for heterosexual men's distancing from gay men is their gender identity and gender-based self-esteem (Falomir-Pichastor & Mugny, 2009).

Even men's choices of food or furniture items are influenced by gender stereotypes (Gal & Wilkie, 2010). If men have enough time, they choose the more masculine items (e.g., a square as opposed to a round sink, "D'Angelo salad" instead of "Martha's Vineyard salad"). This effect was particularly noticeable after doing something nonmasculine. As an illustration, first participants either wrote down things that they would do with their platonic female friends, but not with their platonic male friends (nonmasculine), or vice versa (affirmation of masculinity). After writing about things that they would do with their platonic female friends, men chose only 33% as compared to 50% of the more feminine items.

As we discussed earlier, women also have reasons not to transgress gender stereotypes or to hide it if they do. In particular, they may be punished for transgressions (Rudman & Fairchild, 2004). Behaving in extrafeminine ways may also serve to make up for such transgressions. For example, as mentioned, women portraying themselves in dominant ways could shield against being judged low in hirability by also including information on their social-relations orientation (Rudman & Glick, 2001). In our view, the current state of knowledge on this topic suggests that women are motivated to avoid gender-role transgressions more for external reasons (e.g., fearing social penalties). Women avoid being seen by others as role transgressors. In contrast, it appears that men's reasons for avoiding role transgressions are internal (e.g., feeling ill at ease and becoming anxious). Men do not only worry what others may think if they behave in "feminine" ways, but avoiding everything feminine is so deeply internalized for them that it makes them feel bad even in the absence of being observed. In spite of some possible differences in underlying motivations, there is abundant evidence that both men's and women's behaviors, interests, and skills are shaped by cultural gender stereotypes and that both men and women tend to avoid gender-role transgressions if they can. Next, we look at effects of stereotypes on performance.

Stereotype threat

If you are a woman, imagine a situation where you are about to park your car in a small spot by the side of the road, just big enough for the car to fit in. The moment you start driving backward, you see a group of construction workers chatting while watching you. Does that change the situation for you, psychologically? What would you be thinking about? And could your thoughts possibly affect your performance in the "parking task"? Many women report they would start thinking about unfavorable stereotypes ("women cannot drive"); they would absolutely not want to confirm this stereotype that they assume the workers hold; and they will probably do worse in the "parking task" than they would if they were not being watched by men.

In the last 20 years, one striking effect of stereotypes on women's (and not only women's) behavior has fueled much research interest. Although many psychological studies use self-report data (How do you feel about…? Do you think that person is competent? etc.), research on stereotype threat is mostly concerned with "hard data": performance on math tests or other demanding tasks. We first describe an early study and then review the literature with an emphasis, of course, on gender.

People sometimes wonder what effects coeducational schools as opposed to segregated schools may have regarding interest and performance in stereotyped domains. For example, do girls who attend girls-only schools develop more interest and higher academic self-concepts in physics than those at coed schools? (This is discussed in more detail in Chapter 9 on STEM fields). Based on similar reasoning, a long time ago a research program by Katz and colleagues investigated the effects of desegregation "on the intellectual performance of negroes" (Katz, 1964). They argued that the presence of White teachers and peers could be detrimental in several ways to Black students' performance, most importantly, "failure threat" might result as a situational threat (p. 388). A fear of failure could induce extra stress on Black students, which in turn might lower their performance. In one experiment the author reviews, Black students were given a difficult task that was either described as a hand-eye coordination task or as a test of intelligence, and it was either administered by a Black or a White experimenter. In the presence of a White experimenter, the instruction that the test measured intellectual ability considerably lowered Black students' performance.

Stereotype threat can be defined as a situational threat that may negatively affect the performance of members of groups about which negative stereotypes exist (see Steele, 1997; Steele & Aronson, 1995). As we tried to illustrate using the parking example, the apprehension triggered by the threat can interfere with performance (for reviews, see Maass & Cadinu, 2003; Schmader, Johns, & Forbes, 2008). To the degree that people after stereotype activation worry that they could make mistakes, they perform worse (Keller & Bless, 2008). Women expect to perform worse in the stereotype threat situation (Cadinu, Maass, Rosabianca, & Kiesner, 2005). The more negative math-related thoughts women have in the stereotype threat situation (e.g., "I am not good at math"), the worse their performance.

Reminding women of negative math-gender stereotypes impairs their performance on difficult math tests, and it also reduces their interest in math (e.g., Davies, Spencer, Quinn, & Gerhardstein, 2002; Spencer, Steele, & Quinn, 1999). These findings have also been observed in students at the high school level (e.g., Huguet & Regner, 2007; Keller, 2007). Often, stereotypes are activated subtly, just by informing participants that a given test usually reveals a gender difference between men and women (see Krendl, Richeson, Kelley, & Heatherton, 2008; O'Brien & Crandall, 2003). Another situation that provokes threat and lowers performance is finding oneself as the only woman in a group performing a math test, as compared to a situation in which other women are present (Sekaquaptewa & Thompson, 2003). Even more strikingly, and with immediate practical consequences, indicating one's race or gender on the first page of a test may suffice to lower performance as compared to a condition where demographic information is collected at the end (see Maass & Cadinu, 2003). Being exposed to commercials that depict women in gender-stereotypic ways can undermine women's performance on a math test, make them avoid math tests, and undermine their interest in math-intensive fields (Davies et al., 2002).

Decreased test performance after stereotype activation is pervasive (but limited to difficult tasks, e.g., O'Brien & Crandall, 2003). In fact, it can be created by informing people that they belong to a group they have never heard of (Martiny, Roth, Jelenec, Steffens, & Croizet, 2012). For example, participants learned that there are two different styles of attentional focusing, with some people working best at the beginning and end of a task and others being most concentrated in the middle. They learned which of the groups they belonged to and that this group is thought to perform worse at attention-demanding tasks than the other group. Those to whom this newly learned group membership meant something (i.e., who identified with the group) performed worse when given the instruction about the stereotype. It is typical that stereotypes reduce performance only in individuals who identify highly with the stereotyped group (e.g., Keller & Molix, 2008; for a review, see Martiny & Götz, 2011).

The stereotype threat phenomenon has fueled so much interest in researchers and practitioners because it shows that performance differences between groups can be created situationally: The existence of a negative stereotype puts the stereotyped group at a disadvantage and makes the group appear less able. It appears that women, for example, are worse at math than men, but this gender difference is not stable and is (at least partly) created in the test situation. A situation appears fair, but members of disadvantaged groups are handicapped by it. Moreover, stereotype threat can lead to disengagement from the stereotyped domain (e.g., talented women may leave math-intensive fields): As a result of these two mechanisms, because stereotypes exist, they become true (Martiny & Götz, 2011).

Ironically, much research corroborates the idea that the individuals who are most committed to an academic domain (e.g., women who are math-identified) are most vulnerable to stereotype threat (Brown & Pinel, 2003; Cadinu, Maass, Frigerio, Impagliazzo, & Latinotti, 2003; Johns, Inzlicht, & Schmader, 2008; Schmader & Johns, 2003; Spencer et al., 1999): Because domain-identified women are motivated to excel (Steele, 1997), when they are reminded of negative stereotypes, they spend effort on the achievement task at hand while at the same time being vigilant about disconfirming the relevance of the stereotype on their own behavior. According to one model trying to explain the negative effects of stereotype threat, this increased vigilance depletes working memory capacity needed to excel on complex cognitive tasks, producing the very result—poorer performance—that these women are trying to avoid (Schmader, 2010).

It is our reading of the literature that most of that research relied on participants who were somewhat math identified but not math vanguards. If women from STEM majors were the study participants, a different picture emerged. Under the same conditions that stereotype threat was observed for non-STEM students, STEM students showed a stereotype challenge effect. The students performed better when told that a test produces gender differences (e.g., Crisp, Bache, & Maitner, 2009). It is as of yet an open question why this is so. There are some hints in the literature on conditions that alleviate stereotype threat.

A growing body of evidence shows that stereotype threat effects can be eliminated by various means (e.g., Alter, Aronson, Darley, Rodriguez, & Ruble, 2010; Good, Aronson, & Inzlicht, 2003; Johns, Schmader, & Martens, 2005; Marx & Roman, 2002; McIntyre, Paulson, Taylor, Morin, & Lord, 2011). For example, recent research has shown that the stereotype threat effect is limited to women with a fragile mathematical self-concept, that is, to women with a high math self-concept according to explicit questionnaires but a low math self-concept according to implicit reaction-time tasks (Gerstenberg, Imhoff, & Schmitt, 2012). The stereotype inoculation model suggests that the implicit activation of negative stereotypes about one's own group does not necessarily result in worse performance (Dasgupta, 2011; Stout, Dasgupta, Hunsinger, & McManus, 2011). Rather, protective factors such as female role models can impede this under certain conditions (see Chapter 11 on role models).

Stereotype threat also has negative intrapersonal effects, such as decreased satisfaction and commitment in the stereotyped domain, and negative interpersonal effects, such as dismissal of feedback (for a review, see Kang & Inzlicht, 2014). Stereotype threat also interferes with ability building, such as test preparation (Appel, Kronberger, & Aronson, 2011). More generally, another factor that contributes to the practical consequences of stereotype threat is stereotype threat spillover (Inzlicht & Kang, 2010). Coping with negative stereotypes requires effortful self-control and thus interferes with processing efficiency and the ability to do well at the task at hand (Kang & Inzlicht, 2014). Thus, stereotype threat can have a host of undesirable consequences at the workplace. For example, members of a stereotyped group may perform worse because of thinking of negative stereotypes. Or, if they manage to perform well in spite of those negative stereotypes, they may feel more stressed and drained afterward. In the long run, this puts an extra burden on them.

As such, stereotype threat spillover is reminiscent of minority stress (Meyer, 2003). As suggested in the minority stress model, because of their status, minority members face extra stress that adds to the "normal" stress other individuals experience. For example, fear of discrimination may be taxing even if no discrimination is experienced. Given this extra stress, coping strategies are used that may not always be viable in the long term (e.g., drug abuse, Hatzenbuehler, 2009; Sandfort, de Graaf, Bijl, & Schnabel, 2001).

Summary

In our societies, gender is regarded as one of, if not the most, fundamental social categories. Therefore, boys and girls will grow up carefully constructing their selves in line with the social group to which they belong and in opposition to the group to which they do not belong. This occurs in constant feedback loops with their surroundings. Gendered self-construction may comprise conscious decisions to refrain from ballet dancing and wearing pink or playing soccer and selecting physics. More insidiously, it may comprise uneasy feelings when crossing the border and performing counterstereotypical behavior. Situations that appear objective and fair are not always so. The mere existences of negative stereotypes may lower the performance of individuals who belong to stereotyped groups, undermine their ability-building and interests in counterstereotypic fields, mentally deplete them, and finally drive them away from such fields. We return to many of these mechanisms from Chapter 9 on when we look at negotiations, STEM fields, and other topics. For now, we conclude that gender stereotypes massively influence men's and women's interests, abilities, choices, and eventually their careers.

· 5 ·

GENDER ATTITUDES

Social psychologists define attitudes as evaluations of people or objects (discussed in Chapter 1). Thus, gender attitudes are general evaluations of women and men, comprising spontaneous gut reactions of like or dislike and more elaborate cognitions that may be positive or negative. Attitudes are a central construct in social psychology because they are important predictors of behavior. When looking at work on gender, there is considerable consensus on the following, pattern of findings: Attitudes toward women are more positive than attitudes toward men. Eagly and Mladinic (1989; see also Eagly, Mladinic, & Otto, 1991) examined attitudes and beliefs about men and women. Results showed that both female and male participants expressed more favorable attitudes and beliefs toward women than toward men. This effect was especially pronounced for female participants and particularly large for the so-called feminine-positive traits. More concretely, the most important source of women's stronger favorability was participants' tendency to ascribe warmth to women, which comprised attributes such as helpful, kind, and understanding, thus leading future researchers to refer to this finding as the *women-are-wonderful* effect.

Why are attitudes toward women so positive? One factor may pertain to social desirability (Eagly & Mladinic, 1989): The stronger favorability of women could have reflected participants' monitoring of their responses to avoid appearing prejudiced against women. As mentioned earlier, people's motivation to appear in a socially acceptable way is a common difficulty when approaching socially delicate topics (such as gender issues) using self-report measures. Thus, using implicit measures should help to further understand the women-are-wonderful effect. More precisely, if the female preference were predominantly due to self-presentational pressures, it should be substantially diminished when using implicit measures. During the last decade, several studies have examined implicit gender attitudes (Ebert & Steffens, 2013; Nosek & Banaji, 2001; Richeson & Ambady, 2001; Rudman & Goodwin, 2004; Skowronski & Lawrence, 2001; Steffens & Plewe, 2001). The majority of the findings mirror those reported by Eagly and colleagues, that is, a consistent pattern of stronger implicit favorability toward women than men. The implicit preference for women was particularly pronounced among female participants. Male participants showed a rather inconsistent pattern, including sometimes indicating a rather small preference for men (e.g., Nosek & Banaji, 2001).

The convergence in findings on explicit and implicit gender attitudes is surprising when looking at common findings on intergroup relations and intergroup attitudes revealing that typically high-status groups exhibit strong in-group favoritism, whereas low-status groups exhibit less in-group favoritism or even an out-group preference (we discuss this more fully in Part II). Thus, when considering research on status and intergroup attitudes, one would expect exactly the reversed pattern: Women, who constitute the lower status group in Western societies, should show a smaller in-group preference compared to men, who themselves, as the higher status group, should reveal a relatively strong in-group preference. So why do attitudes toward men and women depart from these regularities commonly applicable to intergroup relations? As Rudman and Goodwin (2004) pointed out, gender relations represent a special case of intergroup relations. Different from common in-group-out-group situations, men and women are in permanent and close contact with each other, their relations are characterized by mutual dependency, and the aspect of heterosexual relationships creates an exceptional psychological and physical intimacy between men and women. Rudman and Goodwin examined several potential correlates of the implicit female preference. They showed that only women possessed a balanced gender identity, revealing that men lack a mechanism that promotes implicit preference for one's own group. Furthermore, they found profemale bias to the extent that participants automatically favored their mothers over their fathers or associated male as opposed to female gender with violence. And finally, for sexually experienced men, more implicit liking of sex corresponded to implicitly preferring females. Surprisingly, the authors did not find the expected link between an automatic gender stereotype describing women as warm and men as powerful on the one hand and implicit gender attitudes on the other hand.

Sexism

If attitudes toward women are so positive, is sexism a thing of the past? We regard gender attitudes as one aspect of gender belief systems (e.g., Deaux, 1985): Interrelated beliefs about what men and women are like (attitudes and stereotypes). Gender beliefs include respective norms concerning behavior and roles in society—what men and women should be like (prescriptive stereotypes and gender roles). Also, one's own assessment regarding gender-related traits is part of the gender belief system. For example, part of a person's gender belief system would be whether she or he applies double standards, in other words, thinks there are behaviors that are okay for men but not for women and vice versa.

What is sexism? Obviously, it is not a negative attitude toward women (i.e., a simple dislike)—women are liked very much in our societies. Instead, at the heart of sexism is women's social, political, and economic position in society. The function of sexist attitudes is to keep women in inferior positions and limit their development (see McHugh & Frieze, 1997). Components of sexism include hostility toward nontraditional women and skepticism regarding equal rights. Sexism also includes evaluating women, but not men, on the basis of their outer appearance. For example, if female, but not male, politicians' attractiveness were under scrutiny, this would qualify as sexist.

There are different conceptions of sexism, and these have been refined over time. *Old-fashioned sexism* scales measure attitudes toward women's roles and rights, differential treatment of men and women, and stereotypes of women's incompetence. An example item is this: "The intellectual leadership in a community should be largely in the hands of men" (see Spence & Buckner, 2000). Sexism is not only related to gender equality; it predicts it. One study examined 57 nations (Brandt, 2011). The more people agreed with sexist statements such as, "men make better business executives than women," the higher was objective gender inequality in that nation a few years later (measured with an objective United Nations' gender equality measure). This is strong evidence showing that sexist attitudes toward women hinder their advancement. The deeper ingrained in a culture the belief that women cannot choose or should not choose certain careers, the less successful women are.

As one can easily imagine, the percentage of people who tend to agree with blatant statements such as men's intellectual superiority has much declined since the 1970s. In newer studies, egalitarian attitudes have emerged (see McHugh & Frieze, 1997). An instrument that is supposed to measure sexism is helpful only if people differ markedly in their responses (as long as sexism exists). As more and more people support nontraditional gender roles, traditional measures of sexism become less helpful (Kite et al., 2008). Therefore, several newer scales have been developed.

Modern sexism is more subtle and covert than blatant old-fashioned sexism and therefore scales measuring modern sexism can detect differences in sexist attitudes that an old-fashioned sexism scale could not (see McHugh & Frieze, 1997). Modern sexism scales are supposed to measure denial of women's continued discrimination (Eckes & Six-Materna, 1998), lack of support for policies enhancing the status of women in society, and opposition against women's movements to obtain equal rights (Swim, Aikin, Hall, & Hunter, 1995; Swim & Cohen, 1997). An example statement is this: "In Western countries, gender equality has long been achieved." People who agree would be classified as modern sexists.

The most influential theory on a modern version of sexism was developed by Peter Glick and Susan Fiske (e.g., Glick, Diebold, Bailey-Werner, & Zhu, 1997; Glick et al., 2000). The authors started by analyzing gender relations in patriarchal societies. As they reasoned, on a societal level, patriarchy is characterized by male dominance. However, relations differ within heterosexual dyads: On the relationship level, men depend on women. Thus, men hold the power in society, but sexual reproduction lends women power when it comes to personal relationships. This complicated situation leads to ambivalence toward women. Because of this ambivalence, the group of women is divided into different subtypes that are evaluated very differently—the Madonna-whore dichotomy (Glick & Fiske, 2001; see also "marianismo" in Latino cultures, e.g., Torres, Solberg, & Carlstrom, 2002). However, ambivalence can also be directed at different aspects of the relationship with a single woman. As the name implies, *ambivalent sexism* is comprised of both negative and positive aspects of gender relations.

Hostile sexism bears a similarity both to typical prejudice measures and to modern sexism—it contains both negativity toward women and denial of discrimination. For example, prejudice is expressed in statements such as, "Women are too easily offended," and closer to a denial of discrimination comes this: "When women lose to men in a fair competition, they typically complain about being discriminated against." These items share a negative tone regarding women.

The more innovative aspect of ambivalent sexism theory is *benevolent sexism*, which ironically is the much more dangerous form. Benevolent sexism is defined as "interrelated attitudes toward women that are sexist in terms of viewing women stereotypically and in restricted roles but that are subjectively positive in feeling tone (for the perceiver) and also tend to elicit behaviors typically categorized as prosocial (e.g., helping) or intimacy-seeking (e.g., self-disclosure)" (Glick & Fiske, 1996, p. 491). Both hostile and benevolent sexism justify inequality between men and women. A first ingredient in benevolent sexism is benevolent paternalism. It reflects a relationship between men and women that is similar to that between a father and child: Whereas the father dominates and makes the decisions, he also protects his offspring: "Women should be cherished and protected by men" illustrates this attitude. The second ingredient is complementary gender differentiation, referring to positive female stereotypes. "The favorable traits ascribed to women compensate for what men stereotypically lack" (Glick & Fiske, 1996, p. 493). For example, "Women, as compared to men, tend to have a more refined sense of culture and good taste." The woman is a man's "better half." The final ingredient of benevolent sexism is heterosexual intimacy. According to Glick and Fiske (1996), this is a powerful source of men's ambivalence toward women because women are the gatekeepers of resources that men really want to have, such as sex. (According to popular stereotypes, men always want sex, and women at times grant it.) An example statement is this: "Every man ought to have a woman whom he adores." Such statements suggest that men are incomplete without a beautiful woman at their side.

Why do we consider benevolent sexism dangerous? It allows privileged groups (i.e., men) to maintain a positive self-image: As compared to "unjustified inequality in gender relations," protecting women and providing them with what they need sounds much more acceptable. Although these representations of women seem subjectively positive, exposure to them can have negative consequences. We discuss this more fully in Chapter 8 on maintaining social hierarchies. For these purposes, it is sufficient to point out that women accept benevolent sexism much more than hostile sexism. Women tend to accept benevolent sexist statements as much as men do (see Glick & Fiske, 2001). So benevolent sexism tricks women into accepting inequality disguised as differentiation. Also, hostile and benevolent sexism are positively related. This means that the people who endorse hostile sexism also tend to endorse benevolent sexism. This is the case both within a given culture and across cultures: "Nations in which hostile sexism was strongly endorsed were those in which benevolent sexism was also embraced, indicating that at the systemic level these ideologies are complementary, mutually supportive justifications of patriarchy and conventional gender relations" (Glick & Fiske, 2001, p. 112). Additionally, both hostile and benevolent sexism are related to objective gender inequality present in a given nation (Glick et al., 2000). The endorsement of benevolent sexism can be reduced by providing information on its harmful effects (Becker & Swim, 2012).

According to ambivalent sexism theory, positive attitudes toward women are constrained to those women who conform to the traditional role of women (Glick & Fiske, 1996). For example, Haddock and Zanna (1994) found more positive attitudes toward housewives compared to feminists. This is similar to the stereotype content model (Fiske et al., 2002), according to which positive attitudes are typically directed to groups higher in warmth and lower in competence (e.g., homemakers), whereas groups higher in competence and lower in warmth are liked less (e.g., feminists; see Eagly & Mladinic, 1989). Whereas hostile sexism predicts negative attitudes toward women who violate traditional gender roles, such as business women, benevolent sexism predicts positive attitudes toward traditional women, such as homemakers (see Glick & Fiske, 2001). Thus, women can choose between roles in which they are cherished and those for which they are punished—a very elaborate strategy for maintaining gender inequality.

It typically goes without saying that sexism is directed at women, but there is also sexism against men. This is an interesting example where typical speech patterns are reversed. Normally, there is "soccer" and "women's soccer"; there are managers and female managers. Maleness is taken for granted unless otherwise mentioned (for an in-depth discussion, see Part II on communication). With sexism, it is the reverse: It is assumed that it is directed at women unless otherwise mentioned. Ambivalent sexism against men also consists of a hostile and a benevolent component (Glick & Fiske, 1999; Glick et al., 2004). "Men will always fight to have greater control in society than women" and "Even if both members of a couple work, the woman ought to be more attentive to taking care of her man at home" illustrate these factors, respectively.

Summary

Although attitudes toward women are at least as positive as attitudes toward men, attitudes toward gender equality do not follow suit. Instead, sexism remains well and alive. The more people believe that women should have different roles in society than men and that men are more competent in high-status roles than women, the less gender equality there is. A subtle and modern form of sexism is denying that women are still discriminated against. Even more subtle is benevolent sexism, a subjectively positive, chivalrous attitude toward women that nevertheless is closely related to hostile sexism and to the discrimination of women, particularly to those in nontraditional roles.

· 6 ·

GENDER DIFFERENCES

Social-psychological research on differences between women and men has a long tradition (see, e.g., Deaux, 1984, for an early review). In part, this is due to the "convenience of using sex as a variable in analysis" (Deaux, 1985, p. 56). However, as Deaux also pointed out, an atheoretical or even opportunistic search for gender differences is not very fruitful. What have we explained if we know that the fact of whether someone is male or female is related (typically in some small way) to some psychological outcome? A person's gender "serves only as a gross marker" (Deaux, 1984, p. 108). What we want to know is what underlies such a difference, psychologically. Nevertheless, for practical rather than theoretical purposes, it could be informative to know, for example, whether vocational interests of women and men differ (even if the search for answers will probably yield underlying psychological factors). Therefore, in this context, what we are interested in are responses to the question of whether there are differences in abilities, interests, and behavior between women and men that may explain gender segregation at work (i.e., why men and women end up in very different occupations).

Before turning to differences between women and men, two words of caution are necessary to avoid misinterpretations. First, as pointed out earlier, gender distributions overlap largely, and gender differences are comparatively small. Men and women are much more similar than different in most social-psychological aspects, particularly those related in any way to work (see Abele, 2000).

Related to the fact that average differences (i.e., mean differences) between men and women are typically quite small, as compared to the wide range of scores within each gender group, is the question of whether studying these means actually provides the responses we are looking for in many contexts (see Ceci et al., 2009, for an in-depth discussion). Briefly, means are most adequate when we are interested in the average man or the average woman: Is the average woman a better leader than the average man? Is the average woman less inclined to take risks than the average man? Does the average woman negotiate as successfully as the average man? So, are these the individuals we are interested in? In this context, typically they are not. Rather, we are interested in those who are above average or even far above average with regard to certain traits and skills (i.e., very intelligent, with exceptional leadership abilities, etc.). Whereas one may start out assuming that distributions of men and women are similar along a given trait or skill, it is by now clear that this often is not the case. Instead, many traits vary a bit more among men than among women. For example, nowadays, often no gender difference is found in average intelligence, but boys are overrepresented both among the few who are highly intelligent and among the few with the least intelligence (for a review, see Ceci et al., 2009). The gender differences that have been found at the extremes of the distribution are much larger than any mean differences we know of, pertaining to the same factors. For example, among those with the very highest scores in mathematic reasoning (the 1% best) according to some studies, there are 7 times more men than women (but data suggest this proportion may be declining over time). To the degree that being much above average in mathematical reasoning is important for career success, such a difference could explain that men outnumber women among the highly successful. A former president of Harvard University, Lawrence Summers, referred to such numbers when providing his view on the lack of social diversity in science and engineering and thus provoked a heated debate in the United States (see Williams & Ceci, 2007).

Note that it is unclear how important mathematical reasoning is for a career in STEM fields (see Ceci et al., 2009). Also, it is hard to imagine that verbal abilities, associative memory, and perceptual speed are not needed for a top scientist. These are skills in which women outnumber men among the

5% best (Ceci et al., 2009). The cognitive differences found among the most talented most likely do not explain the proportions of women and men we observe in top positions. For example, if there were twice as many men as women among the 5% with the highest abilities, then we should observe 33% women in top positions—not 15% or fewer.

As we will see, there are certainly other factors that are very important for career success. For example, if one holds a very visible position, one needs the necessary social skills to know not to make public remarks about historically disadvantaged groups that upset a whole nation (Summers resigned as Harvard president not long after the cited speech). The point we are making here is that mean differences between men and women are often small and relatively uninteresting, and gender differences among those with the highest abilities may often be more telling.

Second, it is perfectly ambiguous, if differences are found (pertaining to means or extreme values), whether these are genetically based or have their roots in the different upbringing of girls and boys. Often, whether one is male or female is a marker of some underlying differences rather than the cause (see Deaux, 1993). As we discussed earlier, gender stereotypes contribute to domain-specific ability concepts, which, in turn, determine effort, interests, and, finally, abilities (see Chapter 1 on gender stereotypes). As another example, classroom observations demonstrate that teachers treat boys and girls differently (see Ceci et al., 2009). Parents are also more likely to explain science to their sons than daughters (see Hyde, 2007). More generally, parents encourage gender-typical activities in their children (for a meta-analysis, see Lytton & Romney, 1991). Gender socialization begins at birth, when parents start to see their daughters as finer featured and handle their sons more roughly even before they are three months old (for a review, see Stern & Karraker, 1989). One can easily imagine that gender differences in interests result from such differences in early interaction and encouragement. Several experiments found that unknown infants are described as more feminine when being introduced as girls and as more masculine when labeled boys, but other experiments failed to replicate this finding (see Stern & Karraker, 1989). Cross-culturally, some differences between the socialization of boys and girls can be observed: There is no culture in which girls are more encouraged toward physical aggression than boys (Sidanius et al., 1994). Early learning accounts for many adult gender differences (see Deaux & Major, 1987). These findings strongly suggest influences of socialization on adult gender differences. If girls and boys are encouraged, from the first months of their lives on, to perform different behaviors, if they are praised and warned in different ways, if parents, teachers, and their whole social environment, even unconsciously, treat them in ways that reinforce gender stereotypes and gender differences, it is hard to imagine that this would not leave a mark:

> From the moment of birth, a child's gender influences the opportunities she or he will experience. Within a few years of life, children begin to form their own ideas about gender that subsequently guide the types of activities they practice, what they find interesting, and the achievements they attain. As children develop, their gender self-concepts, beliefs, and motives are informed and transformed by families, peers, the media, and schools. (Leaper & Friedman, 2007, p. 561)

Thinking one step further, if, due to factors in the environment, boys get away more easily than girls with being "one-track minded" (e.g., playing around with numbers all day without contributing to housework or watching younger siblings throughout childhood and youth), differences among those with the highest abilities in a given domain will emerge. Moreover, as the previous section on stereotype threat indicates, gender differences can clearly be socioculturally based, for example, created in testing situations. We have also seen that stereotypes and others' as well as our own expectations with regard to the social groups to which we belong affect behavior. Therefore, differences observed between men and women who are put into the objectively same situation may also depend on the fact that the situation does not feel identical to men and women. All of these factors, and maybe others as well, comprise gender-specific socializations that will most probably provoke adult gender differences. After these words of caution, we turn to the evidence on gender differences, first in abilities and then in interests and behavior, with a focus on differences related to assertiveness, competence, and warmth.

Gender differences in abilities

Whereas it is part of the male stereotype to be good at math and of the female stereotype to excel in languages (e.g., Steffens et al., 2010), many findings suggest that there are no gender differences in children's primary abilities underlying math performance (for a review, see Spelke & Grace, 2007). Often, no gender differences in math performance are found (e.g., Hall, Davis, Bolen, & Chia, 1999). Also, cross-cultural comparisons show that girls are better at math than boys in several countries (e.g., Hyde, 2007), and differences between cultures in math performance are much larger than gender differences within the cultures: "Culture is considerably more important than gender in determining mathematics performance" (Hyde, 2007, p. 140). Also, whether girls or boys perform better on a math test depends on the specific mix of questions this test consists of (Ceci et al., 2009). And one reason why standardized tests underpredict women's abilities is that women approach these tests with more conscientiousness, thus working more slowly (Kling, Noftle, & Robins, 2012).

One reliable gender difference relates to spatial ability (e.g., Hyde, 2007). Interpreting this gender difference, it should not be overlooked that spatial ability can be vastly improved quite easily through practice. Boys who play computer games have higher mental rotation scores than those who do not (e.g., Quaiser-Pohl, Geiser, & Lehmann, 2006). If boys spend more time playing computer games that train spatial ability, it is to be expected that they are better at this, and if girls play such games often, their spatial abilities improve massively (see Newcombe, 2007). Do the increased outdoor play activities of boys as compared to girls provoke differences in spatial ability that, through some unknown causal path, later result in a higher proportion of men than women in STEM careers? As Ceci and colleagues (2009) pointed out, this suggestion is surprising, as the stereotypes of the sports-mad guys and the nerds do not appear to have much in common, and they appear to apply much less to the same subgroup of boys. Thus, it appears far-fetched to use the sports-mad guys for explaining the under-representation of women in STEM top positions.

Moreover, as meta-analyses have shown, gender differences in spatial ability depend on gender roles, specifically, on masculine (not feminine) gender-role identity (i.e., the degree to which people describe themselves as ambitious, determined, having leadership qualities, etc.). For example, with regard to one component of spatial ability (i.e., mental rotation), the likelihood of being at least average increased from 38% for feminine women (35% for feminine men) to 62% for androgynous (i.e., women with both feminine and masculine traits) or masculine women (65% for androgynous or masculine men; Reilly & Neumann, 2013). In other words, gender roles are more important than gender in explaining gender differences in spatial ability (see also Abele, 2000). According to Ceci and colleagues (2009), although it is often claimed, the causal role of spatial ability for success in math-related domains has not convincingly been shown.

As mentioned earlier, with regard to verbal abilities, associative memory, and perceptual speed, women outnumber men among the 5% best (Ceci et al.,

2009). Taken together, there appear to be some small differences between men and women in abilities, alternately favoring women or men. These differences appear to be declining as gender socialization is becoming less rigid over the decades. They are certainly too small to explain gender segregation at work.

Differences in interests and behavior

In several sections of this book, we discuss whether it could be the case that fewer women than men are interested in pursuing high status and prestige careers or in gaining money. For example, if more women than men were interested in having a fulfilling job, and more men than women would "trade" that against making more money, then we would arrive at a gender difference in careers and income that would not be due to the restrictions imposed on any gender. On the one hand, the literature on work values suggests that indeed, men do value income, status, and prestige more than women (for a review, see Pratto et al., 1997). On the other hand, even after accounting for many relevant factors, the effect of gender on career progress remained, with more women than men working in inadequate positions that they are over-qualified for (Abele, 2000). Specifically, the author asked 1,500 participants to respond to a set of questions over the course of several years. That allowed her to compute which factors lead to more successful careers. For example, type of major and achievement motivation turned out to be relevant. But given the same major, achievement motivation, etc., women were still less successful than men. This hints at a difference between men's and women's opportunities, in addition to possible differences in interests and behavior that we discuss more fully later.

But before looking at specific gender differences, we want to highlight that gender differences in interests and behavior should not be regarded as stable across situations. Rather, whether gender-related behavior is displayed depends on situational cues, on the strength of identification with one's gender, on interactions with perceivers, and other factors (Deaux & Major, 1987). For example, there are "strong" situations, with immediate situational demands, where everyone behaves similarly, and there are no gender differences. At work, an example could be that if you find yourself alone with a high-status guest, you offer the person something to drink, no matter whether you are a warm person or not, male or female. A weaker situation would be that the same guest meets with a gender-mixed team in the conference room, and the boss indicates that first, the guest should be served something to drink. This could activate the gender-related self-concept in a female subordinate ("I am a person who cares well for others; I will get the refreshments") but not in her male colleague. This could particularly be the case if the guest looked at her, indicating that he perceives her in a gender-specific way. In this situation, then, gender differences in behavior could be observed. As this indicates, there will be a lot of variability in observed gender differences, depending on the dynamics of the situation and on the individuals involved, including their goals. Interestingly, a consequence of this reasoning is that one perceiver may be confronted with much more gender-typical behavior than another, depending on their own expectations. A boss who expects, based on her gender stereotypes, female subordinates to cooperate and male subordinates to take charge, will observe more differences between male and female subordinates than a boss who thinks that there are no gender differences between subordinates (see Deaux & Major, 1987). This is an instantiation of the more general concept *self-fulfilling prophecy*, where perceivers end up seeing what they expected in the first place. As reviewed by Deaux and Major (1987), experiments showed that a colleague expected to be female is assigned more feminine tasks and less attention is paid to her preferences than if the colleague is expected to be male. Conversely, there is more self-disclosure and help offered toward the alleged woman than man and more aggression toward him. Both women and men modify their self-presentations and behavior to match the expectations and values of perceivers. Given different expectations conveyed by perceivers, targets are active agents who decide how to act upon them. Returning to the example, the female colleague may fulfill others' gender-based expectations, or openly refuse to serve the drinks, or charmingly ask her male colleague who stands closer to the bar to follow the request. This would, in turn, make it difficult (but not impossible) for him to turn down the proposal. Over time, if targets fulfill others' gender-related expectations, they may adapt their self-concepts, thus becoming the people others expected them to be (Deaux & Major, 1987). For example, a woman expected to take the minutes at meetings who follows this request, and then is praised for their quality, may incorporate into her ability self-concept that she excels at this type of task, whereas her male colleague may never find out how good he would be at it. Conversely, the male colleague who keeps being asked to fix others' computer problems may end up thinking that he is the computer wizard in the team, never knowing that his female colleague who has never been asked for help surpasses him in this ability. Taken together, whether gender differences are observed depends on an interaction among the situation, the person, and the perceiver.

Differences related to assertiveness and competence

Gender differences related to agency (i.e., assertiveness and competence) are very interesting in this context because individuals with more agentic self-concepts have more successful careers than those with less agentic self-concepts (e.g, Abele, 2003). An important finding of Abele's longitudinal study was that individuals became more agentic after more career success (i.e., they rated themselves higher on traits such as "self-confident" and "independent"). Such findings remind us that individual traits are nothing static but change with the social roles individuals fulfill (see Chapter 7 on social role theory).

Some gender differences have been reliably found in many studies. Women are more oriented toward equality in intergroup relations than men, whereas men are more politically conservative, ethnocentric, racist, and militaristic than women: Men are more oriented toward "ranking" and women towards "linking" (see Sidanius et al., 1994). Although it is not immediately obvious why such a difference matters in the work context, that context, in fact, is replete with social hierarchies (i.e., some people have more power than others; there are bosses and subordinates). Therefore, it is possible that men find their place in such hierarchies more smoothly than women, who could feel more ill at ease in these hierarchies. The historical position of women as subordinates is, of course, another reason why it could be more difficult for women than men to assume and negotiate a position of power.

Richard, Bond, and Stokes-Zoota (2003) reviewed all 83 available meta-analyses on social-psychological gender differences (i.e., they excluded gender differences in cognitive abilities). The review is based on over 5,000 original findings and yielded the following average gender differences related to assertiveness and competence: Men are more aggressive than women; men are more likely than women to think their performance was due to ability, whereas women are more likely than men to think their performance was due to luck; women's successes as compared to men's are deemed more from effort; men are more assertive and have higher self-esteem than women. Generally, men tend to overestimate their abilities, whereas women make rather realistic estimates (Roberts & Nolen-Hoeksema, 1994; see also Sieverding, 2003).

It is often thought that men's career motivation is higher than women's, but this idea "is more consistent with gender stereotypes than with empirical evidence" (King, 2008, p. 1686). For example, those male and female alumni of an MBA program who were not entrepreneurs reported similar career motivations (DeMartino, Barbato, & Jacques, 2006). Male and female college students also report an equally strong commitment to their educational objectives (see Devos et al., 2008). As assertiveness is stereotypically male, one would imagine a consistent finding: Men describe themselves as more assertive than women. Does current research corroborate this assumption? Differences in self-ascriptions in line with stereotypes appear to be small and have grown smaller over the decades (Twenge, 2001). For example, in one unpublished study from our lab, we asked university students whether traits such as "self-assured" and "easily makes decisions" are more typical of men, more typical of women, or anything in between. On average, these traits were rated as more typically male, in line with stereotypes. The same students also rated whether each trait applies to them. Both men and women rated themselves on average as rather assertive, with no gender difference. We have observed this pattern of findings many times, on the most common questionnaires internationally used to assess assertiveness. As Abele (2003, p. 768) summarized, "in specific samples of university graduates, one even finds no sex differences in agentic traits at all" (see also Evers & Sieverding, 2014; Sczesny et al., 2004). We believe this pattern of findings is telling with regard to the slowness with which socially shared beliefs about social groups change (see, e.g., Abele, 2000): It takes much evidence to the contrary, for a sustained period of time, until people perceive that the stereotype is no longer true that the average man is considerably more assertive than the average woman.

A willingness to work long hours can be conceived as something that is also related to an individual's ambition and career motivation. A larger proportion of men than women with high abilities worked exceedingly long hours (i.e., over 50 or even over 60 hours per week) and were willing to do so in the job of their first choice (see Lubinski & Benbow, 2007). Note that this is not a mean difference but one pertaining to those with the highest abilities. As other research showed, if women work fewer hours than men, they still do their work, but they miss networking time (see Mölders & van Quaquebeke, 2011). Because networks have a positive influence on careers, this may eventually have negative effects on their careers.

If careers such as medicine or science hinge on people investing over 60 hours a week for several years, women may choose to opt out (also because they are less likely to have a family that does not object to this, as we discuss in Chapter 7 on social roles). As a university professor of medicine once told me, one major difficulty in recruiting female junior scientists was that he could not convince the women that "a normal person even wants to have the job given the circumstances under which men performed it" (e.g., research hours confined to nights and weekends after weekdays filled with hospital work, insecurity of obtaining tenure, etc.). Is there anything to this observation? Are there jobs that women do not want? If we look at jobs in which the proportion of women has increased over time versus stagnated, an exceeding work load could be one factor that makes a difference. Other factors are introduced later.

Risk taking

Among potential gender differences related to job success, risk taking has drawn much attention. Many studies have found gender differences in risk taking (for reviews, see Eckel & Grossman, 2008; Powell & Johnson, 1995). A decision is riskier than another if the variance in possible outcomes is greater (Mishra, 2014). For example, if you choose an investment that yields a profit of 3%, this is less risky than an investment that yields either 0% or 6%. Why is risk taking important? As Johnson and Powell (1994) elaborated, effective decision making lies at the heart of management—a good manager is essentially a person who makes good decisions. Most if not all of these decisions are made under uncertainty, so the subjective assessment of gains and costs (i.e., risks) associated with these decisions plays an important role. Whether decision makers seek out or shy away from risks can have serious consequences for an organization and even for the world economy as a whole, as the most recent economic crisis has vividly demonstrated. It is important to know if and under what conditions men systematically take more, or fewer, risks than women.

One may assume that risk-taking propensity is a general personality trait. Research has clearly shown that this is not the case. The willingness to take a risk depends on the task, the context, expertise with a given domain, and so on (see, e.g., Eckel & Grossman, 2008; Harris, Jenkins, & Glaser, 2006; Hyrsky & Tuunanen, 1999). For example, entrepreneurs are more willing to take risks in domains where they are experts. Cultural factors also play a role, with a higher risk-taking propensity among Americans than Europeans (e.g., Hyrsky & Tuunanen, 1999). In fact, no significant gender difference was found in Hyrsky and Tuuanen's (1999) study. At the same time, there was a cultural difference: Finns scored more than 3 points lower than U.S. Americans on a

0–20 scale. Also, higher education goes along with a higher risk propensity (Moreschi, 2005). Although most organisms are risk averse, even birds may become risk-prone, depending on the context (Mishra, 2014). Precisely, if there is a need that cannot be fulfilled with the less risky option, birds become risk-prone. An example in the human sphere would be this: Only if you have pressing debts of $1,000 that you cannot pay will you prefer a gamble where you either win $1,000 or nothing to one where you get $500 for sure (i.e., an amount that does not fulfill your need). In short, risk taking cannot be judged, in general, independent of context (Figner & Weber, 2011).

Some time ago, it was concluded that there is no consensus among researchers "on the size of gender differences" in decision making or on any context and study factors that make differences more or less likely to be observed (Powell & Ansic, 1997, p. 607). In other words, the evidence is complex. Many studies in the context of financial decision making have found that women make less risky investment decisions than men, which may lower their incomes and pensions (see Eckel & Grossman, 2002, 2008). One may wonder whether this is still the case after the last economic crisis in which men presumably lost more of their pensions than women.

Women also perceive financial risks to be higher than men (Figner & Weber, 2011). As an example pertaining to income, one study found that female CEOs gained less than their male counterparts because the women preferred fixed compensation whereas the men were more likely to opt for performance-contingent components (cited in Eckel & Grossman, 2002). In the presence of gender stereotypes on risk aversion, it is also possible that women receive more conservative advice than men. In fact, both women and men, but men to a larger degree, judged individual women to be more risk-averse than individual men (Eckel & Grossman, 2002).

The willingness to take job-related risks could have potentially large effects for men's and women's different career outcomes. For example, if taking risks as a middle manager leads to highly visible success with a certain (small) probability, and only a small number of middle managers get promoted, then men's chances to get promoted may be increased as compared to those of women. As a second example, if faced with the choice between two jobs, one involving a risk of total failure or, alternatively, big success, and the other implying moderate success but no risk, and men were more inclined than women to choose the first option, then more men than women would end up having big success (see also Booth & Nolen, 2012). As a side note, men would also be more likely to suffer total failure than women; we do not know any respective statistics, but anecdotal evidence from scandals that made the news supports this idea. The scope of this book is limited in that we are more concerned with the success side.

As observed in a meta-analysis of 150 different studies on risk taking, whether gender differences are observed and how large they are depend on the task at hand and also on the age of the study participants (Byrnes, Miller, & Schafer, 1999). For example, the gender difference in risky driving (and also as a pedestrian; see Powell & Johnson, 1995) and in tasks involving physical skills is much bigger than that for drinking or risky drug use. Often, women estimate the associated risks to be higher than men, and also, they judge the negative consequences to be more severe than men (Harris et al., 2006). Typically, regarding the social domain, no gender differences in risk propensity are found (see Harris et al., 2006). This domain is assessed with questions such as "discussing opposing viewpoints with a friend." All of these are, of course, not the risk context we are most interested in. Of particular interest, although choice-dilemma tasks as investigated in the laboratory yielded a small gender difference, tasks classified as intellectual risk taking yielded a rather large effect (Byrnes et al., 1999). These were, for example, mathematical reasoning tasks in which participants chose their preferred level of task difficulty. The authors observed that women were disinclined to take risks even under circumstances where this would be beneficial to them. As they concluded, "men and boys would tend to encounter failure or other negative consequence more often than women and girls... women and girls would tend to experience success less often than they should" (Byrnes et al., 1999, p. 378).

On average, men reported enjoying such risky activities as gambling and skydiving more than women (Harris et al., 2006). In the gambling and health domains, differences in enjoyment, perceptions of the probability, and perceptions of the severity of negative consequences explained the gender differences in risk taking. This means that no gender differences were observed when these factors were taken into account statistically. One may interpret these findings as follows: Those who enjoy risk taking and underestimate the probability and severity of negative consequences have an increased risk propensity, and among them there happen to be more men than women.

The overall gender difference that was found across all tasks can be illustrated as follows: 53% of men and 47% of women would take a certain risk (numbers are taken from Byrnes et al., 1999). First, these numbers, once again, point to the large overlap between men's and women's behavior that is typically observed—gender does not appear particularly informative for predicting who will take a risk and who will not. Second, say that one million middle managers of each gender were faced with a risky situation. Then, 60,000 more men than women would choose to take the risk. Say, hypothetically, that the risk entails a 25% chance of success. Then, 15,000 more men than women would take home that success. We can imagine that such differences in behavior contribute to explaining the scarcity of women in top positions. These findings need to be considered in light of the observation that managers who are assigned challenging jobs (or seek them out?) move up the hierarchy faster (Martell et al., 2012).

Risk taking in women is more negatively regarded than in men, and how far individuals describe themselves as masculine or feminine influences their risk-taking propensity (see Johnson & Powell, 1994; Powell & Ansic, 1997). Familiarity with tasks appears to moderate gender differences in risk taking, which often grow smaller as participants get more experienced with a given task (see Powell & Johnson, 1995).

Gender differences in risk taking are often portrayed as women's failure. From a societal perspective, this may be true. For example, if female entrepreneurs overestimated their chances of success, as men do, and thus founded more start-ups, then a handful of successful ones would remain, strengthening the economy. But how good would this be for the individual woman? An intervention provoking the overestimation of one's success in the face of likely failure would ethically appear very questionable to us. We discuss entrepreneurship more fully in Chapter 9.

The quality of the decisions taken by men versus women did not differ in many studies conducted after 1980 (Powell & Johnson, 1995). Some researchers have also suggested that gender differences in risk propensity are growing smaller (see, e.g., Moreschi, 2005). A crucial question, of course, is how the quality of decisions is assessed: What counts as a good decision? A traditional (normative) economic view is that the best decisions are those with the largest expected payoff: "Risk aversion is a normatively irrational behavior" (Rydell, Loo, & Boucher, 2014, p. 387). For example, a 50% chance of gaining $200,000, with a complementary 50% chance of gaining nothing, has an expected outcome of $100,000 (200,000 *.50 + 0 *.50). An alternative option, with a 50% chance of gaining $100,000, with a complementary 50% chance of gaining $60,000, has an expected outcome of only $80,000 (100,000 *.50 + 60,000 *.50). So a manager, faced with the choice between both options, should choose the former one. Women choose the latter, less risky option more often than men. In one experiment, 35% of the men and

13% of the women chose the most risky option that yielded the largest expected payoff (Eckel & Grossman, 2002). Note that "35% of the men" implies that the majority of the men did *not* choose this option. In spite of that, there is little discussion on the question of how men's risk aversion can be countered. Moreover, readers can make up their own minds whether they would prefer their bosses (or the managers they supervise or even their spouses) to take the first option under any circumstances. In general, empirical research has demonstrated again and again that human decision making does not follow such normative theories (for a recent review, see Mishra, 2014). Personally, I would certainly invest a portion of my pension where the payout will either be $100,000 or $60,000, rather than one returning either $200,000 or nothing. But then, of course, I am a woman.

Gender differences in abstract gambling contexts are well established, with men generally taking higher risks than women (for reviews, see Eckel & Grossman, 2008; Powell & Johnson, 1995). One British study compared women's and men's strategies when betting in (real) horse and dog races (Johnson & Powell, 1994). Men made riskier decisions than women. Conversely, women made more decisions that protected their investment (i.e., yielded some payout), corroborating men's greater risk propensity. Interestingly, there was no evidence at all that women's decisions were inferior to men's. In an additional study, the authors tested how far the risky decisions differed for female and male management students after three years of formal training in decision making. Among them, 40% were practicing managers (part-time students). No gender differences in risk propensity were found. In line with this, it has been concluded that neither male and female managers nor male and female entrepreneurs differ in risk propensity (e.g., Powell & Johnson, 1995).

This is an important finding because it demonstrates that gender differences found in the general population (or in undergraduate student samples) cannot be generalized to those who have undergone formal training. After formal training that guides one's work-related decisions, the influence of gender-stereotypical behavior may be minimized. However, another study, also using such populations, did find that women were more risk-averse than men (Powell & Ansic, 1997). Participants were asked to make several decisions in an insurance context and in a financial-market context. As a compensation for taking part in the experiment, one randomly selected decision was paid. Interestingly, the women gained more than the men in both experiments, even though the difference in gains was not statistically significant. We take this as an indicator that being risk-averse was a good strategy across these contexts. In other words, it is somewhat surprising that researchers never ask the following: Why are men too inclined to take risks, as compared to women? And what can be done to change this? As we see in Part II of this book, Bruckmüller and colleagues (Bruckmüller, Hegarty, & Abele, 2012) elaborated on different ways in which gender differences are framed.

Yet another study found that Indian female managers were more inclined to take risks than Indian male and American male and female managers (cited in Hyrsky & Tuunanen, 1999). Given the discrepancies in findings of such economic studies, it appears timely to ask under which conditions and with what type of tasks do which groups of men and women show different risk propensities and what are the underlying (psychological) causes for the emerging pattern of findings? There are too many differences among the studies to identify with certainty the crucial differences (see Eckel & Grossman, 2008).

Another limitation concerning the generalizability of findings was demonstrated by Schubert and colleagues (Schubert, Brown, Gysler, & Brachinger, 1999), who found gender differences in line with stereotypes in an abstract gambling context. However, when identical decisions had to be made, but they were framed as "investment" and "insurance" (i.e., concrete), the gender differences disappeared. These findings suggest that gambling tasks may overestimate existing gender differences in real-life risky decision making. We believe gambling is a male-typed behavior, thus being more in line with men's than women's gender role. The evidence on gender differences in risk propensity in more contextualized tasks is mixed (see Eckel & Grossman, 2008, for a review).

When taking equally good choices, men were more confident in their decisions than women, who thought their performance was due more to good luck (e.g., Powell & Ansic, 1997; for a review, see Johnson & Powell, 1994). Generally, men report greater confidence in their decisions than do women (see Powell & Johnson, 1995). It would be interesting to test the role of stereotypes in the differential risk-taking propensity of men and women by misinforming participants that women make riskier decisions in regard to certain tasks than men.

Evolutionary psychologists assume that gender differences in risk taking are due to different adaptations of men and women in hunter-gatherer societies (see, e.g., Eckel & Grossman, 2002; Harris et al., 2006). Basically, women could be more risk-averse than men because they had to protect their vulnerable offspring for an extended time period. We do not want to go into the details of this theoretical position (for a general critique concerning its assumptions, see Newcombe, 2007). However, we do want to point out that several research findings are not well in line with these ideas. First, as we have already mentioned, gender differences in risk taking are not independent of task and context. If there is no general enduring personality trait "risk propensity" that differs between men and women, different gender roles concerning childcare 200,000 years ago can hardly explain, for instance, risk propensity in games where one has to steer tanks across mine fields (see Powell & Johnson, 1995). Second, we believe cultural differences in risk propensity (e.g., Hyrsky & Tuunanen, 1999) are more easily explained by socialization than hereditary factors. But of course, it is possible that Finns, given the specific climate where they live, evolved to take fewer risks than U.S. Americans. If gender differences decrease within 30 years, as research indicates, this is "evidence of the strength of cultural factors in determining such outcomes, because biology has not changed over this period" (citing Ceci et al., 2009, p. 218, who refer to the representation of both genders in science).

Both enduring and situational gender stereotypes affect risk taking. It appears that men can get away with being daredevils, but women should not act like that. A recent experiment compared British teenagers from single-gender and coed schools when gambling in same-gender versus gender-mixed groups (Booth & Nolen, 2012). As Booth and Nolen (2012) stated, genetic differences between people living in Essex versus Suffolk can safely be assumed to be rather small. First, that experiment replicated the overall gender differences, with girls (privately) choosing the risky gamble less often than boys. The differences that were observed within gender groups are more interesting. The gender difference in risk propensity was large for girls and boys from coed schools and nonexistent for those from same-gender schools. Also, girls assigned to gender-mixed groups took fewer risks than those assigned to all-girl groups. Also, stereotype threat affected women's risk propensity (e.g., Rydell et al., 2014). In the Booth and Nolen experiment, boys' risk propensity did not depend on group composition (but on type of school). These findings held up when confounding factors such as parents' educational level were considered. In the context of financial decision making (i.e., deciding how much of a large sum of money they would invest in a risky decision), girls from all-girl schools even invested more than boys from coed schools. These findings strongly suggest that gender stereotypes and gender socialization are important factors in explaining men's higher risk propensity than women's. Long-term (i.e., schooling) and short-term (i.e., current) gender-related group composition affects an individual's risk propensity. Note that this explanation implies that women are first culturally socialized to be good, cautious girls, and then their lack of risk propensity is held against them. Ironically, this is the case even if the women gain as much or more money with their more careful strategy as the men in the experiments.

Differences related to relationships

We now turn to the second main dimension of gender stereotypes, warmth or relationship orientation. Whereas it is often believed that boys are interested in objects and girls in people, many studies provide no evidence for this (for a review, see Spelke & Grace, 2007). However, as adults, women as a group tend to prefer to work with people and men with things (see Lubinski & Benbow, 2007). More generally, men construct their self in a more *independent* way, whereas women tend more toward *interdependent* self-construal (Cross & Madson, 1997). Thus, a man's self-definition is based more on his unique abilities and attributes and on what distinguishes him from others. In contrast, a woman's self-definition is based more on her relationships with other people. As the literature on work values suggests, women value helping others and equality among individuals more than men (for a review, see Pratto et al., 1997). Consequently, jobs attract different proportions of men and women. For example, with the same degree, men would rather work with the elite and women with the disadvantaged (Pratto et al., 1997).

What do we know about warmth-related gender differences? A somewhat dated meta-analysis shows that women are more easily influenced than men (Eagly & Carli, 1981). It is also interesting that this overall small gender difference was larger in the older than younger studies included in that research, providing some hint that it was diminishing. A common stereotype is that women depend more on feedback than men do. Women are indeed more responsive than men to the evaluations they receive from others (e.g., Roberts & Nolen-Hoeksema, 1994). It appears that men rather discount feedback as irrelevant, whereas women consider its informational value. However, this also depends on factors of the situation, as we see later.

In the realm of warmth, a construct that is somewhat difficult to define is empathy (for a review, see Eisenberg & Lennon, 1983). It has been defined as the ability to understand the affective or cognitive state of others or as affective response to others' emotional states (such as crying because they are sad). Sensitivity to social cues is also part of the parcel. The ability to infer the content of others' thoughts and feelings is referred to as empathic accuracy (Gesn & Ickes, 1999) or social sensitivity. According to a review, women are highly accurate in decoding nonverbal cues (Hall, 1978). Also, using self-report measures, women indicate that they react more emphatically than men, but more objective measures of emphatic responding did not yield corroborating evidence (Eisenberg & Lennon, 1983). Eisenberg and Lennon (1983) also posited that the gender difference in decoding nonverbal cues is smaller than Hall (1978) interpreted, and when it comes to detecting deception, the gender difference is nonreliable, according to these authors (i.e., there is no gender difference in detecting deceptive nonverbal cues, such as others' lying). The review of meta-analyses cited earlier reported that gender differences in the expression and understanding of emotions were consistently found (Richard et al., 2003). Notwithstanding these different views on the interpretation of the evidence, the interesting question is this: Can we generalize these findings from the 1970s to contemporary gender differences?

Female undergraduate students in the United States were found to be superior to males when judging the correct emotion from faces, even when presented briefly (Hall & Matsumoto, 2004). It needs to be considered that stereotype threat (discussed in Chapter 4) does contribute to finding such a gender difference: Both men and women believe that women do better at social-sensitivity tasks, in line with the self-report findings reported earlier (Eisenberg & Lennon, 1983). In one telling study, only in the presence of an instruction mentioning this gender difference, did men perform worse than women (Koenig & Eagly, 2005). Thus, it depended on the situation whether a gender difference was found. And this is but one demonstration that men also suffer from stereotype threat in counterstereotypic tasks.

Better skills in decoding nonverbal information are related to higher social vulnerability (Ambady, Hallahan, & Rosenthal, 1995). Similarly, women fear negative evaluation more than men do (e.g., Carleton, Collimore, & Asmundson, 2007). They also score higher than men on emotionality (Ashton, Lee, & de Vries, 2014). Typical traits used to measure this include vulnerable and sensitive but not fearless and tough.

As early as 1984, it was concluded that gender differences in assertiveness, competence, and warmth, even if typically found, are generally small in magnitude (Deaux, 1984). Earlier we questioned whether it is the case at all nowadays that men are considerably more assertive than women. Regarding warmth, a somewhat different picture emerges, with both stereotypic ascriptions ("women are more relationship-oriented than men") and self-ascriptions favoring women (e.g., Abele, 2003). It is also interesting that the average man in that study described himself more in terms of warmth than assertiveness/competence. In other words, men would be categorized as more feminine than masculine. However, it is possible that the warmth-related traits are on average more socially desirable than the others (Abele, 2003), so people might describe themselves as more relationship-oriented than they are to appear in a favorable light.

We believe that, as more and more young men go beyond the restrictions of their gender role, taking parental leave, refusing to be 80-hour-a-week breadwinners, gender differences in warmth will diminish as well. It can be regarded as a case in point that for graduates from engineering, science, law, and economics in Abele's (2003) study, no gender differences were observed: One's study major is more informative than gender in judging someone's assertiveness, competence, and warmth.

A recent study tested whether women's unwillingness to make unethical compromises could be a factor steering them away from careers in business (Kennedy & Kray, 2013). Ethical compromises may be defined as decisions where ethical values (e.g., fairness, honesty) stand in opposition to less noble values such as monetary gains. Kennedy and Kray (2013) elaborated that such compromises may be particularly relevant in business contexts because profit is the primary aim of businesses. As the authors reviewed, probably because of women's socialization to be relationship-oriented, several gender differences have been observed that provide indirect evidence for this hypothesis. For instance, women were less willing than men to use deception or unethical tactics in negotiations. Men's ethical reasoning also was more egocentric than women's, in other words, it depended on their own perspective (Kray & Haselhuhn, 2012). In the study by Kennedy and Kray, voluntary participants read several descriptions of a person making a moral compromise (e.g., a defense attorney deciding to defend someone he knows to be guilty, for which he will gain a lot of money, but, among other negative consequences, many employees will lose their retirement savings; a father who decides to take on an important work project immediately after a baby is born to secure a large bonus, even though this includes spending nights and weekends at the office). Women reported more moral outrage and agreed less than men that the descriptions described acceptable business practices. However, the interpretation of this gender difference is complicated by the fact that several of the stories were related to gender roles. Also, half of the stories were related to status hierarchies (e.g., behavior intended to teach those lower in the hierarchy not to voice good ideas during meetings). Thus, an alternative explanation for the findings is that women took a different perspective than men on the gender-role related stories and that they have a different attitude toward status-related behavior. In fact, as we have seen, women may also be punished for dominant behavior (Rudman & Glick, 1999), so it is no big surprise that they agree less with it than men.

The authors' second experiment with U.S. undergraduate students as participants used different stories and found that women reported a lower interest in specific jobs as compared to men if these jobs were described as involving ethical compromises (e.g., staying silent about the mistreatment of a supervisor who will decide how much your bonus will be), but not in the absence of such compromises (Kennedy & Kray, 2013). The authors found that women's reported moral reservations accounted for these findings. Taken together, there is first evidence that women consider certain jobs less attractive than men if these jobs involve moral compromises. Future research needs to test how far "making ethical compromises" is indeed part of job stereotypes and whether this is related to the proportion of women found in these jobs.

Summary

What can we conclude about gender differences? Some small differences between women and men can reliably be observed, even though many of them are culturally dependent and have grown smaller over the past decades. It needs to be kept in mind that they are typically not invariant across situations, even if abilities that appear quite stable such as math or negotiating are considered: "The eye of the beholder does not affect perceptions alone, but can affect behavior as well" (Deaux, 1984, p. 114). Also, on the basis of the small magnitude of these gender differences, the work segregation between women and men, the large differences between their power and status, and even the course of their lives in general, would come as a surprise. We have already seen that gender stereotypes, both their descriptive and their prescriptive aspects, may be a more potent explanation.

From the next chapter onward, we turn to more general psychological theories that are needed to paint a full picture of the situational and structural factors that may differently affect women and men. We have, up to now, already referred to some more general cognitive theories. These have not been developed in the social psychology of gender but can help explain gender-related perceptions and actions in work contexts. For example, attribution theories belong to a very general class of theories. These are concerned with explaining why something happened. As we have seen, women's success on masculine tasks tended to be more attributed to effort and men's to ability; for failure, attributions were reversed (Swim & Sanna, 1996). As another example, the stereotype content model has already been introduced. Its main tenet is that stereotypes of social groups in general vary on the dimensions competence and warmth (Fiske et al., 2002). For these purposes, this idea is so similar to more specific conceptions of gender stereotypes that we integrated it earlier even if it is a general cognitive theory. The general theories that we introduce in more detail in the following have had a profound influence on thinking about gender relations.

· 7 ·
SOCIAL ROLE THEORY

Social role theory (Eagly, 1987) offers a social structural account on the contents of gender stereotypes (for a more recent version, see Eagly & Wood, 2012). In other words, current social structures in a given society contribute to gender stereotypes. Specifically, the theory postulates that gender stereotypes are rooted in different social roles assigned to women and men. Traditionally, women are more frequently encountered in the role of the homemaker or in occupations similar to the domestic role (such as kindergarten teacher or nurse; see also Cejka & Eagly, 1999), whereas men typically take over the role of the breadwinner and are more often located at higher levels within the occupational hierarchy. As demonstrated by Eagly and Steffen (1984), the attributes that are perceived as typical for the role of the homemaker correspond to warmth, whereas the attributes that are perceived as typical for the role of the breadwinner correspond to assertiveness and competence.

This distribution has several consequences. First, because they are often observed in these roles, women have become associated with warmth and men with assertiveness and task competence. Second, according to social role theory, women and men adjust to their gender-typical roles by acquiring the specific skills linked to successful role performance and by adapting their social behavior to role requirements (Eagly, Wood, & Diekman, 2000). In other words, both observers and actors are inclined to infer traits from behavior observed in given social roles: Once a person is put into a role, both the person and the observers come to think they have the traits required in that role. Social role theory posits that gender stereotypes are so similar across nations because of the similar distribution of men and women into social roles internationally. In a seminal study, Eagly and Steffen (1984) demonstrated empirically that trait ascriptions follow social roles. Women and men who were introduced as homemakers were ascribed high warmth and low assertiveness/competence, whereas women and men introduced as employees were ascribed high assertiveness/competence and low warmth. Thus, social role trumped gender when forming impressions of people. These findings corroborate what we have concluded in Chapter 3 on stereotypes: Individuating information is more important than gender when judging individuals.

Contemporary gender roles

In Western cultures, remarkable changes in gender roles have been observed recently. That is, the roles of men and women have become more similar over the last decades, primarily accounted for by women's increased entry into the employee role (see Introduction for numbers). In contrast to these observations within the occupational domain, comparable changes regarding the domestic role have not taken place. A large-scale study on contemporary gender division of labor in Germany revealed that women still spend nearly twice as much time on household chores and childcare as men (Kuenzler, Walter, Reichart, & Pfister, 2001). Similarly, the German microcensus of 2005 showed that 56% of working mothers having a child younger than three years of age have taken parental leave, whereas only 3% of the working fathers have made use of this opportunity (German Federal Office of Statistics, 2006). Likewise, in a Gallup Poll in 2008 addressing the division of household chores within married couples living in the United States, 54% of the married respondents reported that the wife cared for the children on a daily basis, whereas only 9% reported that the husband did. A comparable distribution was found for chores such as "prepare meals" (58% vs. 14%), "do laundry" (68% vs. 10%), and "clean the house" (61% to 6%; Newport, 2008). In short, although women are increasingly found in the employee role, men have not entered domestic roles to the same degree (Shelton, 1992). A similar asymmetry can be observed within the occupational domain, in that men have not entered female-dominated occupations to the same extent that women have entered male-dominated occupations (England, 2003).

As mentioned, associations of gender-typical roles and gender-stereotypic traits were found irrespective of the stimulus person's gender (Eagly & Steffen, 1984). Considering this finding, the question arises whether the observed changes in gender roles are accompanied by systematic changes in stereotypic perceptions of women and men, as social role theory would suggest. Diekman and Eagly (2000; see also Diekman, Eagly, Mladinic, & Ferreira, 2005; Wilde & Diekman, 2005) examined perceivers' beliefs about the typical attributes of women and men over a time span of 100 years (starting in the past and projected onto the future) and their relationship with estimates of role nontraditionalism. Participants perceived increasing role equality over time and a corresponding convergence in the perceived characteristics of men and women. This convergence was primarily due to an increase in ascribing masculine personality characteristics (e.g., competitive and dominant) to women, which is in line with the authors' reasoning that the largest change in gender roles is due to women's entry into male-dominated occupations. Furthermore, there was only a modest increase in ascribing feminine personality characteristics (e.g., sensitive and supportive) to men, interpreted as reflecting the very limited movement of men into female-dominated roles. Diekman and Eagly's findings are in line with work on gender differences in self-reported personality traits (Twenge, 1997). A meta-analysis of 63 studies showed an increase in women's endorsement of masculine personality traits and men's continued nonendorsement of feminine personality traits over 20 years. Further meta-analyses covering a time period from 1931 to 1993 showed that women's self-reported assertiveness closely follows trends in their social status and roles (Twenge, 2001). (For an overview of studies examining the dynamics of gender beliefs and gender-stereotyped personality traits, see Sczesny, Bosak, Diekman, & Twenge, 2007.)

One possible concern with such findings is that they are due to demand effects or social-desirability concerns. If you ask people what women were like 50 years ago and what they will be like 50 years from now, it is quite transparent what "good" responses could be. One can easily see that certain responses would leave a strange impression, such as saying "women will be weak, caring, and lacking work-related competence." Therefore, it is interesting to test with implicit measures which characteristics are ascribed more to men than to women and which more to women than to men. If changing social roles had left their traces in people's automatic and spontaneous thinking, some deviation from traditional gender stereotypes should be observed.

When testing at the same time whether men and women are associated with goal-orientation versus social skills, traditional gender stereotypes emerged, as mentioned earlier (e.g., Rudman & Glick, 2001): Men were more strongly associated with goal orientation and women with social skills. These findings are similar to many other dimensions of implicit gender stereotypes that we reported in Chapter 2. However, findings differed if warmth and competence were investigated separately (Ebert et al., 2014). Then, male and female participants still associated women more with warmth than men, in line with traditional gender stereotypes. In contrast, participants ascribed work-related competence to their own in-group: Men associated men more strongly than women with competence, whereas women associated women more strongly than men with competence. We think these findings are best explained with changes in gender roles that provoke changes in gender stereotypes: Men are no longer generally seen as the "competent gender." The finding that both men and women ascribed work-related competence to their in-group is in line with the general tendency to evaluate in-groups more positively than out-groups (see Rudman et al., 2001; social identity theory is discussed in Part II).

The impact of social roles on men's and women's careers

Imagine you woke up on a strange planet, Thera, and you knew nothing about the beings inhabiting it (Peter Glick inspired this example; see Rudman & Glick, 2008). They are different in several regards, but a distinction that appears central to them is that some are nens and others are nenes. For example, if you refer to one of them in the third person, you use a different pronoun for nens than for nenes. After a while, learning more about their society, you understand that they are preoccupied with the small number of nenes who are highly successful in their jobs and reach top positions in various spheres. They are puzzled about this because the nenes are as intelligent as the nens and as well qualified, if not more. A lot of money has been spent in investigating the reasons for this, and measures are taken to support the careers of nenes. As you learn still more about life on Thera, you find out that most nenes have several extra daily chores, as compared to the nens. Most nenes live together with a nen. If they do, it is the nenes who are responsible for taking care of their habitation and their social relations. If they have offspring, the nenes not only do most of the related work, but they are often taken out of their jobs for half a year, a year, or even more. If they work outside their habitation, their flexibility is reduced because of their extra work assignments at home.

You also observe that some nens work around the clock and appear to do nothing else. If they do, their nenes await them at home and support them. You see no comparable example of a nen patiently waiting for their nena. Are you convinced that working a "second shift" in the evening, being put on hold, and the threat of suffering severe family-life consequences if focusing too much on their jobs affect the nenes' career progress? (*Nen* (*nens*) and *nena* (*nenes*) are Catalan for boy(s) and girl(s).)

The most profound effect that social roles have on women's and men's careers is probably related to being in a relationship and, even more, to having children. Women experience work-to-family and family-to-work conflicts as interrole conflicts between their work roles and their family roles (e.g., Andrade & Mikula, 2014). Although older studies showed that women, but not men, expected to experience such conflicts between parenthood and career, more recent U.S. data showed that women's expected conflicts are also declining (see Devos et al., 2008). Still, gender differences in implicit representations were found: Men identified more strongly with college education than parenthood, whereas women identified equally with both concepts. Also, they all linked parenthood more strongly with women (and, as contrasting categories, college education with men).

Some typical choices that heterosexual women make may negatively affect their careers (for recent reviews, see Bathmann, Cornelißen, & Müller, 2013; Quaiser-Pohl & Reichle, 2007). As they tend to choose older partners, the partners are often more advanced in their careers. Also, if educational levels in heterosexual partnerships differ, it is typically the man who has the higher education (i.e., in 30% vs. less than 10% of cases in Germany in 2009). Both differences can work against a woman's equal career opportunities—doesn't it make sense to move with him because of his career if one's own has not started? And who should work part time to take care of the children? Perhaps the younger partner making less money.

Although male and female college students alike indicate that they value jobs that allow them work-life balance and work flexibility, men still reported lower intentions to seek work flexibility than women (Vandello, Hettinger, Bosson, & Siddiqi, 2013). For men, those who believed it would negatively reflect on their perceived masculine traits opted against work flexibility (e.g., career-oriented, not weak, competent). For women, perceived masculine traits were not related to intentions to seek work flexibility. These findings show that first, both men and women value work flexibility. Second, in line with their prescribed social role, many men would not consider choosing the option of working part time.

Given mobility demands, a close relationship can place an extra burden on those with "linked lives," juggling two careers and a common family life (Bathmann et al., 2013). Among couples in Germany, in 13% of the cases, both partners hold academic degrees. They have to find individual solutions for a work-work-life-balance that suits both of them and their ideas about bringing up their children when children are involved. These depend on conditions at the sociopolitical level (e.g., childcare opportunities, convictions on gender roles) and the organizational level (e.g., family-friendly flexible working hours); work-work-life-balance also depends on factors pertaining to the couple (e.g., division of family labor) and to those on the individual level (e.g., convictions about mothering; Mikula, 2012, 2013). As Bathmann and colleagues (2013) reviewed, single women's mobility is as high as single men's. As soon as they live in a relationship, women's mobility drops, thus affecting their careers negatively. Whereas one might be tempted to attribute this to women's choices alone, research shows the following: As soon as women are married, they are offered fewer relocation opportunities (see King, 2008). Thus, it appears that others' gender stereotypes, again, play a role in this equation.

Equal opportunities management often focuses on the individual woman (or other minority person) without taking into account the social context in which she lives. Bathmann and colleagues (2013) carried out a large qualitative study to elucidate how dual-career couples manage their coordination challenges. Their study yielded a typology of career couples. Some couples (but not many) place priority on the woman's career. If they do, they feel the need to explain how this came about, whereas a priority on the man's career is often taken for granted: There appears to be no need to explain it. Also, women are grateful that their partner copes with this unbalanced status. In turn, among the couples interviewed, household chores were often delegated to third parties (other women). Alternatively, the woman was responsible for them, in addition to her career. Household chores were on her plate to compensate for the nontraditional career distribution that can be a blow to a man's self-worth (see also Pierce, Dahl, & Nielsen, 2013). If a woman has more success in her career compared to her male partner, this may put the couple's relationship at risk, particularly if they work in similar domains (Bathmann et al., 2013). It is easier for a man to cope with his wife's larger success if both work in very different spheres with different values. For example, if she were a politician leading an important world economy, and her husband a scientist, the couple's relationship should be less strained than if he were a mediocre politician. If core indicators of success differ among fields (e.g., societal power versus scientific awards), direct social comparisons cannot be undertaken, and there is less strain on the couple's relationship. "Breaking the gender hierarchy in the professional sphere needs a more traditional doing gender in the private sphere in order not to put the stability of the relationship at risk." (p. 125). In our view, such a division of household chores is a clear disadvantage for women who compete with men who have similar qualifications. These men have either less qualified wives who support their career or equally qualified wives who typically do two thirds of the housework and coordination (see Mikula, 2012). "Heterosexual marriage has traditionally created a 'second shift' for employed women" (Peplau & Fingerhut, 2004, p. 724)—after their employed work, they do the housework.

It appears that a central ingredient of a woman's career is that the couple never puts her career on the line: If both partners agree that their careers are equally important, they find ways to navigate through pressured phases where a lack of time is the defining theme (Bathmann et al., 2013). Moreover, unsurprisingly, individual convictions as to women's social roles are an important aspect. If one thinks that women should always care for their men as best they can and that children will suffer if the mother works, the situation is much more difficult than if one is convinced of gender equality and that children profit from parents who are happy with their work-life-balance.

Other couples placed priority on both careers, which can imply high costs in terms of coordination and mobility, for example, if they work in different countries and can only meet personally every other weekend (Bathmann et al., 2013). Or they scaled back on both careers to take turns placing a priority on being (more) with the children. Still other couples took a joint career path, such as founding a business together. If they work from home, the boundaries between family and work are almost nonexistent; each domain is able to invade the other any time. An attribution that may disadvantage women in joint career constellations is that people perceive the husband as the driving force of their successes and her as coasting (e.g., Quaiser-Pohl & Reichle, 2007). Some couples put the woman's career on hold for a while, when the children were small, and then women would take relevant career steps later. Finally, of course, there were also those couples that placed a priority on the man's career. In sum, heterosexual relationships affect women's careers more than men's.

What could one expect regarding the distribution of household chores within couples if both possess the same educational level? And what appears fair? As mentioned, in heterosexual relationships, typically, the lioness's share of household tasks firmly rests on a woman's shoulders, even if she is as qualified as her partner and earns as much money (Bathmann et al., 2013; Benard & Correll, 2010; Bodi, Mikula, & Riederer, 2010; Mikula, 2012; Rhoads & Rhoads, 2012). It appears that many couples never question a distribution of chores that they learned early on. In line with this, mothers are perceived as more overloaded than fathers (Etaugh & Folger, 1998). Interestingly, it is not the distribution of chores or the hours needed for household work that determine outcomes (e.g., relationship satisfaction, well-being); instead, perceived justice is the crucial factor (see Mikula, 2013). Whereas public discourse suggests that justice is perceived if both partners contribute equally to household chores, research draws a less rigid picture (Mikula, 2013).

Women in top positions have a much lower probability of being mothers as compared to other women. Men in top positions are much more likely to be parents than women in top positions (Mölders & van Quaquebeke, 2011). In other words, women who place a high priority on their careers have worse chances than comparable men to succeed at combining a family life with such a career (see Spelke & Grace, 2007). Also, for women, important steps in many careers occur at the time when the decision to have children needs to be made—for biological reasons (Halpern, 2007). And women have much lower chances of being promoted if they have children, which is not true for men (see Chapter 12 on parenthood). Parenthood had a negative direct influence on women's, but not men's, work hours and thus indirectly a negative influence on their career success (Abele & Spurk, 2011). Ironically, men who had no children were less successful in their careers than those who had children. In contrast, having children had the most damaging effect on women's careers if they had children at career entry.

Sociostructural factors in the environment can influence behavioral patterns related to social roles. For example, since 2007, German couples receive *Elterngeld* (parenting money; a percentage of one's income) if they take family leave. To care for an infant, one can get subsidized for 12 months if only one parent takes leave. If both do, a total of 14 months of subsidy can be received. Consequently, according to the German federal ministry (Bundesministerium für Familie, Senioren, Frauen und Jugend, 2012), the percentage of fathers taking leave rose to 25% (from close to zero). Such incentivized changes in behavior may, in turn, affect social-role perceptions and thus in the long run lead to the perception that fathers have as much responsibility for taking care of their children as mothers. We believe that this would have profound positive effects on women's careers. First, fewer women would feel they need to choose between motherhood and a top career. Second, mothers would not be so overstrained by work-family and family-work conflict. And third, the stereotypes that restrict mothers' careers will slowly erode (again, see Chapter 12).

Social roles appear to limit women in many ways, and one could be inclined to think that this is not the case for men. This inclination is wrong. One topic that we have sometimes wondered about, even though we know of no research investigating it, is how the traditional social role of men as breadwinners affects their career choice. If a young woman never imagines that her income has to suffice for sustaining a whole family, in consequence does she make different choices than a young man? Would it be sufficient to convince women that they were better off if they had the chance to provide for themselves and their children throughout their lives to reduce the number who choose female-typed professions that are paid poorly? And if men knew they had the chance to choose the vocation they are interested in without worrying about being able to support a family on their income, would more of them choose jobs they consider more fulfilling? These questions point again at the restrictions gender roles imply for men. Dropping out of a 60-hour-a-week career to have time for one's children often does not make women unhappy, as compared to the men remaining in these careers (see Ceci et al., 2009).

What are the social-psychological consequences a man experiences if he cannot fulfill his prescribed social role of being the family breadwinner? Traditionally, husbands have either been the sole providers of family income or at least they outearned their wives. In recent years, the percentage of wives outearning their husbands has increased considerably in many societies (see Pierce et al., 2013). The social comparison with their wives that these men undertake yields the outcome that they do not successfully fulfill their breadwinner role. (As we discussed earlier, couples go some extra miles to avoid this blow to the man's self-worth.) Men outearned by their wives have an increased probability of suffering depression, and reported marital satisfaction by such couples is lower.

A recent intriguing study tested whether the frustration that men suffer when being outearned by their wives can also provoke serious sexual problems (Pierce et al., 2013). Over the course of 10 years, income and medical prescription data of more than 200,000 Danish couples were compared. The more women outearned their husbands, the higher the probability that men were prescribed erectile dysfunction (ED) medication. If the wife slightly outearned her husband, there was a "jump" in ED medication usage by about 20%. As this suggests, the phenomenon is really a psychological one, depending on the social comparison with her, yielding a result subjectively unfavorable to him. This relation was only found in married couples, not in cohabiting, unmarried couples. This additional finding suggests that the negative health consequences found for men depend on the social role of being the family breadwinner that is adopted only after marriage. Also, the relation was found only in couples where men outearned women before they got married. This finding points at social roles again. If a man chooses a different social role for himself, for example, becoming a stay-at-home parent, he does not suffer from the increased family income due to his wife's pay raise.

When interpreting this study's intriguing findings, one needs to keep in mind that the absolute proportion of men being prescribed ED medication is very low: Although the relationship found is strong and meaningful, the large majority of the population is not affected. As the study was conducted in Denmark, a country with high gender equality, it is probable that negative consequences of violating the traditional male breadwinner role are even more severe in other countries with stronger gender-role traditionalism. These findings bring us full circle back to the theory of precarious manhood (discussed in Chapter 4) and demonstrate once more that stereotypes and social roles restrict men as much as they restrict women. As a side note, when talking about this study with married women in Germany, these women wondered how Danish men found out that their wives made more money. Possibly, "hiding my high income from my husband" is a tactic used by some career women to avoid negative relationship consequences.

To more fully digest the irony of such findings, we return to the example of the strange planet Thera. To understand the social relations on that planet, one would need to be able to explain the following phenomenon: What happens if a nen's status in society increases, for example, by moving up the hierarchy in a given organization, bringing about a pay raise? As a consequence, the status of the nena coupled with him *increases*, too, in particular, if the nena's success is less than the nen's. In contrast, what happens if a nena's career advances beyond the nen's? His status *decreases* instead.

We turn to another interesting example from Germany. If an older woman is called "Frau Doktor" or "Frau Professor," it is perfectly ambiguous whether she herself gained that academic title or whether she gained the title because her husband is the local physician or a university professor. In other words, his title is extended to her, as if she were a part of him. The converse is impossible for men. Her title is hers, not his. And in the eyes of others, it may threaten his masculinity and illustrate that he could not fulfill his prescribed social role. The status relation between high-status men and low-status women on a societal level is, in this case, violated within the couple.

It is often assumed that women place a higher priority on having a family than men do (e.g., Ceci et al., 2009). We object to this interpretation that makes it appear purely women's choice. It neglects the larger social and cultural context. The better question is this: What are the consequences for women and men, respectively, of placing a high priority on one's career? As we have seen, for women much more often than for men, this goes along with having no children or spouse (for a review, see Ceci et al., 2009). In other words, it remains to be seen if women make different choices than men in societies in which they do not have to pay a higher price for those choices.

Traditional theories assumed that women are less committed at work because of their family responsibilities. Many research findings show that this is not the case. Instead, employed women devoted as much effort to their jobs as men did and more effort than men with similar household responsibilities (see Reskin & Bielby, 2005). However, when only looking at those who devote the most hours to their work, men are overrepresented as compared to women, as we have mentioned: If one assumes that there are only 84 hours a week left after accounting for some basic activities such as sleeping, eating, and showering, and women need more of these hours for household and childcare work than men do, basic mathematics tells us that there is no time left for working 80 hours a week. Particularly highly qualified mothers invest fewer hours a week into their paid work than women without children or men. The more children they have, the fewer hours do mothers in academia work per week, but ironically, for men, the relationship is reversed (see Ceci et al., 2009): Women with more than three children devoted 42 hours a week to their academic jobs and men about 54. Once more, this does not only appear to interfere with women's careers but also with men's father role, thus restricting both genders. One may be puzzled why change is so slow, then, if gender roles restrict all involved. We focus on this question in the next chapter.

Summary

According to traditional social roles in many societies, men are the breadwinners and women are the homemakers. As social role theory posits, these roles have profound influences both on gender stereotypes and on men's and women's self-concepts. Because men and women are in these roles, stereotypes are shaped, and individuals adopt the respective traits into their self-concepts. Over the last decades, women's roles have become broader, including more of what used to be male turf. For men's roles, less of a change has been observed. Still, traditional social roles determine how heterosexual couples distribute household and child-rearing chores between them. Typically, women are still responsible for all that, working a second shift at home if they are full-time employees. This puts many women in the uncomfortable situation of needing to decide between having children or having the career they planned. Also, that a family moves because of the man's job is much more common than because of the woman's job, which may restrict women's career opportunities. However, traditional social roles restrict men as well, and if they cannot be the primary breadwinner, or opt against it, they risk psychological and health problems.

· 8 ·

MAINTAINING SOCIAL HIERARCHIES

Group-based oppression is pervasive. In most societies, there are social groups that have more access to power, status, and material well-being and other groups that experience stigma and hardship (Pratto, Sidanius, Stallworth, & Malle, 1994; Pratto et al., 1997). In other words, there are dominant and oppressed groups. An example that easily comes to mind is the former apartheid system in South Africa. Similarly, if Blacks are disadvantaged as compared to Whites in the United States, and foreigners are discriminated against in Germany, the same mechanisms are at work. With regard to gender, all societies in the world are unequal (see numbers provided in the Introduction). Most people value equality and justice, which are also embedded in Western countries' constitutions and laws. Given striking examples of injustice, one could imagine an uproar or even a revolution—or at least the implementation of immediate and strong interventions against such inequalities. Isn't it strange that this does not happen?

To explain how hierarchical societies are maintained through social and psychological processes, *social dominance theory* was developed (Sidanius & Pratto, 1999). As the theory states, if there are widely accepted ideologies within societies that legitimize discrimination, intergroup conflict is minimized and intergroup relations are smooth (Pratto et al., 1994). Moral and intellectual justifications for inequalities in power, status, and privilege among groups in a given social system serve to stabilize that system (Sidanius et al., 1994). For example, if there is consensus in a society that 16-year-olds are not yet mature enough to vote or drive a car, there is not much impetus to change this state of affairs. As another example, if, instead, a considerable percentage of the population believes that gay and lesbian couples can bring up children as well as heterosexual couples can, social movements may be formed that fight for these couples' right to adopt children. In other words, if a society, or better, if those in power in that society manage to make people believe in ideologies that legitimize inequality, social hierarchies can be maintained more easily. According to social dominance theory, societies are replete with such hierarchy-legitimizing myths. (Similar to stereotypes, such myths may contain some truth.) If both oppressors and oppressed share myths that make oppression appear legitimate, the oppressed groups contribute to their group's unequal chances. For example, meritocracy indicates that society is fair in that individuals get what they deserve, and if some hold more resources than others, it is because they have worked harder and are more intelligent or more deserving in other ways (Pratto et al., 1994). Another myth that we explained in some detail earlier is benevolent sexism (see Chapter 5): Women are put on a pedestal and honored for possessing warm traits that complement men's assertiveness and task competence. In a similar way, Black slaves were likened with children who would be lost without their masters' caring for them. Slaves believing such myths would be less likely to try to change the social hierarchy.

Social dominance theory postulates that there are hierarchy-enhancing social roles that defend the privileges of the elites and hierarchy-attenuating social roles that serve oppressed groups (Pratto et al., 1997). These roles include jobs. According to the theory, for instance, the criminal justice system defends the privileges of the elites and keeps the oppressed in their place, thus maintaining the hierarchy (for a review of the system's injustice in the United States, see Pratto et al., 1994). In contrast, social workers care for the oppressed, thus diminishing the hierarchy. (This is the case at least at first glance; in the long run, as we see later, making the system appear less unjust stabilizes it.) As Pratto and colleagues demonstrated in a variety of studies, gender segregation at work is partly due to men's disproportionate presence in hierarchy-enhancing and women's overrepresentation in hierarchy-attenuating jobs. Even within the same profession, men and women are attracted to different jobs (e.g., prosecutor vs. criminal defense lawyer). People drawn to hierarchy-enhancing jobs had work values such as gaining personal prestige and having a high status; those drawn to hierarchy-diminishing jobs wanted to work with people and serve the community. It comes as no surprise that there were more men among the first and more women among the second group.

Within the theory, an individual's social dominance orientation indicates how much they believe in ideologies that legitimize inequalities and favor policies promoting group dominance (Pratto et al., 1994). Men score higher on average on social dominance orientation than women. This difference did not vary across cultural or situational factors such as age group, political party preference, ethnicity, or educational level (Sidanius et al., 1994). The gender difference in social dominance orientation explained the gender difference in preferences for hierarchy-enhancing versus hierarchy-attenuating jobs (Pratto et al., 1997). In line with that, people who are higher on warmth, empathy, and altruism (i.e., typically women) score lower on social dominance orientation (Sidanius et al., 1994).

What are the implications of this perspective for these purposes? First, even in the absence of gender discrimination, we should expect gender segregation at work as long as women and men have formed different preferences for hierarchy-enhancing versus hierarchy-attenuating jobs. Second, social dominance theory is one way to explain why feminism has such a negative image. At the core of feminism is gender equality (e.g., Eagly, Eaton, Rose, Riger, & McHugh, 2012). Ironically, along with central feminist ideas such as equal pay for equal work or equal chances in life for women and men, gender equality enjoys wide agreement across the population. At the same time, there are not many people who agree with the statement, "I am a feminist." For example, in recent data that we collected in Spain, average agreement to that item was 5 on a scale from 1 to 9 (i.e., people's position was neutral on average). At the same time, average agreement was 8 when responding to the following prompt: "If women were discriminated against in the organization where I work, I would protest." Thus, people endorse feminist ideas while refusing to identify as feminists. According to social dominance theory, to maintain hierarchies, it is a good idea to ridicule and discount social movements such as feminism. If feminists have a negative image, people will shy away from them, they will have less influence, and social hierarchies can be maintained more easily. Whereas negative images of career women and social backlash against them may appear to be a phenomenon of our times, historians tell us that female writers in the 18th century already suffered similar repercussions, and this went on throughout the following centuries. "Feminists ought to get a good whipping. Were woman (sic!) to 'unsex' themselves by claiming equality with men, they would become the most hateful, heathen and disgusting of beings and would surely perish without male protection." Queen Victoria, who is quoted as saying this, obviously managed to dis-identify with being a powerful woman herself (in the 19th century; we thank Jolanda Jetten for bringing this quote to our attention).

Third, social dominance theory implies that certain individuals should be more likely than others to enforce the maintenance of the gender hierarchy. These should be high-status men with a strong social-dominance orientation. According to the theory, these men should prevent women from access to high-status positions. A recent study provided evidence for this (Inesi & Cable, 2014). In a first study with U.S. military personnel, Inesi and Cable (2014) showed that female but not male subordinates received worse evaluations by their male supervisors if they approached them in organizational rank. In other words, female subordinates were evaluated positively if there was enough distance between their rank and that of the supervisor—if the social hierarchy remained intact. But if the female subordinate approached her supervisor in rank, she received a lower performance evaluation from him. Presumably, such a less positive evaluation also preserves the social hierarchy because it prevents her from being promoted. The authors' subsequent study was an experiment in which performance of a hypothetical subordinate was held constant and his or her degree was manipulated (high school vs. college). All evaluators held a college degree. An ironic pattern of performance evaluation was observed if evaluators were male and high in social dominance orientation: Given identical objective performance, women were evaluated worse if they held a college degree rather than a high school education. In contrast, men with a college degree were never evaluated worse than those with a high school education. An additional experiment manipulated the quality of performance and showed that this ironic pattern is only observed if the subordinate performs well. These findings clearly indicate discrimination of high-performing women if their accomplishments threaten the superior status of their male supervisor and if that supervisor has a high social dominance orientation. Thus, social dominance theory contributes to explaining gender-based discrimination of high-performing women at work. The study not only demonstrates the problem but also suggests a cure. Practically speaking, when supervisors are assigned, enough distance between them and the supervised in the hierarchy helps against any threat that could be perceived by the superior person.

A final, more general implication of social dominance theory is that stereotypes function to maintain the stratified social systems in which we live. For example, if women are believed, and believe themselves, to be good at nursing and to enjoy being nurses, and men are believed to be good as leaders, the small proportion of men in low-paying nursing jobs and the small proportion of women in well-paying leadership jobs does not appear unjust. Pratto and colleagues (1997) concluded the following on stereotypes: "These culturally shared and culturally enacted ideas are perhaps the largest kind of self-fulfilling prophecy because they legitimize themselves and the unequal social systems of which they are a part" (p. 51).

As we have seen, according to social dominance theory, making people believe in legitimizing myths is needed, along with other processes, to maintain and stabilize hierarchical societies in which some groups have more access to power and wealth than others. A theory that goes one step further is *system justification theory* (for reviews, see Jost, Banaji, & Nosek, 2004; Jost & Hunyady, 2005). System justification theory predicts that people are motivated to justify the status quo as fair, legitimate, and as the most desirable state of affairs. "For many people, the devil they know seems less threatening and more legitimate than the devil they don't" (Jost & Hunyady, 2005, p. 262). For example, everything else being equal, if there were 5% of women in top leadership positions as opposed to 50%, people would prefer this distribution, but if there were 50% instead of 5%, people would prefer it to be 50%. Even though this idea may appear far-fetched, psychological research has corroborated it (Kay & Jost, 2003). In one experiment, Canadian female undergraduate students were first reminded that government policies substantially influence people's careers and personal lives. Then half of them were shown a graph suggesting that 20% of female members of parliament is a large proportion, whereas the other half saw the same graph, but the proportion appeared very small (i.e., the axis was 0%–25% in the first and 0%–100% in the second graph). They then responded to questions such as, "To what extent do you believe women should be in politics?" Those who had "seen" that there are many women in politics responded that the presence of women in politics was more desirable than those who had "seen" few women.

Another insidious mechanism comes into play when a few minority members ("tokens") are in counterstereotypical positions, as opposed to none. For example, if there is not a single woman on a board of directors or in a government, then the system appears blatantly unjust. The presence of a few "tokens" changes this perception dramatically (e.g., Brown & Diekman, 2013).

Thus, ironically, tokens stabilize the system, increase support for the status quo, and decrease support for social change.

Such findings imply that it is generally not easy to change the status quo. Not only the powerful but also (many of) those who are actually disadvantaged by the current state of affairs may (unconsciously) be motivated to keep it. And once the system starts to change slowly, this change is again retarded by the apparent increased fairness of the status quo. In spite of the latter finding, in the long run, one practical implication of such findings is the following conclusion: The more women there are in top positions, the easier it will be to get women into top positions. In addition, not only should they be there, but there should be enough of them, and this very fact should be visible, so that people actually are aware of their large numbers.

According to system justification theory, people legitimize the existing social system, even against their very personal and group interests, and regard it as fair, desirable, and even inevitable. This theory can explain the lack of correspondence between self-interest and ideology that is often observed. For example, many poor U.S. Americans vote for the conservative party, which will maintain social inequalities at their disadvantage (Jost et al., 2004). Similarly, the lack of support of feminist movements by the majority of women is a case in point. In line with social dominance theory, stereotypes are used to justify the status quo by stereotyping groups depending on their status in society as, for example, dominant versus considerate. Exposure to such complementary stereotypes serves to justify the social system:

> Above and beyond the use of stereotypes to rationalize specific roles such as homemaker and to flatter individual women into embracing the sexist status quo, then, we propose that warmth-related and benevolent gender stereotypes serve system-justifying ends by counterbalancing men's presumed advantages in terms of agency and status. (Jost & Kay, 2005, p. 499)

In Jost and Kay's (2005) study, some women were exposed to beliefs about women and others were not. Indeed, after women were exposed to stereotypes of women as warm, gender-specific as well as general system justification was increased. This is in line with the idea that warmth-related stereotypes of lower status groups serve to justify the status quo and make it appear more acceptable to all. Benevolent sexism also reduces women's motivation to act against gender inequality (Becker & Wright, 2011) and reduces their interest in power (Rudman & Heppen, 2003).

If the social system is under threat, system justification is even increased (for a review of the evidence, see Jost et al., 2004). Taken together, preserving the status quo is a collaborative enterprise of the dominant and the oppressed groups. People's belief in a just world helps them reduce uncertainty, be confident, and trust the system they live in and highly depend upon. It makes them more satisfied with their social situation and reduces frustration. Particularly implicit measures show that advantaged groups are typically evaluated more favorably than disadvantaged groups (with the notable exception of gender; see Chapter 5 on gender attitudes). At the same time, these rationalizations hinder social movements that would improve the status of disadvantaged groups in society. Only if regime change appears inevitable will people immediately begin to rationalize the new system.

We have already described prescriptive aspects of gender stereotypes, including behaviors that are particularly "forbidden" either for men (e.g., showing weakness) or women (e.g., dominating). It has been suggested that such proscriptions serve to maintain the gender hierarchy: Low-status behaviors are proscribed for men, and high-status behaviors are proscribed for women (Rudman et al., 2012). Assertive and competent women threaten the gender hierarchy, and that is why they are punished. As such, backlash against them can be conceived within system justification theory. People prefer the status quo (i.e., the existing gender hierarchy), and that is why dominant, status-incongruent behavior incurs penalties for women but not men. Indeed, findings showed that only those people who endorsed the gender hierarchy punished women for dominant behavior (Rudman et al., 2012). They also perceived these women as more dominant than they perceived men behaving identically. Endorsing the gender hierarchy was measured with items such as the following: "In general, relations between men and women are just and fair."

In Chapter 3, which discussed backlash, it appeared as if people in general disliked assertive, competent women successful in their careers. The findings we have reported in this chapter indicate that this conclusion was too general (Inesi & Cable, 2014; Rudman et al., 2012). Only those perceivers who are high in social dominance orientation and/or endorse the gender hierarchy should be those who dislike assertive, competent women and sabotage their careers if they can. Such differentiated findings also may explain inconsistencies in research findings reported earlier. If there happen to be many participants in a given study who are low in social dominance orientation or do not endorse the gender hierarchy, no backlash against assertive, competent women would be found. Consequently, researchers need to collect more information on participants' attitudes when conducting studies on these topics. From a practical point of view, it appears to us a viable conclusion that assertive, competent women will be judged more harshly than men behaving in identical ways by perceivers motivated to maintain social hierarchies.

Summary

Taken together, social dominance theory holds that legitimizing myths exist in hierarchical social systems that serve to justify these hierarchies. People differ in their social dominance orientation, that is, in the degree to which they believe group dominance should be preserved. In particular, men with a high social dominance orientation will oppose women's careers in traditionally male domains. System justification posits that there is no need for dominant groups to fabricate legitimizing myths to preserve the status quo. Instead, people are generally motivated to justify the status quo as fair and legitimate. Social change is hampered because people prefer the status quo to any other unknown status. Several stabilizing mechanisms come into play if the social system starts to change. First, the presence of minority tokens, as compared to no minority members in top positions, makes the system appear less unjust, thus increasing system justification again. Second, change increases threat, which again raises the motivation for system justification. Both social dominance theory and system justification theory regard group stereotypes as mechanisms that stabilize hierarchies.

Considering gender-related status disparities within working environments, paternalistic stereotypes that ascribe warmth to those women who adhere to traditionally female (i.e., low status) roles promote their compliance with the status quo because warmth is regarded as high in social desirability (Eckes, 2008). At the same time, envious stereotypes of nontraditional women encompassing the ascription of emotional coldness can serve as a legitimization for derogating and discriminating these women. Thus, both female subtypes serve to maintain power disparities between men and women and counteract any system-threatening developments.

· 9 ·

CAREER CHOICE

In the previous chapters, we have elucidated many theories and findings related to gender at work, and each chapter mirrored different theoretical topics and stances that can be applied to many practical questions. From here, the book is structured differently. Chapters 9 to 14 are organized around practical questions, situations, and topics. All of the previously elaborated theories and findings that are relevant are applied to these situations, with respective recommendations and interventions being deduced. Information from previous chapters is summarized and several chapters review topics that have not been addressed. We begin with career choice.

The choice of a specific major, and subsequently, career, appears to be a highly gendered matter. Very few occupations are chosen by similar numbers of women and men. Conversely, there are many in which we find hardly any women and others in which hardly any men are present. We focus here on two specific domains in which there is a lack of women: STEM fields and entrepreneurship. Before we do so, what can we conclude from the theoretical perspectives?

One cannot think about career choice without starting with gender stereotypes. We concluded earlier that gender stereotypes have a profound influence on individuals' interests, their development of abilities, and the relevant self-concepts. Similar to the lack of fit model that describes how we arrive at the conclusion that another person fits a certain job, people wonder how far their interests and abilities match their stereotypes of jobs. Because many women want to work with people and help them, they do not consider jobs where they imagine to be working like a lonesome cowboy day after day. If men think one needs to be sensitive to others' needs to be a kindergarten teacher, and they think they are not, they will not consider this job. As we have also seen, men generally prefer hierarchy-enhancing jobs and have no problem with hierarchies, whereas women prefer hierarchy-attenuating jobs and generally value equality. Status and income appear to be more important to men than women, whereas flexibility and few work-family conflicts are more important to women than men. Therefore, if a profession requires excessively long workdays, women tend to shy away from it. If a girl holds an implicit stereotype that leaders are male, the probability is low that she will consider a leadership position for herself. Stereotype threat, the fear of confirming negative group stereotypes, will steer women and men away from counterstereotypical fields. Because risk taking is conceived of as masculine and more proscribed for women than men, women will probably not choose jobs that require a high risk propensity. Similarly, if jobs appear to require unethical compromises, it could be that women are less willing than men to choose them.

Why are so few women in STEM fields?

Fewer women than men enter several math-intensive fields, for example, engineering and computer science. Percentages are below one sixth in Germany and below one third in the United States (National Science Foundation, 2006). It appears that women are less motivated than men to excel in some STEM fields, including physics (e.g., Taasoobshirazi & Carr, 2009). Gender segregation in choice of major translates into occupational gender segregation and is believed to explain up to 20% of the gender pay gap (Schneeweis & Zweimüller, 2012).

Superficially, one may assume that the small number of women who are leaders in STEM fields is a "pipeline problem" that will soon be overcome. If few women selected these majors 20 years ago, it is to be expected that it takes 20 years for the increasing number of female students to be reflected in the proportion of female leaders. However, there is no doubt that this "pipeline" leaks: Women get lost at each stage necessary for a STEM career, and it depends on the specific domain where the largest drops are observed. For example, in some countries women leave STEM majors at twice the rate as men (e.g., Ceci et al., 2009). More generally, when one compares the proportion of women at a given career stage with the proportion obtaining respective qualifications within the same generation, the proportion of women decreases at each career stage.

Some professions that were historically male are not anymore, such as medicine, specifically veterinary medicine (e.g., Ceci et al., 2009). Others, such as engineering, appear much less successful in attracting women. However, when it comes to the top positions, there is a scarcity of women throughout. In cross-country analyses, small, if any, relations are found between girls' achievement in math and their proportion in math-intensive fields (see Ceci et al., 2009). For unknown reasons, the largest proportions of women in male-typed fields are found in Turkey, South Korea, and Ireland (Ceci et al., 2009). This appears strange because neither Turkey nor Ireland are stereotyped as particularly progressive regarding gender roles.

There is no consensus regarding the skills that are needed for a successful STEM career (Ceci et al., 2009). As we discussed, parents' estimates of their children's talent in math are gender-biased, favoring boys. Mothers' perceptions influence whether children are good or bad at a given domain more than actual grades do. In other words, a girl with good math grades whose mother thinks she is not talented in math will tend to think of herself as low in math ability. In spite of these correlations, causal paths are unclear, and when looking specifically at the most talented children, few such relations are found (see Ceci et al., 2009). This is reminiscent of what we already discussed regarding the role of gender stereotypes. These do not color judgments in the presence of diagnostic evidence, in this case: If a girl is obviously highly talented in math, parents and teachers will notice.

Do girls who attend girls-only schools develop more interest and higher academic self-concepts in physics than those at coed schools? Indeed, this appears to be the case. Girls at girls' schools do better at math and science than those at coeducational schools, and they are more likely to choose STEM majors (for a review, see Schneeweis & Zweimüller, 2012). It appears that a coeducational environment reinforces gender stereotypes. This may come about because of interactions among boys and girls, but it may also be reinforced by teachers who tend to expect gender-typical strengths. Moreover, different norms may be established in single-gender than gender-mixed environments. For example, if advanced physics is offered at a girls' school, it is obvious that it is offered for girls. At a gender-mixed school, one may instead believe that this course is primarily for the boys. In line with this reasoning, the implicit association between "physics" and "others" as compared to self was larger for girls from gender-mixed than for girls from girls-only schools (Kessels, 2007), demonstrating that girls from gender-mixed schools feel more distanced from physics. Difficulty in interpreting differences between girls who visit girls' schools and those who visit gender-mixed schools arises from the fact that they may differ in the first place. For example, feminist or Catholic parents may be more likely to send their daughters to girls-only schools.

Nevertheless, several studies reinforce the interpretation that coeducational environments undermine girls' interest in STEM fields (see Schneeweis & Zweimüller, 2012). First, women in women-only environments are more likely to switch from a gender-typical to a gender-atypical major than those in gender-mixed environments. Second, similar to complete gender segregation, if only a few male students are present, women choose gender-atypical jobs more often and end up earning more money than if there is a higher proportion of men around. As Schneeweis and Zweimüller (2012) showed, women chose technical schools with a higher probability if the proportion of male students in their class was lower.

In their article, "When Being a Girl Matters Less," Kessels and Hannover (2008) provided unambiguous evidence for the role of coeducational environments in deterring girls from STEM fields. They designed a large experiment in which more than 400 K–12 students were assigned to coeducational or single-gender physics classes during the eighth grade. Students were told the study was about teaching methods. Toward the end of the school year, girls from coed classes reported a significantly lower physics ability self-concept than girls in single-gender classes. There was no such effect for boys. Moreover, boys and girls provided speeded self-ratings on typically masculine and typically feminine traits. Both boys and girls tended to self-describe using relatively more gender-typical traits while being taught in coed than in single-gender classes, and these gender-typical traits were more accessible in coed classes, as inferred from faster reaction times. How can we interpret these findings? While learning math or physics, students are not in a vacuum but in a social environment. As teenagers, negotiating their identities as boys and girls is an important developmental task activated through the presence of the other gender. This may interfere with learning in counterstereotypical domains. As we have seen, people try to balance their identities such that, if they are female, and physics is regarded as male, they distance themselves from physics (e.g., Nosek et al., 2002b). Note that the masculine and feminine traits that Kessels and Hannover measured appear totally unrelated to learning in physics, being more general in nature. Thus, as long as the stereotype is alive and well that math and physics are masculine, the presence of boys undermines girls' motivation to excel at such "boys' tasks." This is likely the case in particular at an age when adult gender identities are being formed and are still insecure.

Stereotype threat may also play a role in females leaving STEM fields. One recent study recorded parts of the conversations that male and female STEM faculty had over several days (Holleran, Whitehead, Schmader, & Mehl, 2011). Participants also responded to questions concerning job disengagement, such as, "Lately, I tend to think less during my work and just execute it mechanically." The researchers were interested in the relation between talking about research (vs. social topics) with one's colleagues and job disengagement. As one would expect, the more men talked about research with their colleagues, the more engaged they were in their jobs. The converse pattern was found for women: The more they talked about research, the more disengaged they were. Separate analyses of the sound files indicated that women appeared less competent while talking to their male colleagues (even though they were as successful on objective indicators of research productivity). A possible interpretation of these findings is that female faculty experience stereotype threat while talking about research with their male colleagues and that this threat leads to disengagement. Further studies are needed to test the causal links and the generality of these findings that until now were observed at only one U.S. university.

Imagine you are a Christian and you enter a hotel in a western European city, thinking about spending the night there. The hotel lobby is filled with objects clearly belonging to Muslim culture. You might feel like you do not belong there, and you walk out, searching for a different hotel where you fit in better. Using this example, it is important to note that objects displayed in an environment play a role when making job-related decisions (Cheryan, Plaut, Davies, & Steele, 2009). In a room filled with objects related to the computer-freak stereotype (such as *Star Trek* posters and technical magazines), women in particular showed less interest in majoring in computer science than in a neutral room. Similarly, a web design company appeared less attractive to women if they were informed that such objects were displayed in the offices.

In other words, one reason why it is difficult to increase the proportion of women in certain domains is that the stereotypes of these domains make them unattractive to women and make them feel like they do not belong there. Complementing these findings are experiments that test the effects of domains' gender associations with men's and women's self-assessment of respective skills and career aspirations. As we have seen, the mere fact that a skill is said to be male-associated provokes a higher assessment of one's own abilities in men than women, and in turn, increased aspirations in respective fields (for a review, see Lips, 2013). In particular, if system justification is made salient, women's own ratings of their math abilities are lowered (Bonnot & Jost, 2014). This is in essence a vicious circle: Again, because STEM fields are masculine, there continue to be more men than women in those fields.

Extending this reasoning a little further, one measure to increase the proportion of women in certain majors would be to adapt the description of the abilities required and of the respective jobs. As we have seen, women value jobs where they can work with people and help others. The expectation that their goals regarding social relations will be fulfilled can help attract them to STEM careers (Diekman, Clark, Johnston, Brown, & Steinberg, 2011). Consequently, "high social skills are required, and you will later work in an inspiring team of smart, like-minded individuals developing gadgets that much improve people's lives" could go a long way in raising female students' interest in computer science (see Eccles, 2007, for a discussion).

It is not only the objects displayed in an environment that make professions and jobs more or less attractive for women. The proportion of men and women present in an environment can also make it appear more or less attractive (Murphy, Steele, & Gross, 2007). Murphy et al. (2007) presented conference videos to participants majoring in math, science, or engineering, and asked them how attractive they would find it to attend that conference. If only 25% of women were present, both men and women felt less desire to participate than if 50% of women were present. If women were shown to be a minority at the conference, the women in the study felt a lower sense of belonging, and additional measures indicated that the situation appeared threatening to them. Other research seconds the importance of feelings of belonging for achievement motivation, expectations of success, and interest in a domain (for reviews, see Cohen & Garcia, 2008; Valian, 2014). Some practical implications are not far-fetched. For example, if a company wants to hire more women, a selection committee consisting of 80% men is not a good idea.

One may also ask the following question: What effects does the image of people in a field have on academic and vocational choices? We might call this image a prototype: the most typical person representing the group in question (Hannover & Kessels, 2004; for details, see Chapter 14 on social identity). As Hannover and Kessels (2004) elaborated, self-to-prototype matching may influence academic choices. People's self-image contains information about what they are like and also what they want to be like. This self-image may be compared with the image of the typical student whose favorite subject is math, for example. The authors asked eighth and ninth graders to rate, on many traits, students whose most or least favorite subject is math, physics, German, and English. Their analyses yielded one "science" prototype (i.e., math and physics) and one "humanities" prototype (i.e., German and English). Although the science prototype was considered intelligent and motivated, it was also rated the lowest in physical attractiveness and social popularity. Overall, participants felt more similar to a student whose least favorite subject is science than to one whose favorite subject is science. The authors' findings can be summarized as this: "The more similar a person's self-image was to his or her prototype of a student preferring a school subject as [a] favorite one, the stronger the person's liking for that subject" (Hannover & Kessels, 2004, p. 61). Put blatantly, students who think those who like science are nerds don't like science if they do not want to be nerds. This relation was strongest for math, presumably because there is a well-developed prototype (i.e., agreement about what students who like math are like). Such research suggests that the negative image of the people in a specific domain may prevent other people from entering that domain.

Career preferences have been identified as a major factor in determining the small number of women in STEM fields (Ceci et al., 2009). If women perceive the prototype of a given field (e.g., engineering) as incompatible with the female prototype that is their ideal for themselves, they may shy away from that field (Cheryan & Plaut, 2010). As Cheryan and Plaut (2010) showed in the United States, women were less interested in majoring in computer science, and they felt less similar than men to computer science majors. This gender difference in perceived similarity statistically accounted for the difference in interest, in line with the interpretation that women are not interested in majoring in computer science because they feel dissimilar to computer scientists. Similar findings occurred for men's interest in majoring in English, suggesting that gender differences in the selection of professions follow gender-related prototypes of domains. The relations held up when expectations of success and stereotype threat were taken into account.

Recently, Wang, Eccles, and Kenny (2013) suggested an interesting explanation for the relative lack of women in STEM fields. Among those with outstanding math ability, women on average outperform men in verbal ability. In Wang and colleagues' own study, almost 1,500 U.S. students were surveyed in the 12th grade, and their abilities (on the well-known SAT) were assessed. Fifteen years later, participants were most likely to be in a STEM career if they had high math and *moderate* verbal abilities (30% of them were women). In contrast, a STEM career was less likely for those who had high math *and* high verbal abilities (63% among these were women). Thus, the authors concluded that women with high math abilities have more career choices and may decide to select intellectually challenging majors outside of STEM, such as law. In line with this, participants who also had high verbal abilities valued working with people more than those with only high math abilities, and those who valued working with people chose non-STEM occupations. In Lubinski and Benbow's (2006) opinion, it should not be regarded as a loss of talent if people with exceptional math abilities choose careers outside of math and science. Rather, quantitative and reasoning skills also contribute positively to performance in many other professions.

Ceci and colleagues (2009) held that Goldberg paradigm studies investigating gender bias in STEM fields are largely missing (for an exception, see Moss-Racusin et al., 2012). The authors opined that structural barriers and gender stereotypes, including stereotype threat, most likely only explain a small proportion of the gender difference in STEM positions. However, in our view, Ceci and colleagues underestimated the evidence on gender stereotypes. For example, whereas they point out that the youngest cohorts may not hold gender stereotypes that math is male, recent studies have shown that they do, from an early age on and even pertaining to their automatically activated components (e.g., Cvencek et al., 2011; Muzzatti & Agnoli, 2007; Steffens et al., 2010). Also, the larger the implicit gender-science stereotypes are in a nation, the larger is the achievement gap between boys and girls in math and science in eighth grade (Nosek et al., 2009). Such impressive findings clearly show that STEM fields are automatically perceived to be a masculine domain, which has a host of negative consequences for girls' and women's achievement-related self-concepts, performance, feelings of belonging, endurance when facing obstacles, and career motivation.

Ceci and colleagues (2009) concluded that women's preference for working in other fields is, among other things, a much bigger factor in explaining their scarcity in STEM fields. We do agree that this preference is important. However, while drawing together all the evidence in this book, we were particularly struck by the all-embracing role of gender stereotypes. To illustrate, women's and men's preferences for working in STEM or other fields should also be interpreted as based on gender-role socialization, on the interplay between self-images and images of the fields—taken together: on gender stereotypes.

Entrepreneurship

The economic welfare of modern societies depends on the activities of successful entrepreneurs acting as driving forces in economic innovation (see, e.g., Hyrsky & Tuunanen, 1999): Creating enterprises engenders economic growth (see Baron et al., 2001). Thus, it is an important research aim to identify what influences a person's decision to become an entrepreneur. What distinguishes successful entrepreneurs from those whose business fails? What conditions in the social and economic context are needed to increase the chances of success of those starting their own business? Women become entrepreneurs less often than men (even though the proportion is rising, at least in the United States; see DeMartino et al., 2006). Two factors we have extensively discussed figure prominently in this equation. First, entrepreneur is a strongly male-typed profession. Traits such as assertive, achievement-oriented, and confident distinguish entrepreneurs from managers (e.g., Baron et al., 2001). In other words, entrepreneurs are more strongly male-typed than managers, the group typically regarded as a prototype of a male-typed profession (e.g., "think manager-think male"; Schein, 2001). A recent study tested whether the male stereotype of entrepreneurship contributed to women's lower propensity of choosing entrepreneurship (Gupta, Turban, & Bhawe, 2008). In line with theories on the influence of stereotypes on individuals' decisions, male as compared to female business students had higher intentions of becoming entrepreneurs when no information was presented (i.e., when participants relied on their own masculine stereotype of the profession); but when the stereotype was nullified by explaining that entrepreneurs show typically male *and* female characteristics, this gender difference disappeared by raising women's and (unfortunately!) dampening men's intentions. In line with the self-to-prototype matching ideas introduced earlier, it appears that people evaluate how similar they are to those in a given field: Changing the prototype to make women fit better thus made men feel as if they fit worse. It would be good if a profession's image could be based on gender-unrelated traits (e.g., rigorous, trustworthy), so that both women and men feel like they fit in.

A second factor that needs to be considered for explaining why women become entrepreneurs less often than men is that a high risk-taking propensity is an essential trait for entrepreneurs. As we have seen, women are in many contexts less risk-oriented than men. According to an overview by DeMartino and colleagues (2006), the businesses of male entrepreneurs grow faster than those of their female peers. The question has been asked why female entrepreneurs are less successful than male entrepreneurs. One response is related to differences in time commitment and motivation: Female entrepreneurs are more motivated than male entrepreneurs to balance work and family demands and choose entrepreneurship because of the associated flexibility. For example, a single mother may choose to open her own small business because that step allows her perfect flexibility to juggle childcare and work as she personally deems appropriate. Generally, some entrepreneurs are more oriented toward earning a family income; others are profit- and growth-oriented (e.g., Hyrsky & Tuunanen, 1999). As DeMartino and colleagues reviewed, male entrepreneurs devote more time to their business than female entrepreneurs. These gender differences are augmented for entrepreneurs who have children. Comparing MBA alumni who were entrepreneurs or not, DeMartino and colleagues found that the career and personal-life orientations of female entrepreneurs and nonentrepreneurs did not differ, whereas the career orientations of male entrepreneurs were higher than those of nonentrepreneurs. By implication, "to make it big" drove many men's decisions to become entrepreneurs but not women's. Given this difference in motivation, it does not come as such a big surprise that more men than women have fast-growing businesses.

Chapter 11 on role models has further implications for career choice, both for the number of women in STEM fields and for entrepreneurship.

· 10 ·

THE ROLE OF ORGANIZATIONAL CULTURES

This chapter focuses on different aspects at the intersection of individuals and organizations: job search, job success, negotiations, and diversity in organizations.

Job search situations

What should additionally be taken into account regarding job search situations? Job advertisements should be phrased in a way that attracts both male and female applicants (see also Part II of this volume). Moreover, one should consider that men, in comparison to women, estimate their own abilities to be higher. As a consequence, women may need more active encouragement than men do to consider high-ranked jobs at all. We have also discussed that men self-promote more than women do (and are allowed to do) and that self-promotion during job interviews increases apparent ability.

The aforementioned findings and considerations on the influence of stereotypes on impressions of others can be summarized in the following recommendations: (a) As much information as possible should be available about applicants and (b) this information should actually be used by evaluators (e.g., by rating each applicant on each criterion, taking enough time, and being held accountable for decisions); (c) research on the role of selection criteria shows that these should be specific (see Heilman & Parks-Stamm, 2007; Reskin & Bielby, 2005; Swim et al., 1989). If these recommendations are followed, there is much less room for gender stereotypes to color judgments.

Why selection criteria need to be defined in advance was intriguingly demonstrated in a study with the telling subtitle, "Redefining Merit to Justify Discrimination" (Uhlmann & Cohen, 2005, p. 474). After reviewing men's and women's applications, participants indicated how important each of several criteria was to success at the job (that was typically male or typically female: police chief or women's studies professor). The experiments demonstrated that importance ratings of criteria mirrored the qualifications of the preferred applicant. Whenever the man held certain qualifications, these were rated as important for the police chief. If the woman was portrayed to hold the same qualifications, they were rated as less important. However, for the professor of women's studies, it was reversed. Whenever the woman held certain qualifications, these were rated as more important than when the man held them. As another example, if you favored an applicant for a faculty position at your university and she was stronger in attracting funding than the other applicant but weaker in publishing journal articles, you would judge attracting funding as more important than publications, and vice versa, if her qualifications were the opposite (see Valian, 2007, for a discussion). Interestingly, participants felt they were objective while making these biased decisions—after all, they did use true differences in qualifications on relevant criteria. This effect of "redefining merit" disappeared if the importance of each criterion was rated before applications were reviewed, clearly indicating that this measure helps in practice avoid this pitfall.

Job success

What does career success depend on? Career success can be defined as positive work-related and psychological outcomes related to work experiences (see Ng, Eby, Sorensen, & Feldman, 2005). Following Ng and colleagues (2005), two important perspectives have been widely discussed in the literature. We call the first the merit theory: Those get ahead who show good performance on the job. We call the second the networking theory. According to this view, sponsoring by established elites is important for getting ahead (e.g., being selected for challenging tasks, receiving training opportunities). For example, managers who are more visible to those in the upper echelons by working in closer proximity to the decision makers move up the hierarchy faster (Martell et al., 2012). Of course, to the degree that networks are important, there may be biases in favor of established groups (e.g., men) or against certain historically disadvantaged groups (e.g., women or those with low socioeconomic status). As a meta-analysis by Ng and colleagues showed, both merit and networking were related to all measures of career success. Women's career success was smaller than men's according to the criterion "salary," and, to a lesser degree, with regard to "promotion." The relation between gender and salary was smaller in more recent studies, indicating declining gender differences. Gender was unrelated to career satisfaction, a more subjective indicator of career success.

For women, the relations between education and salary and between hours worked and salary were stronger than for men, which may imply that women have to do more than men to be successful (e.g., have unambiguous credentials). Unfortunately, whether the relationship between networking and career success was larger for one gender than the other could not be tested because there were too few studies investigating these factors. However, for women, the relationships between networking and career satisfaction as well as education and career satisfaction were stronger than for men.

As elucidated in the section on the effects of stereotypes on impressions of others, women may appear less promotable than men while performing as well. Additionally, concrete evidence of performance should be available and used immediately for evaluations—after some delay, much diagnostic information is forgotten again, and stereotypes fill in the blanks when ratings are made.

Negotiations

Stereotype threat plays an important role for men's and women's success in negotiations (Kray, Thompson, & Galinsky, 2001). In female-male dyads, framing the negotiation task as diagnostic of ability increased men's and decreased women's outcomes. Similar findings were generally obtained when stereotypes were implicitly activated, specifically when participants had learned that being rational and assertive increases success and being emotional and accommodating reduces it. When stereotypes were explicitly activated by adding that these personality traits are related to gender, interestingly, the pattern of findings reversed: Women obtained better outcomes than men by making more demanding opening offers. Kray et al. (2001) explained this as men "choking under pressure"—too high expectations lead to failure— and women actively distancing themselves from gender stereotypes, for example, by demonstrating that they are not emotional. Supplementing these findings, women's success in negotiations is also increased if the negotiation topic is not male-typed (Bear & Babcock, 2012). Instead of negotiating the prize of motorcycle headlights, the topic was changed to "lamp-work beads used to make jewelry." After this simple intervention, women negotiated as well as men.

Negotiators whose first offer is accepted are often less satisfied with the negotiation than those who achieve the very same result after several rounds of negotiating (see Kray & Gelfand, 2009). However, women may experience relief if their first offer is accepted, believing that the process was not as tough as they had feared. Women face higher risks in negotiations than men and may be punished for behaving in the exact same way. For example, compensation negotiations appear greedier when initiated by women than by men (see Kray & Gelfand, 2009).

Because research has shown that women feel less entitled to high salaries and that they fare worse than men in negotiations (e.g., Kray et al., 2001), the solution appears straightforward: Teach women that they deserve more, and teach them to demand more. However, recent research has shown that this is not the correct diagnosis or cure (Amanatullah & Morris, 2010). Instead of subscribing to a trait model (i.e., "women do not have the personality traits it takes to negotiate successfully"), Amanatullah and Morris (2010) postulated that bargaining one's salary assertively would come across as greedy when done by a woman (but not by a man), because it is not congruent with the prescriptive stereotype that women are warm. Thus, the authors described women as "savvy impression managers navigating the environment" (p. 257). It is, however, congruent with female stereotypes to bargain for others: Excelling for someone else's best interest is clearly social-relations oriented. Amanatullah and Morris corroborated these ideas in an experiment. They demonstrated that women requested a lower salary in a simulated negotiation only when negotiating for themselves. In contrast, they did as well as men when negotiating for someone else. This difference was fully due to anticipated social backlash (responses to questions such as, "How much do you think you can reasonably ask for without causing the hiring manager to punish you for being too demanding?"). Social backlash was expected at much lower salaries for women negotiating for themselves than for any of the other three groups. In other words, women had a feeling of how much they could ask for before being punished, and that was the reason they did not ask for more; thus they were behaving in a socially strategic way.

The computer negotiation paradigm Amanatullah and Morris (2010) created paves interesting avenues for future research. For example, participants can be put into the salary manager's shoes, and it can be tested how they react to the demanded salaries, depending on employee gender. Focusing on the interaction between both, one could test whether women are more sensitive to ambiguous signals sent by their negotiation partner.

Organizational cultures and diversity

The larger social environment at work also puts minority members into less comfortable positions than majority members. The rules and customs of work contexts have been shaped by men and reward traditionally male behavior (see Johnson & Powell, 1994). "Women are forced to acquiesce to male norms in order to gain promotion" (Johnson & Powell, 1994, p. 127). As one example, men are socialized to avoid emotional expression more than women: They learn to conceal their vulnerability (Sieverding, 2009). The author's job interview study showed that men tried to conceal their emotions in a job interview more than women did and that those who concealed their emotions were judged more competent than those who did not. By implication, women tended to appear less competent than men because—following female prescriptions—they tried less to suppress, for example, their nervousness.

The social situation in institutions that used to be male turf (or still are) differs in many respects for women and men. A group that forms the minority is more visible and viewed more in terms of group stereotypes (see Eagly & Karau, 2002). For example, during a business meeting attended by 50% women, a woman's contribution is weighted less according to gender than the same contribution if she is the only woman (see Lyness & Thompson, 2000). Moreover, exclusion from networks may result (often called "old boys'" networks). Minority members often report that it is a barrier to their success that a majority of White men are already in place who feel most comfortable around their own kind. Conversely, women may feel they fit less into a male-dominated culture (e.g., senior management). The higher the proportion of women already employed, the higher the probability that other women will be hired or promoted (for reviews, see Eagly & Karau, 2002; Reskin & Bielby, 2005). What happens if women invest extra time into networking (which they often fail to do—for example, if the children are waiting to be picked up)? It turns out that networking may be difficult for women in male-dominated occupations. For example, male rituals and men's activities may have been established where women perceive that they do not fit in (e.g., male-only sports competitions, strip bars, etc.; Mölders & van Quaquebeke, 2011).

How far do the career paths of female and male executives differ? Lyness and Thompson (2000) compared women and men concerning perceived barriers and facilitators, challenging experiences, and career histories. Women rated four out of six barriers higher than men: lack of culture fit, fewer opportunities for geographical mobility, exclusion from informal networks, and less challenging experiences. Challenging experiences are associated with being promoted (see also Martell et al., 2012). In the Lyness and Thompson study, women gave higher ratings than men on the facilitators having a good track record (i.e., unambiguous evidence of success) and developing relationships. Among these factors, challenging job assignments were the best predictor of success. Additionally, mentoring helped men's success more than women's. Taken together, successful female executives reported barriers to their success but had strategies that helped them overcome them, such as making sure their strengths were obvious and actively seeking out challenging jobs if they were not offered to them (see also Bowles, 2012).

London, Downey, Romero-Canyas, Rattan, and Tyson (2012) demonstrated that women differ in their sensitivity to being rejected because of their gender. Women high in gender-based rejection sensitivity suspect more often than others that they may be treated differently because of their gender, and as a consequence, they self-silenced and thus lost opportunities for advancement (e.g., they did not volunteer to speak or missed a professor's office hours). Comparable concerns were nonexistent for the majority of men who took part in that research (but, for example, Black or gay men may fall prey to the same situational cues).

Several field studies have shown that companies with a higher proportion of women in top management fare better financially than those with predominantly male governing bodies (see Ellemers, Rink, Derks, & Ryan, 2012, for details). It is important to note that these studies are correlational: It cannot be concluded from such evidence that hiring women at the top is the *cause* of positive outcomes. Other factors could be responsible for the relation. For example, a progressive and open corporate culture could have both consequences, that more women make it to the top and that all employees try to give their best for the organization (see Mölders & van Quaquebeke, 2011). The result would be exactly the observed relation—that more female executives go along with better financial outcomes.

Anyway, rather than the presence of women per se, a diverse composition of a group may provoke positive outcomes. Managing diversity is the art of creating a common in-group in which each person feels he or she is a valued member of the whole but also a respected individual (see Ehrke & Steffens, 2014). A pertinent danger is creating an atmosphere in which discrimination is negated. This can have a range of negative consequences, particularly for minority members (e.g., Apfelbaum, Pauker, Sommers, & Ambady, 2010; Holoien & Shelton, 2012). For example, the color blindness ideology proposes equal treatment of all, regardless of skin color. It minimizes group differences and thus negates discrimination. The more White employees that endorsed the color blindness ideology, the less engaged at work and the less identified with the company were their minority coworkers (Plaut, Thomas, & Goren, 2009).

Managing diversity is an important aspect in determining the success of diverse groups. Given a proactive diversity-management strategy, the relationship between team diversity and organizational performance is stronger than in the absence of such a strategy (Cunningham, 2009; see also McKay, Avery, & Morris, 2008). Proactive diversity management comprises, for example, integrating diversity into an organization's mission statement and informing all employees of it:

> A true diversity climate permits men and women in the organization to hold multiple identities and to display the leadership style that best suits their individual abilities and personal preferences. It should focus on individual merit, instead of allowing for the perpetuation of gendered beliefs and stereotypic expectations. (Ellemers et al., 2012, p. 181)

Proactive gender diversity management may also make organizations more attractive to women (Martins & Parsons, 2007). Furthermore, a climate in which sexism toward women is present "chills" not only women's but also men's climate perceptions (Settles, Cortina, Buchanan, & Miner, 2012). In other words, all members of an organization may profit from a true diversity climate.

Diversity management has been reviewed from a social-psychological perspective by Ehrke and Steffens (2014). Diversity management is about handling social diversity in an adequate and sensitive way. Keep in mind, however, that there is no consensus of what constitutes diversity, although the core diversity dimensions of gender, age, ethnic-cultural background, (dis)ability, sexual orientation, and religiosity have been defined (henceforth, social-group diversity). This classification overlooks social class, appearance, and weight, as well as diversity pertaining to attitudes, values, and beliefs. Finally, diversity of functions and status is an important aspect of diversity in organizations.

In the United States, the roots of diversity management are the civil rights and antiracism movement, whereas in Europe, gender inequality at work is its foundation (see Ehrke & Steffens, 2014). On the one hand, diversity management is seen as inevitable because of the growing social-group diversity in multicultural societies and because of antidiscrimination laws. For example, perceived discrimination at work provokes lower job satisfaction and higher turnover intentions (Madera, King, & Hebl, 2012). Therefore, organizations should make sure that little discrimination occurs. On the other hand, the value-in-diversity hypothesis promises more organizational effectiveness from more diverse teams, such as more creativity and better solutions. Studies testing the value-in-diversity hypothesis have yielded inconsistent results. For example, social-group diversity appeared more important in recently constituted than in long-established teams, where diversity in values reduced the satisfaction of team members and team cohesion. In established teams, informational diversity improved outcomes. An important moderator that influences the effect of team diversity is task complexity. Complex tasks profit from diverse teams, whereas simple tasks are carried out most effectively by homogeneous teams. Also, if team members believe in the value of diversity, they identify more strongly with diverse teams (van Knippenberg, Haslam, & Platow, 2007). Overall, effects of team diversity on performance are rather small (see Ehrke & Steffens, 2014). In one study, ethnical diversity increased the number of different ideas generated by a team, whereas gender diversity reduced it. Taken together, positive effects of social-group diversity can be productivity, innovation, and creativity, whereas among negative effects, less fluid communication and value conflicts have been reported. What the inconsistent findings tell us is that it is of little value to pose very general questions such as this: "Does diversity increase productivity?" Rather, we need more specific models of outcomes of specific aspects of diversity given certain beliefs, tasks, instructions, team compositions, and the like.

One of the most important ingredients of diversity management is diversity training (see Ehrke & Steffens, 2014). A typical aim of such training is awareness raising; another is skill building. Often, such training focuses on differences, neglecting communalities. This may have unintended negative consequences. For example, if White men are construed as perpetrators and minority members as victims, members of all of these groups may be unsatisfied with the training (see also Stevens, Plaut, & Sanchez-Burks, 2008). If diversity is stressed in a one-sided fashion, those group members who consider their own group as prototypical may react with negative attitudes toward diversity and toward out-groups (Steffens, Reese, Ehrke, & Jonas, 2015). For example, U.S. Americans who thought their group was the prototype of "North Americans" felt threatened when thinking about the diversity of North Americans, which was related to less positive out-group attitudes (for similar findings, see Morrison, Plaut, & Ybarra, 2010; Plaut, Garnett, Buffardi, & Sanches-Burks, 2011; Roccas & Amit, 2011; Verkuyten, 2011). In addition, if differences between groups are stressed, differences within groups are often neglected, thus increasing out-group stereotyping (e.g., Brauer & Er-rafiy, 2011). Such negative effects of diversity interventions are not uncommon (see Ehrke & Steffens, 2014).

Although billions are spent on diversity training, the respective measures are evaluated very infrequently (e.g., Paluck & Green, 2009). In addition, these interventions are often not based on social-psychological theorizing (see Pendry, Driscoll, & Field, 2007). Conversely, that theorizing is often tested only in the laboratory, so that the real-world implications of our most important theories go untested. We recently developed a diversity training program based on the in-group projection model (Mummendey & Wenzel, 1999; Wenzel, Mummendey, & Waldzus, 2007). This model is based on social identity theory and self-categorization theory (see Part II). It suggests that groups are compared with reference to an inclusive group providing relevant comparison dimensions. When the inclusive group is evaluated positively, as is typically the case, group members tend to ascribe features of their in-group to the inclusive group and therefore generally perceive a congruency between the in-group and inclusive group. For instance, psychology students are likely to conceive of students in general as being more like psychology students (e.g., emotional), whereas business students are likely to think that students in general are more like business students (e.g., career-oriented; see Wenzel, Mummendey, Weber, & Waldzus, 2003). Similarly, primary school teachers think they are more typical of teachers in general, whereas high school teachers think they are the more typical group (Waldzus, Mummendey, Wenzel, & Boettcher, 2004). Consequently, other groups (i.e., out-groups) are perceived as less prototypical, which legitimizes a less positive evaluation and treatment of out-group members. Taking into account that members of each subgroup tend to perceive their respective group as prototypical, the model predicts that they will disagree on the representation of the inclusive group, resulting in a perspective divergence between the different subgroups. For example, employees in accounting, as opposed to employees in marketing, will think they are more prototypical of the organization as a whole. A large number of studies have confirmed that in-groups are indeed perceived as more prototypical for inclusive groups relative to out-groups (for recent evidence, see, e.g., Bianchi, Mummendey, Steffens, & Yzerbyt, 2010; Machunsky, Meiser, & Mummendey, 2009; Reese, Berthold, & Steffens, 2012). Moreover, there is a negative relationship between perceived prototypicality and attitudes toward a relevant out-group (e.g., Berthold, Mummendey, Kessler, Luecke, & Schubert, 2012).

According to that model, if diversity is regarded as a feature of the inclusive group, then differences between in-groups and out-groups are not seen as deficits of the out-group (Waldzus, Mummendey, Wenzel, & Weber, 2003). Instead, these differences are conceived of as valuable additions to the inclusive group. On this basis, we developed a diversity training program that highlighted the diversity of the inclusive group (in that case, adults; Ehrke, Berthold, & Steffens, 2014). Participants were graduate students who volunteered to take part in the training to receive a certificate. Sexist attitudes were treated most extensively during the training, and the restrictions that gender roles pose on both women and men were discussed. We evaluated this training using a waiting control group design in which attitudes were measured for all participants before training; then again, after half the participants had received training; and finally, after all participants had received training. Half of the participants were assigned to the early training group and half to the late training group. Thus, if attitude change occurs, we can be sure that it was because of the training (not because of measurement or some other unknown factors). As a consequence of training, adults were perceived as more diverse, and this reduced sexism. In addition, ageism and negative attitudes toward the out-groups, East and West Germans, respectively, were also reduced. Similar but weaker effects were observed in undergraduate students who took part in a shorter diversity training program covered as get-to-know activities on their first day at a university. In other words, even though they did not know they had taken part in a diversity training program, the training improved out-group attitudes. These findings show that a social-psychological model can fruitfully be used as a theoretical basis for developing and implementing diversity training.

· 1 1 ·

ROLE MODELS

We start our discussion on role models by looking at mentoring. Following Blickle and colleagues (2008), this is a one-on-one professional relationship between a less and a more experienced person, intended to facilitate the growth of the less advanced person. Mentoring is positively related to many indicators of achievement (e.g., income, promotion). Women sometimes report a stronger need for mentoring than men do (see Lyness & Thompson, 2000). At the same time, only female mentors can provide same-gender role models to women; in contrast, relationships with male mentors have been found to be more vital to career success, presumably because of the men's more central role in companies and networks. Men can get both aspects at once from a male mentor: a role model and a central network figure.

As we have seen, people often self-stereotype, behaving in manners that are considered appropriate for the social groups to which they belong. For example, girls form non-STEM school interests because they associate STEM fields with boys. But, this being said, there are also girls and women who choose counterstereotypic interests and occupations, thus provoking social change: Fields such as medicine are no longer stereotypically male, although they definitely were several decades ago. When considering under what conditions women pursue counterstereotypic interests, an important ingredient is the role model. Seminal studies have demonstrated the importance of role models for considering and performing new behaviors (Bandura, 1965). It is widely believed that role model gender is important—female role models are believed to work better for girls than male role models (see Cheryan, Siy, Vichayapai, Drury, & Kim, 2011). The number of female role models has manifold positive consequences for women in STEM disciplines, such as increasing their commitment (see Young, Rudman, Buettner, & McLean, 2013). Competent female role models may also alleviate stereotype threat effects (e.g., Marx & Roman, 2002; McIntyre et al., 2011). After a short interaction with a female (rather than a male) advanced peer, female STEM majors increased their effort on a difficult math test, held more positive implicit attitudes toward math, and implicitly identified with math more (Stout et al., 2011). Similarly, as a subsequent study showed, reading biographies of female rather than male successful engineers improved female engineering students' implicit math attitude. More strongly identifying with these engineering role models was related with stronger intentions to pursue a career in engineering. Such effects appear promising for mentoring and role model interventions. Unfortunately, of course, in domains in which women are underrepresented, few role models are available, so underrepresentation may self-perpetuate.

In Chapter 2, we discussed the fact that counterstereotypic exemplars such as female leaders can affect implicit gender-leadership stereotypes (Dasgupta & Asgari, 2004). Similarly, female math teachers had an immediate positive effect on female STEM students' implicit math attitudes and their implicit identification with math (Stout et al., 2011). Further, female students expected higher grades from female rather than male professors, and they identified more with female professors. Male students were unaffected by the presence of a female versus male professor, presumably because enough role models and stereotypes that math is for men had been available throughout their lives and continued to be in the other classes they attend.

As other research has shown, role models only influence individuals successfully if they identify with them and if they regard their success as attainable (see Asgari, Dasgupta, & Stout, 2012). For example, if girls adore their female math teacher and think they could accomplish what she did, their interest in STEM fields should increase. In contrast, if girls dislike her and they think they could never become as good at math as she is, this role model should not affect positively their interest in pursuing math-related fields. A recent study showed such effects on implicit science-related cognitions (Young et al., 2013). Participants were female students in engineering and chemistry courses. These students implicitly identified more with science if they saw their female professor as a positive role model, and their implicit associations of science with male were reduced as compared to female students who did not identify with their female professor. These findings show positive influences of female role models—if and only if students identify with those role models.

Other research has shown that role models may backfire. First, as clarified in Chapter 8 on maintaining social hierarchies, the presence of a few (female) tokens makes the system appear fair and thus decelerates need for social change (Brown & Diekman, 2013). Moreover, extending research on self-to-prototype matching, Cheryan and colleagues (2011) recently showed that women who interacted with a stereotypical computer science major (male or female) for two minutes or less thought it was unlikely they could be successful in that field. The reason why success beliefs were lower than those of women who interacted with a nonstereotypical computer science major was that women felt dissimilar to the stereotypical individual. No such negative effect was obtained for (a small sample of) men. The stereotypical individual was dressed in an unfashionable way, wore a T-shirt that read, "I code. Therefore I am," and indicated stereotypical hobbies such as playing video games. A follow-up study showed that after interacting with a stereotypical individual, women were also less likely to indicate they could imagine majoring in that field (Cheryan, Drury, & Vichayapai, 2013). This effect persisted for two weeks. In the comparison group, women interacted with the same student, but the student was not acting in a stereotypical manner. In both experiments, it did not matter whether the interaction partner was male or female—if he or she was a nerd, women shied away from the field. By implication, if there are only a few visible women in certain positions (e.g., on the executive board of a company, in national politics), but these provoke in many women the reaction, "I definitely do not want to be like her," then women will be less likely to pursue that career given "role models" than if there were no women at all.

Although one may assume that feminine role models are necessary to attract more girls to certain careers, a recent study indicated that this may also backfire (Betz & Sekaquaptewa, 2012). Specifically, it appeared that the girls considered the success of these role models particularly unattainable and were therefore not motivated to try to follow their example. Similarly, Rudman and Phelan (2010) observed a contrast effect of priming female participants with counterstereotypic role models. After priming, women implicitly ascribed less leadership to themselves and showed a lowered interest in masculine occupations. The authors discussed these somewhat unexpected findings as contrast effects caused by threatening upward social comparison processes with the female vanguards (see also Parks-Stamm, Heilman, & Hearns, 2008).

A recent study by Asgari and colleagues (2012) shed more light on the processes underlying positive and negative effects of role models. As these authors showed, perceived (dis)similarity of the role model to other women, including the self, played a crucial role. All participants were presented biographies of women in counterstereotypic domains. The only difference was whether they were presented as possessing extraordinary early talent that made them differ from most other women or as working extremely hard after ordinary beginnings. As expected, the college students who took part in the research felt more similar to the hard-working than to the talented woman, and their implicit self-leadership associations were increased only after having been presented with those hard-working role models. Further studies replicated these findings and extended them: Participants who felt similar to successful female leaders also rated their own leadership qualities as higher than those in the other conditions and indicated more ambitious career goals. On top of these positive effects, women in leadership positions can also be regarded as agents of change (Huffman, 2013).

If we think about men's and women's roles in today's societies, role models may not only be important for encouraging women to develop career aspirations that they may otherwise not envision. Role models may also help to overcome the traditional division of labor at home that we discussed earlier as a major barrier to women's careers (see Chapter 7 on social roles). Gender role beliefs may be easily transmitted from parents to children because children observe very closely, and daily, how their parents share domestic work (Croft, Schmader, Block, & Baron, 2014). Such early and frequent observation may establish implicit stereotypes that may influence children's own thinking in many ways. In a Canadian study, the authors tested the correspondence between children's and parents' perceptions. That study found several indicators linking parents' beliefs about the division of labor, their self-stereotyping, and their implicit gender role associations and their children's stereotyping and expectations regarding their own future roles. In particular, fathers' explicit beliefs, their contributions to domestic work, and their implicit gender role associations predicted their daughters' career aspirations. These findings show that both aspects, work and family, cannot be regarded as independent from each other. They second what we concluded earlier: The key to changing men's and women's career paths is changing traditional domestic roles. Couples who live gender equality daily in their homes will have children who are less restricted by traditional gender roles, both inside the home and beyond.

· 1 2 ·

PARENTHOOD AND WORK-RELATED IMPRESSIONS

In addition to having effects on women's overall burden and the conflicting tasks they try to juggle (see Chapter 7 on social roles), parenthood also affects how working women are perceived by others. Mothers appear to embody the essence of womanhood (e.g., Okimoto & Heilman, 2012). What does this imply for the careers of women (and men) who have children? Several experiments have tested this, generally using the Goldberg paradigm: Written information about women and men who had children or not was provided to different participants, who rated them on competence, job commitment, and the like. These experiments show that parenthood is costly in several respects to both women and men. For example, both mothers and fathers were perceived as less committed to their jobs, less available, and less assertive/competent than childless applicants or the "ideal worker" (Fuegen et al., 2004). Also, the information that someone had taken a parental leave of absence resulted in lower recommendations for overseas assignments for both mothers and fathers (Allen, Russell, & Rush, 1994). A sample of female employees working full time perceived parents working full time as more career and less family oriented than were perceived those with reduced working hours (Etaugh & Moss, 2001). Similarly, working parents appeared less warm than stay-at-home parents (Bridges, Etaugh, & Barnes-Farrell, 2002; see also Park, Smith, & Correll, 2008).

In spite of these findings indicating costs of parenthood for both women and men, much additional evidence suggests that parenthood is more damaging to working mothers than to working fathers. The lack of fit model (Heilman, 1983) suggests that mothers, because they represent typical women more than childless women, should appear less competent and less fitting for male-gender typed jobs than women without children or fathers (Heilman & Okimoto, 2008). This has been termed the "motherhood penalty" or the "maternal wall."

Working mothers are liked less than working fathers and are assumed to be worse parents than working fathers and nonworking mothers, in particular when they decide to work for personal fulfillment instead of financial necessity (Brescoll & Uhlmann, 2005; Okimoto & Heilman, 2012). It is important to note that it is not known whether these findings generalize to mothers with children beyond preschool age. Similar prejudice was observed against men violating traditional gender roles: Stay-at-home fathers were liked less than stay-at-home mothers (Brescoll & Uhlmann, 2005). Fathers working full time appeared more competent than those with reduced working hours (see also Vinkenburg, van Engen, Coffeng, & Dikkers, 2012), but the same benefit was not observed for mothers working full time (Etaugh & Folger, 1998).

Interestingly, fathers were held to lower standards than both mothers and men without children, with regard to, for example, the time commitment raters would require of the applicant before hiring (Fuegen et al., 2004; Fuegen & Endicott, 2010). In other words, fathers would be required to show up less in the office than both men without children and mothers (see Benard & Correll, 2010, for similar findings). Mothers were less likely to be hired or promoted compared to women without children, but for male applicants, parental status did not lower their respective chances (Cuddy et al., 2004; Fuegen et al., 2004; Heilman & Okimoto, 2008). When asked which applicant should not be considered further for a male-gender typed leadership position, 62% of participants eliminated the mother as opposed to the father and the childless woman or man (Heilman & Okimoto, 2008). Mothers were given lower screening recommendations than the other three applicants because participants regarded them as less assertive (e.g., independent, leaders) and competent (including productive and effective) than the others (also see Cuddy et al., 2004).

A large experiment yielded a particularly consistent and troubling set of findings. Mothers appeared lower in competence than nonmothers and men with or without children and less committed to work. Participants required mothers to have higher test scores to be hired than the other groups. At the same time, mothers were allowed fewer days late and were offered lower salaries. They received lower hiring recommendations as well as a lower likelihood to be recommended for management or promotion (Correll et al., 2007). Childless women were six times more likely to be recommended for hiring than mothers were. Fathers, in contrast, appeared more committed than nonfathers, were allowed more days late, were offered higher salaries, tended to be recommended more often for management, were more likely to be recommended for promotion, and were somewhat more likely to be hired than men without children (Correll et al., 2007). This pattern was generally replicated in a more recent study (Benard & Correll, 2010). Complementing their laboratory findings, in a second study, Correll and colleagues sent out more than 1,200 (fake) applications in response to job offers. Childless women received more than twice as many callbacks as equally qualified mothers.

A study in the context of U.S. academia collected data both from junior faculty themselves and from the perspective of supervisors or senior faculty (King, 2008). Even though occupying formally similar positions, mothers made less money than fathers. Senior faculty expected less career advancement of mothers than of fathers. At the same time, mothers reported more involvement in their work and a higher commitment than fathers. Whereas mothers and fathers reported no differences in desire and flexibility for advancement, supervisors perceived mothers as less involved and less flexible than fathers. In turn, supervisors' ratings were related to career advancement. This study is intriguing because it shows a perspective divergence between mothers and their supervisors concerning work performance (i.e., the supervisors judge mothers lower than mothers judge themselves), and it shows that supervisors' impressions partly determine career success. Gender stereotypes can possibly explain the perspective divergence: Because of the motherhood penalty, mothers' work commitment and work-related achievement motivation are underestimated. However, in the absence of objective performance indicators, we believe it cannot be excluded that mothers may overestimate their own performance as compared to fathers. For example, an identical response on a subjective scale (e.g., "strongly agree") to an item such as, "I want to advance quickly," may objectively have a different meaning to a mother than to her colleagues if she is more burdened with childcare than they are (see shifting standards in Chapter 3); concretely, it could be that fathers mean, "I want to obtain tenure within two years," and mothers mean, "I want to obtain tenure within three years" when indicating strong agreement. This ambiguity notwithstanding, the findings are important because first, gender stereotypes are a likely explanation for them, too, and second, the findings imply that mothers will feel they have less career success than they deserve, as compared to fathers. Future research should test if such a perspective divergence is observed in work contexts other than academia. Ellemers, van den Heuvel, de Gilder, Maass, and Bonvini (2004) reported a similar perspective divergence for female and male postdocs in the Netherlands and Italy who were not parents.

In the context of blue-collar work, a simple gender bias was observed on most ratings: Regardless of parental status, women were judged as warmer, less assertive and competent, and less committed to the job, and they were hired with a lower probability than men (Güngör & Biernat, 2009). In this context, mothers were also seen as more unavailable than fathers. These findings are a case in point that we cannot generalize from the conditions that were investigated in several experiments to other conditions that were never targeted (in this case, blue-collar work). For example, expectations regarding the distribution of gender-related domestic work may differ between these contexts.

When unambiguous information about job-related success was added, female participants regarded mothers as less likable than fathers, held them to higher standards, and recommended them less for promotion (Benard & Correll, 2010). Hiring discrimination occurred because participants disliked mothers. It appears that female participants discriminated against mothers because they felt threatened by a woman who excels at work and manages having children at the same time—in other words, an extremely successful woman (for evidence of this, see Parks-Stamm et al., 2008). Typically, though, no gender differences in discrimination of highly successful women are found (e.g., Heilman et al., 2004). Still, it is possible that women and men discriminate against them for different reasons (discussed later).

Mothers are not only often judged as less competent than others, but working mothers are also judged as less warm than those staying at home (Riggs, 1997) and than working fathers (Etaugh & Folger, 1998), which boils down to a "no-win situation" for working mothers (Cuddy et al., 2004, p. 702): "Women lost perceived competence and gained perceived warmth when they became mothers," whereas "when working men became fathers, they maintained perceived competence and gained perceived warmth" (Cuddy et al., 2004, p. 711).

Not all studies converge on similar patterns of findings. In one recent study, mothers were hired with the same probability as fathers and women without children, and parents were suggested for promotion more often than those without children (Fuegen & Endicott, 2010). Can women escape the motherhood penalty? A recent Spanish study showed that they can by making their devotion to work clear and explicit (Aranda & Glick, 2014). Mothers who indicated their devotion to work received hiring recommendations similar to work-devoted and family-devoted fathers. Only mothers who indicated their devotion to their families received lower recommendations. A similar pattern was found for the allocation of resources and work opportunities.

Interestingly, if mothers were portrayed to be lesbians, impressions of them were also similar to those of working fathers: They did not lose on career orientation but appeared more family-oriented (Peplau & Fingerhut, 2004). These findings, along with those discussed earlier in the context of blue-collar work, are strong evidence that the discrimination of working mothers depends on their perceived social roles—stereotypes of working mothers depend on "the presence of a male provider and the expectation of strong family obligations" (Peplau & Fingerhut, 2004, p. 720). In other words, the key to ending discrimination of working mothers based on stereotypes of mothers is that the unequal distribution of housework and childcare between working mothers and fathers stops or at least the perception that women will be devoted to housework and childcare instead of to their jobs (Aranda & Glick, 2014). Women who are devoted to their jobs should be sure to correct wrong assumptions in work-related contexts.

But how are fathers perceived if they live less traditional social roles? An economic questionnaire study with fathers of young children in Germany demonstrated that there was indeed a negative relationship between identification with one's employer and taking parental leave: Their jobs and the organizations where they worked mattered less to fathers taking leave than to those who decided against it (Vogt & Pull, 2010). Also, deciding against leave was related to expecting more negative consequences for one's career. And as one would expect, fathers who took leave held less traditional gender role beliefs than those who did not. Other important predictors pertained to family orientation, the partner's career, and economic questions (e.g., income differences with partner, compensation during leave).

Mothers working for financial reasons appeared less warm than fathers working for the same reason, but at the same time, these mothers also appeared more assertive and competent than these fathers (Riggs, 1997). In that study, the child was a year old and the parent either planned to stay at home throughout the childhood years or not. We believe the best explanation for such a pattern of findings rests on social role theory. If one opts to choose a gender-atypical role, this behavior appears more telling than if one acts in line with traditional gender roles. So if a father decides to stay at home with his children, he must be very warm, and if a mother decides to work, she must be very interested in doing so.

Several studies investigated how information on leaves of absence in general, or parental leave in particular, affects impressions formed of women and men. Somewhat counterintuitively, an experiment with human resources professionals as participants demonstrated that women were considered more likely to be interviewed and more hirable if their resumes contained several employment gaps, as compared to none or one (Smith et al., 2005). A reason for this could be that participants thought they had finished having children. Moreover, men were "punished more" than women if their resumes indicated periods of unemployment. Men's commitment and hirability were judged lower than women's only in the presence of employment gaps. Presumably, this information violates the male, but not the female, stereotype.

One experiment found that parental leave of absence did not affect men more negatively than women (Allen et al., 1994). No statistically significant effects were found regarding factors such as perceived organizational commitment and allocation of rewards (e.g., recommending the person for training or promotion). However, there are at least two likely causes why the authors failed to find an effect. First, all ratees were portrayed as high-performing employees. As we concluded earlier when discussing the influence of gender stereotypes, effects of stereotypes are most likely in the presence of ambiguity. Second, the sample was rather small (on average, less than 20 participants per group), so even quite substantial effects may turn out as "not statistically significant." It is thus conceivable that leave of absence information damages fathers more than mothers.

Corroborating this reasoning, a follow-up experiment yielded different findings (Allen & Russell, 1999). Study participants were undergraduate business students, most of whom were currently employed. In the authors' experiment, performance level appeared high, intermediate, or low. Given a parental leave of absence, women were more likely to be recommended for the allocation of rewards than men. Women's and men's work commitment appeared similar in the absence of parental leaves, but given a leave, women received higher ratings than men.

Similarly, an experiment with U.S. introductory psychology students as participants found that women who took 12 weeks of unpaid leave after a child was born were seen as better organizational citizens (i.e., more altruistic toward coworkers by, e.g., helping them with problems) than men taking leave for the same reason (Wayne & Cordeiro, 2003). Men were also perceived as less altruistic than men in a no-leave control condition.

Corroborating these findings, men who missed one and a half days of work because of a sick child received lower performance ratings and lower reward recommendations than men who did not, whereas there was no negative effect for women who missed work (Butler & Skattebo, 2004). Notably, the sample of that study consisted of workers, the majority of whom had children.

In contrast, a recent experiment with psychology students from a small Midwestern university found that male and female newspaper reporters who had taken 12 weeks of leave were evaluated more positively than those taking no leave and those becoming stay-at-home parents (Coleman & Franiuk, 2011). More positive overall impressions were reported of those taking leave; they appeared as warm as stay-at-home parents but warmer than working parents and as competent as working parents but more competent than stay-at-home parents. Female participants also reacted more favorably than male participants toward those breaking gender roles. These findings suggest that traditional views of men taking parental leave are changing.

Vandello and colleagues (2013) found that men were not penalized more than women for taking afternoons off for childcare. Both men and women were seen more negatively in terms of job-related characteristics if they had switched to half time, but at the same time, they were rated as warmer (for similar findings, see Park et al., 2008). It appears that independent of target gender, "typically female" behavior led to the ascription of less masculine and more feminine traits. Squarely contradicting the motherhood-bias hypothesis, across work arrangements, the mother was evaluated more positively than the father in that study (e.g., dependable, dedicated, should be recommended for promotion). Similarly, she was rated as more career-oriented and higher in self-esteem and related masculine traits, including competence, than he was.

In another recent experiment, Rudman and Mescher (2013) did find that introductory psychology students penalized men for requesting a leave. In that study, the employee requested an intermittent leave to take care of a child with leukemia (i.e., not 12 weeks in a row but a reduction in working hours for a more sustained time period). There was no female employee comparison condition. Men who requested leave were regarded as lower in organizational citizenship than those who did not, and they received fewer rewards (e.g., suggestions for training) and more penalties (e.g., salary reduction). Also, as compared to men who did not request leave, those who did were seen as warmer, weaker, less competent, and less dominant. In other words, they lost ascribed masculinity and gained femininity. Findings generalized across Black and White target men.

Of course, that experiment did not include a female target condition, so we cannot know whether men were judged more strictly than women for the same behavior. Based on the findings by Vandello and colleagues (2013), one may assume that female targets would have suffered similar penalties. We do know that the findings contradict those of Coleman and Franiuk (2011), as discussed earlier, on perceptions of newspaper reporters in that men were not rewarded but punished for requesting leave. An important difference between study procedures is that in all previous studies, the leave period was in the past, possibly signaling that no future leave is to be expected (see Smith et al., 2005), whereas Rudman and Mescher's (2013) participants were put into the shoes of an employer who has to deal with a leave that is about to take place. That context should be more sensitive for finding negative effects.

A recent study from our own laboratory tested the perception of mothers and fathers who indicated that they were single parents, that is, who were bringing up their children on their own, instead of with a partner. We reasoned that this context equates women's and men's social roles—both should be perceived as primary caregivers. Indeed, in the first experiment, raters in leadership positions rated the work-related competence of single fathers lower than that of men in the other conditions (i.e., married or without children). A follow-up experiment with students as participants yielded that the impressions of married mothers and fathers diverged and those of single mothers and fathers converged. Whereas married fathers were perceived to be more assertive and less warm than married mothers, single mothers and fathers were rated in between and similar on both dimensions.

Taken together, findings are in line with the idea that social roles determine impressions independent of target gender. Mothers are not discriminated against because they are women but because they are expected to have a social role that demands a considerable amount of family commitment. In turn, work commitment is expected to suffer. Studies on fathers who do not follow a traditional breadwinner role have demonstrated that this can be costly regarding impressions formed of their competence, organizational citizenship, and the like. So fathers who deviate from their traditional social roles may suffer negative consequences.

· 1 3 ·
CONCLUSIONS

Why is there a gender pay gap?

The gender pay gap is both a final practical topic to which the theories and findings from the first section of this book can be applied, and it is the first section of the conclusions: Many of the considerations brought up so far are mirrored in this chapter.

All over the world, women earn less than men (see Introduction). Why is this the case? As has become clear, lack of education is not a reason for this because women are highly qualified in North America and many European countries today, and in fact, women's qualifications often exceed men's. Then why does this investment in education pay off less well for women than for men? First, as mentioned earlier, choice of major may explain up to 20% of the gender pay gap (Schneeweis & Zweimüller, 2012). Women as compared to men choose majors and thus occupations that pay less on average. As such, this factor appears purely economical. For example, if you want your educational investment to pay off, it is better to invest in engineering than educational sciences, and men tend to make "better" choices in this regard. Conversely, social psychology comes into play: Salaries are lower in typically female than in typically male jobs, and if more women enter a field, over time, salaries drop (see Reskin &

Bielby, 2005). In addition, men in typically female occupations earn more than their female colleagues on average (unless noted otherwise, these considerations are based on an excellent review by Lips, 2013). According to U.S. data, there is no occupational category in which women earn as much as men. Similarly, within each educational level, men's and women's salaries differ, and rather than decreasing, the difference tends to increase with higher education levels (in spite of women's better grades). A study on men and women within medicine found that assertiveness and competence, high grades in school, and field of specialization predicted men's later incomes but not women's (Evers & Sieverding, 2014).

All of the latter findings challenge a simple economic model in which output (e.g., income) is determined from input: investments such as education, experience, and hours worked. Such human capital models try to compute "objectively" different inputs invested by women and men and determine how much unexplained variance in income remains that is apparently due to discrimination (e.g., Evers & Sieverding, 2014). According to such models, around 40% of the gender pay gap cannot easily be explained by economic factors.

Lips (2013) generally criticized the human capital approach. Whereas it pretends that income is determined in rational and objective ways, this is not true. Hardly any one thinks it is justified that a top CEO earns over $4,000 on average for an hour's work or that an accountant receives a large bonus after nearly ruining not only the company but also contributing to a crisis of the world economy. In other words, which job should be rewarded with how much pay is probably more in line with system justification theory (see Jost & Hunyady, 2005, and Chapter 8) than with objective facts.

An additional factor that is included in human capital models is working part time, which, of course, decreases income. Women work part time much more often than men. Of course, women's preference for part-time work is not a simple question of choice but hinges on social roles such as primary responsibility for child rearing and housework, as explained in Chapter 12. Moreover, the very existence of sabbaticals demonstrates that some career interruptions are more economically valued than others.

In line with these factors, according to studies conducted in the United States, the wage gap is reduced for lesbians, who hold higher degrees, choose less female-typed jobs, hardly ever work part time, and earn more than comparable heterosexual women (see Peplau & Fingerhut, 2004, for an overview). This hints once more at gender roles as an important factor in explaining the gender pay gap: The gap is reduced for women with nontraditional gender roles (i.e., those who are not heterosexual and married).

A third factor needed to explain the gender pay gap is more insidious and psychological and not in line with human capital approaches. Experiments show that women with exactly the same qualifications as men are offered lower salaries (e.g., Smith et al., 2005). The flip side is that women also demand less than men for the same work. As we saw in Chapter 10 on negotiations this is the case because women fear backlash: They know they will not get away with demanding as much as men do (Amanatullah & Morris, 2010). Put simply, men's work is culturally more valued than women's work. If we have no idea how valued a given work is, then the hint that a man is doing it is sufficient to make it appear more valued.

As we pointed out in the previous chapter, parenthood "traditionalizes perceptions." Everything else being equal, fathers are often offered higher salaries than men without children and women. Mothers, in contrast, are viewed as less motivated to pursue a career than fathers and childless women and are offered fewer opportunities for advancement. These findings clearly show that gender stereotypes and social roles lead to discrimination of women: The mere fact of being male makes a person appear entitled to a higher salary and, in line with their social roles, fathers' career opportunities and income grow disproportionally. The more children they have, the lower is mothers' income, but fathers' income increases with the number of children (Evers & Sieverding, 2014).

Taken together, at least the following factors contribute to the gender pay gap:

1. Women's and men's choices of majors/professions.
2. Societal value assigned to men's versus women's jobs.
3. Part-time work contingent on women's larger share of family work.
4. Salaries offered to individual women and men.
5. (Negative) discrimination of mothers along with positive discrimination of fathers.

Why are more men than women in top positions?

The best established metaphor for the scarcity of women in top positions is the *glass ceiling:* It is a solid barrier on women's way to the top, but it is so subtle that you will not easily notice it from a distance (see Bruckmüller, Ryan, Haslam, & Peters, 2013, for a discussion and critique of these metaphors). We previously mentioned also the *leaky pipeline:* While women are transported from bottom to top, several of them get lost at every stage on the way. More recently, the metaphor of a *labyrinth* was coined (Eagly & Carli, 2007). As Eagly and Carli (2007) argued, there is no longer a glass ceiling—after all, some women "break" the ceiling and make it to the top. However, the way there is more difficult to find for women than men, and there are many potential crossroads where a woman can get lost, so her way to the top resembles a labyrinth. What can we conclude concerning the factors constituting this labyrinth?

If we draw together all the theories and findings discussed in the theoretical perspectives, what we arrive at looks more like a "hurdles woman" than a labyrinth (see Figure 1). It is a coarse model, and it cannot be interpreted in a strict sequential way. Also, several of the mechanisms (in circles) could be depicted at several stages. We start at the lower left corner with a young individual with counterstereotypical talent. As everyone else in our societies, this person will be swamped with gender-stereotypical messages, in turn forming both explicit and implicit ideas of what is typical and appropriate for males and females. Given this massive exposure, it appears a small wonder that not everyone ends up with a gender-stereotypical ability self-concept, with interests and behaviors following suit, ending up in a gender-stereotypical career. If a girl or woman manages to get past that hurdle, she will excel in a counterstereotypical domain (e.g., physics or leadership). Then, prescriptive gender stereotypes and hierarchy-maintaining mechanisms kick in, and she experiences social sanctions, which may either lead her back to the gender-specific "path of virtue" or, alternatively, diminish her success (that is what sanctions do). Up to this point, the situation would be equivalent for boys with counterstereotypical talents.

In spite of these hurdles, some women persistently excel in counterstereotypic domains. Then, more subtle, paternalistic, and benevolent stereotyping can lead them back to gender-stereotypical domains. Apparently, this Pied Piper, though successful, does not catch them all. Subsequently, there are several factors that may prevent her excellence from being adequately noticed, among them stereotype threat decreasing performance and perceivers' attributions and shifting standards that prevent them from seeing excellence. The result is a reduction in perceived competence, again provoking less success than she deserves, based on her talent. Nevertheless, some women's excellence does not go unnoticed. As we have seen, these women are often disliked, particularly by sexists and those high in social dominance orientation or system justification. Being disliked leads to weaker networks, which, in turn, diminishes success.

Even if excellence is clearly demonstrated, a remaining big hurdle is women's social role in the domestic sphere, provoking a "second shift" for many of them that, again, keeps them from networking after work and thus leads to the same negative outcome. Finally, on traditional male territory, women often feel they do not belong. Such alienation can lead to disengagement.

If a woman takes all these hurdles, she can have a stellar career in a counterstereotypic domain, including leadership. While writing this, it occurs to me that a percentage such as "20% of those who make it to the top are women" is quite an impressive number. How did they get past all these hurdles? Maybe we are only beginning to understand this side of the coin.

In a nutshell, the role of the social context cannot be overestimated when explaining the scarcity of women at the top (see also Eagly et al., 2012). More than we had expected, the personal sphere plays a role here, in other words, gender role expectations in heterosexual relationships and families. Along with other authors, we hope the following: "With increased behavioral role and economic equality between women and men, changes in the personal sphere may follow at last" (Kite et al., 2008, p. 228).

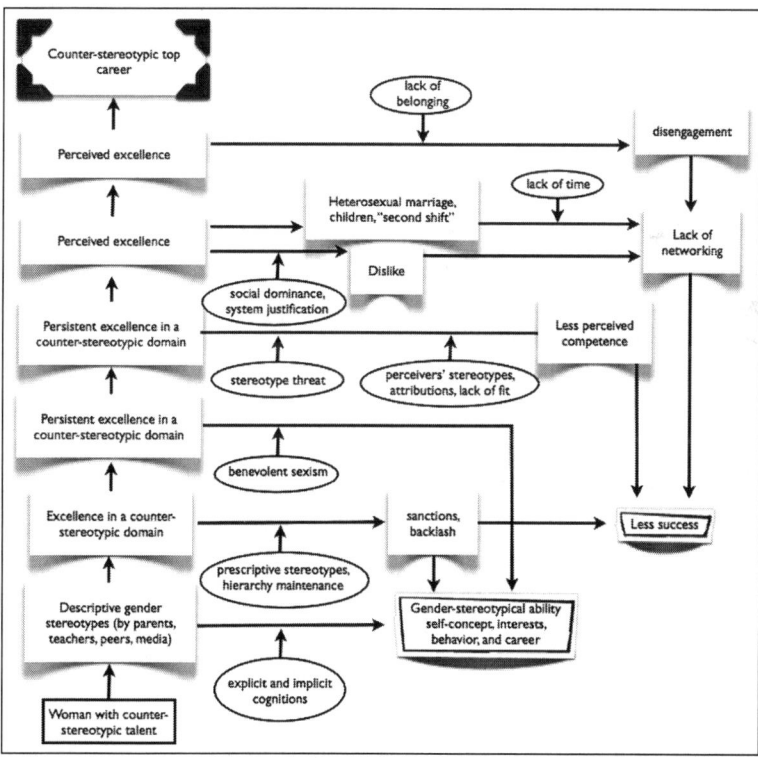

Figure 1. A woman's pathway to a counterstereotypic top career. Each arrow toward the top needs to be followed to arrive there. Each arrow to the right symbolizes a hurdle where "the pipeline leaks." Circles show reasons why women do not succeed.

Which interventions could be effective?

The circles in Figure 1 summarize some central mechanisms that interventions could target. Throughout the previous text, such interventions have been introduced. For example, implicit gender-leadership stereotypes are reduced by long-term exposure to female leaders (i.e., role models). Women who demonstrate warmth in addition to assertiveness and competence suffer less from backlash provoked by prescriptive stereotypes (etc.). Instead of reiterating these factors here, in the following we draw specific conclusions for companies, bosses, and individual employees.

What should companies do?

A review of 27 intervention studies that tried to reduce gender bias in hiring ended with the recommendation that as much job-relevant information as possible should be considered to allow individuating information to trump the use of stereotypes (Isaac et al., 2009). Women should comprise at least 25% of the applicant pool, if at all possible. As we have seen, selection criteria should be determined *before* candidates are known (Uhlmann & Cohen, 2005), and concrete ratings of each applicant on each dimension should be made. Raters should not be distracted and take enough time, and interviews should be structured in order to be comparable. The job should not be described in a language that elicits a male prototype (e.g., chairperson is preferable to chairman). Finally, training should alert employees in human resources to these biases (Isaac et al., 2009).

Regarding gender stereotypes' influence on salary negotiations, companies are well advised to make salaries dependent on objective performance indicators (including the performance of the group led by a leader) rather than on individual negotiations (Amanatullah & Morris, 2010). Which promotion models reduce discrimination? Hiring several people simultaneously rather than sequentially benefits minorities (Martell et al., 2012), presumably by drawing attention to the (lack of) diversity among those hired.

Self management and career planning are important for career success (see, e.g., Abele & Wiese, 2008). Women profit more than men from career management systems (see Lyness & Thompson, 2000). Organizations should also break down the following barriers for women: perceived lack of culture fit, fewer opportunities for geographical mobility, exclusion from informal networks, and less challenging experiences.

How masculine an image does the organization display (Cheryan et al., 2009)? Does the selection body signal to women (and other minorities) that they do not belong? Are men taking paternal leave displayed as role models, or are they targets of jokes (Bathmann et al., 2013)? Are there organizational structures that take into account childcare emergencies and irregular working hours? Flexible work schedules have been shown to positively influence productivity, (lack of) absenteeism, organizational commitment, and satisfaction with the job and the work schedule (see Padgett, Harland, & Moser, 2009).

Most couples expect nowadays that an organization will offer a career option to the partner if it wants to hire someone for a leadership position (Bathmann et al., 2013). Organizations should do their best to establish professional services and join forces with others in the closer environment to increase the chances that such "couple hires" will be successful and to help the couple with all the tasks that their mobility implies (find a place to live, childcare facilities, schools, etc.). Here is a side note: Promising support and not being able to deliver it is probably worse than not promising anything at all.

Several decades ago, within a couple, typically, one person worked extensive hours, whereas the other did not have a job outside the home. Nowadays, there are couples where both are expected to work long hours. It is easy to see that this change has its drawbacks. Employers should take into account that employees need to reserve time to do other things but work in the organization (Bathmann et al., 2013). Is it possible for leaders to sometimes work from home? Is part-time leadership possible?

Given the normality of dual careers, it appears somewhat fallen out of time that organizations still expect young leaders to go abroad for years. At the same time, many organizations do not feel responsible at all for the dual-career implications of such a step. Or leaders are expected to spend every day in a different country, even though video conferences could obtain the same aim (Bathmann et al., 2013).

"While much discussion of family-friendly workplaces focuses on 'leave' policies—and these are indeed important—the present work suggests that we focus more attention on 'stay' policies, which facilitate caring for children while continuing to work" (Benard & Correll, 2010, p. 641).

What should supervisors do?

As a team leader, how should one act? First, one should try not to stereotype or make assumptions. It is possible that the guy with the glasses is the computer wizard, but others may be better than him. Also, it could be that the mothers in the team lack geographical mobility, but one can ask them anyway if they want to lead the overseas project. The more gender-stereotypical the lens one uses, the more gender-stereotypical behavior one will observe. One should try to balance assignments and tasks, give equal opportunities to all in the team, and allow the women to quarrel as much as the men without negatively stereotyping them. Members of disadvantaged groups, due to their historically disadvantageous position, may need more encouragement to use opportunities; they may not volunteer as much even if they are highly qualified for a certain task. For performance evaluations, one should take enough time and think carefully, and one should use as much information as possible, as soon as possible (e.g., do performance evaluations immediately afterward, not in a delayed fashion).

What should individuals do?

The following section is a bit delicate to write. On the one hand, we do not want to leave unmentioned the traps that individuals can avoid if they are informed of them. On the other hand, we do not want to "blame the victims" for changing a state of affairs that they have not caused. Readers are advised to use the following information at their discretion—and to ignore and sabotage what they consider inadequate. Similar to Elle in the movie *Legally Blonde*, you can succeed at Harvard in pink. But it may be a bit harder than in dark blue.

Isaac and colleagues (2009) ended their literature review with several recommendations for women. First, women should make sure that their objective credentials cannot be missed. Women at the top considered unambiguous evidence of their excellence an important ingredient in their career. Given current gender subtypes, some people are inclined to think that women who excel in counterstereotypic domains lack the niceness prescribed for women. Therefore, it is to a woman's advantage if her relationship orientation is noticeable. For both women and men, it has been found that very feminine attributes (e.g., dress, perfume, manner of speaking) may provoke lowered competence ascriptions. Similarly, excessive self-promotion may backfire, whereas modesty is clearly not appropriate in job interviews.

In terms of family planning, late motherhood can be better for a woman's career than early motherhood (Abele & Spurk, 2011). If a woman already has several years of experience in her job, organizations find it more attractive to win her back, and she is in a better position to negotiate the conditions as well as invest in excellent childcare (Bathmann et al., 2013). Although mothers may take it for granted that they have high career aspirations, this is often not the case for perceivers. An easy remedy is making it very clear that one puts a high priority on one's career. Similarly, mothers should explicitly inform their supervisors regarding their commitment and achievement motivation.

What can women do to avoid the gender trap concerning salary negotiations (see Amanatullah & Morris, 2010)? They could frame the situation differently and make it clear that they need more money not for their own personal greed, but, for example, because they are responsible for their family's income: A mother fighting like a lioness so her daughter can afford a good education is congruent with gender stereotypes. If possible, women can also switch roles, taking turns negotiating their best friend's salary.

Additional perspectives

The aforementioned applied perspectives and conclusions are based on the theories and findings that we elaborated on earlier. They clearly show that gender stereotypes are an important factor on which differences in women's and men's career trajectories depend. The other big factor we identified were social roles, in particular pertaining to the division of labor in heterosexual couples with children—and as a mirror-image, expectations concerning mothers' job disengagement. But is this the whole story? Are there perspectives that we have left out? Indeed, there are. Two of them are of particular weight. First are people's social identities: The groups that matter to them, that they want to be part of, and whose images they want to fit. Second are communication processes at work that reify and perpetuate social hierarchies. We turn to these topics in Part II of this book.

PART II: SOCIAL IDENTITIES, COMMUNICATION, AND GENDER

Introduction

Communication is an everyday activity that is intertwined with human life as a whole so thoroughly that sometimes we overlook its importance and complexity. Every aspect of our daily life depends on communication with others (Giles, 2012; Giles, Reid, & Harwood, 2010). This includes messages from people we do not even know. Much research in organizational psychology has dealt with communication problems between women and men at work as essentially an "interpersonal" phenomenon (Tajfel, 1982), a phenomenon that is mainly influenced by people's personal characteristics and preferences when they interact. According to this view, people are isolated from the social context, and social interaction is treated as a simple relationship between people (Coates & Johnson, 2001).

Thus, problems of miscommunication (Coupland, Giles, & Wiemann, 1991) in the workplace due to gender were considered as alleged personal shortcomings. Therefore, solutions based on individual education and training were emphasized: Women should be taught to communicate in a more appropriate manner (e.g., to communicate like men or use strategies that do not contradict established standards of workplace communication). Men were taught to avoid undesirable sexist behaviors and were punished if they did not comply (e.g., threatened with loss of promotions and even with lawsuits).

However, if we approach gender interactions in the workplace as a strictly interpersonal phenomenon, we overlook key pieces of the puzzle (Boggs & Giles, 1999). Examining the social context in the workplace where problems occur, we find evidence that the dynamics of communication "between groups" can lead to negative relationships between male and female colleagues (Hirigoyen, 2001; Williams & Giles, 1978). Recognition of the intergroup nature of gender conflicts at work can point the way to finding solutions to women's subtle discrimination.

Our starting point is the social identity perspective, one of the more, if not the most, important psychological perspectives that explains the intricate mechanisms underlying intergroup communication, in our case, communication between men and women as groups. We address specifically the relationship between men and women with a high level of responsibility in a workplace with a traditionally male dominant culture (for example, engineering companies).

We have no intention of providing a prescriptive self-help guide or a trainer's manual but rather to offer a base (logically incomplete) of knowledge, ideas, and some solutions that can be mined in various ways to configure different institutional and organizational programs to achieve gender equality. We hope that the reader finds the chapters exciting and brimming with possibilities for applicability, to achieve a better world for all.

· 14 ·

SOCIAL IDENTITY PERSPECTIVE

All human creatures are part of larger groups. Since the beginning of our existence we have socialized within groups that have helped shape our personalities, beliefs, and attitudes (e.g., family, school), and we continue into adulthood as a part of groups (e.g., working groups, friends) that exert a great influence on us (Tajfel, 1982). As if this were not enough, our gender, age, culture, and nationality also place us in a series of larger groups or social categories that shape our view of the world and determine how we are perceived or treated by other people.

One of the most influential theoretical influences in intergroup communication studies is the social identity perspective (Abrams & Hogg, 2010; Turner, Hogg, Oakes, Reicher, & Wetherell, 1987). Under this label, two theories are summarized: social identity theory and self-categorization theory. The social identity perspective states that people categorize themselves into groups and do the same with others, placing them in certain groups and not others. This process of categorizing ourselves in groups we value helps define our social identity and makes social comparisons easier. Social comparison, in turn, involves an exaggeration of differences between groups and an exaggeration of the similarities between people within groups.

Focusing on gender categorizations, these do not have the same meaning for everyone. Women cannot be treated as a unified group because there are too many women with different identities to include them all in one group. When we are introduced to a woman, we are definitely assigning to her certain beliefs that we have about the "group of women" (see Giles, Reid, & Harwood, 2010). However, our beliefs assignation that comes about because of belonging to the "group of women" is interfered by other aspects such as membership in other groups. For example, a woman may be a scientist, and membership to this group will add information and transform the features that we had allocated using the mere fact of belonging to the group of women. Also, as we shall see later, context is vitally important. Perceptions of a woman who is introduced to us will be different depending on whether we meet her at a party or at a scientific meeting. This perspective claims that different identities interact and affect each other, for example, to identify herself as a professional puts that woman in a very different position in relation to other groups than if she were identified as a "housewife."

So according to the social identity perspective, people self-define in terms of belonging to one or more groups, and we strive to maintain or improve our social identity. We make comparisons with other groups, which can result in a positive or negative impression of the group to which we belong. If such comparisons are positive, we obtain a satisfactory social identity, and on the contrary, if the comparisons are negative, our social identity is unsatisfactory. To restore or generate a satisfactory social identity, people engage certain processes and strategies.

Researchers have explored many different variables that affect the development of gender identity. The social identity perspective states that persons belonging to high status groups identify more strongly with the group than members of low status groups, because identification with a group of high status makes a positive contribution to self-esteem (Abrams & Giles, 2004). So we have to assume that men identify with their own masculine gender more than women with their gender. On this line, researchers like Williams and Giles (1978) have assumed that women who accept the status quo have internalized their inferiority and have low self-esteem or a negative self-concept.

Two types of identity can be distinguished: personal identity, which refers to an image of the self as one person (the differences between oneself and the in-group would be maximal), and social identity (as a member of one or more groups). This can be represented in terms of a bipolar continuum. At one extreme, the interaction between people, that is, interpersonal behavior, is determined solely by the character and motivations of the person as an individual (personal identity). At the other, the behavior is derived solely from the membership of the person in a group (social identity); this is what we call "intergroup behavior." In making this distinction, researchers suggested that intergroup and interpersonal behaviors are qualitatively different from each other. Group behavior cannot be explained in terms of interpersonal principles (Abrams & Hogg, 2010).

In fact, social identity processes come into play to the extent that behavior is defined in intergroup terms (Maio, Haddock, Spears, & Manstead, 2010). Intergroup communication occurs when parties in a social interaction define themselves or others in terms of group membership (Harwood, Giles, & Palomares, 2005). For example, when a conflict escalates between two companies, workers may be more likely to start thinking of themselves as members of a company.

Along this line, Tajfel (1982) made two important hypotheses. He suggested that when behavior is defined as intergroup, in-group members would be more likely to react uniformly relative to out-group members and consider the out-group as a whole uniform. That is, individual differences among out-group members are disregarded. Therefore, during a conflict, it is likely that the "other side" is treated consensually as if "all of us agree that they are all equal." According to Tajfel, positioning of individuals on the interpersonal-intergroup continuum is a consequence of the interaction between social and psychological factors. Social factors have to do with the objective features of the world with which people are confronted and psychological factors are associated with the individual interpretation of these features. Therefore, the way we see ourselves depends both on the events happening in the world around us and the way we take them.

Salience of social categories

People ponder social categories so that some are more important than others (salience of social categories). Salience is thus a subjective perception of each person and may vary dynamically in a specific relationship. Gender schema are cognitive structures that induce the processing of social information from a gender-based perspective and similar constructions (Bem, 1981). People with gender schema have a gender stereotypical self-perception and tend to behave in a manner consistent with their gender, often trying to avoid gender-inconsistent behavior. For people with a gender schema, gender is usually more salient than for people without a gender schema. Thus, a man with a gender schema will consider himself more masculine than feminine, and a woman with a gender schema will see herself more feminine than masculine. People with gender schema also communicate based on stereotypical notions of gender (e.g., men are assertive, women affiliative). While the female schema often connotes weakness, insecurity, and loss of authority, the male schema connotes strength, self-assurance, and authority. However, the extent to which these gender differences do arise depends on the salience of gender and its prototype (Palomares, 2012). In mixed interactions, gender tends to be more salient than in interactions among men or women.

Some studies on women in traditionally male work environments have focused on the question of how different proportions of men and women affect gender salience (Kanter, 1977). However, there may be other aspects of gender-dominated occupations that influence gender salience. For example, a policewoman may discover that physical risk may increase her gender salience. Macke (1981) found that gender salience increased in people working at a workplace dominated by the opposite gender. She also found that characteristics related to employment played a more important role for the self-esteem of people working in occupations with same-gender dominance than characteristics related to gender. She describes how the asymmetrical proportion of gender has an effect on gender salience in both groups (minority and majority).

Kanter (1977) argued that the relative proportions of the "social types" in a group shape the social relations of its members. She suggested that "as the proportions change," "so do social experiences" (pp. 2,7). Proportions have this effect because they influence how people perceive each other. As an example of how the salience of a category may vary, consider the case where the categories would be used to represent a gender discussion between men and women: Gender categories would be significant if all men in a room are saying one thing and all women another (comparative adjustment); and if, in addition, what men are saying matches our expectations or stereotypes about male behavior and what women say matches our expectations or stereotypes of female behavior (normative adjustment), the salience of gender will increase (Klauer, Wegener, & Ehrenberg, 2002).

A key implication of this conception is that categorization depends on who is present in the *context*. For example, if there are radical feminists and moderate feminists involved in a discussion, the differences between them seem larger and could be categorized as opposing each other. However, if some antifeminists become part of the debate, the differences between the groups (moderate and radical feminists) would be comparatively small compared to the differences between feminists and those who support traditional gender relations. Therefore, the salience would change from "moderate feminist" versus "radical" to "feminist" versus "antifeminist."

Prototypes

An important contribution of the perspective of the social identity is the concept of prototype. A prototype is the set of characteristics that best defines a category (Turner et al., 1987; see Reid, Giles, & Harwood, 2005). When we talk about a person's "prototype" of an in-group, we mean one that best represents the position of the group on some dimension relevant to the group. A prototype is a fuzzy set of attributes (perceptions, beliefs, or opinions, attitudes, feelings, behaviors) that describe a group and distinguish it from other relevant groups. Prototypes obey the principle of metacontrast (maximize intergroup differences and minimize intragroup differences, emphasizing group entitativity). Group entitativity is the property of a group that makes it seem a unitary entity, coherent and distinct (Turner et al., 1987). Group prototypes are not simply the average of the attributes of the group, and the most prototypical person in a group is not its average member.

Since prototypes are cognitive representations of groups, they are very closely related to stereotypes. However, from the social identity perspective, a prototype is a stereotype only if it is recognized as such by out-group members (Tajfel, 1982). Finally, prototypes depend on the context. This means that the content of a specific prototype changes depending on the out-group compared with relevant members of the in-group (Turner et al., 1987). When we classify ourselves it is exactly the same: We define, perceive, and evaluate based on our group's prototype, and we behave according to that prototype. The categorization of the self produces in-group normative behavior (compliance with group norms) and self-stereotyping and, therefore, is the process that causes us to behave like a group member.

Within groups, prototypical members exert more influence than nonprototypical members, and people pay more attention to the first than the second as reliable sources of information on group norms and social identity

(Hogg, 2010). In addition, prototypical members tend to occupy positions of leadership, and leaders are more effective if they are perceived as prototypical (Hogg, 2007). The clear consequence of this is that when people feel insecure, they will pay even more attention to their leaders and feel more inclined to give them power and follow and crave their recognition and validation.

We want to facilitate the understanding of what is a prototype and how it can help us analyze the performance of a group through the following examples: Analyze the situation of a woman engineer who, because of her skills and high preparation, would deserve to hold a position of responsibility in a company. A first example can be placed in a company in which the prototype is autocratic; that is, there is a prevailing male culture based on traditional hierarchical organization. This company develops technology products, and the prototype is defined as a "middle-aged man with technological expertise and leadership ability and the ability to resolve conflicts between people and the ability to deal with competitors." All of these factors are associated with male gender in this corporate culture. The company is identified with this prototype. When technically prepared candidates begin to appear, women's gender salience increases because the stereotypical "woman" does not match the expectations, regulations, or prototype stereotypes imposed by the dominant group. These women find it very difficult to progress because the company as a group placed them far from the prototype.

Now imagine another company newly created by young people, university colleagues in which the prototype, consequently, will be a creative person with capacity for innovation, who values talent and teamwork. Gender in this second company is not salient and the prototype is based on values that are not assigned to one or the other gender. Clearly, women will not have the same problems as in the previous example.

Finally, we could consider a third company dedicated to the care of people in which the prototype is defined by the ability to care, communality, and empathy. These values are mainly attributed to the female gender and, therefore, this company is gender salient and fits the female prototype. At first glance we might say, simplifying, that women should have no problem ascending to high positions of responsibility. We are aware that these are very simplified examples, but they are useful to understand the concept of prototype.

In summary, the concept of prototype is the result of two forces: One force puts the prototype at the point where greatest proximity for the largest number of people in the group is achieved, and at the same time, another force puts it at a point of maximum differentiation from the relevant comparison out-group. The result of these two forces is what defines the prototype of the group. If a large number of highly educated women enter into a group, this may change the position of the prototype attached to this new group, to the extent that it gains importance.

What happens is that this progress will be very slow due to the resistance of the dominant group.

Summary

In this chapter, we have explored some foundations of the social identity perspective, with particular attention on communication between gender groups. In many ways, these are the foundations from which all other chapters follow and are the basis for much of our thinking about gender equality developed in the overall conclusions of this Part II.

In the next chapter, we look at the diverse ways in which professional women cope with their devaluated gender identity at the workplace with male dominance. That is, after having explained the foundation on which the social identity perspective is built, we talk about behavioral strategies, which, in this perspective, have been identified to restore, maintain, or achieve a positive self-esteem. We focus particularly on gender in the workplace.

· 15 ·

IDENTITY MANAGEMENT STRATEGIES

When people are not satisfied with their social identity, they have three possible alternatives for a more positive assessment: individual mobility, social creativity, or social competition. The strategy or direction of the behavior adopted by the person depends on the perceived legitimacy of the situation, the stability of intergroup relations, and the permeability of group boundaries (Tajfel, 1982). As we have seen, the social group "women" has been stigmatized for centuries by the patriarchal system, and the prototypical woman has been the housewife. Let's examine the strategies women might develop to improve their situation in the workplace.

Individual mobility is seen to be associated with a general belief in the possibility of social mobility, while social creativity and social competition are conceptualized as aspects of a belief system of social change. The latter system of beliefs is likely to dictate the behavior of people when the feeling of belonging to a group is very strong and when they are aware that they must act either to enhance or defend their status.

In the workplace, for example, women who perceive that there is a "glass ceiling" may believe that their best strategy for advancing at work is to progress as an individual (for example, act as "one of the boys") instead of trying to establish collective action to improve the way women are treated and their status in general (Ellemers & van Laar, 2010; Haslam, 2004; Schmitt, Ellemers, & Branscombe, 2003). The widespread system of meritocracy beliefs makes it easier for women to adopt beliefs of individual mobility.

Individual mobility has been considered as an effective and attractive strategy for people of discriminated social groups to combat limiting stereotypes and discrimination (Ellemers & van Laar, 2010). It has been shown that individuals who have sufficient merits and who invest enough effort should be able to prove their personal value and hence move up in the status structure, despite the prejudice and discrimination directed toward their group. Ellemers and Barreto (2008) focused on the limits of individual mobility as a strategy in addressing negative group-based expectations about the self. They argued that due to the mechanisms addressed here, individual mobility beliefs and the behaviors thus elicited tend to reinforce, rather than challenge, group-based inequality.

Social creativity and social competition, on the other hand, are strategies associated with beliefs about changes in the social system, which are destined to improve the negative conditions or keep the positive ones of the in-group. Such strategies may arise when people believe that group boundaries are impermeable and, therefore, they cannot improve themselves by moving among groups (see Paulsen, Jones, Graham, Callan, & Gallois, 2005). Here individuals are forced to face the reality based on their own group (Wright, 2010). Social creativity strategies are based on changing the values attributed to the in-group; in the case of the female gender group, a social creativity strategy would be to focus on a different comparison dimension (e.g., not on job-related success or money) and emphasize that women have better tastes than men, are more socially sensitive, and are nicer people.

Social competition strategies are also likely to arise when boundaries are perceived as low in permeability. Thus, group members who perceive real and unfair boundaries that hinder their progress at work (e.g., women or people with disabilities) and who can imagine a way to improve their situation can act collectively to change their circumstances through confrontation with the other relevant group.

Even more aggressively, members of a high-status group who feel their comparative advantage is in danger (e.g., some men related to the women out-group) may engage in collective action to resist change (Weatherall & Gallois, 2005). Because this strategy places the in-group directly against the interests and values of the out-group, it is more likely to produce some kind of social conflict and open hostility than individual mobility strategies or social creativity (since both accept or avoid directly challenging the interests and values of the high-status group). In this sense, social competition represents a direct and open path to challenge or maintain the status quo in a way that other strategies do not.

Gender, status, and identity management strategies

In their research on strategies for social change for women and response strategies from the dominant group of men, Williams and Giles (1978) reviewed gender relations from the social identity perspective. Two key ideas of the study are that (a) the social identity of women derives from the comparison with men, and (b) their social identities are negative because they have internalized the dominant ideology that men hold a higher status than they do. Note that nowadays, the status of women has improved greatly, but women still lag behind men on many indicators of social participation (see the Introduction in this volume).

Comparisons between groups of men and women in the organizational context reflect a perception of inferior status and a negative identity in women, whereas they show opposite implications concerning the identity of men (Schein, 2001). Such group comparisons tend to encourage the identity of the male group, since they are usually favored in the context of the organization (Hoyt, 2010). However, men's social identity is threatened whenever women gain ground and enter any field that is traditionally occupied by them, thus directly challenging the positive, distinguishing features of men in contexts of high relevance in the construction of their group identity (Schmitt, Ellemers, & Brascombe, 2003). Just as Giles and his collaborators have shown (Giles, 2012), people who are dependent on their group, who consider it as an essential part of their being, who feel solidarity toward it, and who consider their social identity as threatened, will be prone to see encounters among groups in group terms.

This threatening perception occurs when it is considered that the out-group jeopardizes the well-being and the resources of the group itself (Quinn, Kallen, & Spencer, 2010; Stephan & Renfro, 2003; Stephan & Stephan, 2000). Effectively, from the point of view of social identity, the perception of a decrease of the differences between women and men motivates the latter to identify more strongly with their own gender group and makes them protect their status as well (Giles, 2012; Haslam, 2004;

Turner & Haslam, 2001). In fact, in experimental contexts, the members of high-status groups tend to identify more strongly with the in-group (by closing barriers) when members of other groups with a lower status have the opportunity to join the ranks of the high-status group. For example, in work-related contexts, some men who think that their high status is being threatened by women might respond with an unusual expression of insults. Sexual harassment or the display of pornographic images of women (Glick & Rudman, 2010) are examples of men reacting to their male identities being threatened.

As a result of their negative social identity, women should be motivated to regain a positive social identity through the embrace of any of the three identity management strategies, based on general social structural perceptions such as the legitimacy of their status quo, the permeability of group boundaries that they perceive between their gender in-group and the male out-group, and the stability of the relationships between men and women (Giles & Viladot, 1994).

Collective strategies of gender identity management

An important trend of research in the field of identity focuses on the relationship between feminist identity and collective action (Becker, 2012; Becker & Wright, 2011; Derks, van Laar, & Ellemers, 2009; Esses, Jackson, & Bennett-AbuAyyash, 2010; Liss, Crawford, & Popp, 2004; Williams & Giles, 1998). These research projects have shown that the strong feminist identity that some women adopt is directly related to the strategies of social competence and political or collective action (see Simon & Klandermans, 2001). This subgroup of women has the belief that the differences between men and women, in terms of status, are illegitimate and unstable as well (e.g., that the situation of gender inequality can be turned into one of equality; Faludi, 2000). Effectively, when women perceive that their in-group has a lower social status and there are strong barriers between them and the male out-group, attempts to achieve social change through collective action will be more likely. However, to definitely participate in collective strategies, women, along with believing that the relationships between the groups could be changed, must have a strong sense of belonging to their gender in-group (Kalbfleisch, 2010).

In the case of groups of a lower status, under certain structural conditions, especially when strong boundaries are perceived between the compared groups and the sense of inferiority is considered stable (that it cannot be changed easily through any form of social action), the esteem of the group can be recovered through social creativity strategies (Tajfel, 1982), just like some studies conducted by Jetten and her colleagues (Jetten, Schmitt, Branscombe, & McKimmie, 2005) have suggested. Therefore, women who believe that individually joining the male group is not possible but who consider the status of their group as stable (that it cannot be changed easily through any form of social action), will identify with their group but they will avoid any confrontation with the male group, and they will adopt creative social responses.

Creativity strategies have the effect of improving the sense of belonging to the in-group. It has been discovered that when the in-group loses in a task, or when it is considered responsible for the favorable conditions of the out-group, or when its involvement in a very important dimension is seen as inferior, it will attempt to recover its value by disregarding the merits of the out-group or by emphasizing the importance of the positive virtues of the in-group to recover its self-esteem (Branscombe, 1998). In any case, attempting to recover the value of the in-group occurs mainly in people (men or women) who have a high sense of belonging to the in-group (Tajfel, 1982).

A series of different social creativity strategies have been defined, all of which focus on the increase of the in-group's value and on the promotion of gender identity. Women will adopt such strategies when they consider that their gender identity has been disregarded, or when the boundaries between men and women are practically impossible to overcome, or if the in-group imposes severe punishment or sanctions on those who do not act as having a sense of belonging to it. In other words, social creativity strategies will be adopted in this case by people for whom leaving the group is impossible and for whom identifying with it is inevitable.

One such strategy would be to avoid "painful" comparisons with the out-group, comparisons that produce a negative in-group perception. If no intergroup comparisons are made, the evaluative differences will be dissolved and the presence of an identity that is perceived as negative will be less evident. This is accomplished by either looking for other groups that are disregarded as well, with which people can make favorable comparisons, or by making comparisons within the in-group, instead of with other groups. For instance, Western women can compare their situation to that of women in the East, such as those in Islamic cultures.

Another creativity strategy would be to reconsider the characteristics of the group that may bring forth a negative connotation (e.g., emphasizing the fact that women are better than men in many aspects or that the women of our day and age are better off than women from previous generations; Kellerman & Rhode, 2007). This is about changing the way the characteristics of the group are valued. In that sense, great effort has been made to reevaluate the contributions women have made to history, art, and the academy. Meanwhile, at another level, attempts to establish the social value of the so-called traditional roles of women (housekeeping and babysitting) have continued (even when they have had little success). To summarize, social creativity strategies pursue changes in the way stigmatizing features of the in-group are considered, and thus a positive social identity is achieved by eliminating painful comparisons between the in-group and the out-group.

We should note that the level of subjective importance the sense of belonging to a group has to a person determines whether that individual will respond to the perceived strength of the boundaries that stand between the groups (Giles & Viladot, 1994). People who identify strongly with their group (when it is one that is disadvantaged) tend to remain loyal to it, even when given the possibility of leaving it and entering another that presents more advantages.

Individual strategies of gender identity management

When in the intergroup relationship, the status of each group is considered legitimate and stable (i.e., women believe there is little likelihood that the status difference between men and women will be modified) and the possibility of large-scale social changes is discarded (Bettencourt, Charlton, Dorr, & Hume, 2001). As a result, women who seek leadership may perceive individual mobility as the only way of improving their personal position, even when they are not completely sure whether the boundaries between the prototypical group of men and their group actually exist. That way, certain conditions indicating that change (on a group level) is not likely can cause women to see individual mobility as the only way to improve their status (Ellemers, 2001). In brief, it is only when women consider that their gender group has a low status and this will not change, or when they also have a low sense of belonging to their gender group and they consider the possibility of joining the high status group of men, will they believe in social mobility.

Sociopsychological studies show that individual mobility is, for group members who are discriminated, the preferred method for dealing with their low social status. For centuries, women have reached positive social identities through that strategy (Williams & Giles, 1978), by denying that their gender is fundamental to their social identity, and they have considered themselves in terms of male standards by adopting male roles and behaviors to gain prestige. By acquiring such characteristics, self-esteem grows, which brings forth a feeling of a positive social identity for these women (Ellemers, 2001; Ellemers & van Laar, 2010).

This strategy is used even when there are reasons to doubt the fairness of the system due to the scarce possibilities of success (Kellerman & Rhode, 2007). The belief in the value of individual merits is held in spite of concrete evidence of the existence of systematic differences in the accomplishments that are reached by professional women in the work setting (Ellemers & van Laar, 2010), for example, women in decision-making positions that are traditionally occupied by men. As we have seen, in the U.S. Fortune 500 list, women represent only 16% of company employees and 15% of high-level executives (data from Catalyst, 2007). This, again, is a reflection of the concept of individual meritocracy, which defines people as individuals who act independently from the group to optimize their individual accomplishments and their own well-being. But all of that does not explain in a satisfactory way the systematic differences that are observed in the successes and failures that occur when women attempt to improve their position in the social scale of the organization (Cleveland, Stockdale, & Murphy, 2000; Eagly & Carli, 2007; Hoyt & Burnette, 2013).

Women who are leaders, who believe in the possibility of social change, attempt to succeed in male-dominated settings and do not perceive this in terms of competition with the male gender. They tend to see the differences between genders as something symbolic (Jetten, Brascombe, Schmitt, & Spears, 2001; Schmitt, Branscombe, Kobrynowicz, & Owen, 2002; Schmitt, Spoor, Danaher, & Branscombe, 2009). They also deny being discriminated; they believe that other women are, but that they, themselves, are not (Schmitt, Branscombe, & Postmes, 2003), and these characteristics make it easier for the dominant male group to explain the lower position of women in certain work settings as a consequence of their personal traits.

Denying social category-based discrimination (on belonging to groups) legitimizes the existent differences of social position, keeping the socially dominant gender group of higher status from feeling guilty for its advantages and making it less likely that the group would try to change the rules of the system or renounce members' privileges (Barreto, Ellemers, Cihangir, & Stroebe, 2009; Ellemers, 2001). And the most surprising thing is that women are also reluctant to recognize that they are discriminated (Schmitt, Branscombe, & Postmes, 2003). Even though attributing the few or bad accomplishments of female leaders to discrimination may contribute to maintaining self-esteem, as long as such discrimination is the cause of an external factor, they do not always feel comfortable thinking that their belonging to a specific social group is what hinders the success of satisfactory, work-related accomplishments.

It seems that the denial of personal discrimination is helpful from a psychological point of view for several reasons (Crosby, Stockdale, & Ropp, 2007). First, women have the impression that they are in control of their lives; if they thought they would inevitably suffer constant personal discrimination, they would feel powerless in facing their future. In addition, denying personal discrimination offers a justification for not applying affirmative measures against those who discriminate against them; in fact, many times women do not even try to change the discriminating actions that are done to them because doing so would be of great cost and it would put their work situation at risk. That is, in fact, the reason why belief systems based on meritocracy are so powerful; no matter the objective opportunities that society offers, meritocratic beliefs maintain the conviction that the barriers between groups do not really exist, and the message they convey to professional women is that individual mobility is the best way to enhance their careers and be perceived better by the dominant group consisting of the executives of the organization (Barreto et al., 2009). In spite of the fact that individual progress can be objectively possible or even encouraged through the concept of meritocracy, the fact of knowing that only few women have had success in the past reduces subjective expectations of having success (Barreto, Ellemers, & Palacios, 2004).

That way, even when some women have had success in the past, it does not necessarily make the mobility of other women any easier. In fact, the conditions those women faced may convince other women not to try. Also, if those women who achieved work and social success convey the message that gender stereotyping has not been applied to them, this self-declared "exceptionality" will reinforce the stereotypes that society gives to the rest of the women (Ellemers, Rink, Derks, & Ryan, 2012). This has important consequences. First, it is likely that women who have achieved success and claim that they are not considered as part of stereotypes will not be motivated to help other women. Second, given the fact that the ones who have achieved success try to convince other women that the negative stereotype of the group is not applicable to them make great efforts to demonstrate that they are different from the other women. The need, for example, to adjust to behavioral rules of the dominant group easily leads these women who are successful in the work setting to an excess of compensation, like when they tend to adopt male-like styles (Eagly & Karau, 2002; Ellemers & van Laar, 2010), making it less likely that other women from the same group will consider them as attractive models in relation to the socially relevant role they perform.

Sometimes single women among male colleagues work hard to demonstrate that they possess all of the masculine characteristics required for the job. They describe themselves as very different from "regular" women and in stereotypically masculine terms. In contrast, they see "a typical" more junior woman in stereotypically female terms and end up supporting young women's careers less than they support young men's careers and less than senior men support both young men and women. This has been termed the "queen bee effect" (Madera et al., 2012). Importantly, research shows that this is not part of women's personality but determined by the environment: having been a token among a majority of men and having been treated in terms of gender while preferring not to be. For example, older female faculty of an Italian university perceived typical female doctoral students as less committed to their career than male doctoral students.

In summary, taken together, this suggests that women can either identify with their gender group, which may harm their careers individually, or they disassociate, which may in turn damage the careers of other women.

A study that analyzed existing letters of recommendation in academia found an interaction that can be interpreted as supporting evidence for the "queen bee" effect. Madera et al. (2012) found that female applicants were described less in active terms (e.g., ambitious) by female as opposed to male supervisors (e.g., professors). We can conceive an explanation for this along the lines of the "queen bee" effect: If a female professor sees herself, but not her younger colleagues, in stereotypically masculine terms, she will see herself as very assertive, in contrast to the younger women, and thus she will rate these younger women as less assertive.

The widespread belief, among men as much as among women, in the meritocratic nature of differences in accomplishments is reinforced to a great extent because, in contemporary societies in which direct demonstrations of prejudice and segregation are considered as unaccepted social behaviors, discrimination is, in many cases, subtle and concealed (Dovidio, 2001; Eagly & Carli, 2007). As a result, gender-based discrimination is less evident, since at least, seemingly, society offers women new opportunities (through legislation and policies of affirmative action), and instances of individual success seem to prove the meritocratic nature of modern society (Barreto et al., 2009). That way, then, the subtlety of modern prejudices reinforces the idea that individual mobility is an effective strategy for dealing with the disadvantages that are based on belonging to a low-status group; it appears that if women have enough merits and work hard enough, they should be capable of improving their position in the structure of society (Ellemers & van Laar, 2010; Ellemers, Plagiaro, & Barreto, 2013).

One way of attempting to fit in the dominant group could be to apply a strategy that is opposed to the aforementioned one, in which people cling to their own social identity, instead of denying its salience. Instead of renouncing to a group-based identity, women can try to use it to get their individual mobility by claiming that their belonging to their group is what gives them certain valuable features (Bird & Rhoton, 2011). A professional woman, for instance, might argue that she can contribute with traits that are considered feminine (for example, emotional and social sensitivity), which the current group lacks. Alternatively, women could also appeal to legal requisites (affirmative action and quota), which require the presence of a certain number of women among a group of executives. It is important to point out that the value that is given to the characteristics that are related to the group is based, in this case, on their lack of representation in the high status group. The unique and distinctive contribution of these characteristics will be reduced when some women have success in their attempts at individual mobility (Benschop & Verloo, 2011). That way, even if professional women use their belonging to their gender group as a personal benefit when they present prototypical features of their group as a source of value and diversity, it is possible that this helps them or makes it easier for them to achieve their personal goals but not those of the gender group (Bettencourt et al., 2001).

Costs of subtle discrimination

Despite the fact that individual mobility may seem an attractive strategy, there are several mechanisms that reduce its effectiveness or attractiveness. The most evident limitation is that it does not necessarily make people who occupy key positions (professors, recruiting personnel, executives, and supervisors) change their stereotypes, prejudice, and low expectations of the female gender group (Steele, Spencer, & Aronson, 2002; Wheeler & Petty, 2001). In their study, Schmitt, Branscombe, and Postmes (2003) found that the perception of a discriminatory action due to the prejudices of others may have important negative consequences for the psychological well-being of people, even more so if these people are aware of their belonging to a social group that faces a systematic devaluation on behalf of a dominant group. Also, it was shown that when women generally occupy a disregarded position in the social structure in relation to men, the perception of gender discrimination brings negative effects on women's psychological well-being. Another discovery that was made was that this effect was less negative for women who identify more strongly with the group. The negative effect of perceived discrimination on members of disregarded groups could be reduced if the sense of belonging to the in-group increases.

Thus, a strategy (i.e., based on psychological well-being) that can help stigmatized people reduce the negative effect of discrimination is to promote a greater sense of belonging to their group.

This prejudice and discrimination reduce the probability that women will try to move up in the organization and that those attempts will be successful, creating uncertainty effects (Hogg, 2007, 2012), self-discrimination, and disidentification from the organization (Benschop & Verloo, 2011). Effectively, important studies have shown that negative intentionality is not necessary for discrimination to be produced, but that in many cases, it is the result of automatic processes (de Lemus, Moya, Bukowski, & Lupiáñez, 2008). Thus, discrimination may be subtle and indirect, and in many cases, women may doubt if they have been subject to discrimination or if their lack of accomplishments has been the result of personal inadequacy (Major, Quinton, & Schmader, 2003). This uncertainty causes professional women to be victims of prejudice and it makes it harder for observers to be aware of their unfair treatment (see Hogg, 2012). In fact, it is very unlikely that professional women who are victims of modern, subtle, and indirect prejudice forms and who are not capable of identifying them would question such forms. As a result of that, forms of subtle prejudice (in comparison to the other more direct and traditional forms) may have worse consequences for the women who suffer from them, in the sense that not only do they decrease their well-being but also their self-confidence (Steele & Aronson, 1995; Steele et al., 2002). Even when women who have high responsibilities try to improve their position and become aware that they are being treated unfairly, battling subtle discrimination can have considerable social costs. Due to their belief in meritocracy, other people, especially those in the high-status male group, are more comfortable perceiving women's failure as an indication of a lack of individual merit (Ellemers, 2001; Schmitt, Ellemers, & Branscombe, 2003). Consequently, professional women who attribute their negative results to discrimination are considered as problematic or dissatisfied, unable to accept responsibility for their failures. Although this can be especially true when discrimination is subtle, it also occurs when it is direct (Garcia, Horstman Reser, Amo, Redersdoff, & Branscombe, 2005; Kaiser, 2006; Kaiser & Miller, 2003).

That way, the current discrimination, expressed in an implicit and ambiguous manner, puts women in work settings in a dilemma. The fact that they do not recognize that their personal accomplishments are the result of negative treatment that is based on their belonging to their gender group reduces their level of well-being, their motivation, and their performance (Barreto, Ellemers, & Palacios, 2004). However, recognizing such discrimination and fighting against it also has negative interpersonal and social consequences (Barreto et al., 2009).

Gender-based prejudices can affect the achievements obtained by women in academic and work situations, even when the discriminating part is absent (Inzlicht & Ben-Zeev, 2000; Steele & Aronson, 1995; Steele et al., 2002). We have seen how stereotype threat studies show that the mere presence of negative stereotypes in a context can cause women to have feelings of anxiety that distract their attention from the task at hand, negatively affecting their work performance (Steele & Aronson, 1995).

Having gone through experiences of negative stereotypes, prejudice, and discrimination represents a reality that can promote the work motivation of women by affecting their expectations and their value, the two essential components of motivation. Such experiences can make many women believe that getting positive results will turn out to be harder or even impossible (van Laar, 2000), anticipating that achieving them will cause them a considerable level of stress and difficulty (Cadinu et al., 2003). That way, experiences of previous discrimination make people from stigmatized groups (in comparison to those from groups that are not) evaluate their own opportunities in a less favorable way (Barreto et al., 2004). Therefore, the perception of negative expectations that result from prejudice and discrimination can discourage women (as a disregarded group and one that has a relatively lower status than the dominant group that is formed by the male gender), making their performance unsatisfactory. In brief, even when the context does not show concrete evidence of prejudice or it is not likely to imply direct discrimination, the application of negative expectations based on the belonging to groups to oneself, and the decrease of the expectations of discriminating treatment, make it less possible for the members of stigmatized groups to show the necessary level of competence in taking advantage of the opportunities of individual mobility (Steele et al., 2002).

To the degree that leading women perceive the attitude the male group show toward them (Sinclair & Huntsinger, 2006), they experience interaction anxiety and a greater rejection sensitivity (Tropp, 2006). As a consequence, discriminated women tend to reduce the value they give to success in an area, withdrawing psychologically from it and focusing their attention on other areas in which they do not have to face negative stereotypes (van Laar & Derks, 2003). This disassociation with the area in question has been observed in women when it comes to mathematics and regarding general academic achievements (Castaño & Webster, 2014). This anxiety takes place when people feel uncomfortable and do not know how to interact with members of the gender out-group. This type of anxiety can be produced in the leading male group when members interact with leading women who, as we said before, represent a group that has been stereotyped negatively. Those negative stereotypes come to represent, in a certain way, a threat to the male gender group. That means that if it is believed that leading women have values or forms of leadership that alter the favorable privileges of the male group, the mere presence of a female leader in the group will make the men feel threatened (Stephan & Stephan, 2000).

Summary

To summarize, the social identity perspective (a psychological perspective on how we relate to others) argues that having an identity that is respected is gratifying and has an effect on people by providing them with positive self-esteem. Women leaders in traditionally male work environments constitute a group that is valued more negatively than the group of men. The feeling of a negative identity disrupts the essence of who they are and causes emotional distress. We have seen how the social identity perspective proposes seemingly constructive ways for people (in our case, women leaders) to avoid negative feelings using diverse strategies or facing the thought of being a member of a group devaluated by gender. An important feature of such a perspective is its dynamic character. As has been shown, many professional women seek to assimilate into the dominant group of men. But if the privileged group of men perceives a threat on its social vitality and gender identity, because men think that women are trying to level the playing field, it will not remain idle and won't accept what could generate an uncomfortable new status quo. Assimilation involves disidentification from the gender group, and this fight at an individual level to reach the top of the organization endangers the psychological well-being of these women. Many of them end up self-discriminating, leaving their careers and seeking alternative solutions better suited to their status of women. How do women self-discriminate? Let's talk about this in the next chapter.

· 16 ·

DISCRIMINATION AND SELF-DISCRIMINATION OF WOMEN AT WORK

In the previous chapter we explained that people choose certain strategies to keep, change, or upgrade their gender identity. Work discrimination against women is changing gradually toward greater equality; the occupational areas that offer more resistance are those traditionally dominated by the male gender, up to the point that many women, after having tried different strategies to manage their gender identity, abandon their careers. It is often argued that women self-discriminate themselves. The economic experiments on risk aversion clearly illustrate these self-discriminatory processes of women. This is why we are interested in these investigations. But the research does not explain the underlying motives of women's self-discrimination. Certainly, before self-discriminating, women have suffered discrimination. We return to this subject later.

As we discussed, because of the mere fact that many adults live and work with people of different genders, they erroneously assume that we have overcome gender discrimination. Many workplaces are significantly segregated, either physically or in terms of the type of work. For example, in the military, women traditionally do not participate in the fighting, and at the U.S. Military Academy, most theoretical disciplines are fundamentally taught by men, while women are concentrated in the descriptive and applied disciplines like "support." Moreover, since many friendships between men and women are perceived as sexualized, it is difficult for both to form close relationships, devoid of sexual load, unless one party is openly gay or lesbian or the relationship is within a group of friends or couples (Hajek & Giles, 2005).

Many female researchers and feminists (e.g., Faludi, 2000) have reported that some women, especially younger women, invoking the concept of meritocracy, believe women as a group have achieved equality with men in society (Ellemers & van Laar, 2010). However, this is not true, at least not with women leaders in traditionally male dominated occupations, who are perceived as having a lower status than men (Carton & Rosette, 2011; Williams & Giles, 1978) due to women's historical absence in those professions. This has obvious consequences for the behavior of each group, its self-esteem, and its communicative processes (Collins & Clément, 2012; Dovidio, Hewstone, Glick, & Esses, 2010; Giles, 2012; Nelson, 2009; Major, Quinton, & Schmader, 2003; Steele, Spencer, & Aronson, 2002). The fact is that stereotypes based on associations like "think as a manager—think as a male" make men appear better suited for leadership than women (Heilman & Okimoto, 2008). These stereotypes also place women who are in positions of leadership in a tricky crossroad (Cook & Glass, 2013; Eagly & Sczesny, 2009). Likely due to these stereotypes, men still earn significantly more than women (Kulich, Trojanowski, Ryan, Haslam, & Renneboog, 2011) and are more likely to be promoted even when factors as important as level of education, hours worked, experience, or qualifications are on a par (Hoyt, 2010). This bias, however, far from being a problem for executive positions, seems to operate at all levels of the organizational hierarchy (Carton & Rosette, 2011). The fact that there are differences between the support networks of men and women represents an added difficulty for women when it comes to breaking the glass ceiling. At the same time, the support networks help men to journey by their labor trajectories and professional careers in a more fluid manner (Eagly & Sczesny, 2009; Livingston, Rosette, & Washington, 2012; Roth, 2007, 2009). We discuss this further in the next chapter.

A large-scale study on stereotypes, sponsored by IBM, found that top managers (30% of the sample) and other managers from the United States and Europe perceive differences between women and men leaders (Catalyst, 2007). According to the study, men perceive women leaders as more effective than men in the "caregiver" role, providing support and rewards to their subordinates. Moreover, they perceive male leaders as more effective than women in delegation and problem-solving roles. In particular, the study found that these perceptions were not supported by research on effective leadership behavior. The findings show that because of stereotypes, the leadership talent of women is routinely underrated and underutilized in organizations, even though these same organizations need female talent to succeed, as several studies have shown (see, e.g., Brunet & Rodríguez-Soler, 2013).

Essentially, because of these stereotypes, women who want to be seen as leaders face a dilemma: If they act like women (in traditionally female ways), they are assumed to be weak. If they take on the attributes associated with men, they are seen as too aggressive. Neither option is best; hence the term "double-bind" is given, meaning a situation in which a person (in this case, a woman) must choose between equally unsatisfactory alternatives, a detrimental and unavoidable dilemma (Bosak & Sczesny, 2011; Ellemers et al., 2012). For example, McIlwee and Robinson (1992), in their study of engineering graduates and engineering work environments, found that the association of the engineering career with men created conflicts for female engineering students. They found that women engineers perceived that attention afforded to them, because they were few, undermined their credibility as engineers because the focus was on the fact that they were women (there was strong gender salience). On the other hand, the acceptance of their peers as engineering students undermined the well-being of female students as feminine women. For example, jokes about the lack of physical attractiveness of women engineers demonstrated the existence of an unambiguous picture: either engineer or attractive woman, but not both at once. Other studies have suggested that women face disadvantages due to the overwhelming masculinity of the engineering culture that forces them to choose between denial of their gender or being perceived as the "otherness" (Ceci & Williams, 2007; Franzway, Sharp, Mills, & Gill, 2009).

While discrimination in the first instance is a phenomenon that is experienced, it is also internalized, and it can lead women to self-discriminate. When a woman is criticized, she might think that these criticisms are true and assume them as such, adjusting her behavior according to the standards expected from her discriminators (Fiske, 2000). Self-discrimination is the saddest form of discrimination because it is the woman herself who performs it; it is the woman herself who self-censors. It could be described by the following mechanism: First, the "different" characteristics of discriminated women cause in the discriminators stereotyped behaviors and expectations. Second, these expectations involve different treatments, judgments, and behaviors against discriminated women. Third, discriminated women internalize these differential judgments and behave differently, according to what is expected by the discriminators.

Ergun, Garcia-Muñoz, and Rivas (2012) reviewed the literature on gender differences in economic experiments on risk aversion, trust, deception, and leadership. They explored environments where self-discrimination emerges and through various experiments have characterized a series of behaviors that, extrapolated to work, family, and social environment, may lead to self-discrimination. Some of the behaviors associated with women are aversion to risk and competition, prosocial behavior, generosity, and cooperation (Aguiar, Brañas-Garza, & Miller, 2008; Andreoni & Vesterlund, 2001; Benito, Brañas-Garza, Hernández, & Sanchis, 2011; Brañas-Garza, Espinosa, & Rey-Biel, 2011). At an equal skill level, it appears that women abstain more than men in choosing or searching for jobs associated with challenges or unknown risks (Niederle & Yestrumskas, 2008). This differential preference is associated with differences in self-perception that men and women have of their ability to work in new and challenging environments and differences in their attitudes toward risk and uncertainty in general (Brañas-Garza & Rustichini, 2011). A study by Niederle and Yestrumskas (2008) found that men more often attributed failure in a specific task to bad luck and success to their ability. Women more often attributed failure to their lack of skill and success to good luck. Croson and Gneezy (2009) also reviewed a series of experiments on gender differences in competition and risk, concluding that, in general, women are more risk averse and more sensitive to social issues, and they have a lower preference for competitive environments. According to the findings, gender differences in career choices and speed of promotions could be caused by women's desire to avoid competitive situations. No one takes her away from there; she leaves by herself. The work of Niederle and Vesterlund (2007) is much more conclusive. During their experiment, men and women performed a real chore. When collecting the salary for the task, they were asked if they preferred to collect money directly or through a competitive system (the best job earns more): Women preferred the first and men the second option. Again, when asked, women freely withdrew from the competition. This type of behavior gives an alternative explanation for the lack of women business leaders. That is, many women do not compete for internal promotions and allow male peers to do it. What this work fails to explain is whether the decision to withdraw from the competition is taken freely (personal preference) or, conversely, is a result of the internalization of gender roles (Eagly & Karau, 2002; Fiske, 2000) that lead to self-discrimination.

Eckel and Grossman (2008) reviewed economic experiments that explore gender differences in abstract games, finding that there are no gender differences when people are exposed to risks. In the absence of risk, however, they observed systematic gender differences in the sense that women make decisions that are more communal. Together, these results explain, for example, that women give up a career in favor of their husbands because they do not accept the idea of competing with them and are more generous (cooperate on behalf of another); their expectations also play an important role. They know that their husbands expect their resignation and feel bad when they do not do what is expected from them (do not meet the expectations of their partners) or do not follow roles imposed by society. Given that men and women tend to play different social roles, both behave differently, adjusting to these roles (Eagly & Sczesny, 2009).

There is a theory that risk aversion is associated with feminine attributes, showing that for both sexes, high scores of femininity (as measured by tests of identification and gender roles) reduce risk propensity (Meier-Pesti & Penz, 2008). Eckel and Grossman (2002) argued that if women are stereotyped as more risk averse, this could negatively affect them in many ways, such as accepting lower wages than men. However, several studies have found that gender differences are mitigated by experience and professionalism (see Niederle & Yestrumskas, 2008). Using a male and female sample of executives, Atkinson, Boyce Baird, and Frye (2003) found no gender differences in how those men and women managers administered their funds in terms of risk. Revisiting this topic, Johnson and Powell (1994) found that in a population with no management training, women were less willing to take risks, but these differences were not observed in a population with leadership training. Therefore, it seems that providing training on organizational or corporate governance reduces the fear of risk. It could also be that women who study executive subjects have inherently less fear of risk. In any case, Niederle and Yestrumskas (2008) suggested that to prevent self-discrimination of women with high work skills, social work norms should be created whereby women can try different tasks without a strict initial commitment. In this way, women could assess their ability *in situ* and remove or ratify their initial prejudices about their ability to perform the task.

Without a doubt, self-discrimination can be learned. Within the family and society, negative values are learned and internalized. These values ultimately have an impact on personal decisions and on relationships with third parties (Foss, Domenico, & Foss, 2012).

Let us consider promotion to a senior position in a company: A woman can be discriminated by the company and not be promoted, despite having the same qualifications as male candidates (discrimination per se). However, she can also resign herself to not being promoted because she does not believe she will be chosen or because she believes the job is not suited for a women (self-discrimination). Both explanations are plausible but not exhaustive; there is at least a third one: It may be that women give up because they have different preferences and simply are not interested. In this case, one could not talk about self-discrimination. However, the distinction between self-discrimination and women's preferences is difficult to establish. Many women prefer to postpone a promotion and have less social salience to devote more time to their family; however, this decision may be the result of a learned model where a woman should be devoted to her husband and family, or on the contrary, it may be a decision freely taken by a woman whose priority is her family.

There is no doubt that in many cases, self-discrimination serves to protect the individual welfare of women, enabling them to seek social support in other women and highlight alternate fields (see Esteban-Guitart, Viladot, & Giles, 2014, for the importance of support networks for self-esteem). But it also reduces their contact with the dominant and controlling male group, thus limiting their access to knowledge and resources that are in the hands of that male group. So if women stop valuing their academic and professional achievements, they may jeopardize their chances of achieving a better social position (Barreto et al., 2004).

Finally, it is important to consider neurobiological research. This suggests that behavior in favor of a society that characterizes women (cooperation, generosity, trust in others, etc.) may be due to the presence of estrogen and a female hormone called oxytocin (see Derks, Scheepers, & Ellemers, 2013). According to these theories, women's withdrawal from competition could be a preference, a chosen option (one could not talk about self-discrimination), and not a decision subject to the acceptance of roles imposed by society. Differences in female hormones and estrogen within the population would explain differences in risk propensity, for example, that women are generally more cautious than men. Some of the biological factors that influence willingness to take risks have already been explored (Bosch-Doménech,

Brañas-Garza, & Espín, 2014). An experimental study by Apicella, Dreber, Campbell, Gray, Hoffman, and Little (2008) showed that risk behaviors are positively correlated with levels of testosterone (the male sex hormone) measured in saliva samples (a marker of exposure to the hormone at puberty). In addition, testosterone was found to be one of the factors associated with sensation seeking (a personality characteristic highly associated with predisposition to risk), and biological features associated with this trait have been studied in depth (Zuckerman, 2007).

These results should not be underestimated when analyzing the factors involved in the discrimination of women. Knowing to what extent socialization is involved and to what extent biology (the eternal debate) should be important in establishing structural policies. Coherent information from social psychology and communication should require the integration of the various research trends on gender in biosocial interaction theories that recognize the causal role of biological and social influences on the psychology of women and men (Eagly & Wood, 2012). However, research on the differences and similarities between men and women lacks comprehensive models that integrate behavioral, cognitive, biological, and environmental concepts (including social). It is important to mention that research on motor behavior in men and women shows evidence that experiences can alter neurophysiology. Studies suggest that gender differences in motor coordination or speed between the two genders cannot be explained solely by biological factors. Specifically, Chalabaev, Brisswalter, Radel, Coombes, Easthope, and Clément-Guillotin (2013) suggested that the activation of gender stereotypes could "lead to gender gaps in motor performance through motivational processes (e.g., effort)" (p. 147). If these results were the same in reference to other behavioral differences found, once again, we could counter the studies that encapsulate women and men in biological determinism. However, we think that even if there are biological characteristics for each gender, these differences should be assessed on their own, without negative connotations. Later we discuss diversity concepts as they relate to these differences.

In sum, to achieve positions of high responsibility, the way of women is certainly much more intricate than that of men. They have to overcome obstacles that block access to positions of high leadership that don't exist for their male counterparts. Unlike women, men tend to follow a straighter path and face less obstacles. How can determined women navigate the winding road that they must follow to reach the executive suite? Next we discuss some of the strategies.

"Female identity" versus "work identity"

Men's occupational identity is more integrated with their gender identity, while the occupational and gender identities of women are often separated and can be a source of stress (see also the discussion of work-family conflict in Chapter 7). Also, those responsible for making decisions in the workplace tend to assume that women have important domestic responsibilities and, therefore, they do not promote them (Sabattini & Crosby, 2009; see also Chapter 12).

How can one cope with a negative social identity at work? Pronin, Steele, and Ross (2004) showed that when people feel threatened by stereotypes applied to their social group, they selectively disidentify from the components of group identity that affect their self-esteem, while at the same time maintaining a positive identification with their group. This process of identity bifurcation or partitioning implies that people reduce their sense of identification with those aspects of belonging to a group that are perceived, in a particular field or context, as associated with negative stereotypes. Similarly, to resolve the tension they feel regarding the reconciliation of their female identity with their occupational identity at the workplace, many women choose to deflect the threat by disidentifying with the stereotyped group itself (von Hippel, Issa, Ma, & Stokes, 2011). That is, by separating their female identity from their professional identity, they can emphasize their professional role within the organization, even when such skills are counterstereotypical for women. Thus, women who experience stereotype threat may respond to this threat by differentiating between women's roles and professional roles at the workplace. See the following, for example:

> When Jane is working she might consider herself persuasive, influential, analytical, and independent. Jane may see these characteristics as her 'work-self.' When Jane is not working, she might consider herself sensitive, warm, tender, accommodating, and gentle. Jane may see these characteristics as her 'female-self.' In this way, Jane maintains a clear distinction between her work self and female self, and she prevents her female qualities from serving as a source of weakness or stereotypicality at work (while simultaneously retaining them as a valued aspect of her self-concept). (von Hippel et al., 2011, p. 152)

However, we must remember that stereotypes are not merely descriptive but mostly prescriptive, for example, prescribing how men, women, or managers should be. And because of this fact, women in leadership roles are often at risk of not being perceived as leaders if they do not show typically male behavior, but they risk rejection if they try to solve this problem by behaving in an aggressive and masculine way (Eagly & Karau, 2002; Gartzia & van Engen, 2012). For this reason, women who have split their identity and succeed in leadership roles tend to be seen as competent and instrumental, but they also could be perceived as less warm and not "feminine" enough (Cikara & Fiske, 2009; Ellemers et al., 2012; Heilman, 2012; Lakoff, 2003). That is, gender stereotypes and the expectations they generate about women and their behavior can lead to isolation, hostility, devaluation of their performance at work, denial of their success, or punishment for being too competent (Eagly & Karau, 2002; Ellemers et al., 2012; Heilman, 2012).

Although men in positions of power also face challenges, in the case of women, these challenges are exaggerated. Moreover, these gender-based beliefs or expectations (strongly rooted in stereotypes) tend to become "self-fulfilling prophecies." This phenomenon occurs when someone who is holding a particular expectation about another person behaves toward this person in a way that leads to a confirmation of that person's initial expectation (for example, not giving women many opportunities to speak and, therefore, confirming the belief that they cannot do this well; for a classic study, see Word, Zanna, & Cooper, 1974).

It is known that these biases in perceptions may result in "self-fulfilling prophecies" when, for example, managers unknowingly cause confirmation behaviors in members of the stereotyped group (Operario & Fiske, 2001). In other words, according to these effects, it is possible that once we have an expectation, we tend to act in a manner consistent with it; and so, quite often, the expectation becomes reality, as if by magic (Word et al., 1974).

In summary, we can say that our schema and beliefs about men and women (or even about ourselves or events) are loaded with expectations that somehow influence our behavior and that of others, coming to induce compliance with them. Thus, our gender schema and attitudes are reinforced, as there are numerous situations in which what we expected is exactly what happens (Barreto et al., 2009).

We explained that, at the workplace, many women exhibit a distinct identity separate from their feminine identity. Due to stereotypical beliefs about the female gender, many women choose to distance themselves from the female behavior that could harm their professional image. Since male stereotypical beliefs are associated with the executive world, the professional identity of many women is constructed based on the work behaviors associated with men. Certainly, the professional identity of women is much more complex than that of men.

Summary

Although stereotype due to gender refers to consensual beliefs about the attributes of each gender as a group and their members (men and women), discrimination targets those behaviors that deny equality in the treatment of women because of their attachment to the social category "woman."

In macrosocial terms, discrimination against women refers to a complex system of relationships between "men" and "women" who produce and reproduce inequalities in access to resources, for example, to restrain women in their employment opportunities. At this level of analysis, discrimination against women refers to the institutions, norms, and social practices responsible whereby their exclusion by virtue of belonging to the social category "women" is perpetuated and legitimized.

In psychological terms, discrimination (behavioral) refers (in the context of this volume) to differential and unfair treatment faced by women at work in terms of their responsibilities and their daily interactions, by the mere fact of belonging to the social category to which they belong. In many cases, women leave the profession to seek jobs with less stress to avoid a highly masculinized environment that harms them and, when they become mothers, to gain flexibility.

In the field of organizations, "risk" conducts have been widely studied. The explanation of self-discrimination observed in women is very complex, since it has not been elucidated to what extent is due to the internalization of "structural" discrimination and to what extent other factors are involved, preferential and biological. In that sense, here we have made notoriously evident the lack of comprehensive theories that allow us to understand the complex network of relationships between the variables studied. We refer to more general models that attempt to coherently integrate the many scattered results.

Precisely because research shows that factors associated with the antagonistic communication between genres are numerous and are located at different levels of analysis, the challenge is to identify those that are truly important. The exclusion of relevant variables as well as the inclusion of irrelevant variables are two of the most difficult problems to solve in specifying our models of explanation.

For now, the closest perspective to the described profile is the social identity perspective, in its attempt to integrate (a) cognitive processes underlying the distorted perception of out-groups, (b) psychological needs responsible for such distortions, and (c) the impact of objective social relations in these cognitive and motivational mechanisms. This perspective is particularly appropriate for examining specific communicative processes and general mechanisms of behavior between genders. The vast amount of research inspired by social identity perspective, both in the field of intergroup communication and intergroup harmony, is just an indicator of the benefits of this theoretical model, large enough and at the same time parsimonious enough to provide general conceptual tools and specific hypotheses that can be subjected to empirical testing.

· 17 ·

CONSERVATIVES VERSUS LIBERALS

Although the presence of women in the labor market has increased significantly in recent decades, we are still far from full gender equality in the workplace. And even more far the higher up we go in the hierarchy of organizations.

A recent study by the firm PayScale on salary increases provides new evidence in this regard. This study, conducted in late 2014 in the United States from a sample of more than 30,000 people has a positive outcome: It belies the widespread belief that women ask less than men for salary increases. It also shows that the percentage of employees who get the requested increase is similar in men and women.

However, when we apply the zoom, look up and focus on the group of professionals who have an MBA, what we see is worrying. When we look at what happens to these people, mostly directors, we discover that they don't enjoy so much gender equality. Among the MBAs, 63% of men who requested a salary increase got everything they asked for, versus only 48% of women. But there's more: Only 10% of men did not get anything, compared to 21% of women (PayScale, 2014).

Although most people prefer a male boss, this trend has decreased, and the preference for a female boss and the percentage of people "without preference" has increased (see Gallup Poll Survey, 2013). This is probably due to a general change in society, among other factors. In this regard, Hoyt (2010, 2012) and Hoyt and Burnette (2013) showed that the people who supported the status quo of gender roles ("conservatives") discriminated against women in employment decisions and supported men for leadership roles, while people who actively rejected the status quo ("liberals") showed a greater tendency to promote female candidates. Compared with liberals, conservatives depended more on their gender and leadership prototypes to make their assessments of men and women in work environments. This predicts a likely discrimination against women wishing to achieve levels of power (Hoyt & Burnette, 2013; Rudman & Kilianski, 2000; Simon & Hoyt, 2008).

Conservatives showed a tendency to use prototypical stereotypes as the basic unit of analysis; they held the belief that behaviors are consistent across time and situations. Liberals were more likely to focus on the big picture and consider that past behavior does not always predict current behavior. For example, students were asked to view a slide show of a child who changed schools; the boy deceived and lied to make a good first impression on his new schoolmates. When students were asked what they thought the boy would be like several years later, the conservatives were much more likely than progressives to predict that he would be a troublemaker (Erdley & Dweck, 1993). Erdley and Dweck's (1993) study showed how identical situations can be processed and interpreted differently when forming an assessment or a value judgment. This is important in understanding the unique differences in the ease or difficulty professional women face in their organizations, depending on the type of leadership, conservative or liberal, that they have to contend with.

Most of the research on role congruence and leadership focuses on prejudices experienced by women leaders, because leadership roles are incompatible with the social expectations that are prescribed for them (Eagly & Karau, 2002). The study by Hoyt and Burnette (2013) expanded this perspective, showing a bias in favor of women that can arise when people hold liberal attitudes toward women in positions of authority.

Thus, this research contributes to an emerging literature that demonstrates that gender bias in the workplace and leadership do not always work against women. Attitudes toward gender roles proved to be important in predicting evaluations of women in incongruous contexts, with the people who reject traditional roles being more likely to support women in these positions (Hoyt, 2012).

In short, unlike liberals, conservatives rely on their gender stereotypes and leadership prototypes and attitudes when positioning their evaluations. Conservatives, compared with liberals, pay more attention to stereotype-consistent than stereotype-inconsistent information, and they rely more on social group membership and less on information related to individual characteristics of people.

In our view, one of the interesting theoretical aspects of this body of work is that the focus is on the behavior of men. If we consider research on gender discrimination at work as a whole, we immediately realize that these studies focus almost exclusively on women and their experiences (Bruckmüller, Ryan, Haslam, & Peters, 2013). So far we have seen different situations and factors that hinder the advancement of women to leadership positions, predisposing them to leave, making their careers particularly difficult and complex. More generally, we tend to compare the lower status groups with the higher status group that is considered the background, in the same way that less typical groups are compared with the prototypical groups (Hegarty & Bruckmüller, 2013).

The overwhelming tendency to put the spotlight on women seems to us natural because of the challenges they face in overcoming inequality in the workplace. However, this turns against them. What happens is that research comparisons between men and women usually are not conducted in a symmetrical manner; the tendency is to analyze the characteristics of women with respect to men (Coates & Johnson, 2001). That is, men are positioned as barely visible "background" and women are compared with this background, settling an asymmetrical relationship. Investigations that have examined which groups are being considered as "the effect to be explained" and which are placed in the "background" have shown that both lay people and scientists, and both men and women, explain gender differences by examining women more than men (Bruckmüller et al., 2013).

Since men generally enjoy a higher social status than women (Williams & Giles, 1978) and are often perceived as more prototypical leaders than women (Eagly & Sczesny, 2009), it is not surprising that explanations of gender discrimination at work usually focus on women. Only traditionally female-dominated work environments (e.g., social work, nursing, or primary school teaching) are an exception. It has been shown that in these occupational areas where women are more prototypical, men advance faster to leadership positions (called "glass escalator"; C. L. Williams, 1992); when asking why, once again, the less prototypical group (in this case, men) becomes the effect to be explained.

An obvious consequence is that, by highlighting the experiences of women and the boundaries they face, it is likely that discussions on gender inequality end up focusing on the attributes, characteristics, and stereotypes of women (Eagly & Karau, 2002), including but not limited to their careers and family planning choices. If this happens, most studies to date could obscure other aspects of gender inequality, such as stereotypes about men (e.g., Bruckmüller et al., 2013) or organizational culture and practices, such as work-related networks within the "old boys' club" (Castaño & Webster, 2014). And importantly, the fact that the explanations of gender differences focus on women may imply that women, rather than men, are the ones who should change their behavior to reduce the differences (Hegarty & Pratto, 2001).

In short, the fact that the focus of the explanations falls on women makes gender discrimination a greater problem for women than for men. It implies that what generates gender inequality is up to the women themselves and, therefore, it is women who have to change behaviors to reduce this inequality (Bruckmüller et al., 2013). In this sense, too many studies focusing on women avoid confronting men with uncomfortable truths about their own advantages and privileges (Branscombe, 1998).

Recent work also shows that the status quo is changing. The work of Croft, Schmader, Block, and Baron (2014) focused on the masculine, proving that the role of fathers in housework chores is a key element when predicting academic choices and occupations, mostly for daughters. The most revealing fact of the research is the influence of equalitarian fathers on the daughters: They tend to choose careers linked to male stereotypes, rather than the usual female professions related to the care and service occupations. This study shows that women's advancement in traditionally male fields, such as engineering and science, is in the hands of men.

Summary

In the previous chapters, we discussed how women leaders react to discriminatory processes in the workplace. We discussed the strategies they use to manage their gender identity at the workplace, how they split their identity at work, and the reasons why they self-discriminate and abandon their careers. We have seen how discrimination against women is linked (is explained or is conditioned) to the ideology that underlies the attitudes of men toward them. In the next chapter, we discuss other harmful situations that some women have to cope with at work. Sexual harassment is probably the most negative situation for women at the workplace. This phenomenon entails dire psychological consequences for women and leads to workplace instability.

· 18 ·

INTERACTIONS BETWEEN GENDER AND POWER: SEXUAL HARASSMENT

Before addressing the issue of sexual harassment, we will place it in its appropriate framework.

Power and the way it is conceived and used through interpersonal communication provides the framework within which is located the destructive phenomenon of sexual harassment in the workplace. We affirm that sexual harassment would not exist if there wasn't inequality—favoring men—between genders regarding social vitality and power. The link between gender and sexual harassment begins with the recognition of what Fiske (2000) called *power asymmetries*.

Giles and others in the 1970s formulated a theoretical base for the analysis of the vitality (power) of social groups (e.g., age, gender, ethnicity; Esteban-Guitart, Viladot, & Giles, 2014; Giles & Viladot, 1994; Viladot & Esteban-Guitart, 2011; Viladot, Esteban-Guitart, Nadal, & Giles, 2007; Viladot, Giles, Bolaños, & Esteban-Guitart, 2013; Viladot, Giles, Gasiorek, & Esteban-Guitart, 2012).

Status and institutional support are the two causal factors for measuring gender vitality. We can certainly say that women as a gender group have less social vitality (less social power) than men as a gender group. That is, social, economic, language, and sociohistorical status seem to favor male vitality.

Men have more rights and privileges. They exhibit their privileges and power and produce them in every communication situation (Kabat-Farr & Cortina, 2014; see also Collins & Clément, 2012). Some men believe they have the right to exercise their power and force women to have sex. This is a phenomenon that goes against the most basic human rights. Sexual harassment in the workplace is a prime example of the use of power (Pörhölä & Kinney, 2009). Let's talk about it.

In intergender communication, interpersonal control strategies are particularly important (Wiemann, 2009), that is, the maintenance of interpersonal control in its relation to power or the status difference between men and women. Where power differentials exist, language and communication are often used to stabilize inequality (Giles, Coupland, & Coupland, 1991; Giles & Ogay, 2007). These power differences are not natural but socially created and, therefore, their generation will be observable in language and social interaction (Collins & Clément, 2012; Gasiorek & Giles, 2012). Consequently, many differences in social behavior that appear to be gender differences can be best described as differences in power.

The definition of sexual harassment is controversial because the phenomenon comprises various causes, modalities, and consequences, nuanced and mediated by the culture of the social group in which the phenomenon occurs (Kabat-Farr & Cortina, 2014). In relation to women, men disproportionately hold control over resources and results in business enterprises and other contexts. Men who harass are in a position to control the reinforcements and punishments that can inflict women. Consequently, subordinate women who report harassment or even resist the sexual advances of a director or manager can suffer devastating economic consequences, such as wage loss (if they are dismissed from their jobs) or opportunities for advancement (loss of promotion or recommendation letters from the sexual stalker; García-Izquierdo, Meseguer, Soler, & Sáez, 2014). Thus, it is probable that men harass partly because they have a good chance of getting away with it (Hirigoyen, 2001; Pörhölä & Kinney, 2009).

Sexual harassment behaviors range from sexist and degrading acts commonly used in social life, to unwanted sexual advances, blackmail, and coercion, up to physical attacks for sexual purposes (Piñuel & Oñate, 2002). Therefore, sexual harassment is a form of violence. It violates fundamental rights and the free exercise of sexuality. The force used can range from physical coercion to the use of power by offering rewards, privileges, or denial of vested rights (Ibañez, Lezaún, Serrano, & Tomás, 2007). The aim often is to obtain some type of sexual contact with the harassed woman. The type of sexual harassment that usually comes to mind is that related to men in higher positions who threaten their subordinates with the loss of their jobs if the requests for sexual favors are not met (Kabat-Farr & Cortina, 2014). Data show that 60% of sexually harassed women do not confront their harasser and only 30% face the aggressor (Ibañez et al., 2007). The escape response can be explained by the serious risk the woman faces when confronting the perpetrator. He can use many tricks to cast doubt on a possible complaint and discredit the victim. For example, the attacker can invoke a misunderstanding, a trap, or an exaggeration.

Cultural conceptions about women as traditional (housewife), modern (nontraditional women), or sensual (sexy women) contribute to the way they are treated at work (Glick & Rudman, 2010). In particular, women classified as sensuous are perceived as preoccupied with their appearance in order to arouse men (Hirigoyen, 2001). This feminine stereotype awakens sexual urges in men and sexual harassment of such women reflects a desire for lasting intimacy or male domination. In contrast, women classified as modern are perceived as having masculine qualities and assuming masculine gender roles. These women will be the target of sexual harassment to assert not only male dominance but traditional gender roles as well. In each case, power possession has a direct influence on the impressions men form of subordinates, which has an impact on the way they treat them. For example, a woman perceived as "sexy" is more likely to experience sexual harassment than one perceived as a housewife (Glick & Rudman, 2010). This differentiation into subtypes within the general assemblies of men and women helps to explain the level where prejudice, stereotypes, and finally, discrimination take place.

However, researchers rush to say that only a minority of men in power positions at organizations sexually harass their subordinates. Why is that so if men have more power in enterprises than women? One reason is that harassing conduct has to be seen as permissible or normative at a given workplace (Cantisano, Depolo, Domínguez, & Morales, 2007). The authors' extensive literature search yielded 86 empirical studies with 93 samples. The meta-analysis obtained confirms that environmental factors are the main predictors of harassment. For example, Pryor (1995) analyzed data from reports of sexual harassment gathered in two large, national, U.S. surveys. He tested the hypothesis that in organizations in which management is perceived to condone or ignore complaints of sexual harassment, women are more likely to suffer.

The results of each survey showed that complaints of sexual harassment were higher in companies where employees felt that management tolerates such conduct or ignores the complaints. In spite of the correlational nature of the study, these data are consistent with the notion that men who abuse their power and harass women often believe that their sexual advances are tolerated in the organizational culture.

In experimental investigations, Pryor and colleagues (Pryor, 1995; Pryor, LaVite, & Stoller, 1993) showed that only men who associate the concepts of power and sex are likely to harass women when they perceive that the organization condones their behavior. To identify men's predisposition to harassment, Prior conceived a scale (LSH, Likelihood to Sexually Harass). The scale consists of 10 situations describing a man with a power advantage over an attractive woman. For example, in one situation, the manager of a restaurant notes that a pretty waitress deliberately alters her friends' bill. Men are asked to imagine themselves in each of the situations and score the likelihood that they would use their power advantage (e.g., the threat of dismissal for the waitress) for getting sexual favors from her. The higher the overall probability that a man would use his power for his sexual pleasure, the stronger was his association between power and sex. It appears that a man with high scores on this scale has a willingness to take advantage of a woman if he thinks the organization supports the harassing behavior.

Several studies supported this prediction (Pryor, 1995). In one experiment, Pryor and colleagues (1993) asked men with high and low scale scores to help an attractive woman (a colleague) perform a text processing task at the computer. Before the experiment, half of the participants observed how a male authoritarian figure (a confederate of the experimenter) sexually harassed the woman through body contact and suggestive comments. The other half observed that he addressed her in a friendly but professional way. When participants were later asked to help the woman, those with high scale scores who had observed harassment made more unsolicited physical contact and sexual comments. However, none of the men harassed the woman. In a similar vein, men who believe that other men accept rape myths respond with higher rape proclivity (Kabat-Farr, & Cortina, 2014). As Pryor and colleagues elaborated, rape myths are beliefs that deny, trivialize, or justify men's sexual aggression toward women. If male students believed the social norm was that sexual aggression was okay, they responded that they would be more likely to use power for sexual pleasure in situations like those described earlier, and they would enjoy it more. These and similar results show that some men tend to take advantage of a woman when they perceive that the organizational climate tolerates this behavior.

Do men who harass recognize that their behavior is harassment? And do they look for situations in which they can abuse their power? Bargh, Raymond, Pryor, and Strack (1995) argued that many harassing men are not aware that their behavior is damaging to their female victims. Bargh and colleagues showed that the association between power and sex is strong and that it influences behavior in an unconscious and automatic way. According to this reasoning, a man with a high score on Pryor's scale automatically activates sexual ideas in response to power, and this activation is unconscious and not subject to his control. Because these men do not realize that their sexual thoughts were activated by power, they ascribe them to something they are currently focusing on, that is, a woman. Therefore, they interpret her friendly behavior as a form of reciprocity of sexual interest. This helps explain why, according to Fitzgerald (1993), many men accused of sexual harassment are surprised and upset. They dismiss the damage caused by their behavior, they deny that they have done it intentionally, and they offer a different interpretation for their behavior (e.g., that it was a compliment).

However, there is also intentional sexual harassment as a strategy that solidifies male dominance and women's subordination at the workplace by strengthening gender-power relations (Ibañez et al., 2007). Such harassment undermines women's self-confidence and self-appreciation as autonomous and lovable individuals (Kabat-Farr & Cortina, 2014). Therefore, sexual harassment can be used by the harasser as a way to maintain intergroup boundaries and to achieve both sexual goals and personal power. Research indicates that, at least in some cases, sexual harassment is one of the strategies that is used to intimidate and push women out of labor areas considered male territory (Altés–Tárrega, 2002). Several studies have found that sexual harassment is a major problem for many women who hold traditionally male positions (Hirigoyen, 2001; Maass & Cadinu, 2006). There is evidence that men treat women occupying traditionally male positions different from female colleagues in typically female positions (Popovich & Warren, 2010); these women may be the target of derisive speculations on the nature and extent of their sexual life and their physical attributes.

Unambiguous evidence for sexual harassment's function to preserve power differences between women and men comes from a series of experiments designed from a social identity perspective (Maass, Cadinu, Guarnieri, & Grasselli, 2003). Maass and colleagues (2003) assumed that men would become more likely to sexually harass if their identity as men was threatened. They argued that if the status difference between genders was threatened, men would react with harassment, in particular men for whom their male identity is very important. The authors developed a computer harassment paradigm to test their predictions. Interestingly, that paradigm allows both close experimental control and investigations in which no woman needs to suffer from the harassment provoked, which would be a research ethics problem. In this paradigm, men believed they were chatting, via connected computers, with a woman, and they believed the study was about picture recognition. Each of the two participants, the man and the woman (who does not really exist), had to choose pictures to send to the other participant. Some of the files from which they could choose pictures were labeled "models" and "porno." The interesting question was how many of those pictures the participant would send to the woman. Any time one of those pictures was sent, the woman protested.

The woman they believed they were chatting with either introduced herself as a traditional woman or as a feminist intending to become a bank manager. The latter should pose a threat to the legitimacy of the gender status difference. In line with the authors' hypotheses, participants sent more pornographic images to the feminist than to the traditional woman, particularly if they highly identified with the male group. Those who harassed also felt "more manly" after proving their male identity in this way.

The authors found evidence for the role of another type of threat. They argued that the threat of not being a prototypical group member could provoke harassment. They gave participants a test of masculinity and femininity (self-ratings on traits such as considerate, dominant, etc., which was discussed earlier). They either learned that their result was as expected or that it was typical for a woman but atypical for a man. Again, this type of threat increased the number of pornographic images the men sent, mainly if the men were highly identified with their gender group. As observed earlier, harassment increased male identity. Thus, "a strong identification as a male appears to be a risk factor for harassment; in turn, harassment seems to reinforce such an identity, suggesting that harassment feeds back into a self-maintaining cycle" (Maass et al., 2003, p. 865).

Summary

In this chapter, we presented strong objective evidence of the function of sexual harassment to keep men's superior status in the social hierarchy and women "in their place." Additionally, this evidence is related to the findings on precarious manhood. If men feel threatened in their male identity, they try to affirm their identity (Maass & Cadinu, 2006). This is done not only by choosing masculine behaviors such as punching balls; it also leads to all kinds of undesirable behaviors directed at out-groups, such as harassing women and gay men.

Women promoted to executive positions previously held exclusively by men can also be subject to rumors that "they slept their way to the top" (Pearce & Robinson, 2011). Hostile behavior manifestations at the workplace can be multiple and varied; Hirigoyen's (2001) Scandinavian study found a clear gender difference in the distribution of victims of harassment: Of those who were victims, 70% were women and 30% were men. However, these percentages should be interpreted in their sociocultural context. Scandinavia generally exhibits a genuine concern for equal opportunities for both genders. In other European countries, a macho atmosphere prevails. Many men think that a working woman is the cause of an unemployed man. In general, there are more harassed women than men at the workplace, and women are harassed in a different way, with sexist connotations (Altés–Tárrega, 2002; Pernas, Román, Olza, & Naredo, 2000; Popovich & Warren, 2010).

Let us now enter into a field of study that explains how people (and groups) manage the communication between them. We will see the other side of the coin: the behavior and reactions of the male group in the workplace (in areas traditionally dominated by this group) in their relationships and contacts with professional women.

· 1 9 ·

COMMUNICATION ACCOMMODATION THEORY AND INTERGENDER BOUNDARIES

We have a wide variety of ways to start a conversation with our neighbors, friends, relatives, and acquaintances. These forms express the degree of closeness or social remoteness that we maintain with our partner (Gallois, Ogay, & Giles, 2005; Giles & Gasiorek, 2013). The choice of how we address the other is both a reflection of the relationship we want to have and the social definition of the type of situation we are in (Giles, Willemyns, Gallois, & Anderson, 2007). For example, depending on the interlocutor and the situation, we can address our interlocutor formally or familiarly, marking distance or not. Such markers are cultural and socially well defined, but their improper use can cause communication problems (Coupland, Giles, & Wiemann, 1991).

Adapting to others is an essential part of interpersonal interaction and social success. We do not speak to our colleagues the same way we speak to our partners or to our parents the same way we speak to our children; rather, we adapt communication to the present circumstances (Giles & Gasiorek, 2013; Giles et al., 2007). The Communication Accommodation Theory (CAT) developed by Howard Giles and colleagues (Gallois et al., 2005; Gasiorek, 2013; Gasiorek & Giles, 2012, 2013; Giles et al., 2007; Shepard, Giles, & Le Poire, 2001), influenced by the social identity perspective, analyzes communication as "something more" than an exchange of individual linguistic behavior. It explores the different ways in which we settle our communication, our motivations for doing so, and their consequences. Communication is not only an exchange of information on facts, ideas, and emotions (often called "referential communication"); membership in salient social groups during an interaction is negotiated through the accommodation process.

The dynamic variation of away and approach communicative behavior between interactants is called accommodation. We use certain strategies to adapt our verbal and nonverbal behavior to express the degree of interest in maintaining a particular communication, and these are discussed next (Gallois et al., 2005; Giles et al., 2007).

Accommodative convergence and divergence

We use convergence when we want to approach our interlocutor. The purpose is to extend the communication, achieve a greater degree of closeness (Coupland, Coupland, Giles, & Henwood, 1988), and promote a relaxed interaction (Gallois et al., 2005). When two people effectively converge, they engage with each other and find each other more attractive, predictable, and easy to understand. Convergence is a means of signaling attraction to, and/or seeking the approval of, the other person. Social power is an important component of CAT: Salespersons, interviewees, and those in socially inferior roles will converge more respectively to clients, interviewers, and those in socially dominant roles and vice versa. An important feature of CAT is that people converge not so much toward where others are located in a physical sense but where they *believe* them to be. In addition, people can be accommodating to where others expect (or wish) them to be (Giles & Gasiorek, 2013). This might occur in romantic situations where males take on more macho stances (e.g., speaking with a deeper pitch) while females might sound more feminine (e.g., softer tones—a tactic called "speech complementary").

However, we negatively evaluate any attempt at convergence used in mockery, to tease others, to ruin their reputation, and so forth (Major, Sawyer, & Kunstman, 2013). For example, in a workshop, the boss can say the following to a woman in front of the whole group to discredit her: "Maybe lately you haven't provided all we expected, but it's great to have you in the meetings, no one makes the coffee as good as you." At first, the boss's comment may seem to be an attempt at convergence, but quickly we realize that the comment will draw attention to any further comments the woman may make, enhancing their sensitivity and highlighting a female stereotype.

In situations where a "them" versus "us" stance is unlikely to be perceived, women and men tend to converge in their communication, thus reducing gender differences. If the intergender context were not friendly and personal enough, divergence could arise (Shepard, Giles, & Le Poire, 2001). Giles and Smith (1979) argued that in situations where group membership is salient, speech divergence (shifting the language style to make it dissimilar to the interlocutor's) reflects a group identity maintenance process, that is, a strategy to mark oneself as distinct from another social group. For example, a woman wanting to emphasize her femininity may exaggerate the features associated with women's language in a mixed-gender interaction (Weatherall & Gallois, 2005). In her conversation, she might use more diminutives and a sweeter tone than she would use normally.

We use the divergence (nonaccommodation strategy) when we want to emphasize the social distance (see Gasiorek & Giles, 2012). However, the levels of awareness of divergence appear to be higher than those of convergence. That is, we converge toward others, in a more automatic or peripheral mode; however, we diverge from the interlocutor in a more cognitive way, in a way that is more aware. Individually, the divergence may serve to accentuate differences or to show contempt for the other. At the group level, the divergence can be used to emphasize a valuable in-group identity (Gasiorek & Giles, 2012, 2013). This may threaten the male in-group as women enter areas of managerial responsibility within the company and strengthen intergroup barriers, thus putting into operation nonaccommodative strategies. No doubt an influential factor is the gender schema of each person (Bem, 1981). In fact, it has been found that men who conceived gender less traditionally converged more toward women than those who had a more conservative schema on gender (Hoyt, 2012; Hoyt & Burnette, 2013).

Analysts have shown that informal conversations between men at work are based heavily on familiar themes of their lives, such as team sports, mainly football, cars, video games, technology, politics, work and business, and male sexuality (Bird & Rothon, 2011). Talking about these issues may represent a divergent strategy by men, playing a role in creating and marking intergroup barriers in two ways. First, even when men do not intentionally discuss these issues, the conversations can serve as a reminder to women that they lack such experiences, thus placing them into an external group (out-group), the "otherness," compared to the male in-group. But this can also be a tactic men use when they consciously want to remind women to stay out of their territory (Williams & Giles, 1978).

Studies have found that in situations where men and women interact, men use sexual innuendo and dirty jokes more than they do when they are in a group of only men. As demonstrated, these forms of communication are strategies men use to highlight their superior capabilities and skills of leadership and authority with respect to women (Popovich & Warren, 2010). The lack of accommodation by the higher status group is a strategy to defend the privileges of that group (male), barring the out-group (females) from sharing those privileges.

Another factor, perhaps the best documented, perpetuating gender inequality in the field of senior management, is the almost absolute restriction of women into the casual networks of support and "in-group" patronage (favoritism) exerted by the "old boys' club." These causal social networks are retained by men and act as a communication strategy of divergence. It has been found that informal social networks play a central role in career success. For example, in a study of senior businesswomen in the Boston area, 78% of them viewed casual networking as "helping to a great extent" in their development as leaders, and 70% cited informal mentoring relationships (Manuel, Shefte, & Swiss, 1999, p. 11). Roth (2007, 2009) also found that women's competition was seen as suspect and was closely monitored. In addition, Roth discussed the strategies women used to successfully overcome intergroup dynamics with men. Some developed individual strategies, such as finding powerful mentors (Cleveland, Stockdale, & Murphy, 2000), to work in a unique area; some demonstrated endurance in facing these situations; and others sought different occupations where it was more likely that their work would be objectively evaluated.

Employees need access to informal networks to learn the requirements and procedures that lead to job success; these informal networking situations occur mostly outside of formal structures (Roth, 2009). Through these informal communication networks, professionals can find mentors to help them in developing their careers and to be considered and treated as full members of the organization by their peers (Rhode & Williams, 2007). When men, whether consciously or unconsciously, exclude women from these informal networks (Bird & Rothon, 2011), not only are the women being denied important opportunities to enhance their careers, but it is also a way of subtly reinforcing in-group boundaries (Giles, Coupland, & Coupland, 1991), thus excluding women as a labor out-group. This is a clear divergence of communicative behavior at the group level.

Social activities can also be organized around activities that are traditionally male, such as sporting events, or are held in places that usually do not include women, such as private clubs and country clubs with facilities "for men only" (Eagly & Carli, 2007; Hirigoyen, 2001). In addition, women may not be invited to join a group of male colleagues for dinner or drinks. Sometimes the exclusion is indirect since, despite being invited, family care responsibilities, assigned to the female gender, prevent or hinder women's participation in these informal areas after working hours. Eagly and Carli (2007) noted the following: "Those who create social capital through good relationships with colleagues, both within and outside their organization, are more likely to rise to positions of authority" (p. 173).

In turn, men may not be willing to develop mentoring relationships with women for fear that their colleagues could attribute a sexual component to the relationship or because they do not expect that women can succeed in management positions. In addition, men may interpret the efforts of women to participate in informal networks as indicative of sexual interest and not as gestures of friendship or business (Cárdenas et al., 2014; Eagly & Carli, 2007).

Thus, the inner and outer circles of contacts and support from superiors and colleagues are important resources for employment success, and the lack of this support is a good predictor of job stress. Because men tend to have better access than women to these informal networks, this means that not only can men climb stairs more easily, but they also do so without the stress of feeling excluded, an experience that usually leads women to give up higher positions more often than men.

Overaccommodation and gender

The intrinsic characteristics of the communication agents (differences in age, social status, economics, etc.) also find differences in the use of accommodation strategies. For example, people with higher status are less accommodating to their interlocutor, while those with lower status are more accommodating (Gasiorek & Giles, 2012). When we talk to very old people, because of our negative stereotypes associated with age, such as hearing and interpretation problems, we usually employ a significant amount of "overaccommodation" or patronizing talk (for an overview, see Giles & Gasiorek, 2011; Giles et al., 1991; Giles, Davis, Gasiorek, & Giles, 2014; Giles & Williams, 1994; Giles, Zwang-Weissman, & Hajek, 2004; Viladot & Giles, 1998), resulting in hyper-simplified speech (Hummert & Ryan, 2001; Viladot & Giles, 1998). Overaccommodation is defined as overcompensation in terms of interactional adjustment (Ryan & Bannister, 2009).

Therefore, we overaccommodate when a speaker is exceeding or surpassing the level of communicative behavior necessary for successful interaction (Viladot & Giles, 1998; Ytsma & Giles, 1997). In this vein, Brown, Giles, and Thakerar (1985) found that slow speech is considered unfavorable and can be attributed to benevolent and overprotective reasons (for example, trying to explain difficult issues to women). In intergenerational meetings, forms of paternalistic communication when trying to help have been considered more polite and appropriate than the patronizing speech attributed to negative reasons (e.g., disapproval, exercising authority; Giles & Williams, 1994; Viladot & Giles, 1998).

In the workplace, nicknames and other forms of patronizing speech (overaccommodation communication) serve to trivialize the contributions of professional women. For example, let us imagine Rosa, a young executive, who just graduated from a prestigious U.S. university. During a department meeting at her company, a veteran colleague called her "cute" and "babe" without anyone objecting. Or there is the example of a male calling the secretarial staff at his company "office girls," which questions their maturity, capacity, and competence and may serve to legitimize the low wages of female secretaries and their lack of promotion opportunities. Describing a female manager as "the iron lady" or "the slut" can be a means to marginalize women who may be perceived as having excessive or inadequate power in the organization (Bird & Rhoton, 2011; Popovich & Warren, 2010). Comments related to a woman's sex appeal, clothing, or marital status in response to her professional presentation point out to other listeners that her message is irrelevant and need not be taken seriously in deliberative processes (Eagly & Carli, 2007). Furthermore, the practice of apologizing to a woman before using obscenities serves to mark her as the "other" and to imply that she is weak and unable to properly cope with her colleagues (i.e., treating her as a child and not as an "adult"; Barreto et al., 2004).

Vescio, Gervais, Snyder, and Hoover (2005) defined patronizing behavior as a form of sexism that implies a positive side, such as high praise, and a negative side, such as devalued competition. Benevolent sexism includes three subcomponents: protective paternalism (e.g., the belief that women should be protected and served by men), complementary gender differentiation (e.g., the belief that women are the "best" sex and have special qualities as a superior moral sensibility that few men possess), and heterosexual intimacy (e.g., the belief that women play off the romantic needs of men). Although these three representations seem subjectively positive, exposure to the condescending behaviors resulting from these three subcomponents can undermine cognitive performance (Becker & Wright, 2011; Dardenne, Dumont, & Bollier, 2007; Vescio et al., 2005). Moreover, the "positive" vision implicit in benevolent sexism may be available only to women who behave in accordance with the requirements and denied to women who are dissatisfied with the status quo, such as feminists. Therefore, presenting women as wonderful but childish, incompetent, needing men to protect them, which is the strategy described in the CAT overprotection, justifies gender inequality (Jost & Elsbach, 2001).

Thus, the strategy of overaccommodation may promote gender inequality by increasing the tolerance of discrimination against women, where hostile sexism would likely be recognized and provoke resistance from women (Becker & Wright, 2011). Also, overprotection leads women to counternegotiate individually and interpersonally and is very unlikely to challenge the system as a whole (Glick & Rudman, 2010). Subtle forms of discrimination against women are more difficult to recognize and resist. If men discriminate subtly, in friendly ways that are not necessarily perceived by women, it is likely that women will respond in a convergent mode with kindness, becoming more submissive, thereby unknowingly strengthening male dominance (Moya, Glick, Expósito, de Lemus, & Hart, 2007). The result of this ambivalent behavior, covert discrimination, is that women are discriminated without realizing it, often without objection, believing that the men are being kind. Moreover, these overaccommodation behaviors (by men against women) implicitly involve an attack on women's dignity and self-esteem (Kaufman & Grace, 2011).

How can we counter these overprotective and paternalistic behaviors that diminish women's gender identity? Responding to them assertively is an effective strategy, but we must remember that men who are overprotective in this manner are not always acting with the intention to harm women. Some men are fully convinced that they are to help the women. So, if women aggressively and assertively face the overprotective behavior of men, they may be attacking the identity (self-esteem) of those men who believe their behavior is supporting and helping women. Ryan and Bannister (2009) identified a strategy called *appreciative* that women can use when receiving overaccommodations from men. This strategy is a response to humor. Through humor, the identity and self-esteem of women, along with men, are not affected (as they are when women respond to men in an aggressive or even assertive way).

Let us take an example of each of the three possible responses to attitude overaccommodations by men. We will start with the appreciative response (based on a humorous attitude).

A male production manager and a female planning director of a company are in the lobby waiting for the elevator to their offices. When the elevator arrives, the production manager gives way to the planning director, so she enters the elevator first. On the way up, the production manager says, "It is evident that the planning department is headed by a woman. You notice that the details are cared for; count on me for any assistance you may need. I will be happy to help." She, sensing the condescending and overaccommodated tone, replies with a smile: "Hi, man, as it is offered, I would appreciate if you take my gym bag; between the computer and the bag, I hold a heavy burden." The director takes his cue and picks up her bag.

An assertive response might be this: "In my department, we try to be the most professionally competent. To plan effectively, we need to hold regular meetings with the production department." An aggressive response might be this: "I take care of everything rather than just the minor details. And, by the way, I would like to talk to you, because I've found great imbalances in the production department, which does not pay attention to the planning instructions we send to you."

Another strategy of nonaccommodation, besides divergence and overaccommodation, is *maintenance*. It is defined as the absence of adaptive adjustments, that is, people maintain their communication style by "default," without taking into account the characteristics of their interlocutors. However, it may be a strategic statement about the preservation of social identity, in particular, intergroup contexts (Giles, Reid, & Harwood, 2010), and, as such, is an active statement of one not wanting to adapt (see Sachdev & Bourhis, 2005). This strategy is particularly interesting to consider in the context of organizations.

To finish, let us talk about the strategy of *subaccommodation* (Gasiorek & Giles, 2012). For example, participants attend to their interlocutor's knowledge of, or sophistication about, a particular topic that is being discussed. Supposedly, communicatively competent speakers should, for example, attenuate the complexity of their speech and reduce jargon, thereby promoting comprehension, coherence, and clarity. Obviously, the goal here is to establish mutual ground with an interlocutor, yet it is quite easy to overlook another's lack of understanding and "underaccommodate" (Gasiorek & Giles; 2012; Gasiorek, 2013) that person—a stance that is often interpreted as insensitive and egotistic (Williams & Nussbaum, 2001).

It is likely that women in high levels of an organization with a male majority have lost track of the number of times they have experienced underaccommodation and maintenance strategies. Imagine a professional woman who is part of a company with an overwhelming male majority. During a heated discussion—speaking clearly and out loud—she says something that no one appears to hear. A man repeats it minutes, maybe seconds later, to accolades and group discussion. Or, for example, she is participating in a group interview of a candidate. When he answers the questions, he looks directly at the men in the room and never or rarely looks at her—even when she is the one to ask the question. He asks questions of the men only, even when she clearly is the most appropriate person to address.

Imagine now a woman at a party. The topic of physics (or cosmology, or data science) comes up. A man she has just met proceeds to describe to her a *New York Times* article he has read on the subject. She says that she has a PhD in this subject and is an expert. Instead of using this as an opportunity to ask *her* questions and learn from *her*, he continues to talk about what *he* knows. He turns to her boyfriend—who isn't a physicist or a data scientist—and asks him questions about the topic.

Here is another example: A professional woman keeps trying to participate in a male-dominated discussion, but she is repeatedly interrupted and talked over. The only way to be heard is to interrupt back, talk over people herself, or call out the behavior and ask others to let her finish. All of these options feel overly aggressive and make her uncomfortable, so she ends up remaining silent, not contributing to the discussion.

Of course, there are plenty of men who do not behave this way and many conversations that don't go this way—but there are many that do. Interrupting, ignoring, over-talking, and dismissing also happen as the result of differences in class and social status, but research shows that gender is a dominant factor in this dynamic (Eagly & Carli, 2007). It may be difficult for a professional women subgroup to maintain a positive social identity, as these women are constantly bombarded with verbal and nonverbal messages that are devalued and unimportant.

We have shown that women managers endure more pressure than men managers in workplaces dominated by men; stressors include the following: infrequent feedback and communication, less access to training, less control (ideas are not heard; there is less opportunity to participate in decision making), difficulties in maintaining a healthy work-life balance, job insecurity, lack of credit for achievements, isolation and/or lack of support from others, and inequalities or lack of transparency in remuneration and benefits.

Perhaps of all of these factors, the most important is control (or lack of it). Women feeling that they have little influence in decisions or events (especially those that could potentially have a direct and negative impact on them) is one of the main causes of stress in the workplace. Also, taking control is one of the most effective stress management strategies (Cleveland et al., 2000; Kellerman & Rhode, 2007). Is there a sense in which having control can be a positive pressure? There it is, and it generally takes the form of responsibility. As men, women who seek out and succeed in senior management positions welcome this responsibility because of the implicit positive challenge pressure. They like to feel stretched and they feel sufficiently confident in their ability to cope with the pressure the position brings—although confidence is very complex and the best leaders experience doubts at times (Cleveland et al., 2000).

Related to the other factors mentioned, one of the reasons many of them are potentially stressful is because they take away the women's ability to influence events and actively manage the situation to avoid a negative outcome for themselves, their colleagues, and even their families. Take the example of infrequent feedback and communication, which entails stress and implies that senior managers (men) do not consider women when communicating; they do not think that women need feedback to improve their performance, although they believe men do (Bird & Rhoton, 2011; Bosak & Sczesny, 2011; Kellerman & Rhode, 2007). As everyone knows, "information is power," and without it, women are disadvantaged in their attempts to meet objectives, advance their careers, establish a secure future for themselves and their families, and so on. The issue is similar when women are troubled by a lack of transparency in remuneration and benefits—given transparency, women feel better equipped to judge whether the situation is unfair and to take action by arguing their case or looking for another job.

In summary, we think that one of the most serious problems that women leaders face are the nonaccommodations of the organization in its various manifestations; we are referring to the lack of involvement of the subgroup of women leaders, who are not represented or are discriminated when trying to enter senior management positions.

Summary

In this chapter, we have shown how communicative processes underlie issues that are not normally addressed when studying organizational communication, which is essential if one wants to minimize communicative issues between the genders. We have relied on CAT, one of the most complete and heuristic theories of interpersonal and intergroup communication.

Several studies conducted in the United States and Europe showed little female presence in organizational management. Knowing what happens within organizations in regard to their level of communication and their processes is essential in preventing gender discrimination.

In general, it seems that the male culture dominates the executive offices of organizations ("boys' club"), which ensures that the most important tasks are conducted by men. It appears that there is a global culture, and it is clearly masculine. The shadow of Don Draper of *Mad Men* is still present.

How can an organization change the status quo that discriminates against women leaders? Depending on the subjective perception of gender relationships, situations in the workplace can be considered in either terms of cooperation or competition, as opportunities for personal enrichment or as threats.

Let's start with the issue of contact in the organizational field between established groups by reason of gender, men and women. Can contact between them improve the intergroup situation?

· 2 0 ·

INTERGROUP CONTACT, GENDER, AND LEADERSHIP

The intergroup research that has been conducted thus far seems to show that one of the central characteristics of workplace discrimination against female leaders is the existing unfavorable attitudes toward them. Such attitudes are sustained by social ideologies as well as, among other factors, a general lack of knowledge about female leaders (Pettigrew & Tropp, 2011; van Laar, Levin, & Sidanius, 2008). There is a relatively small number of women in traditionally male-dominated industries. When contact between men and women is first established in these types of industries, it creates anxiety, especially in men, due to the negative consequences that this can bring about to the individual as well as to the privileged group (Stephan & Stephan, 2000). One of the biggest barriers that needs to be overcome is perhaps intergroup anxiety; it is therefore critical to be able to obtain information about individuals from the out-group (Stephan & Stephan, 2000; Turner, Hewstone, & Voci, 2007; Turner, Hewstone, Voci, & Vonofakou, 2008). This anxiety has at least four origins: (a) the sensation that one's existence, well-being, political power, organizational power, and so forth, within the group, are being threatened; (b) the perception that individuals from the out-group are a threat to the values, beliefs, ethics, and norms of the in-group; (c) the perception that one's I is being threatened (e.g., fear of rejection), which is felt during interactions within the group; and (d) a fear of anxiety within the group (whether it has already been experienced, is imagined, or anticipated) based on negative stereotypes of life outside the group. For example, a man who has never had one may react to the prospect of a new female boss with more insecurity than if he gets a new male boss. However, under the right circumstances, contact may reduce anxiety and intergroup attitudes and relations (Brown & Hewstone, 2005; Pettigrew & Tropp, 2006, 2011; Turner et al., 2007; Turner et al., 2008). Research shows that the level of identification within the group alleviates anxiety and threatens perception in a contact situation. For individuals who strongly identify with the group, threats are more likely to mediate the relationship between contact and positive attitudes.

According to the contact hypothesis, contact should be effective only under certain conditions (Allport, 1954). Contact should be prolonged and involve a cooperative activity rather than a casual purposeless interaction. It must occur within the framework of official and institutional support. For example, the European Union aims, through affirmative action programs, to ensure that by 2025, 30% of CEOs are women. Although legislation against discrimination or equal opportunities alone is not enough to abolish prejudice, it provides a social environment that is conducive to the emergence of more tolerant social practices. Additionally, contact should involve people of equal status, such as colleagues. Contact with people of a different status is more likely to confirm stereotypes, further stabilizing existing prejudice.

There is a wide body of evidence that supports Allport's (1954) central idea that cooperation, shared objectives, status equality, and the support of local authorities and norms are key preconditions for a positive change in intergroup attitudes. The meta-analysis of Pettigrew and Tropp (2006) showed that contact can positively affect attitude. However, there are certain critical issues that are linked specifically with the way contact can affect (see Pettigrew & Tropp, 2011) the group of women who legitimately wish to access positions of power. One of these issues is the process of generalization of the attitudes to women as a group.

The results from various investigations (see Pettigrew & Tropp, 2011; Tropp & Pettigrew, 2004, 2005) have given considerable support to the basic notion that contact between groups can be effective in reducing prejudice, and it can also change attitudes toward groups in general, not just toward individuals from the out-group who we are in contact with. Therefore, attitude changes toward a female leader due to sustained contact with her in the workplace might entail a general attitude change in the group toward female leaders as a whole. However, it is still necessary to keep in mind that, as has been noted before, this can only happen under certain conditions. Intergroup contact is by definition a communicative event, and specific communication processes might yield different outcomes (Harwood & Joyce, 2012). Therefore, it is entirely possible that the opposite results: Contact might heighten the perception of the male in-group of being threatened by females in the out-group (Tropp 2006), putting into motion intergroup strategies of communicative divergence (Giles & Gasiorek, 2013). It would seem that group awareness needs to be relatively high for attitudes toward an out-group member to translate to attitudes about the out-group as a whole. Additionally, the specific out-group member (e.g., a professional women) must be seen in some way as typical or representative of the group for generalization to occur. When out-group members are perceived in some way as atypical of their group, they will likely be treated as exceptions and thus will not be influential in determining more general intergroup attitudes. This phenomenon is known as *subtyping* (Brown & Hewstone, 2005).

Supporting this idea, the investigation on intergroup contact indicates that intergroup attitudes due to gender are not simply a matter of ignorance or lack of familiarity between male and female leaders; rather, they reflect a real conflict of interest between male and female leaders. This is often sustained by the existence of social categories. Ironically, it has also been found that contact reduces the wish for social change in groups that suffer from discrimination (Harwood & Joyce, 2012). In short, the contact that is most likely to generalize is not the contact that is most likely to yield positive attitudinal outcomes.

Recent work has examined *self-disclosure* as an important communication variable in this context. Individuals whose intergroup relationships are high in self-disclosure have less negative attitudes about out-group members than those with more superficial intergroup relationships. They have intergroup contact that is more satisfactory and friendly (Soliz & Harwood, 2006). (Regarding gender, we can relate these findings with the ones found by Hoyt, 2012, and Hoyt & Burnette, 2013, cited in another chapter). Self-disclosure develops depth in relationships and reveals more detailed information about individuals. This allows for a more developed cognition on individuals in the out-group. It also helps refute harmful stereotypes and allows the group to be perceived as heterogeneous and diverse from the out-group (Harwood & Joyce, 2012).

A promising variant of the interpersonal contact hypothesis called *the effect of the extension of contact* has been proposed by Wright, Aron, and Tropp (2002). They suggested that intergroup attitudes can improve if people see or have knowledge of satisfying intergroup friendships between others (e.g., if my friend Pedro has close friends in the out-group, it is likely that the out-group is not as bad as I think it is). This can happen because people of the same group have a common identity that links them and allows them to include the other person in the self, meaning that it lets individuals develop a degree of intersubjectivity that allows them to perceive others as themselves (Wright et al., 2002).

Let us now turn to a promising line of research on intergroup contact. We have seen how, under certain circumstances, groups polarize when they perceive that their identities are being threatened. Research shows that if we can get closer, cognitively, to the "other," many of the barriers that hinder positive intergroup contact would vanish.

The perspective of the other

If we could adopt the perspective of other people and perceive the world as they do, we would be less likely to harbor negative and harmful attitudes toward others and more likely to behave prosocially toward them. Currently, there is evidence that adopting another's perspective can improve intergroup attitudes (Pettigrew & Tropp, 2011; Vescio, Sechrist, & Paolucci, 2003), which does not necessarily entail paternalism or overaccommodation.

Regardless, the way in which we act with "others" is configured in part by the way we imagine them. Still, the descriptions of these images prove our difficulty in describing other people and everything they entail and experience. This is true regardless of whether we are describing a friend or someone we barely know, although the problem is worsened when the person is a stranger. Discrimination against female leaders drives the search for individual solutions in organizational settings, so that these discriminations no longer take place. Some solutions could entail a frame of "generosity" that entrusts men with the important task of spontaneously "imagining" the female leaders in their workplace and to do so on a daily basis. On the contrary, alternative solutions could try and solve the problem of the "otherness" of female leaders through planned actions. If this second solution were implemented, it is highly likely that individual spontaneous behaviors would produce positive results toward female leaders (see Harwood & Joyce, 2012). But if planned solutions are not implemented, daily practice and spontaneous generosity, although praiseworthy, will have little effect; that is, they will not be very effective and will also not be generalized toward female leaders as a whole.

Imagining others has multiple difficulties; for example, we can be in front of a female leader who is disoriented and stressed due to systematic workplace discrimination and not realize it. The ease with which the male outgroup ignores, whether consciously or unconsciously (non-accommodation strategies), that the well-being of female leaders is called into question is what facilitates continuous discrimination. There is thus a circular relationship between the commission of discrimination and its consequences on the well-being and health of women in positions of power and the problem of otherness. How far does the ability to imagine reach? When we speak about imagination during our daily conversations, we usually believe that it has a higher capacity than other, more usual sensations. However, if we try to close our eyes and focus on the imaged face of a friend, and then open our eyes, we realize that our imagined friend lacks the vitality and vivacity of the friend we were basing it on. And what we do not do well singularly, we do even worse in plural. The human capacity to stigmatize and discriminate against the outgroup has always been bigger than we imagine it. We could perhaps even say that the capacity to discriminate against people (with its negative effects on the psychological well-being of people) is extremely large precisely because our capacity to imagine it is small.

Recategorization

The model of Gaertner's common group identity (Gaertner & Dovidio, 2000) suggests that if people from the out-group that served as the basis of comparison can be stimulated to be reclassified as people of the same group, intergroup attitudes, by definition, not only improve but even disappear. This process, however, as we see later, has great limits and is not always feasible. Promoting contact between men and women in the context of organizations seems to be, at first, the least discriminatory and prejudiced way to approach intergender relationships; it would imply completely ignoring the differences between both groups. This is the "melting pot" policy, or the so-called policies of assimilation, in which all of the social groups are treated as equals. However, the "melting pot" is not at all a melting pot but rather a pot in which women will try to assimilate into the dominant out-group, thus ceasing to exist and yet continuing to be discriminated against. We have spoken about this previously.

The alternative to assimilation is pluralism (see Sachdev & Bourhis, 2005), the acceptance of diversification. This approach directs the attention to the reality of intergender diversity and responds to it in an effort to improve negative attitudes and redirect disadvantages, at the same time that it preserves the integrity of the differences that exist in female leaders and their mode of leadership. This approach attempts to reach positive relationships between men and women and harmonious intergroup relationships between groups of both genders (Hornsey & Hogg, 2000).

However, some recent events also indicate that diversity would need to be implemented with extreme care to ensure that no hidden conflicts remain. The efficiency of providing a superordinate goal has been confirmed by other studies (Gaertner & Dovidio, 2000; Hogg & Giles, 2012). Organizations are the perfect natural environment to observe the effect that a superior order identity (e.g., the company) has on the relationship between the subgroups. A superordinate goal that is particularly effective will result in resistance to the threat shared by a common enemy. This is the base that alliances can use to temporarily improve relationships between individuals who were previously adversaries. However, there is an important requisite. The superordinate goal will not reduce intergroup conflict if the groups do not achieve the end goal. Unsuccessful cooperation toward achieving a superordinate goal seems to worsen intergroup and intergender relationships only when the fault can be attributed, whether correctly or incorrectly, to the actions of the female out-group. If there is enough external justification and the female out-group is not blamed, intergroup relationships have a tendency to improve (Hogg & Giles, 2012).

One final point about the relationship of superordinate goals and social harmony can be quickly understood by an analysis of zero-sum and not-zero-sum objectives (see, e.g., the chicken game, game theory, decision theory, the prisoner's dilemma, strategic dominance, the strategy game, the tragedy of the commons, and the zero-sum game). When two groups consider their goal relationships as zero-sum, they are classifying the relationship as competitive: If they get a lot, we get little. The pie to be divided is limited; therefore, others' actions frustrate our goals. This is the case, for example, if men say that each working woman takes away a man's job.

When two groups consider their goal relationships as not-zero-sum, they are classifying those relationships as cooperative: If they get a lot, we get a lot. The pie can become bigger if we work together; therefore, others' actions help us achieve our goals. For example, this is the case if members of a steering committee think that if each of them does an excellent job, the company's profits will grow.

These relationships that start from the establishment of superordinate goals are subject to ideology and rhetoric—zero-sum rhetoric associated with sexism and prejudice toward women. Other men believe that the integration of female leaders will have positive consequences because women bring abilities, energy, and enthusiasm, as well as additional benefits—not-zero-sum rhetoric that is associated with positive attitudes toward women and female leadership.

In this sense, data provided recently by Harwood (2014) clearly suggest that the effects of contact experiences on specific attitudes are tied to context. Starting with the results obtained by Harwood about gay people in the military, we could say that attitudes about women in upper management are tied more closely to the quality of contact with men in the workplace than contact with them outside the workplace—even when those women contacts outside the workplace are perhaps close friends and family members. Attitudes about women in upper management are tied to the quality of experiences with women in those roles. Higher quality contact may reduce the feeling of being threatened, which in turn improves intergroup attitudes (Harwood, 2014; Tropp, 2006).

Summary

In summary, we can say that optimum contact between male and female leaders can reduce intergroup prejudices. Such is the case particularly when the contact is planned specifically to obtain a positive result. Contact by itself does not have the ability to change negative attitudes toward a relevant outgroup. Thus, the question is not whether contact reduces prejudice but rather how it needs to be structured for the contact to be effective. Contact by itself does not represent anything, given that, as we have seen, it can even go so far as to increase prejudices and discrimination between groups. That is to say, the contact will be positive if it is structured to be positive.

Indeed, given the objective differences between social groups, it is sometimes impossible and counterproductive to deny the psychological boundaries between in-groups and out-groups. However, a situation that promotes interaction through customization or a common social identity seems to be a critical condition to disconfirm stereotypes and facilitate intergroup friendship. However, if the optimal contact occurs only at the interpersonal level, intergroup attitudes remain intact. This apparent paradox has been addressed by Pettigrew and colleagues (cited in Pettigrew & Tropp, 2011) in their longitudinal model of intergroup contact.

Obviously, the use of intergeneric contact as a means to improve communication between genders in the areas of professional liability depends largely on extrinsic variables to the situation of optimal contact. Some of these variables are linked to the particular characteristics of the participants in the interaction, including expectations and past experiences. Aspects such as intergroup anxiety or the importance attached to intergroup contact are just some interindividual variables that may moderate or mediate the effects of contact on intergeneric attitudes. Finally, we cannot forget that essential conditions to foster common cause intergroup relations are given by the social structure that determines the relation between groups and their members. A deep transformation of the social order is essential for the development and maintenance of solidarity and intergroup harmony.

· 21 ·

LEADERSHIP AND GENDER IDENTITY IN ORGANIZATIONS

The workplace plays a critical role in the development and enactment of people's social identity. Organizations are "minicultures" that provide people with a sense of self and belonging (Haslam, 2004). More specifically, organizations contribute to the construction of people's identities in at least two specific ways: by placing people in particular roles and by developing norms that regulate how members interact with others (Morton, Wright, Peters, Reynolds, & Haslam, 2012). Through these processes, organizations create leaders and subordinates (Haslam, Reicher, & Platow, 2011).

In spite of the important entry of women into the workplace and despite the growing interest of many professional women in working in traditionally male professions, gender has not been considered as an important variable in the communications among male and female professionals in these fields. There still exists glaring occupational gender segregation; many occupations are dominated by either one gender or the other. Gender segregation is a taken-for-granted feature of the workplace (Castaño & Webster, 2014).

Research on how businesses operate and theories on organizational structure have barely considered how gender in the workplace can be used to interpret social realities. Moreover, the perspective of examining gender roles the workplace is overshadowed by the emphasis on optimizing business management through leadership. Can we speak here of nonaccommodation strategies? We believe so. There are many studies that examine the social-psychological and sociostructural factors barring women from the top positions. In addition, the elements that hinder their access to higher level positions also lead women away from more traditionally male career trajectories (Haslam, 2004). How could the social identity and communication perspectives shed light on why women frequently encounter a glass ceiling in an organizational environment?

Organizations are socially structured and distinct entities. Their effective functioning depends on something more than the specific qualities of individuals. Social identity theorists have highlighted the critical role that the sense of shared belonging plays in the group in order to structure organizational dynamics and create the conditions for success or failure (Morton et al., 2012). This sense of shared identity creates effective channels of communication, thus contributing to the success of the organization; however, in this success, female employees are often forgotten, especially those employed in areas traditionally dominated by men. The effect of social identity (i.e., feeling like part of a group) on communication is not only motivational (as in, not only determined by who we are willing to communicate with) but also contextual (e.g., the context determines how we communicate). Communication is a social process. Effective communication is characterized by mutual understanding and influence that encourage appropriate actions (Gasiorek, 2013; Gasiorek & Giles, 2012, 2013; Giles & Gasiorek, 2013). It also depends on the relationships between people and not exclusively on the words used. But the aforementioned people belong to groups, and one of the most important groups to consider is that created by gender (Palomares, 2012). Each gender group is associated with stereotypes and has certain roles prescribed in society. In traditionally male work environments, male gender is afforded high status, while the status of women in the same environment is questionable. For this reason, it is extremely important to keep in mind the communication processes between gender groups. We now explore some of the relational forces shaping the flow of communication between genders in predominantly male organizations, focusing especially on those that contribute to the overall success of the organization (Morton et al., 2012; Haslam, Postmes, & Ellemers, 2003).

Recall that the self-concept is multifaceted, and both personal and social identity are considered equally true aspects of the self (Turner et al., 1987). The context determines whether personal or social identity is salient. But when social identity is salient, individual thought, feeling, and action are regulated by norms and values associated with group membership (e.g., specific in-group rules; Hogg & Giles, 2012). Since the rules are shared representations, situations that lead people to define themselves in terms of membership to a common group also result in behavior that is coordinated in relation to other group members (see also, Gaertner & Dovidio, 2000). This is the psychological mechanism that makes group life possible. In addition, people are motivated to achieve or maintain a positive self-concept and uniqueness (Tajfel, 1982).

When situations define the self solely in terms of individuality (e.g., when personal identity is salient), people are likely to engage in an internal dialogue to understand the world around them and their place in it. However, when the self is socially defined, this dialogue becomes external. Under these conditions, people will interact with others to answer any questions they may have about the world. Other people are included in their concept of self as a result of shared group membership and therefore are an important and valuable source of information and understanding. For this to happen, people must be willing to share information and be equally willing to pay attention to what others say. We have already seen that this is not what happens in communication between genders in traditionally male work environments. That is, communication significantly revolves around people's motivation, values, and group norms. The social identity approach draws our attention to the fact that these motivations (e.g., to share information, to listen carefully, and to act on others' information) are socially structured (Giles, 2012; Mulac, Giles, Bradac, & Palomares, 2013).

Although the two genders are generally less willing to share information with out-group people than with in-group people, this trend is amplified when they perceive the relationship between both gender groups as competitive rather than cooperative (Mulac et al., 2013). Women working in traditionally male domains represent a quintessential example of such a situation. Think of the "old boys' clubs" where privileged information is circulated and women are excluded.

A study by McGarty, Haslam, Hutchinson, and Turner (1994) established that people are more easily persuaded by communications that originate from a member of the in-group than by a member of the out-group, even if the message content is identical. One of the reasons for this is that people pay more attention to messages that originate from the in-group (Morton et al., 2012).

Therefore, as long as the message itself is convincing, people are more likely to be influenced by in-group sources. One consequence of this for women is that being influential requires more than just creating a compelling message containing strong arguments. First and foremost, to be persuasive, it is necessary to have a public that is willing to listen to what you have to say (Muñoz, 2011). It is more likely that this will occur when communicators share with their audience membership in a salient group. So we can infer that professional women in traditionally male work environments have little influence and struggle to be heard (Eagly & Carli, 2007).

Supporting this point, recent research on leadership suggests that to be able to influence others, leaders must engage first in acts of corporate identity to cultivate a sense of shared identity with and among aspiring followers (Gaertner & Dovidio, 2000; Haslam, Postmes, & Ellemers, 2003; Hogg & Giles, 2012). More specifically, leaders need to work to create and maintain a coherent sense of "we" and "us" and also to define what "us" means (and what it does not mean) for followers (Hogg & Giles, 2012; Steffens, Haslam, Stephen, Platow, Fransen, Yang. et al., 2014). In this case, the use of "we" certainly helps (Haslam, Reicher, & Platow, 2011). But also, shared in-group membership provides a basis for trust that makes it easier for people to accept forms of communication more complex and potentially threatening, such as negative comments or criticism.

Communication between genders within the organization will be more effective when it is framed in a global sense of organizational identity and all people identify with this collective self-definition. To quote Gaertner and Dovidio (2000), "if members of different groups are induced to imagine that they are all part of one group and not of separate groups, attitudes toward former out-group members will become more positive due to a number of cognitive and motivational processes, including the tendency to favor one's own group members" (p. 46).

When alternative shared identities are not available, Wright, Reynolds, Haslam, and Willingham (2011) showed that when the success of intergroup communication is within the group interest, it is possible that members feel more motivated to communicate effectively, shifting the in-group boundaries because it is in their own interest (see Morton, Postmes, & Jetten, 2007). Thus, in situations where higher order identities are not available or are not viable, an alternative way to facilitate communication and cooperation within an organization is to capitalize on the interests of the organization's subgroups.

In terms of behavior in organizations, Morton et al. (2012) confirmed important predictions derived from the principles of the social identity perspective: They pointed out that people work with others with more kindness and effectiveness when they perceive that those other people share their social identity. They support the idea that this effect is created by the processes by which people send and receive information, namely that they cooperate better when they perceive themselves as members of the same group. However, the results showed that communication can transcend in-group boundaries when people believe that cooperation with an out-group favors the interests of their own in-group. Consequently, when communication is necessarily intergroup by nature, those who manage the communication (the organizational leadership) should consider ways to strategically utilize the interests of each group to maximize the probability of effective and productive communication between them. The importance of this matter to prospective female leaders in traditionally male domains cannot be underestimated.

However, with regard to the subgroup of professional women in organizations with a traditional male majority, it is vital to recognize that communication is not just a neutral vehicle through which information and ideas are transmitted (Giles & Gasiorek, 2013). As demonstrated through accommodation (described earlier), communication can create (or jeopardize) the connections between people and, therefore, it plays a key role in shaping social relations (Haslam et al., 2011; Hogg & Giles, 2012; Gasiorek & Giles, 2012, 2013). In this respect, the relationship between identity and communication is bidirectional (Gallois et al., 2005; Giles, 2012). One consequence of this is that the ways in which organizations provide opportunities for communication with certain people (e.g., men in decision-making positions) and not with others (e.g., women in decision-making positions) will also have consequences for the ways in which people perceive themselves within the same organization (Haslam, 2004; Hogg & Giles, 2012). Among other things, this means that the way in which business organizations manage communication will be a key factor in preserving (or undermining) the diversity of social and gender identities in the workplace. This concept is extremely important.

A powerful way to break up the shared identity among a group of employees is by depriving them of the company of others. In this sense, the boundaries imposed on women, for example, by the old boys' club, are a way to block shared identity between men and women and, therefore, keep women from obtaining top decision-making positions. Boundaries are also created by overprotective communication (which we discussed earlier) and patronizing speech (see Giles et al., 2004; Viladot & Giles, 1998). Here it is also appropriate to discuss the uncertainty that prevents women leaders from fully identifying with the group of male leaders in the organization (because of the very real boundaries perceived) and therefore, their inability to identify with the organization because men are perceived as the best organizational representation. This also causes a negative impact on women's psychological well-being (Hogg, 2012; Stroebe, Dovidio, Barreto, Ellemers, & John, 2011). Women also may be victims of bullying or rude behavior as a result of the perceived uncertainty and threat their presence invokes in the male workers (see Hogg, 2010, 2012).

According to the social identity leadership theory (Hogg, 2007), the prototypical members tend to occupy positions of leadership, and leaders are more effective if they are perceived as prototypical. The clear implication is that self-uncertainty will make people pay even more attention to their leaders and feel prone to give them power in exchange for the leaders' acknowledgment and validation (Hogg, 2010). In these circumstances, people need to feel that they are valued and that they can trust their leaders, even if these feelings are nothing more than an illusion (Haslam et al., 2011).

So, in traditionally male organizations (engineering, for example), values transmitted by the prototypical leader are of great importance for the integration of women and to prevent them from being seen as the "other" (see Haslam et al., 2011). We are discussing "integration" rather than "assimilation." Assimilation involves the search for individual acceptance by acquiring the values and norms of the prototypical group.

According to an important model on impression formation (see Fiske & Taylor, 2008), the perception of others takes place along a continuum that goes from perceptions based on categories to more individualized impressions, either because, when building our impressions, we process information very quickly or in a more systematic way. These different ways of processing information are influenced by the degree to which people rely on preexisting attitudes and social categories or launch a perceptual process focused on the person as an individual. According to Hoyt and Burnette (2013), the most conservative people will use a limited amount of information, that is, their judgments about someone will be based on preexisting attitudes. In contrast, people with more liberal beliefs will make a deeper and thorough analysis, relying less on preexisting attitudes, to gain an understanding of the person and to make assessments. If the values of the prototype (the leader of the organization) are based on diversity and democratic values (Rai & Fiske, 2011), and talent is assessed as the defining characteristic of group excellence (Cleveland, Stockdale, & Murphy, 2000), without the assessment being influenced by stereotypes that discriminate against women, the possibility that they reach the top of their careers on equal footing with men can become a reality (Benschop & Verloo, 2011). We are talking about the need to ensure that there is no salience of gender in organizations for values that are supported by stereotypes and norms that discriminate against women in the workplace. Promoting this strategy of creative identity management for social change and giving value to characteristics that distinguish women from men would be a way of neutralizing gender salience within organizations when it affects women leaders in a negative way. The moral value of diversity is therefore of utmost importance within organizations. It is not about avoiding differences but valuing differences at the same level without negative bias impacting the treatment of women in the workplace (Boulouta, 2013).

Expanding these observations, we can deduce that just as it is important to encourage certain forms of communication with others within the organization, how this process is managed will show to what extent gender identities are valued by the organization as a whole. The actions of leaders not only directly promote specific identities (e.g., facilitating certain forms of interaction) but also indirectly provide information on which identities are valued and which are not. This is important because it breaks the disastrous cycle that leads to nonaccommodation in the form of subaccommodation addressed to the women's group (Gasiorek, 2013; Gasiorek & Giles, 2012). There is evidence that people are very sensitive to information that is critical of their behavior in the workplace. In particular, it determines the degree to which they participate in their relevant organizational identities or if they feel excluded or alienated (Heilman & Okimoto, 2007; Williams, 2003). In the words of Haslam et al. (2011), "... it is impossible to lead a group unless one first understands the nature of the group that is to be lead" (p. 207). In organizational contexts, this means discovering the nature of social identities in terms of how employees define themselves. Once leaders have reflected on the nature of the groups they aspire to lead, they need to represent this group. Therefore, if the prototypical leaders neglect these sensitivities to the subgroup of women, the mountain women need to climb to obtain leadership positions will be insurmountable for most (Akerlof, 2011).

So far, our analysis provides clear evidence that communication processes within organizations are highly contingent on membership in groups and on concerns about the employees' associated identity (Gardner, Cogliser, Davis, & Dickens, 2011). However, a key question is whether this theoretical understanding can lead to practical advice. How can an appreciation for the dynamics between gender groups be used to take advantage of the power of shared identity without falling into the trap of the limits created by group distinctiveness? Successfully managing communication requires attention to people's motivation to communicate with others within their organizations. The social identity perspective provides evidence that the motivations for interacting with others are based on the understanding of what people are, for example, on identities that are salient to them and that structure their relationships with others (Cleveland et al., 2000). Where there exists a sense of shared identity within a given team, in a country or in an organization as a whole, there is a solid basis for positive communication between the parties. The shared identity opens people to dialogue with others, because others are relevant and important components of their social selves (Dezsö & Ross, 2012). This is why a key strategy to improve communication consists in creating (and certainly not destroying) a sense of shared identity that will bind those who need to communicate with each other (Haslam et al., 2011).

Yet, it must be made clear that this is not always possible. When communication requires crossing the boundaries imposed by the group (e.g., crossing the boundaries created by gender stereotypes), we must recognize from the start that the likelihood of problems arising is greater (Kaufman & Grace, 2011). However, when relationships between men and women leaders are reasonably good, these problems are surmountable. Human touch, intense or prolonged mutual assistance to reach a shared objective, can gradually remove boundaries between groups (Gaertner & Dovidio, 2000).

While this may seem like an ideal solution to the problems women leaders face when trying to be accepted on equal footing with men, it may actually have the opposite effect (backfiring). Although groups may have higher or superordinate goals, they may also want to keep their individual identities and thus resist the perceived threat of becoming a single entity. In this way, new conflicts to keep the perceived distinctiveness can arise. Hornsey and Hogg (2000) carried out a research program that suggests that a balance between higher order identity and the positive distinctiveness of subgroups (men and women) can be a promising project for social harmony.

This order works because by preserving different cultural identities, there is no danger of causing intergroup hostility, while the existence of a higher identity or an identity of higher order can make it so that subgroups are seen as distinct groups with complementary roles, and all people are working on the same team with integration objectives.

More broadly, the idea suggests that the answer to intergroup problems can consist in building groups that are not only based on the tolerance of diversity but actually celebrate diversity as a defining characteristic of their social identity (Costea, 2011; Desvaux, Devillard-Hoellinger, & Baumgarten, 2007; Diversity Inc., 2013; Wright et al., 2002). Therefore, it's not about promoting paternalism but embracing diversity over performance and financial results of the company or organization. But also, the concept of diversity management appreciates and takes advantage of the talents of individual differences. These differences, in turn, transform the various skill sets of each employee to the advantage of the organization (Davidson & Burke, 2000).

In this situation, it is necessary not only to recognize the challenges that this will entail but also the opportunities that might encourage male leaders in traditionally male workplaces to engage more effectively with the subgroup of women (Haslam et al., 2011). So, fighting nonaccommodation is again very important (see Gasiorek, 2013; Giles & Gasiorek, 2013). When group disagreements can be transcended through some significant identity of higher order (e.g., human rights or acceptance of human diversity; Boulouta, 2013; Costea, 2011), the obstacle of intergroup differences should be reduced as individual motivations are recalibrated to align with others who are included in this wider group membership. Actually, we have already seen that in a shared identity of higher order that includes two subgroups; communication can be as effective as it is within the limits of the subgroups (Wright et al., 2011).

Perhaps members of the dominant male group could be encouraged to recognize the value of the feminine gender identity by realizing that cooperation benefits their own group (Wright et al., 2011). A recurring problem is the existence of various (self) discrimination mechanisms (e.g., the threat of stereotypes and self-stereotypes); these mechanisms even affect women who succeed (remember that they represent a gender group with lower status in relation to men in the same conditions) who still feel devalued. However, even though it has been shown that women in situations of discrimination at work show a low level of well-being, anticipate more failure than success, and have reduced performance in work contexts dominated by the male out-group, studies have also shown that these threats and negative effects on performance can be mitigated when the characteristics of the stigmatized groups are explicitly valued (Derks, van Laar, & Ellemers, 2007, 2009; Joy, Carter, Wagner, & Narayanan, 2007).

On a more general level, recent studies confirm the importance of respecting people's social identity as a key element for wellness, motivation, and performance of people belonging to groups perceived as having a lower status (Akerlof, 2011; Boulouta, 2013; Cameron & Lalonde, 2001; Costea, 2011). This suggests that, rather than deny or ignore the devalued social identity of the people in those groups, it is important to recognize, affirm, and value the fact of specifically belonging to disadvantaged groups (Cameron & Lalonde, 2001).

Recall that the "taking of the perspective of the other" is the experience of imagining the world from the point of view of another person; when we engage in perspective taking, in essence we are seeing things through (what I imagine to be) the eyes of another person. The attempt to take the perspective of someone else (empathize with others) increases the overlap of mental representations of others and of oneself and the psychological sense of similarity and feeling of mental and behavioral connection among people. Indeed, we are talking about the importance of empathy as a mediator (Pettigrew & Tropp, 2011). Maybe promoting perspective-taking in organizations could be an important way for women to overcome the glass ceiling (Boulouta, 2013; Ryan & Haslam, 2005; van Vianen & Fischer, 2002), but let us emphasize that we are not talking about paternalism (overaccommodation; e.g., Ryan & Bannister, 2009). Paternalism requires a lengthy consideration that does not apply here. Suffice it to say that in intergroup terms, the group in power is the dominant group of men, and to get a real existing equality, this group should cede some of its power. To what extent does this not imply paternalism? To what extent would men not be making a concession to women? And what are the reasons for this concession? Major et al. (2013) provided an interesting debate about the suspicions that paradoxically generate in minority groups' the attitudes and behaviors of the dominant groups. A historical example of a grant given from men to women is the right to vote; however, once this prerogative was reached, the following generations of women no longer had to fight to get it. The first generation of women who got it paid a price and subsequent generations reaped the rewards of their efforts.

Anyway, it is clear that researchers have yet to fully engage with the complexity of the dynamics of communication between the genders in contemporary organizational life. The success of organizations (and of the whole world) lies in taking seriously people's identities (Boulouta, 2013; Coates & Johnson, 2011; van Knippenberg & Schippers, 2007). When women leaders experience attachment to their gender group, and when they understand that gender group membership is embedded within their organization and is valued by it, we will have achieved equality. Unlike the point of view that women at work can act independently to optimize both their own accomplishments and their comfort level, we have emphasized the extreme importance of taking into account the fact that gender identity is at stake and that this has important psychological and behavioral consequences.

Summary

The relevance of the study of leadership from the perspective of interpersonal and intergroup communication is associated with the need for organizations not only to lead teams composed of all kinds of people but of integrating women in senior positions in management teams. This increases interest in the issue of communication and may lead to solutions for issues that arise from contact between genders.

The identity of individuals (both personal and social identity) is one of the most important aspects negotiated in communication processes. So the quality of the elite leadership's interpersonal and intergroup communication is essential for the elimination of employment discrimination against women.

In this sense, the role of managers is of great importance, since they are the most active and influential actors and are creators of culture. What ideas do they start from? What do they transmit? What do women see that male managers often are unaware of? Communication is inherent in the role of managers, and this is of varying quality depending on initial conditions that affect, from the beginning, interactions between genders. Managers, as a kind of sonar, emit signals that are picked up by others (women) and have different backgrounds. The less noise they emit, the better their initial conditions, and the greater the likelihood that they will succeed in their communication. Regarding integration and increasing women in leadership roles, this is an issue of great and wide importance that we have analyzed generally.

The study of communication is complex, but the fascination for a better understanding of the communicative phenomena that contributes to greater personal and professional development for men and women has led us to develop this volume.

· 2 2 ·
CONCLUSIONS

Over the past decades, women have been gaining confidence, skills, and experience in the workplace. There is nothing, at the moment, preventing them to think that they cannot take the next step on the professional scale. However, statistics tell a very different story (see De Madariaga, 2013). What can they do to be included in that small minority of women who manage to reach the highest levels?

Women are urged to promote themselves and to follow courses of training, mentoring, and leadership to develop skills and confidence to apply for high-level jobs. Nowadays, there are many young women who have no problem applying for such jobs or promoting themselves.

In our opinion, telling women what to do and how to improve suggests that the reason they are not in top positions is because they are not suitable for those positions. It has also been said that the few women who have reached high levels deny help to other women and that this is partly the reason for the underrepresentation of women in positions of responsibility.

In our view, the only way in which the current scarcity of women in top positions can change is through the elimination of systemic and structural bias in policies and procedures that favor men (and specifically White men).

The issue of pipeline shrinkage for women in the academic world is a well-known and researched phenomenon and refers to the fact that women enter universities at the same rate as men, but they are less likely to enter and succeed in academia than their male counterparts, particularly in science and engineering disciplines (Ellemers et al., 2012). Why is this? What are the hidden motives or factors? It seems that powerful structural factors are intervening.

Several researchers in the area of personnel selection procedures have highlighted a language selection bias, which is based on variations of language as a structural attribute and a tool used by committee members to differently portray selected and rejected applicants (see, e.g., Douglas & Sutton, 2014).

Effectively, there are not only factors acting at the individual level (through interpersonal interactions); inequalities can also be strengthened through structural-level factors that influence judgments and preferences in such ways that serve to preserve group inequality and the prevailing status quo. Although these characteristics at the structural and systemic level may be less noticeable and are much less studied, we believe they are partly responsible for the stagnation in the progression of women into areas of leadership. Current research highlights systemic characteristics and shows its potential impact on the maintenance of inequality. By doing so, it provides useful advances in the understanding of gender inequality in the labor force. In this regard, we believe that mechanisms should be implemented to force human resource departments of various organizations and academic tribunals to consider the most current findings on the gears operating in subtle discrimination applied to women (e.g., among many other investigations, Gaucher, Friesen, & Kay, 2011; Mulac et al., 2013).

So far, the evidence provided on job discrimination against women has been the basis for established public policies aimed to counteract such discrimination with positive laws that, for example, require a minimum percentage of women in certain levels within public institutions or allow for the possibility that a woman can sue a company for not being hired or promoted if she can prove that the decision was due to her gender. Quota programs invite companies with a low female presence on their boards to make a deliberate effort to find potential female candidates whenever a vacancy has to be filled on the board, especially for independent positions. These measures effectively raise the proportion of women in academic and industrial areas. Obviously, for the in-group of women, the mere existence of such programs can be a motivating factor, as they convey the message that society, or at least part of it, recognizes and attempts to improve their situation (Matsa & Miller, 2013). However, there is also the concern that these policies actually make it more difficult for their beneficiaries to prove that they are worthy of the opportunities they receive (van Laar, Levin, & Sinclair, 2008). If affirmative action policies are not clearly informed or the credentials of the candidates are not explained to organizations that have open positions, this may cast doubt on the competence of the beneficiaries, and, in turn, candidates may begin to doubt their own abilities (see Crosby, 2004; Heilman, 2012).

These doubts interfere with motivation and performance when undertaking tasks involving a challenge, reducing the chances of success (see Crosby, 2004). Thus, the unsatisfactory implementation or lack of explanation in regard to the level of women's competence can easily backfire, generating resistance against both these programs and the beneficiaries (Federico & Sidanius, 2002). As a result of this lack of knowledge, the need for affirmative action has been questioned, arguing that the disadvantages based on membership to the in-group of women have ceased to exist (Ellemers & Barreto, 2008; Schmitt, Ellemers, & Branscombe, 2003). That conveys the idea that the different results obtained by women only reflect differences in individual merits and that disadvantages and discrimination caused by group membership have nothing to do with these results (Cleveland, Stockdale & Murphy, 2000; Eagly & Carly, 2007). However, Carter and Silva (2010) found that men begin their professional careers at higher levels than women. This finding cannot be attributed to the fact that women do not aspire to the top positions; the data are still valid when only women and men who say they are aiming for senior executive positions are included. This data also cannot be attributed to the fact that motherhood slows down women's careers, because even among women and men without children living at home, men still begin at higher levels.

As a concrete example, we would like to close our conclusions by discussing the recent controversy provoked by Facebook and Apple when they offered to allow their female workers to freeze their eggs for free. This controversy is neither trivial nor marginal. Is it an acceptable measure to attract female talent? Is it an acceptable measure to achieve the reconciliation of work and family life? Is it an acceptable measure to offer equal opportunities for both men and women? From the very start, offering egg freezing openly tells us that in work environments of this type, the work of women is not compatible with motherhood. But what happens is that at the same time, motherhood is necessary for the social, cultural, and economic prosperity of countries.

These technology giants are real male ghettos. On Twitter, for example, 70% of the 3,000 workers, 90% of information technology specialists, and 80% of its leaders are men. Most of these women work in marketing, public relations, or sales departments, and rarely in technological areas (Williams, 2014). Women are often excluded from the male worlds that are unique to the careers called STEM (the acronym to describe science, technology, engineering, and mathematics), since they do not identify with them. Even the physical work environments of these organizations are the kind that women cannot identify with. It is a masculine world made and designed by and for men. Therefore, not only is there an impermeable barrier created by the male world, but women themselves often lack motivation to trespass it. Offering egg freezing to attract candidates is useless until we change the stereotypes that prescribe certain fields of study and certain jobs solely for men.

But also, we must consider that today, the number of births in Catalonia, Spain (children per woman in 2013, 1.39; Idescat, 2014), and the European Union (children per woman in 2014, 1.60; CIA, 2014), is so low that it is not able to maintain the age pyramid. The aging population poses challenges for our societies in cultural, organizational, and economic terms. Each worker provides the economic means for a growing number of elderly dependents. In Spain in 2050, people over 65 will account for over 30% of the population, and octogenarians will come to exceed the figure of 4 million (Fernández, Parapar & Ruíz, 2010).

In general, we accept neoliberal capitalism as the only form of economic organization, and this system requires full availability of the people as a sine qua non for a successful career. Although this may be good for enterprises, it is lethal for the medium and long term for the whole society, because it harms the age pyramid and women, to whom society transfers the responsibility of solving this problem at the expense of their personal fulfillment and freedom. Women should be mothers and housewives, should be working outside the home to earn money, and must care for an increasingly aging population. It is intended that they work intensively, that they consecrate their younger years to companies with total dedication, and all this with low wages. And when they reach higher wages, the company grants them all kinds of maternity leaves with a consequent reduction in salary on a higher base. But also, once they have become mothers, they are perceived as less competent, assertive, and committed.

The key to ending discrimination against working mothers based on stereotypes is to stop the unequal distribution of housework and childcare between parents or at least stop the perception that women are devoted to housework and childcare at the expense of their jobs. Leaders of organizations can do much to change these perceptions. Motherhood is a social problem serious enough and with too many consequences for us to relegate it to short-term goals and for the maximum benefit of enterprises. Society and public authorities must intervene vigorously to correct these problems, to achieve greater happiness for women and society with a balanced age pyramid. If not, we know what awaits us: Prospective data have notified us that in the Europe of 2030, the population pyramid will be reversed (I+DTinfo, 2014).

EPILOGUE

The aim of this book was to shed light on the question of why there is no gender equality at the workplace, also taking into account that the secondary and postsecondary education of women is equal to that of men. More specifically, our goal was to analyze the factors and mechanisms that lead to women's discrimination regarding their careers.

Together, the two parts of this volume cover the major aspects and approaches of research in this area from the point of view of social psychology and communication. We concluded Part I with the metaphor of a "hurdles woman," a struggle in which a woman has to jump many hurdles to succeed. To reiterate, gender stereotypes play a chief role among the hurdles that impede women's success in counterstereotypic tasks or jobs (including leadership positions): Parents, teachers, and peers expect different behavior from girls than from boys. As one consequence, they will explain girls' and boys' successes differently (e.g., as evidence of talent vs. effort). Additionally, girls' and boys' self-concepts of ability tend to be tainted by these stereotypes. For example, due to gender stereotypes, boys are more likely to come to believe in their math talent than girls, given equal individual talent. The stereotype-threat phenomenon shows that stereotypes may become what is known as "self-fulfilling prophecies": Because a stereotype exists, respective differences in performance will occur.

There are two further insidious aspects of such gender stereotypes. First, there is an implicit, automatized component to them that is hard to counteract. And second, they comprise prescriptive elements: Some behaviors are more forbidden for girls than for boys and vice versa. For example, girls should be more modest and less assertive than boys, a stereotype that is hard to reconcile with a (future) leadership role. Women and men may be penalized by others for violating prescriptive stereotypes. Women who nevertheless excel at male-typed tasks risk being disliked by more conservative individuals, and they risk working in a profession in which they sometimes feel they do not belong.

The other "big" factor we have identified in Part I as affecting women's careers are social roles in relationships and families. Presently, heterosexual women still do the larger share of family work. More generally, they are more likely to behave like satellites circling around their husbands' lives than vice versa. Employers also expect less mobility, work commitment, and ambition of women once they are married and particularly when they become mothers. No such negative effects of parenthood occur in the perception of fathers (unless they follow nontraditional gender roles, e.g., asking for paternal leave). These are the hurdles we have elaborated in Part I of this volume.

In Part II, we addressed the phenomenon of work discrimination of professional women from a different angle: from the processes and communication strategies between men and women at the workplace, relying on the social identity perspective.

The starting point of this analysis was the recognition that human beings are irrevocably social, interacting with each other based on the groups they belong to, rather than simply interacting as unique individuals. Fundamentally, people incorporate the values, norms, and behaviors of the groups they feel a belonging to. Therefore, when two people engage in a communicative process, each brings a particular interpretation of the social environment and a specific perception of their communication partner. Successful communication requires that each participant overcomes inadequate expectations. Problems occur when this does not happen. As stereotypes are rigid constructions that establish expectations, they can therefore affect the quality and type of social interactions. Furthermore, stereotypes unconsciously direct intergroup communication because they are based on automatic categorization.

Clearly, intergroup attitudes (stereotypes and prejudices) reside in the heads of people and certainly there are idiosyncratic differences in the specific content of individual beliefs of the members of a given social group. However, the most significant intergroup attitudes are widely shared by members of society. Intergroup attitudes gain their power and importance because of these beliefs, beliefs that not only members of a society know very well but that are also shared over time by social groups. In this sense, intergroup attitudes become part of our common understanding of who "we" are and who "they" are. Men and women form two gender groups to which stereotypes and roles are allotted, and this, in part, channels processes and communicational strategies. Since humans are social beings by nature, the identity of each is necessarily constructed in relation to others (through teaching, imitation, etc.). And in these relations of knowledge, power is always mixed. Therefore, identities and ideologies are always linked.

The goal of most intergroup interaction researchers is to understand these interactions and propose ways to improve them by building nonthreatening situations for some (the men) that do not discriminate against others (the women). This is especially important to consider in work areas where men and women interact in positions of similar responsibility but with male preponderance. How do men and women manage their gender identity when engaged in roles of responsibility at the workplace? Which strategies do they use to preserve their self-esteem when they perceive that their individual and gender identities are being threatened?

The most problematic aspects of intergroup communication are precisely those that involve strong emotions and powerful feelings. Many men, as we observed in this second section, not only frequently interpose barriers to job advancement of women but also experience anxiety and disgust when they have to interact with them. This anxiety may come directly from an anticipated negative effect as shame, rejection, and ridicule, and, more indirectly, worry about how to behave from possible deep-rooted negative feelings. When deep-rooted negative feelings collide with a system of free and egalitarian values, prejudice can take the form that is now called *subtle prejudice:* prejudice that inadvertently leaks and eventually leads to discriminatory behaviors.

Of course, there are individual differences in people's beliefs about men and women as groups and even shared intergroup attitudes can be changed consensually. At the same time, there is a strong consistency and agreement not only between people but also over time. This consistency is due to the fact that the content of stereotypes and prejudice about groups is part of a society's culture. This cultural "knowledge," as mentioned earlier, is institutionalized in the norms and practices of a society and transferred to others through the usual channels of socialization: parents, schools, books, media, and other social institutions (e.g., hiring men and women, etc.). Automatic intergroup attitudes are embedded in language, not only in the things we say but more subtly in communication patterns and styles (e.g., the university committees established for the selection of candidates for university professors may favor men). In addition, intergroup attitudes perpetuate and extend through daily interactions between groups and individuals. It is precisely because intergroup attitudes are consensually shared that they form the basis of conflict or cooperation between groups. In other words, intergroup attitudes are institutionalized in discriminatory practices that become part of the structure of social institutions. This institutionalization not only serves to sustain intergroup attitudes encouraging (or even imposing) attitude-consistent behavior, but discrimination may occur in the absence of those original attitudes. That is, once installed, these institutional practices can keep group inequality even if attitudes become more egalitarian. Thus, negative intergroup attitudes of the past have residual effects on intergroup relations in a way that maintains the relative status of the groups, even after these initial attitudes are replaced by more positive ones. We think future research should place special emphasis on these aspects.

We have also emphasized that organizations should incorporate the concept of diversity (the respect and defense of different social identities) to achieve real equality between men and women at work and in particular between men and women with top job responsibilities (where employment discrimination is manifest to a larger degree). When a social identity is routinely ignored, as happens with the vast majority of professional women in male domains, the person may experience anxiety and depression. These feelings have a direct impact on the individual's self-esteem and well-being.

A prevailing belief is that a cordial interpersonal contact between people of different genders is the best way to eliminate gender discrimination at work. However, according to Allport's contact hypothesis, the conditions for optimal effects of contact are these: Contact needs to be extended and cooperative and occur within an institutional and official environment that promotes integration, and the groups should be of equal status. These conditions are virtually impossible to meet in most intergroup contact situations; therefore, contact is not always very effective in changing intergroup relations or improving intergroup attitudes. After all, intense intergroup relations are often associated with groups that are very different and contact may confirm their worst fears. Until there is a change in the perception of intergroup relations, contact simply will provide a forum for conflict. However, it seems that Allport's conditions could be in contacts between men and women leaders in work environments with male dominance.

A specific problem is that, as already mentioned, there may be anxiety associated with intergroup contact, an effect that, of course, makes the interaction relatively unpleasant. However, if contact between groups is not associated with intergroup anxiety, that contact can be nice; in fact, it may be warm enough to encourage the development of lasting friendships that cross group boundaries. However, a close friendship with people of another group does not guarantee that the person lodges positive attitudes toward the group as a whole. It is not often that close friendships between members of different groups improve the image of the other group as a whole. People can like each other as individuals but still harbor negative attitudes toward the group as a whole. Generally speaking, the relationship between intergender contact and gender attitudes in the employment context with male dominance should be explored further.

Given the plethora of interwoven aspects that keep women from climbing the career ladder, one may wonder how some of them succeed at all. However, as the chapter on role models illustrated, the more of them succeed, the more likely it is that society reaches a tipping point: a high percentage of women in top positions across occupational domains. If this happens, change could subsequently be rapid: Gender stereotypes and social roles confining women to lower positions will quickly erode, and so will negative social identities, incompatibilities between women's roles and leaders' roles, and asymmetric communication patterns at work. We have started this book reviewing some changes related to gender roles in society, such as the late official recognition of women's soccer in some countries. Fifty years from now, young students may lay their hands on this book, wondering how come something that seems to belong to a past long gone was written only 50 years earlier. Every woman succeeding in a position at the top, and every woman or man giving a woman the chance to show her abilities, as well as every man doing his share of family work, help make this vision a reality.

To finish, the economic costs of gender inequality are high. As one example, every dollar invested in a man's education pays off better than one invested in a woman's education. Low birth rates in many European countries, particularly among well-qualified women, are the flip side of this serious problem that societies and political institutions need to attend to. Women should *not* be forced to decide between a career and having children. (Likewise, men should not be forced to make such a decision.) The fact that some women freeze their eggs to advance their careers without losing the opportunity to have children is a strong indicator of the perverseness of the situation. Every person should have the opportunity to have both a fulfilling career and children. Because of societal structures that enable and maintain low birth rates, European societies are aging, a serious situation for both women and men. Women and men, individuals and groups, politicians and companies, should work together to change this.

REFERENCES

Abele, A. E. (2000). A dual-impact model of gender and career-related processes. In T. Eckes & H. M. Trautner (Eds.), *The developmental social psychology of gender* (pp. 361–389). Mahwah, NJ: Lawrence Erlbaum.

Abele, A. E. (2003). The dynamics of masculine-agentic and feminine-communal traits: Findings from a prospective study. *Journal of Personality and Social Psychology, 85*, 768–776.

Abele, A. E., & Spurk, D. (2011). The dual impact of gender and the influence of timing of parenthood on men's and women's career development: Longitudinal findings. *International Journal of Behavioral Development, 35*, 225–232.

Abele, A. E., & Wiese, B. S. (2008). The nomological network of self-management strategies and career success. *Journal of Occupational and Organizational Psychology, 81*, 733–749.

Abrams, D., & Hogg, M. A. (2010). Social identity and self-categorization. In J. F. Dovidio, M. Hewstone, P. Glick, & V. M. Esses (Eds.), *The Sage handbook of prejudice, stereotyping and discrimination* (pp. 179–193). London, UK: Sage.

Abrams, J. R., & Giles, H. (2004). An intergroup approach to communicating stigma. In S. H. Ng, C. N. Candlin, & C. Y. Chiu (Eds.), *Language matters: Communication, culture and identity* (pp. 27–62). Hong Kong, China: City University of Hong Kong Press.

Agthe, M., Spörrle, M., & Maner, J. K. (2010). Don't hate me because I'm beautiful: Anti-attractiveness bias in organizational evaluation and decision making. *Journal of Experimental Social Psychology, 46*, 1151–1154.

Aguiar, F., Brañas-Garza, P., & Miller, L. (2008). Moral distance in dictator games. *Judgment and Decision Making, 3*, 344–354.

Akerlof, G. A. (2011). Foreword: The social identity approach to leadership and why it matters. In S. A. Haslam, S. D. Reicher, & M. J. Platow (Eds.), *The new psychology of leadership: Identity, influence, and power* (pp. XIII–XVII). London, UK: Psychology Press.

Alicke, M. A., Dunning, D. A., & Krueger, J. I. (2005). *The self in social judgment*. New York, NY: Psychology Press.

Allen, T. D., & Russell, J. E. A. (1999). Parental leave of absence: Some not so family-friendly implications. *Journal of Applied Social Psychology, 29*, 166–191.

Allen, T. D., Russell, J. E. A., & Rush, M. C. (1994). The effects of gender and leave of absence on attributions for high-performance, perceived organizational commitment, and allocation of organizational rewards. *Sex Roles, 31*, 443–464.

Allport, G. W. (1954). *The nature of prejudice*. Reading, MA: Addison-Wesley.

Alter, A. L., Aronson, J., Darley, J. M., Rodriguez, C., & Ruble, D. N. (2010). Rising to the threat: Reducing stereotype threat by reframing the threat as a challenge. *Journal of Experimental Social Psychology, 46*, 166–171.

Altés–Tárrega, J. A. (2002). *El acoso sexual en el trabajo* [Sexual harassment at work]. Valencia, Spain: Tirant Lo Blanch.

Amanatullah, E. T., & Morris, M. W. (2010). Negotiating gender roles: Gender differences in assertive negotiating are mediated by women's fear of backlash and attenuated when negotiating on behalf of others. *Journal of Personality and Social Psychology, 98*, 256–267.

Ambady, N., Hallahan, M., & Rosenthal, R. (1995). On judging and being judged accurately in zero-acquaintance situations. *Journal of Personality and Social Psychology, 69*, 518–529.

Andrade, C., & Mikula, G. (2014). Work-family conflict and perceived justice as mediators of outcomes of women's multiple workload. *Marriage & Family Review, 50*, 285–306.

Andreoni, J., & Vesterlund, L. (2001). Which is the fair sex? Gender differences in altruism. *Quarterly Journal of Economics, 116*, 293–312.

Apfelbaum, E. P., Pauker, K., Sommers, S. R., & Ambady, N. (2010). In blind pursuit of racial equality? *Psychological Science, 21*, 1587–1592.

Apicella, C. L., Dreber, A., Campbell, B., Gray, P. B., Hoffman, M., & Little, A. (2008). Testosterone and financial risk preferences. *Evolution and Human Behavior, 29*, 384–390.

Appel, M., Kronberger, N., & Aronson, J. (2011). Stereotype threat impairs ability building: Effects on test preparation among women in science and technology. *European Journal of Social Psychology, 41*, 904–913.

Aranda, B., & Glick, P. (2014). Signaling devotion to work over family undermines the motherhood penalty. *Group Processes & Intergroup Relations, 17*, 91–99.

Asgari, S., Dasgupta, N., & Stout, J. G. (2012). When do counterstereotypic ingroup members inspire versus deflate? The effect of successful professional women on young women's leadership self-concept. *Personality and Social Psychology Bulletin, 38*, 370–383.

Ashburn-Nardo, L. (2008). Fairly representing the stereotyping literature? *Industrial and Organizational Psychology, 1*, 412–414.

Ashmore, R. D., & Del Boca, F. K. (1979). Sex stereotypes and implicit personality theory: Toward a cognitive-social psychological conceptualization. *Sex Roles, 5*, 219–248.

Ashton, M. C., Lee, K., & de Vries, R. E. (2014). The HEXACO honesty-humility, agreeableness, and emotionality factors: A review of research and theory. *Personality and Social Psychology Review, 18,* 139–152.

Athenstaedt, U. (2003). On the content and structure of the gender role self-concept: Including gender-stereotypical behaviors in addition to traits. *Psychology of Women Quarterly, 27,* 309–318.

Atkinson, S. M., Boyce Baird, S., & Frye, M. B. (2003). Do female fund managers manage differently? *Journal of Financial Research, 26,* 1–18.

Bakan, D. (1966). *The duality of human existence. An essay on psychology and religion.* Oxford, UK: Rand McNally.

Banaji, M. R., & Hardin, C. D. (1996). Automatic stereotyping. *Psychological Science, 7,* 136–141.

Banaji, M. R., Hardin, C. D., & Rothman, A. J. (1993). Implicit stereotyping in person judgment. *Journal of Personality and Social Psychology, 65,* 272–281.

Bandura, A. (1965). Influence of models' reinforcement contingencies on the acquisition of imitative responses. *Journal of Personality and Social Psychology, 1,* 589–595.

Bargh, J. A. (1994). The four horsemen of automaticity: Awareness, intention, efficiency, and control in social cognition. In R. S. Wyer, Jr. (Ed.), *Handbook of social cognition* (pp. 1–83). Hillsdale, NJ: Lawrence Erlbaum.

Bargh, J. A., Raymond, P., Pryor, J., & Strack, F. (1995). Attractiveness of the underling: An automatic power, sex association and its consequences for sexual harassment and aggression. *Journal of Personality and Social Psychology, 68,* 768–781.

Baron, R. A., Markman, G. D., & Hirsa, A. (2001). Perceptions of women and men as entrepreneurs: Evidence for differential effects of attributional augmenting. *Journal of Applied Psychology, 86,* 923–929.

Barreto, M., Ellemers, N., Cihangir, S., & Stroebe, K. (2009). The self-fulfilling effects of contemporary sexism: How the well-being and behavior of women is affected by the subtle discrimination they encounter. In M. Barreto, M. Ryan, & S. Schmitt (Eds.), *The glass ceiling in the 21st century: Understanding barriers to gender equality* (pp. 99–124). Washington, DC: American Psychological Association.

Barreto, M., Ellemers, N., & Palacios, M. S. (2004). The backlash of token mobility: The impact of past group experiences on individual ambition and effort. *Personality and Social Psychology Bulletin, 30,* 1433–1445.

Bathmann, N., Corneließen, W., & Müller, D. (2013). *Gemeinsam zum Erfolg? Berufliche Karrieren von Frauen in Paarbeziehungen* [Joint towards success? Careers of women in relationships]. Wiesbaden, Germany: Springer.

Bavishi, A., Madera, J. M., & Hebl, M. R. (2010). The effect of professor ethnicity and gender on student evaluations: Judged before met. *Journal of Diversity in Higher Education, 3,* 245–256.

Bear, J. B., & Babcock, L. (2012). Negotiation topic as a moderator of gender differences in negotiation. *Psychological Science, 23,* 743–744.

Becker, J. C. (2012). The system-stabilizing role of identity management strategies: Social creativity can undermine collective action for social change. *Journal of Personality and Social Psychology, 103,* 647–662.

Becker, J. C., & Swim, J. K. (2012). Reducing endorsement of benevolent and modern sexist beliefs: Differential effects of addressing harm versus pervasiveness of benevolent sexism. *Social Psychology, 43,* 127–137.

Becker, J. C., & Wright, S. C. (2011). Yet another dark side of chivalry: Benevolent sexism undermines and hostile sexism motivates collective action for social change. *Journal of Personality and Social Psychology, 101,* 62–77.

Bem, S. L. (1981). Gender schema theory: A cognitive account of sex typing. *Psychological Review, 88,* 354–364.

Benard, S., & Correll, S. J. (2010). Normative discrimination and the motherhood penalty. *Gender & Society, 24,* 616–646.

Benito, J. M., Brañas-Garza, P., Hernández, P., & Sanchis, J. A. (2011). Sequential versus simultaneous Schelling models: Experimental evidence. *Journal of Conflict Resolution, 55,* 60–84.

Benschop, Y., & Verloo, M. (2011). Gender change, organizational change, and gender equality strategies. In E. Jeanes, D. Knights, & P. Y. Martin (Eds.), *Handbook of gender, work & organization* (pp. 277–290). Chichester, UK: Wiley.

Berthold, A., Mummendey, A., Kessler, T., Luecke, B., & Schubert, T. (2012). When different means bad or merely worse. How minimal and maximal goals affect ingroup projection and outgroup attitudes. *European Journal of Social Psychology, 42,* 682–690.

Bettencourt, B. A., Charlton, K., Dorr, N., & Hume, D. L. (2001). Status differences and ingroup bias: A meta-analytic examination of the effects of status stability, status legitimacy, and group permeability. *Psychological Bulletin, 127,* 520–542.

Betz, D. E., & Sekaquaptewa, D. (2012). My fair physicist? Feminine math and science role models demotivate young girls. *Social Psychology and Personality Science, 3,* 738–746.

Bianchi, M., Mummendey, A., Steffens, M. C., & Yzerbyt, V. (2010). What do you mean by European? Evidence of spontaneous ingroup projection. *Personality and Social Psychology Bulletin, 36,* 960–974.

Biernat, M. (2003). Toward a broader view of social stereotyping. *American Psychologist, 57,* 707–724.

Biernat, M., & Kobrynowicz, D. (1997). Gender- and race-based standards of competence: Lower minimum standards but higher ability standards for devalued groups. *Journal of Personality and Social Psychology, 72,* 544–557.

Bird, S. R., & Rhoton, L. A. (2011). Women professionals' gender strategies: Negotiating gendered organizational barriers. In E. L. Jeanes, D. Knights, & P. Y. Martin (Eds.), *Handbook of gender, work and organization* (pp. 245–262). Chichester, UK: Wiley-Blackwell.

Blair, I. V. (2002). The malleability of automatic stereotypes and prejudice. *Personality and Social Psychology Review, 6,* 242–261.

Blair, I. V., & Banaji, M. R. (1996). Automatic and controlled processes in stereotype priming. *Journal of Personality and Social Psychology, 70,* 1142–1163.

Blair, I. V., Ma, J. E., & Lenton, A. P. (2001). Imagining stereotypes away: The moderation of implicit stereotypes through mental imagery. *Journal of Personality and Social Psychology, 81,* 828–841.

Blau, F. D., & DeVaro, J. (2007). New evidence on gender differences in promotion rates: An empirical analysis of a sample of new hires. *Industrial Relations, 46*(3), 511–550.

Blau, F. D., & Kahn, L. M. (2000). Gender differences in pay (No. 7732). *Journal of Economic Perspectives, 14* (4), 75–99.

Blickle, G., Schneider, P. B., Perrewé, P. L., Blass, F. R., & Ferris, G. R. (2008). The roles of self-disclosure, modesty, and self-monitoring in the mentoring relationship: A longitudinal multi-source investigation. *Career Development International, 13*, 224–240.

Bodenhausen, G. V. (1990). Stereotypes as judgmental heuristics: Evidence of circadian variations in discrimination. *Psychological Science, 1*, 319–322.

Bodi, O., Mikula, G., & Riederer, B. (2010). Long-term effects between perceived justice in the division of domestic work and women's relationship satisfaction testing for moderation effects. *Social Psychology, 41*, 57–65.

Boggs, C., & Giles, H. (1999). The canary in the cage: The nonaccommodation cycle in the gendered workplace. *International Journal of Applied Linguistics, 22*, 223–245.

Bonnot, V., & Jost, J. T. (2014). Divergent effects of system justification salience on the academic self-assessment of men and women. *Group Processes & Intergroup Relations, 17*, 453–464.

Booth, A. L., & Nolen, P. (2012). Gender differences in risk behaviour: Does nurture matter? *Economic Journal, 122*, F56–F78.

Bosak, J., & Sczesny, S. (2011). Exploring the dynamics of incongruent beliefs about women and leaders. *British Journal of Management, 22*, 254–269.

Bosch-Domènech, A., Brañas-Garza, P., & Espín, A. M. (2014). Can exposure to prenatal sex hormones (2D:4D) predict cognitive reflection? *Psychoneuroendocrinology, 43*, 1–10.

Bosson, J. K., Prewitt-Freilino, J. L., & Taylor, J. N. (2005). Role rigidity: A problem of identity misclassification? *Journal of Personality and Social Psychology, 89*, 552–565.

Bosson, J. K., & Vandello, J. A. (2011). Precarious manhood and its links to action and aggression. *Current Directions in Psychological Science, 20*, 82–86.

Boulouta, I. (2013). Hidden connections: The link between board gender diversity and corporate social performance. *Journal of Business Ethics, 113*, 185–197.

Bowles, H. R. (2012). Claiming authority: How women explain their ascent to top business leadership positions. *Research in Organizational Behavior: An Annual Series of Analytical Essays and Critical Reviews, 32*, 189–212.

Brañas-Garza, P., Espinosa, M. P., & Rey-Biel, P. (2011). Travellers' types. *Journal of Economic Behavior & Organization, 78*, 25–36.

Brañas-Garza, P., & Rustichini, A. (2011). Organizing effects of testosterone and economic behavior: Not just risk taking. *PLoS ONE, 6*, e29842.

Brandt, M. J. (2011). Sexism and gender inequality across 57 societies. *Psychological Science, 22*, 1413–1418.

Branscombe, N. R. (1998). Thinking about one's gender group's privileges or disadvantages: Consequences for well-being in women and men. *British Journal of Social Psychology, 37*, 167–184.

Brauer, M., & Er-rafiy, A. (2011). Increasing perceived variability reduces prejudice and discrimination. *Journal of Experimental Social Psychology, 47*, 871–881.

Brescoll, V. L., Dawson, E., & Uhlmann, E. L. (2010). Hard won and easily lost: The fragile status of leaders in gender-stereotype-incongruent occupations. *Psychological Science, 21,* 1640–1642.

Brescoll, V. L., & Uhlmann, E. L. (2005). Attitudes toward traditional and nontraditional parents. *Psychology of Women Quarterly, 29,* 436–445.

Brescoll, V. L., & Uhlmann, E. L. (2008). Can an angry woman get ahead? Status conferral, gender, and expression of emotion in the workplace. *Psychological Science, 19,* 268–275.

Brewer, M. B. (1988). A dual process model of impression formation. In T. K. Srull & R. S. J. Wyer (Eds.), *Advances in social cognition, Volume 1: A dual process model of impression formation* (pp. 1–36). Hillsdale, NJ: Lawrence Erlbaum.

Bridges, J. S., Etaugh, C., & Barnes-Farrell, J. (2002). Trait judgments of stay-at-home and employed parents: A function of social role and/or shifting standards? *Psychology of Women Quarterly, 26,* 140–150.

Brown, B. L., Giles, H., & Thakerar, J. N. (1985). Speaker evaluations as a function of speech rate, accent, and context. *Language Communication, 5,* 207–220.

Brown, E. R., & Diekman, A. B. (2013). Differential effects of female and male candidates on system justification: Can cracks in the glass ceiling foster complacency? *European Journal of Social Psychology, 43,* 299–306.

Brown, R. J., & Hewstone, M. (2005). An integrative theory of intergroup contact. In M. P. Zanna (Ed.), *Advances in experimental social psychology* (Vol. 37, pp. 255–343). San Diego, CA: Elsevier.

Brown, R. P., & Pinel, E. C. (2003). Stigma on my mind: Individual differences in the experience of stereotype threat. *Journal of Experimental Social Psychology, 39,* 626–633.

Bruckmüller, S., Hegarty, P., & Abele, A. E. (2012). Framing gender differences: Linguistic normativity affects perceptions of power and gender stereotypes. *European Journal of Social Psychology, 42,* 210–218.

Bruckmüller, S., Ryan, M. K., Haslam, S. A., & Peters, K. (2013). Ceilings, cliffs, and labyrinths: exploring metaphors for workplace gender discrimination. In M. K. Ryan & N. R. Branscome (Eds.), *The SAGE Handbook of Gender and Psychology* (pp. 450–464). London, UK: Sage.

Brunet, I., & Rodríguez Soler, J. (2013). Empresas spin-off y género: Diferencias entre hombres y mujeres en la creación de empresas de base tecnológica [Spin-offs and gender: Differences between men and women in the creation of technology-based companies]. *Comunitania: International Journal of Social Work and Social Sciences, 6,* 9–36.

Bundesministerium für Familie Senioren Frauen und Jugend. (2012). *Elterngeld-Monitor* [Parenting money monitor]. Retrieved from http://www.bmfsfj.de/BMFSFJ/Service/Publikationen/publikationsliste,did=184556.html

Butler, A. B., & Skattebo, A. (2004). What is acceptable for women may not be for men: The effect of family conflicts with work on job-performance ratings. *Journal of Occupational and Organizational Psychology, 77,* 553–564.

Byrnes, J. P., Miller, D. C., & Schafer, W. D. (1999). Gender differences in risk taking: A meta-analysis. *Psychological Bulletin, 125,* 367–383.

Cadinu, M., Maass, A., Frigerio, S., Impagliazzo, L., & Latinotti, S. (2003). Stereotype threat: The effect of expectancy on performance. *European Journal of Social Psychology, 33*, 267–285.

Cadinu, M., Maass, A., Rosabianca, A., & Kiesner, J. (2005). Why do women underperform under stereotype threat? Evidence for the role of negative thinking. *Psychological Science, 16*, 572–578.

Cameron, J. E., & Lalonde, R. N. (2001). Social identification and gender-related ideology in women and men. *British Journal of Social Psychology, 40*, 59–77.

Cantisano, G. T., Depolo, M., & Domínguez, J. F. M. (2007). Acoso laboral: meta-análisis y modelo integrador de sus antecedentes y consecuencias [Workplace bullying: Meta-analysis and integrative model of its antecedents and consequences]. *Psicothema, 19*, 88–94.

Cárdenas, M. C., Eagly, A., Salgado, E., Goode, W., Heller, L-I., Jaúregui, K.,…Godoy, M. J. (2014). Latin American female business executives: An interesting surprise. *Gender in Management, 29*, 2–24.

Carleton, R. N., Collimore, K. C., & Asmundson, G. J. G. (2007). Social anxiety and fear of negative evaluation: Construct validity of the BFNE-II. *Journal of Anxiety Disorders, 21*, 131–141.

Carter, N. M., & Silva, C. (2010). Pipeline's broken promise. *Catalyst*. Retrieved from http://www.catalyst.org/publication/372/pipelines-broken-promise

Carton, A. M, & Rosette, A. S. (2011). Explaining bias against black leaders: Integrating theory on information processing and goal-based stereotyping. *Academy of Management Journal, 54*, 1141–1158.

Castaño, C., & Webster, J. (Eds.). (2014). *Género, ciencia y tecnologías de la información* [Gender, science and information technology]. Barcelona, Spain: Aresta.

Catalyst. (2007). *The double-bind dilemma for women in leadership: Damned if you do, doomed if you don't*. New York, NY: Catalyst.

Ceci, S. J., & Williams, W. M. (2007). *Why aren't more women in science? Top researchers debate the evidence*. Washington, DC: American Psychological Association.

Ceci, S. J., Williams, W. M., & Barnett, S. M. (2009). Women's underrepresentation in science: Sociocultural and biological considerations. *Psychological Bulletin, 135*, 218–261.

Cejka, M. A., & Eagly, A. H. (1999). Gender-stereotypic images of occupations correspond to the sex segregation of employment. *Personality and Social Psychology Bulletin, 25*, 413–423.

Chalabaev, A., Brisswalter, J., Radel, R., Coombes, S. A., Easthope, C., & Clément-Guillotin, C., (2013). Can stereotype threat affect motor performance in the absence of explicit monitoring processes? Evidence using a strength task. *Journal of Sport & Exercise Psychology, 35*, 211–215.

Cheryan, S., Drury, B. J., & Vichayapai, M. (2013). Enduring influence of stereotypical computer science role models on women's academic aspirations. *Psychology of Women Quarterly, 37*, 72–79.

Cheryan, S., & Plaut, V. C. (2010). Explaining underrepresentation: A theory of precluded interest. *Sex Roles, 63*, 475–488.

Cheryan, S., Plaut, V. C., Davies, P. G., & Steele, C. M. (2009). Ambient belonging: How stereotypical cues impact gender participation in computer science. *Journal of Personality and Social Psychology, 97*, 1045–1060.

Cheryan, S., Siy, J. O., Vichayapai, M., Drury, B. J., & Kim, S. (2011). Do female and male role models who embody STEM stereotypes hinder women's anticipated success in STEM? *Social Psychological and Personality Science, 2*, 656–664.

CIA. (2014). Total fertility rate (children born/woman). *The world factbook.* https://www.cia.gov/library/publications/the-world-factbook/rankorder/2127rank.html

Cikara, M., & Fiske, S. T. (2009). Warmth, competence, and ambivalent sexism: Vertical assault and collateral damage. In M. Barreto, M. Ryan, & M. Schmitt (Eds.), *The glass ceiling in the 21st century: Understanding barriers to gender equality* (pp. 73–96). Washington, DC: American Psychological Association.

Cleveland, J. N., Stockdale, M., & Murphy, K. R. (2000). *Women and men in organizations: Sex and gender issues at work.* Mahwah, NJ: Lawrence Erlbaum.

Coates, L., & Johnson, T. (2001). Towards a social theory of gender. In W. P. Robinson & H. Giles (Eds.), *The new handbook of language and social psychology* (pp. 451–463). Chichester, UK: John Wiley & Sons.

Cohen, G. L., & Garcia, J. (2008). Identity, belonging, and achievement: A model, interventions, implications. *Current Directions in Psychological Science, 17*, 365–369.

Cole, E. R. (2009). Intersectionality and research in psychology. *American Psychologist, 64*, 170–180.

Coleman, J. M., & Franiuk, R. (2011). Perceptions of mothers and fathers who take temporary work leave. *Sex Roles, 64*, 311–323.

Collins, K. A., & Clément, R. (2012). Language and prejudice: Direct and moderated effects. *Journal of Language and Social Psychology, 31*, 376–396.

Cook, A., & Glass, C. (2013). Research notes and commentaries above the glass ceiling: When are women and racial/ethnic minorities promoted to CEO? *Strategic Management Journal.* Advance online publication.

Correll, S. J., Benard, S., & Paik, I. (2007). Getting a job: Is there a motherhood penalty? *American Journal of Sociology, 112*, 1297–1338.

Costea, B. (2011). Diversity, uniqueness and human resourcefulness. In E. Jeanes, D. Knights, & P. Y. Martin (Eds.), *Handbook of gender, work and organization* (pp. 333–346). Chichester, UK: John Wiley & Sons.

Coupland, N., Coupland, J., Giles, H., & Henwood, K. (1988). Accommodating the elderly: Invoking and extending a theory. *Language and Society, 17*, 1–41.

Coupland, N., Giles, H., & Wiemann, J. (Eds.). (1991). Gender, power, and miscommunication. In N. Coupland, H. Giles, & J. Wiemann (Eds.), *"Miscommunication" and problematic talk* (pp. 18–43). Newbury Park, CA: Sage.

Crisp, R. J., Bache, L. M., & Maitner, A. T. (2009). Dynamics of social comparison in counter-stereotypic domains: Stereotype boost, not stereotype threat, for women engineering majors. *Social Influence, 4*, 171–184.

Croft, A., Schmader, T., Block, K., & Baron, A. S. (2014). The second shift reflected in the second generation: Do parents' gender roles at home predict children's aspirations? *Psychological Science, 25*, 1–11.

Crosby, F. J. (2004). *Affirmative action is dead: Long live affirmative action.* New Haven, CT: Yale University Press.

Crosby, F. J., Stockdale, M. S., & Ropp, S. A. (2007). *Sex discrimination in the workplace: Multidisciplinary perspectives*. New York, NY: Wiley-Blackwell.

Croson, R., & Gneezy, U. (2009). Gender differences in preferences. *Journal of Economic Literature, 47*, 1–27.

Cross, S. E., & Madson, L. (1997). Models of the self: Self-construals and gender. *Psychological Bulletin, 122*, 5–37.

Cuddy, A. J. C., Fiske, S. T., & Glick, P. (2004). When professionals become mothers, warmth doesn't cut the ice. *Journal of Social Issues, 60*, 701–718.

Cunningham, G. B. (2009). The moderating effect of diversity strategy on the relationship between racial diversity and organizational performance. *Journal of Applied Social Psychology, 39*, 1445–1460.

Cvencek, D., Meltzoff, A. N., & Greenwald, A. G. (2011). Math-gender stereotypes in elementary-school children. *Child Development, 82*, 766–779.

Dardenne, B., Dumont, M., & Bollier, T. (2007). Insidious dangers of benevolent sexism: Consequences for women's performance. *Journal of Personality and Social Psychology, 83*, 764–779.

Dasgupta, N. (2011). Ingroup experts and peers as social vaccines who inoculate the self-concept: The stereotype inoculation model. *Psychological Inquiry, 22*, 231–246.

Dasgupta, N., & Asgari, S. (2004). Seeing is believing: Exposure to counterstereotypic women leaders and its effect on the malleability of automatic gender stereotyping. *Journal of Experimental Social Psychology, 40*, 642–658.

Davidson, M. J., & Burke, R. J. (2000). *Women in management: Current research issues. Volume II*. London, UK: Sage.

Davies, P. G., Spencer, S. J., Quinn, D. M., & Gerhardstein, R. (2002). Consuming images: How television commercials that elicit stereotype threat can restrain women academically and professionally. *Personality and Social Psychology Bulletin, 28*, 1615–1628.

Davison, H. K., & Burke, M. J. (2000). Sex discrimination in simulated employment contexts: A meta-analytic investigation. *Journal of Vocational Behavior, 56*, 225–248.

De Houwer, J., Teige-Mocigemba, S., Spruyt, A., & Moors, A. (2009). Implicit measures: A normative analysis and review. *Psychological Bulletin, 135*, 347–368.

de Lemus, S., Moya, M., Bukowski, M., & Lupiáñez, J. (2008). Activación automática de las dimensiones de competencia y sociabilidad en el caso de los estereotipos de género. [Automatic activation of competence and warmth dimensions in the case of gender stereotyping]. *Psicológica, 29*, 115–132.

De Madariaga, I. (Ed.). (2013). *Científicas en cifras 2013* [Scientific figures 2013]. Madrid, Spain: Secretaria de investigación, desarrollo e investigación.

Deaux, K. (1984). From individual differences to social categories: Analysis of a decade's reasearch on gender. *American Psychologist, 39*, 105–116.

Deaux, K. (1985). Sex and gender. *Annual Review of Psychology, 36*, 49–81.

Deaux, K. (1993). Sorry, wrong number—A reply to Gentile's call. *Psychological Science, 4*, 125–126.

Deaux, K., & LaFrance, M. (1998). Gender. In D. T. Gilbert, S. T. Fiske, & G. Lindzey (Eds.), *The handbook of social psychology* (4th ed., Vols. 1 & 2, pp. 788–827). New York, NY: McGraw-Hill.

Deaux, K., & Lewis, L. L. (1984). Structure of gender stereotypes: Interrelationships among components and gender label. *Journal of Personality and Social Psychology, 46,* 991–1004.

Deaux, K., & Major, B. (1987). Putting gender into context: An interactive model of gender-related behavior. *Psychological Review, 94,* 369–389.

DeMartino, R., Barbato, R., & Jacques, P. H. (2006). Exploring the career/achievement and personal life orientation differences between entrepreneurs and nonentrepreneurs: The impact of sex and dependents. *Journal of Small Business Management, 44,* 350–368.

Derks, B., Scheepers, D., & Ellemers, N. (Eds.). (2013). *Neuroscience of prejudice and intergroup relations.* New York, NY: Psychology Press.

Derks, B., van Laar, C., & Ellemers, N. (2007). Social creativity strikes back: Improving motivated performance of low status group members by valuing ingroup dimensions. *European Journal of Social Psychology, 37,* 470–493.

Derks, B., van Laar, C., & Ellemers, N. (2009). Working for the self or working for the group: How personal and social self-affirmation promote collective behavior among members of devalued groups. *Journal of Personality and Social Psychology, 96,* 183–202.

Desvaux, G., Devillard-Hoellinger, S., & Baumgarten, P. (2007). *Women matter: Gender diversity, a corporate performance driver.* Paris, France: McKinsey & Company. Retrieved from http://www.mckinsey.com/locations/paris/home/womenmatter/pdfs/Women_matter_oct2007_english.pdf

Devine, P. G. (1989). Stereotypes and prejudice: Their automatic and controlled components. *Journal of Personality and Social Psychology, 56,* 5–18.

Devos, T., Blanco, K., Rico, F., & Dunn, R. (2008). The role of parenthood and college education in the self-concept of college students: Explicit and implicit assessments of gendered aspirations. *Sex Roles, 59,* 214–228.

Dezsö, C. L., & Ross, D. G. (2012). Does female representation in top management improve firm performance? A panel data investigation. *Strategic Management Journal, 33,* 1072–1089.

Diekman, A. B., Clark, E. K., Johnston, A. M., Brown, E. R., & Steinberg, M. (2011). Malleability in communal goals and beliefs influences attraction to STEM careers: Evidence for a goal congruity perspective. *Journal of Personality and Social Psychology, 101,* 902–918.

Diekman, A. B., & Eagly, A. H. (2000). Stereotypes as dynamic constructs: Women and men of the past, present, and future. *Personality and Social Psychology Bulletin, 26,* 1171–1188.

Diekman, A. B., Eagly, A. H., Mladinic, A., & Ferreira, M. C. (2005). Dynamic stereotypes about women and men in Latin America and the United States. *Journal of Cross-Cultural Psychology, 36,* 209–226.

Diversity Inc. (2013). *Where is the diversity in Fortune 500 CEOs?* Retrieved from http://www.diversityinc.com/facts/wheres-the-diversity-in-fortune-500-ceos

Douglas, K., & Sutton, R. M. (2014). A giant leap for mankind, but what about women? *Journal of Language and Social Psychology, 33,* 667–680. Retrieved from http://kar.kent.ac.uk/id/eprint/41076

Dovidio, J., Hewstone, M., Glick, P., & Esses, V. (2010). Prejudice, stereotyping and discrimination: Theoretical and empirical overview. In J. Dovidio, M. Hewstone, P. Glick, &

V. Esses (Eds.), *The Sage handbook of prejudice, stereotyping and discrimination* (pp. 3–29). London, UK: Sage.

Dovidio, J. F. (2001). On the nature of contemporary prejudice: The third wave. *Journal of Social Issues, 57,* 829–849.

Dunning, D., & Sherman, D. A. (1997). Stereotypes and tacit inference. *Journal of Personality and Social Psychology, 73,* 459–471.

Eagly, A. H. (1987). *Sex differences in social behavior: A social-role interpretation.* Hillsdale, NJ: Lawrence Erlbaum.

Eagly, A. H., & Carli, L. L. (1981). Sex of researchers and sex-typed communications as determinants of sex differences in influenceability: A meta-analysis of social influence studies. *Psychological Bulletin, 90,* 1–20.

Eagly, A. H., & Carli, L. L. (2004). Women and men as leaders. In J. Antonakis, A. Cianciolo, & R. Sternberg (Eds.), *The nature of leadership* (pp. 279–301). Thousand Oaks, CA: Sage Publications.

Eagly, A. H., & Carli, L. L. (2007). *Through the labyrinth: The truth about how women become leaders.* Boston, MA: Harvard Business School Press.

Eagly, A. H., Eaton, A., Rose, S. M., Riger, S., & McHugh, M. C. (2012). Feminism and psychology. Analysis of a half-century of research on women and gender. *American Psychologist, 67,* 211–230.

Eagly, A. H., & Karau, S. J. (2002). Role congruity theory of prejudice toward female leaders. *Psychological Review, 109,* 573–598.

Eagly, A. H., & Mladinic, A. (1989). Gender stereotypes and attitudes toward women and men. *Personality and Social Psychology Bulletin, 15,* 543–558.

Eagly, A. H., Mladinic, A., & Otto, S. (1991). Are women evaluated more favorably than men? An analysis of attitudes, beliefs, and emotions. *Psychology of Women Quarterly, 15,* 203–216.

Eagly, A. H., & Sczesny, S. (2009). Stereotypes about women, men, and leaders: Have times changed? In M. Barreto, M. K. Ryan, & M. T. Schmidt (Eds.), *The glass ceiling in the 21st century: Understanding barriers to gender equality* (1st ed., pp. 21–47). Washington, DC: American Psychological Association.

Eagly, A. H., & Steffen, V. J. (1984). Gender stereotypes stem from the distribution of women and men into social roles. *Journal of Personality and Social Psychology, 46,* 735–754.

Eagly, A. H., & Wood, W. (2012). Social role theory. In P. van Lange, A. Kruglanski, & E. T. Higgins (Eds.), *Handbook of theories in social psychology* (pp. 458–476). Thousand Oaks, CA: Sage.

Eagly, A. H., & Wood, W. (2013). The nature-nurture debates: 25 years of challenges in understanding the psychology of gender. *Perspectives on Psychological Science, 8,* 340–357.

Eagly, A. H., Wood, W., & Diekman, A. B. (2000). Social role theory of sex differences and similarities: A current appraisal. In T. Eckes & H. M. Trautner (Eds.), *The developmental psychology of gender* (pp. 123–174). Mahwah, NJ: Lawrence Erlbaum.

Ebert, I. D., & Steffens, M. C. (2013). Explizite und implizite geschlechtsbezogene Kognitionen heute [Explicit and implicit gender-related cognitions today]. *GENDER. Zeitschrift für Geschlecht, Kultur und Gesellschaft, 5,* 26–40.

Ebert, I. D., Steffens, M. C., & Kroth, A. (2014). Warm, but maybe not so competent? Contemporary implicit stereotypes of women and men in Germany. *Sex Roles, 70,* 359–375.

Eccles, J. S. (1994). Understanding women's educational and occupational choices: Applying the Eccles et al. model of achievement-related choices. *Psychology of Women Quarterly, 18,* 585–609.

Eccles, J. S. (2005). Studying gender and ethnic differences in participation in math, physical science, and information technology. In J. E. Jacobs & S. D. Simpkins (Eds.), *Leaks in the pipeline to math, science, and technology careers* (pp. 7–14). San Francisco, CA: Jossey-Bass.

Eccles, J. S. (2007). Where are all the women? Gender differences in participation in physical science and engineering. In S. J. Ceci & W. M. Williams (Eds.), *Why aren't more women in science? Top researchers debate the evidence* (pp. 199–210). Washington, DC: American Psychological Association.

Eckel, C. C., & Grossman, P. J. (2002). Sex differences and statistical stereotyping in attitudes toward financial risk. *Evolution and Human Behavior, 23,* 281–295.

Eckel, C. C., & Grossman, P. J. (2008). Differences in the economic decisions of men and women: Experimental evidence. In C. Plott & V. Smith (Eds.), *Handbook of experimental economics results* (pp. 509–519). New York, NY: Elsevier.

Eckes, T. (1994). Features of men, features of women: Assessing stereotypic beliefs about gender subtypes. *British Journal of Social Psychology, 33,* 107–123.

Eckes, T. (1997). *Geschlechterstereotype: Frau und Mann in sozialpsychologischer Sicht* [Gender stereotypes: Woman and men from a social psychology viewpoint]. Pfaffenweiler, Germany: Centaurus.

Eckes, T. (2008). Geschlechterstereotype: Von Rollen, Identitäten und Vorurteilen [Gender stereotypes: About roles, identities, and prejudice]. In R. Becker & B. Kortendiek (Eds.), *Handbuch Frauen- und Geschlechterforschung [Handbook women- and gender studies]* (pp. 171–182). Wiesbaden, Germany: VS Verlag für Sozialwissenschaften.

Eckes, T., & Six-Materna, I. (1998). Leugnung von Diskriminierung: Eine Skala zur Erfassung des modernen Sexismus [Denial of discrimination: A scale measuring modern sexism]. *Zeitschrift für Sozialpsychologie, 29,* 224–238.

Ehrke, F., Berthold, A., & Steffens, M. C. (2014). How diversity training can change attitudes: Increasing perceived complexity of superordinate groups to improve intergroup relations. *Journal of Experimental Social Psychology, 53,* 193–206.

Ehrke, F., & Steffens, M. C. (2014). Diversity-trainings—Einstellungen zwischen Gruppen sozialpsychologisch fundiert verbessern [Diversity training—Improving intergroup attitudes based on a social-psychological foundation]. In M. Sauerland & O. L. Braun (Eds.), *Aktuelle Trends in der Personal- und Organisationsentwicklung* (pp. 127–159). Hamburg, Germany: Windmühle.

Eisenberg, N., & Lennon, R. (1983). Sex differences in empathy and related capacities. *Psychological Bulletin, 94,* 100–131.

Ellemers, N. (2001). Individual upward mobility and the perceived legitimacy of intergroup relations. In J. T. Jost & B. Major (Eds.), *The psychology of legitimacy: Emerging perspectives* on ideology, justice, and intergroup relations (pp. 205–222). Cambridge, UK: Cambridge University Press.

Ellemers, N., & Barreto, M. (2008). Maintaining the illusion of meritocracy: How men and women interactively sustain gender inequality at work. In S. Demoulin, J.-P. Leyens, & J. F. Dovidio (Eds.), *Intergroup misunderstandings. Impact of divergent social realities* (pp. 191–208). New York, NY: Psychology Press.

Ellemers, N., Plagiaro, S., & Barreto, M. (2013). Morality and behavioural regulation in groups: A social identity approach. *European Review of Social Psychology, 24*, 160–193.

Ellemers, N., Rink, F., Derks, B., & Ryan, M. K. (2012). Women in high places: When and why promoting women into top positions can harm them individually or as a group (and how to prevent this). *Research in Organizational Behavior: An Annual Series of Analytical Essays and Critical Reviews, 32*, 163–187.

Ellemers, N., van den Heuvel, H., de Gilder, D., Maass, A., & Bonvini, A. (2004). The underrepresentation of women in science: Differential commitment or the queen bee syndrome? *British Journal of Social Psychology, 43*, 315–338.

Ellemers, N., & van Laar, C. (2010). Individual mobility. In J. F. Dovidio, M. Hewstone, P. Glick, & V. Esses (Eds.), *Handbook of prejudice, stereotyping and discrimination* (pp. 561–576). London, UK: Sage.

England, P. (2003). Toward gender equality: Progress and bottlenecks. Retrieved from http://www.ipr.northwestern.edu/publications/docs/workingpapers/2003/IPR-WP-03-13.pdf

Erdley, C. A., & Dweck, C. S. (1993). Children's implicit personality theories as predictors of their social judgments. *Child Development, 64*, 863–878.

Ergun, S., García-Muñoz, T., & Rivas, M. F. (2012). Gender differences in economic experiments. *Revista Internacional de Sociología, 70*, 15–26.

Esses, V. M., Jackson, L. M., & Bennett-AbuAyyash, C. (2010). Intergroup competition. In J. F. Dovidio, M. Hewstone, P. Glick, & V. M. Esses (Eds.), *The SAGE handbook of prejudice, stereotyping, and discrimination* (pp. 225–240). London, UK: Sage.

Esteban-Guitart, M., Viladot, M. A., & Giles, H. (2014). Perceived institutional support among young indigenous and mestizo students from Chiapas (México). A group vitality approach. *Journal of Multilingual and Multicultural Development, 36, 124–125*. Retrieved from http://www.tandfonline.com/doi/full/10.1080/01434632.2014.898645#.U2DZJlV_uSp

Etaugh, C., & Folger, D. (1998). Perceptions of parents whose work and parenting behaviors deviate from role expectations. *Sex Roles, 39*, 215–223.

Etaugh, C., & Moss, C. (2001). Attitudes of employed women toward parents who choose full-time or part-time employment following their child's birth. *Sex Roles, 44*, 611–619.

Evers, A., & Sieverding, M. (2014). Why do highly qualified women (still) earn less? Gender differences in long-term predictors of career success. *Psychology of Women Quarterly, 38*, 93–106.

Falomir-Pichastor, J. M., & Mugny, G. (2009). "I'm not gay... I'm a real man!": Heterosexual men's gender self-esteem and sexual prejudice. *Personality and Social Psychology Bulletin, 35*, 1233–1243.

Faludi, S. (2000). *Stiffed: The betrayal of the American man*. New York, NY: Harper Perennial.

Fazio, R. H., Sanbonmatsu, D. M., Powell, M. C., & Kardes, F. R. (1986). On the automatic activation of attitudes. *Journal of Personality and Social Psychology, 50*, 229–238.

Federico, C. M., & Sidanius, J. (2002). Racism, ideology, and affirmative action, revisited: The antecedents and consequences of "principled objections" to affirmative action. *Journal of Personality and Social Psychology, 82*, 488–502.

Fernández, J. L., Parapar, C., & Ruíz, M. (2010). El envejecimiento de la población [The aging population]. *Lychnos. Cuadernos de la Fundación General CSIC, 2*, edición digital. Spain: Consejo Suoerior de Investigaciones Científicas—CSIC. http://www.fgcsic.es/lychnos/es_ES/articulos/envejecimiento_poblacion.

Figner, B., & Weber, E. U. (2011). Who takes risks when and why? Determinants of risk taking. *Current Directions in Psychological Science, 20*, 211–216.

Fiske, A. P., Haslam, N., & Fiske, S. T. (1991). Confusing one person with another: What errors reveal about the elementary forms of social relations. *Journal of Personality and Social Psychology, 60*, 656–674.

Fiske, S. T. (2000). Interdependence and the reduction of prejudice. In S. Oskamp (Ed.), *Reducing prejudice and discrimination* (pp. 115–135). Mahwah, NJ: Lawrence Erlbaum.

Fiske, S. T. (2010). Venus and Mars or down to earth: Stereotypes and realities of gender differences. *Perspectives on Psychological Science, 5*, 688–692.

Fiske, S. T., Cuddy, A. J. C., Glick, P., & Xu, J. (2002). A model of (often mixed) stereotype content: Competence and warmth respectively follow from perceived status and competition. *Journal of Personality and Social Psychology, 82*, 878–902.

Fiske, S. T., & Neuberg, S. L. (1990). A continuum of impression formation, from category-based to individuating processes: Influences of information and motivation on attention and interpretation. In M. P. Zanna (Ed.), *Advances in experimental social psychology, Vol. 23* (pp. 1–74). New York, NY: Academic Press.

Fiske, S. T., & Taylor, S. E. (2008). *Social cognition: from brains to culture* (1st ed., p. 540). London, UK: McGraw-Hill.

Fitzgerald, L. P. (1993). Sexual harassment: Violence against women in the workplace. *American Psychologist, 48*, 1070–1076.

Foschi, M. (2000). Double standards for competence: Theory and research. *Annual Review of Sociology, 26*, 21–42.

Foss, S. K., Domenico, M. E., & Foss, K. A. (2012). *Gender stories: Negotiating identity in a binary world* (p. 257). Long Grove, IL: Waveland Press.

Franzway, S., Sharp, R., Mills, J. E., & Gill, J. (2009). Engineering ignorance: The problem of gender equity in engineering. *Frontiers, 30*, 89–106.

Fuegen, K., Biernat, M., Haines, E., & Deaux, K. (2004). Mothers and fathers in the workplace: How gender and parental status influence judgments of job-related competence. *Journal of Social Issues, 60*, 737–754.

Fuegen, K., & Endicott, N. F. (2010). Evidence of shifting standards in judgments of male and female parents' job-related ability. *Current Research in Social Psychology, 15*, 53–61.

Gaertner, S. L., & Dovidio, J. F. (2000). *Reducing intergroup bias: The common ingroup identity model* (p. 212). Philadelphia, PA: Psychology Press.

Gal, D., & Wilkie, J. (2010). Real men don't eat quiche: Regulation of gender-expressive choice by men. *Social Psychological and Personality Science, 1,* 291–301.

Galinsky, A. D., Hall, E. V., & Cuddy, A. J. C. (2013). Gendered races: Implications for interracial marriage, leadership selection, and athletic participation. *Psychological Science, 24,* 498–506.

Gallois, C., & Giles, H. (1998). Accommodating mutual influence in intergroup encounters. In M. Palmer & G. A. Barnett (Eds.), *Mutual influence in interpersonal communication: Theory and research in cognition, affect, and behavior* (pp. 135–162). New York, NY: Ablex.

Gallois, C., Ogay, T., & Giles, H. (2005). Communication accommodation theory. In W. B. Gudykunst (Ed.), *Theorizing about intercultural communication* (pp. 121–148). Thousand Oaks, CA: Sage.

Gallup Poll Survey. (2013). Retrieved from http://www.gallup.com/poll/165791/american-prefer-male-boss.aspx

Garcia, D. M., Horstman Reser, A., Amo, R., Redersdoff, S., & Branscombe, N. R. (2005). Perceivers' responses to in-group and out-group members who blame a negative outcome on discrimination. *Personality and Social Psychology Bulletin, 31,* 769–780.

García-Izquierdo, M., Meseguer, M. Soler, Mª. I., & Sáez, Mª C. (2014). Avances en el estudio del acoso psicológico en el trabajo [Advances in the study of psychological harassment at work]. *Papeles del Psicólogo, 35,* 83–90.

Gardner, W. L., Cogliser, C. C., Davis, K. M., & Dickens, M. P. (2011). Authentic leadership: A review of the literature and research agenda. *The Leadership Quarterly, 22,* 1120–1145.

Gartzia, L., & van Engen, M. (2012). Are (male) leaders "feminine" enough? Gendered traits of identity as mediators of sex differences in leadership styles. *Gender in Management: An International Journal, 27,* 296–314.

Gasiorek, J. (2013). I was impolite to her because that's how she was to me: Perceptions of motive and young adults' communicative responses to underaccommodation. *Western Journal of Communication, 77,* 604–624.

Gasiorek, J., & Giles, H. (2012). Effects of inferred motive on evaluations of non-accommodative communication. *Human Communication Research, 38,* 309–331.

Gasiorek, J., & Giles, H. (2013). Accommodating the interactional dynamics of conflict management. *Iranian Journal of Society, Culture and Language, 1,* 10–21.

Gaucher, D., Friesen, J., & Kay, A. C. (2011). Evidence that gendered wording in job advertisements exists and sustains gender inequality. *Journal of Personality and Social Psychology, 101,* 109–128.

German Federal Office of Statistics. (2006). *Leben und Arbeiten in Deutschland, Sonderheft 2: Vereinbarkeit von Familie und Beruf—Ergebnisse des Mikrozensus 2005* [Living and working in Germany, Issue 2: Compatibility of family and work—Results of the Mikrozensus 2005]. Wiesbaden, Germany: Statistisches Bundesamt.

Gerstenberg, F. X. R., Imhoff, R., & Schmitt, M. (2012). "Women are bad at math, but I'm not, am I?" Fragile mathematical self-concept predicts vulnerability to a stereotype threat effect on mathematical performance. *European Journal of Personality, 26,* 588–599.

Gesn, P. R., & Ickes, W. (1999). The development of meaning contexts for empathic accuracy: Channel and sequence effects. *Journal of Personality and Social Psychology, 77,* 746–761.

Gilbert, D. T., & Hixon, J. G. (1991). The trouble of thinking: Activation and application of stereotypic beliefs. *Journal of Personality and Social Psychology, 60*, 509–517.

Giles, H. (2012). Principles of intergroup communication. In H. Giles (Ed.), *The handbook of intergroup communication* (pp. 3–18). New York, NY: Routledge.

Giles, H., Coupland, N., & Coupland, J. (1991). Accommodation theory: Communication, context, and consequence. In H. Giles, J. Coupland, & N. Coupland (Eds.), *The contexts of accommodation* (pp. 1–68). New York, NY: Cambridge University Press.

Giles, H., Davis, S., Gasiorek, J., & Giles, J. (2013). *Successful Aging: A Communication Guide to Empowerment*. Barcelona, Spain: Aresta.

Giles, H., & Gasiorek, J. (2011). Intergenerational communication practices. In K. W. Schaie & S. Willis (Eds.), *Handbook of the psychology of aging* (pp. 231–245). New York, NY: Elsevier.

Giles, H., & Gasiorek, J. (2013). Parameters of non-accommodation: Refining and elaborating communication accommodation theory. In J. Forgas, J. László, & V. Orsolya Vincze (Eds.), *Social cognition and communication* (p. 155–172). New York, NY: Psychology Press.

Giles, H., & Ogay, T. (2007). Communication accommodation theory. In B. B. Whaley & W. Santer (Eds.), *Explaining communication: Contemporary theories and exemplars* (pp. 293–310). Mahwah, NJ: Lawrence Erlbaum.

Giles, H., Reid, S. A., & Harwood, J. (2010). Introducing the dynamics of intergroup communication. In H. Giles, S. Reid, & J. Hardwood (Eds.), *The dynamics of intergroup communication* (pp. 1–16). New York, NY: Peter Lang.

Giles, H., & Smith, P. (1979). Accommodation communication theory: Optimal levels of convergence. In H. Giles & R. N. St. Clair (Eds.), *Language and social psychology*. Baltimore, MD: Basil Blackwell.

Giles, H., & Viladot, M. À. (1994). Ethnolinguistic differentiation in Catalonia. *Multilingua, 13*, 301–312.

Giles, H., Willemyns, M., Gallois, C., & Anderson, M. C. (2007). Accommodating a new frontier: The context of law enforcement. In K. Fiedler (Ed.), *Social communication* (pp. 129–162). New York, NY: Psychology Press.

Giles, H., & Williams, A. (1994). Patronizing the young: Forms and evaluations. *International Journal of Aging & Human Development, 39*, 33–53.

Giles, H., Zwang-Weissman, Y., & Hajek, C. (2004). Patronizing and policing elderly people. *Psychological Reports, 95*, 754–756.

Glick, P., Diebold, J., Bailey-Werner, B., & Zhu, L. (1997). The two faces of Adam: Ambivalent sexism and polarized attitudes toward women. *Personality and Social Psychology Bulletin, 23*, 1323–1334.

Glick, P., & Fiske, S. T. (1996). The Ambivalent Sexism Inventory: Differentiating hostile and benevolent sexism. *Journal of Personality and Social Psychology, 70*, 491–512.

Glick, P., & Fiske, S. T. (1999). The Ambivalence toward Men Inventory: Differentiating hostile and benevolent beliefs about men. *Psychology of Women Quarterly, 23*, 519–536.

Glick, P., & Fiske, S. T. (2001). An ambivalent alliance: Hostile and benevolent sexism as complementary justifications for gender inequality. *American Psychologist, 56*, 109–118.

Glick, P., Fiske, S. T., Mladinic, A., Saiz, J. L., Abrams, D., Masser, B.,... Lopez, W. L. (2000). Beyond prejudice as simple antipathy: Hostile and benevolent sexism across cultures. *Journal of Personality and Social Psychology, 79*, 763–775.

Glick, P., Lameiras, M., Fiske, S. T., Eckes, T., Masser, B., Volpato, C.,... Wells, R. (2004). Bad but bold: Ambivalent attitudes toward men predict gender inequality in 16 nations. *Journal of Personality and Social Psychology, 86*, 713–728.

Glick, P., & Rudman, L. A. (2010). Sexism. In J. F. Dovidio, M. Hewstone, P. Glick, & V. M. Esses (Eds.), *The Sage handbook of prejudice, stereotyping and discrimination* (pp. 328–345). London, UK: Sage.

Glick, P., Zion, C., & Nelson, C. (1988). What mediates sex discrimination in hiring decisions? *Journal of Personality and Social Psychology, 55*, 178–186.

Goldberg, P. A. (1968). Are women prejudiced against women? *Transaction, 5*, 28–30.

Gollwitzer, P. M., & Schaal, B. (1998). Metacognition in action: The importance of implementation intentions. *Personality and Social Psychology Review, 2*, 124–136.

Good, C., Aronson, J., & Inzlicht, M. (2003). Improving adolescents' standardized test performance: An intervention to reduce the effects of stereotype threat. *Journal of Applied Developmental Psychology, 24*, 645–662.

Greenwald, A. G., & Banaji, M. R. (1995). Implicit social cognition: Attitudes, self-esteem, and stereotypes. *Psychological Review, 102*, 4–27.

Greenwald, A. G., Banaji, M. R., Rudman, L. A., Farnham, S. D., Nosek, B. A., & Mellott, D. S. (2002). A unified theory of implicit attitudes, stereotypes, self-esteem, and self-concept. *Psychological Review, 109*, 3–25.

Greenwald, A. G., Poehlman, T. A., Uhlmann, E. L., & Banaji, M. R. (2009). Understanding and using the Implicit Association Test: III. Meta-analysis of predictive validity. *Journal of Personality and Social Psychology, 97*, 17–41.

Gregor, A. (2014). Die Medikalisierung der Geschlechtszuweisung. Das Geheimnis um intergeschlechtliche Körper als Konstituens des kulturellen Systems der Zweigeschlechtlichkeit [The medicalization of gender assignment The secret around intersex bodies as constituting the cultural system of gender binaries]. In S. Klinge & L. Schlicht (Eds.), *Geheimni Wissen—Perspektiven auf das Wissen vom Geheimnis seit dem 18. Jahrhundert* (pp. 241–263). Berlin, Germany: Trafo Verlagsgruppe, Dr. Wolfgang Weist.

Guadagno, R. E., & Cialdini, R. B. (2007). Gender differences in impression management in organizations: A qualitative review. *Sex Roles, 56*, 483–494.

Gunderson, E. A., Ramirez, G., Levine, S. C., & Beilock, S. L. (2012). The role of parents and teachers in the development of gender-related math attitudes. *Sex Roles, 66*, 153–166.

Güngör, G., & Biernat, M. (2009). Gender bias or motherhood disadvantage? Judgments of blue collar mothers and fathers in the workplace. *Sex Roles, 60*, 232–246.

Gupta, V. K., Turban, D. B., & Bhawe, N. M. (2008). The effect of gender stereotype activation on entrepreneurial intentions. *Journal of Applied Psychology, 93*, 1053–1061.

Haddock, G., & Zanna, M. P. (1994). Preferring "housewives" to "feminists": Categorization and the favorability of attitudes toward women. *Psychology of Women Quarterly, 18*, 25–52.

Hajek, C., & Giles, H. (2005). Intergroup communication schemas: Cognitive representations of talk with gay men. *Language and Communication, 25*, 161–181.

Hall, C. W., Davis, N. B., Bolen, L. M., & Chia, R. (1999). Gender and racial differences in mathematical performance. *Journal of Social Psychology, 139*, 677–689.

Hall, J. A. (1978). Gender effects in decoding nonverbal cues. *Psychological Bulletin, 85*, 845–857.

Hall, J. A., & Matsumoto, D. (2004). Gender differences in judgments of multiple emotions from facial expressions. *Emotion, 4*, 201–206.

Halpern, D. F. (2007). Science, sex, and good sense: Why women are underrepresented in some areas of science and math. In S. J. Ceci & W. M. Williams (Eds.), *Why aren't more women in science? Top researchers debate the evidence* (pp. 121–130). Washington, DC: American Psychological Association.

Hamilton, D. L., & Gifford, R. K. (1976). Illusory correlation in interpersonal perception: A cognitive basis of stereotypic judgments. *Journal of Experimental Social Psychology, 12*, 392–407.

Hamilton, D. L., & Sherman, J. W. (1994). Stereotypes. In R. S. J. Wyer & T. K. Srull (Eds.), *Handbook of social cognition, Vol. 1: Basic processes* (pp. 1–68). Hillsdale, NJ: Lawrence Erlbaum.

Hanges, P. J., & Ziegert, J. C. (2008). Stereotypes about stereotype research. *Industrial and Organizational Psychology, 1*, 436–438.

Hannover, B., & Kessels, U. (2004). Self-to-prototype matching as a strategy for making academic choices. Why high school students do not like math and science. *Learning and Instruction, 14*, 51–67.

Harris, C. R., Jenkins, M., & Glaser, D. (2006). Gender differences in risk assessment: Why do women take fewer risks than men? *Judgment and Decision Making Journal, 1*, 48–63.

Harwood, J. (2014): Intergroup contact, prejudicial attitudes, and policy preferences: The case of the U.S. military's "don't ask, don't tell" policy, *The Journal of Social Psychology, 155*, 57–69. Retrieved from http://dx.doi.org/10.1080/00224545.2014.959886

Harwood, J., Giles, H., & Palomares, N. A. (2005). Intergroup theory and communication processes. In J. Harwood & H. Giles (Eds.), *Intergroup communication* (pp. 1–17). New York, NY: Peter Lang.

Harwood, J., & Joyce, N. (2012). Intergroup contact and communication. In H. Giles (Ed.), *The handbook of intergroup communication* (pp. 167–180). New York, NY: Routledge.

Haslam, S. A. (2004). *Psychology in organizations: The social identity approach* (2nd ed.). London, UK: Sage.

Haslam, S. A., Postmes, T., & Ellemers, N. (2003). More than a metaphor: Organizational identity makes organizational life possible. *British Journal of Management, 14*, 357–369.

Haslam, S. A., Reicher, S. D., & Platow, M. J. (2011). *The new psychology of leadership: Identity, influence and power* (p. 267). London, UK: Psychology Press.

Hatzenbuehler, M. L. (2009). How does sexual minority stigma "get under the skin"? A psychological mediation framework. *Psychological Bulletin, 135*, 707–730.

Hegarty, P., & Bruckmüller, S. (2013). Teaching & learning guide for asymmetric explanations of group differences: Experimental evidence of Foucault's disciplinary power. *Social and Personality Psychology Compass, 7*, 701–705.

Hegarty, P., Lemieux, A. F., & McWueen, G. (2010). Graphing the order of the sexes: Constructing, recalling, interpreting, and putting the self in gender difference graphs. *Journal of Personality and Social Psychology, 98*, 375–391.

Hegarty, P., & Pratto, F. (2001). The effects of social category norms and stereotypes on explanations for intergroup differences. *Journal of Personality and Social Psychology, 80*, 723–735.

Hegarty, P., & Pratto, F. (2004). The differences that norms make: Empiricism, social constructionism, and the interpretation of group differences. *Sex Roles, 50*, 445–453.

Hegarty, P., Pratto, F., & Lemieux, A. F. (2004). Heterosexist ambivalence and heterocentric norms: Drinking in intergroup discomfort. *Group Processes & Intergroup Relations, 7*, 119–130.

Heilman, M. E. (1983). Sex bias in work settings: The lack of fit model. *Research in Organizational Behavior, 5*, 269–298.

Heilman, M. E. (2012). Gender stereotypes and workplace bias. *Research in Organizational Behavior, 32*, 113–135.

Heilman, M. E., & Eagly, A. H. (2008). Gender stereotypes are alive, well, and busy producing workplace discrimination. *Industrial and Organizational Psychology, 1*, 393–398.

Heilman, M. E., & Okimoto, T. G. (2007). Why are women penalized for success at male tasks? The implied communality deficit. *Journal of Applied Psychology, 92*, 81–92.

Heilman, M. E., & Okimoto, T. G. (2008). Motherhood: A potential source of bias in employment decisions. *Journal of Applied Psychology, 93*, 189–198.

Heilman, M. E., & Parks-Stamm, E. J. (2007). Gender stereotypes in the workplace: Obstacles to women's career progress. In S. J. Correll (Ed.), *Social psychology of gender. Advances in group processes* (Vol. 24, pp. 47–77): New York, NY: Elsevier.

Heilman, M. E., Wallen, A. S., Fuchs, D., & Tamkins, M. M. (2004). Penalties for success: Reactions to women who succeed at male gender-typed tasks. *Journal of Applied Psychology, 89*, 416–427.

Heyder, A., & Kessels, U. (2013). Is school feminine? Implicit gender stereotyping of school as a predictor of academic achievement. *Sex Roles, 69*, 605–617.

Hirigoyen, M. (2001). *El acoso moral en el trabajo* [Bullying at work]. Barcelona, Spain: Paidós.

Hoffman, C., & Hurst, N. (1990). Gender stereotypes: Perceptions or rationalization? *Journal of Personality and Social Psychology, 58*, 197–208.

Hogg, M. A. (2007). Social psychology of leadership. In A. W. Kruglanski & E. T. Higgins (Eds.), *Social psychology: Handbook of basic principles* (2nd ed., pp. 716–733). New York, NY: Guilford.

Hogg, M. A. (2010). Human groups, social categories, and collective self: Social identity and the management of self-uncertainty. In R. M. Arkin, K. C. Oleson, & P. J. Carroll (Eds.), *Handbook of uncertain self* (pp. 401–420). New York, NY: Psychology Press.

Hogg, M. A. (2012). Uncertainty-identity theory. In P. A. M. van Lange, A. W. Kruglanski, & E. T. Higgins (Eds.), *Handbook of theories of social psychology* (Vol. 2, pp. 62–80). Thousand Oaks, CA: Sage.

Hogg, M. A., & Giles, H. (2012). Normative talk in intergroup communication. In H. Giles (Ed.), *The handbook of intergroup communication* (pp. 373–387). New York, NY: Routledge.

Holleran, S. E., Whitehead, J., Schmader, T., & Mehl, M. R. (2011). Talking shop and shooting the breeze: A study of workplace conversation and job disengagement among STEM faculty. *Social Psychological and Personality Science, 2*, 65–71.

Holoien, D. S., & Shelton, J. N. (2012). You deplete me: The cognitive costs of colorblindness on ethnic minorities. *Journal of Experimental Social Psychology, 48*, 562–565.

Hornsey, M. J., & Hogg, M. A. (2000). Assimilation and diversity: An integrative model of subgroup relations. *Personality and Social Psychology Review, 4*, 143–156.

Hoyt, C. L. (2010). Women, men, and leadership: Exploring the gender gap at the top. *Social and Personality Psychology Compass, 4*, 484–498.

Hoyt, C. L. (2012). *Women and leadership: Theory and practice* (5th ed.). Thousand Oaks, CA: Sage.

Hoyt, C. L., & Burnette, J. L. (2013). Gender bias in leader evaluations: Merging implicit theories and role congruity perspectives. *Personality and Social Psychology Bulletin, 39*, 1306–1319.

Huffman, M. L. (2013). Organizations, managers, and wage inequality. *Sex Roles, 68*, 216–222.

Huguet, P., & Regner, I. (2007). Stereotype threat among schoolgirls in quasi-ordinary classroom circumstances. *Journal of Educational Psychology, 99*, 545–560.

Hummert, M. L., & Ryan, E. B. (2001). Patronizing. In W. P. Robinson & H. Giles (Eds.), *The new handbook of language and social psychology* (pp. 253–269). Chichester, UK: John Wiley & Sons.

Hyde, J. S. (2007). Women in science: Gender similarities in abilities and sociocultural forces. In S. J. Ceci & W. M. Williams (Eds.), *Why aren't more women in science? Top researchers debate the evidence* (pp. 131–145). Washington, DC: American Psychological Association.

Hyde, J. S., Lindberg, S. M., Linn, M. C., Ellis, A. B., & Williams, C. C. (2008). Gender similarities characterize math performance. *Science, 321*, 494–495.

Hyrsky, K., & Tuunanen, M. (1999). Innovativeness and risk-taking propensity: A cross-cultural study of Finnish and U.S. entrepreneurs and small business owners. *Liiketaloudellinen aikakauskirja, 48*, 238–256.

Ibañez, M., Lezaún, Z. Serrano, M., & Tomás, G. (2007). *Acoso sexual en el ámbito laboral* [Sexual harassment in the workplace]. Bilbao, Spain: Universidad de Deusto.

Idescat. (2014). Indicadors demogràfics [Demographic indicators], Catalonia Spain: Institut d'Estadística de Catalunya, Generalitat de Catalunya.

I+DTinfo. (2014). Personas Mayores. Cuando la pirámide se invierte [Senior citizens. When the pyramid is inverted]. *I+Dtinfo. Revista de la investigación europea.* http://ec.europa.eu/research/rtdinfo/49/01/print_article_4105_es.html

Inesi, M. E., & Cable, D. M. (2014). When accomplishments come back to haunt you: The negative effect of competence signals on women's performance evaluations. *Personnel Psychology, 00*, 1–43.

Inzlicht, M., & Ben-Zeev, T. (2000). A threatening intellectual environment: Why females are susceptible to experiencing problem-solving deficits in the presence of males. *Psychological Science, 11*, 365–371.

Inzlicht, M., & Kang, S. K. (2010). Stereotype threat spillover: How coping with threats to social identity affects aggression, eating, decision making, and attention. *Journal of Personality and Social Psychology, 99*, 467–481.

Isaac, C., Lee, B., & Carnes, M. (2009). Interventions that affect gender bias in hiring: A systematic review. *Academic Medicine, 84,* 1440–1446.

Jacobs, J. E., & Eccles, J. S. (1992). The impact of mothers' gender-role stereotypic beliefs on mothers' and children's ability perceptions. *Journal of Personality and Social Psychology, 63,* 932–944.

Jetten, J., Branscombe, N. R., Schmitt, M. T., & Spears, R. (2001). Rebels with cause: Group identification as a response to perceived discrimination from the mainstream. *Personality and Social Psychology Bulletin, 27,* 1204–1213.

Jetten, J., Schmitt, M. T., Branscombe, N. R., & McKimmie, B. M. (2005). Suppressing the negative effect of devaluation on group identification: The role on intergroup differentiation and intragroup respect. *Journal of Experimental Social Psychology, 41,* 208–215.

Johns, M., Inzlicht, M., & Schmader, T. (2008). Stereotype threat and executive resource depletion: Examining the influence of emotion regulation. *Journal of Experimental Psychology: General, 137,* 691–705.

Johns, M., Schmader, T., & Martens, A. (2005). Knowing is half the battle: Teaching stereotype threat as a means of improving women's math performance. *Psychological Science, 16,* 175–179.

Johnson, J. E. V., & Powell, P. L. (1994). Decision making, risk and gender: Are managers different? *British Journal of Management, 5,* 123–138.

Jost, J. T., & Banaji, M. R. (1994). The role of stereotyping in system-justification and the production of false consciousness. *British Journal of Social Psychology, 33,* 1–27.

Jost, J. T., Banaji, M. R., & Nosek, B. A. (2004). A decade of system justification theory: Accumulated evidence of conscious and unconscious bolstering of the status quo. *Political Psychology, 25,* 881–919.

Jost, J. T., & Elsbach, K. D. (2001). How status and power differences erode personal and social identities at work: A system justification critique of organizational applications of social identity theory. In M. A. Hogg & D. J. Terry (Eds.), *Social identity processes in organizational contexts* (pp. 181–196). Philadelphia, PA: Psychology Press.

Jost, J. T., & Hunyady, O. (2005). Antecedents and consequences of system-justifying ideologies. *Current Directions in Psychological Science, 14,* 260–265.

Jost, J. T., & Kay, A. C. (2005). Exposure to benevolent sexism and complementary gender stereotypes: Consequences for specific and diffuse forms of system justification. *Journal of Personality and Social Psychology, 88,* 498–509.

Joy, L., Carter, N. M., Wagner, H. M., Narayanan, S. (2007). The bottom line: Corporate performance and women's representation on boards. Retrieved from http://www.catalyst.org/publication/200/the-bottomline-corporate-performance-and-womens-representation-on-boards

Kabat-Farr, D., & Cortina, L. M. (2014). Sex-based harassment in employment: New insights into gender and context. *Law and Human Behavior, 38,* 58–72.

Kaiser, C. R. (2006). Dominant ideology threat and the interpersonal consequences of attributions to discrimination. In S. Levin & C. van Laar (Eds.), *Stigma and group inequality: Social psychological perspectives* (pp. 45–64). Mahwah, NJ: Erlbaum.

Kaiser, C. R., & Miller, C. T. (2003). Derogating the victim: The interpersonal consequences of blaming event on discrimination. *Group Processes & Intergroup Relations, 6*, 227–237.

Kalbfleisch, P. (2010). Gendered language as a dynamic intergroup process. In H. Giles, S. Reid, & J. Harwood (Eds.), *The dynamics of intergroup communication* (pp. 29–39). New York, NY: Peter Lang.

Kang, S. K., & Inzlicht, M. (2014). Stereotype threat spillover: Why stereotype threat is more useful for organizations than it seems. *Industrial and Organizational Psychology: Perspectives on Science and Practice, 7*, 452–456.

Kanter, R. (1977). Some effects of proportions on group life: Skewed sex ratios and responses to token women. *American Journal of Sociology, 82*, 965–990.

Kasof, J. (1993). Sex bias in the naming of stimulus persons. *Psychological Bulletin, 113*, 140–163.

Katz, D., & Stotland, E. (1959). A preliminary statement to a theory of attitude structure and change. In S. Koch (Ed.), *Psychology: A study of a science* (Vol. 3, pp. 423–475). New York, NY: McGraw-Hill.

Katz, I. (1964). Review of evidence relating to effects of desegregation on the intellectual performance of Negroes. *American Psychologist, 19*, 381–399.

Kaufman, E. K., & Grace, P. E. (2011). Women in grassroots leadership: Barriers and biases experienced in a membership organization dominated by men. *Journal of Leadership Studies, 4*, 6–16.

Kawakami, K., Dovidio, J. F., Moll, J., Hermsen, S., & Russin, A. (2000). Just say no (to stereotyping): Effects of training in the negation of stereotypic associations on stereotype activation. *Journal of Personality and Social Psychology, 78*, 871–888.

Kawakami, K., Dovidio, J. F., & van Kamp, S. (2005). Kicking the habit: Effects of nonstereotypic association training and correction processes on hiring decisions. *Journal of Experimental Social Psychology, 41*, 68–75.

Kay, A. C., & Jost, J. T. (2003). Complementary justice: Effects of "poor but happy" and "poor but honest" stereotype exemplars on system justification and implicit activation of the justice motive. *Journal of Personality and Social Psychology, 85*, 823–837.

Keller, J. (2007). Stereotype threat in classroom settings: The interactive effect of domain identification, task difficulty and stereotype threat on female students' maths performance. *British Journal of Educational Psychology, 77*, 323–338.

Keller, J., & Bless, H. (2008). When positive and negative expectancies disrupt performance: Regulatory focus as a catalyst. *European Journal of Social Psychology, 38*, 187–212.

Keller, J., & Molix, L. (2008). When women can't do math: The interplay of self-construal, group identification, and stereotypic performance standards. *Journal of Experimental Social Psychology, 44*, 437–444.

Kellerman, B., & Rhode, D. L. (2007). *Women and leadership: The state of play and strategies for change* (1st ed., p. 528). San Francisco, CA: Jossey-Bass.

Kennedy, J. A., & Kray, L. J. (2013). Who is willing to sacrifice ethical values for money and social status? Gender differences in reactions to ethical compromises. *Social Psychology and Personality Science, 5*, 52–59.

Kessels, U. (2007). Identifikation mit naturwissenschaftlichen Fächern: Ein Vergleich von Schülerinnen einer monoedukativen und koedukativen Schule [Identification with science: A comparison of girls at a girls' and a coed school]. In L. Herwartz-Emden (Ed.), *Neues aus alten Schulen [News from old schools]* (pp. 161–180). Opladen, Germany: Verlag Barbara Budrich.

Kessels, U., & Hannover, B. (2008). When being a girl matters less: Accessibility of gender-related self-knowledge in single-sex and coeducational classes and its impact on students' physics-related self-concept of ability. *British Journal of Educational Psychology, 78*, 273–289.

Kessels, U., Rau, M., & Hannover, B. (2006). What goes well with physics? Measuring and altering the image of science. *British Journal of Educational Psychology, 76*, 761–780.

Kiefer, A. K., & Sekaquaptewa, D. (2007). Implicit stereotypes and women's math performance: How implicit gender-math stereotypes influence women's susceptibility to stereotype threat. *Journal of Experimental Social Psychology, 43*, 825–832.

King, E. B. (2008). The effect of bias on the advancement of working mothers: Disentangling legitimate concerns from inaccurate stereotypes as predictors of advancement in academe. *Human Relations, 61*, 1677–1711.

Kite, M. E., Deaux, K., & Haynes, E. L. (2008). Gender stereotypes. In F. L. Denmark & M. Paludi (Eds.), *Psychology of women: A handbook of issues and theories* (pp. 205–236). Westport, CT: Praeger.

Kite, M. E., & Whitley, B. E., Jr. (1996). Sex differences in attitudes toward homosexual persons, behaviors, and civil rights: A meta-analysis. *Personality and Social Psychology Bulletin, 22*, 336–353.

Klauer, K. C., Ehrenberg, K., & Wegener, I. (2003). Crossed categorization and stereotyping: Structural analyses, effects patterns, and dissociative effects of context relevance. *Journal of Experimental Social Psychology, 39*, 332–354.

Klauer, K. C., Wegener, I., & Ehrenberg, K. (2002). Perceiving minority members as individuals: The effects of relative group size in social categorization. *European Journal of Social Psychology, 32*, 223–245.

Kling, K. C., Noftle, E. E., & Robins, R. W. (2012). Why do standardized tests underpredict womens's academic performance? The role of conscientiousness. *Social Psychology and Personality Science, 4*, 600–606.

Ko, S. J., Judd, C. M., & Stapel, D. A. (2009). Stereotyping based on voice in the presence of individuating information: Vocal femininity affects perceived competence but not warmth. *Personality and Social Psychology Bulletin, 35*, 198–211.

Koenig, A. M., & Eagly, A. H. (2005). Stereotype threat in men on a test of social sensitivity. *Sex Roles, 52*, 489–496.

Köller, O., Daniels, Z., Schnabel, K., & Baumert, J. (2000). Kurswahlen von Mädchen und Jungen im Fach Mathematik: Die Rolle des fachspezifischen Selbstkonzepts und Interesses [Course selection of girls and boys in mathematics: The role of academic self-concept and interest]. *Zeitschrift für Pädagogische Psychologie/ German Journal of Educational Psychology, 14*, 26–37.

Kray, L. J., & Gelfand, M. J. (2009). Relief versus regret. The effect of gender and negotiating norm ambiguity on reactions to having one's first offer accepted. *Social Cognition, 27*, 418–436.

Kray, L. J., & Haselhuhn, M. P. (2012). Male pragmatism in negotiators' ethical reasoning. *Journal of Experimental Social Psychology, 48*, 1124–1131.

Kray, L. J., Locke, C. C., & Van Zant, A. B. (2012). Feminine charm: An experimental analysis of its costs and benefits in negotiations. *Personality and Social Psychology Bulletin, 38*, 1343–1357.

Kray, L. J., Thompson, L., & Galinsky, A. (2001). Battle of the sexes: Gender stereotype confirmation and reactance in negotiations. *Journal of Personality and Social Psychology, 80*, 942–958.

Krendl, A. C., Richeson, J. A., Kelley, W. M., & Heatherton, T. F. (2008). The negative consequences of threat: A functional magnetic resonance imaging investigation of the neural mechanisms underlying women's underperformance in math. *Psychological Science, 19*, 168–175.

Kuenzler, J., Walter, W., Reichart, E., & Pfister, G. (2001). Gender division of labour in unified Germany. Retrieved from http://www.soziologie.uni-wuerzburg.de/na_rep.pdf

Kulich, C., Trojanowski, G., Ryan, M., Haslam, S. A., & Renneboog, L. D. R. (2011). Who gets the carrot and who gets the stick? Evidence of gender disparities in executive remuneration. *Strategic Management Journal, 32*, 301–321.

Kunda, Z., & Thagard, P. (1996). Forming impressions from stereotypes, traits, and behaviors: A parallel-constraint-satisfaction theory. *Psychological Review, 103*, 284–308.

Kurzban, R., Tooby, J., & Cosmides, L. (2001). Can race be erased? Coalitional computation and social categorization. *Proceedings of the National Academy of Sciences, 98*, 15387–15392.

Lakoff, R. (2003). Language, gender and politics: Putting "women" and "power" in the same sentence. In J. Holmes & M. Meyerhoff (Eds.), *The handbook of language and gender* (pp. 161–178). Malden, MA: Blackwell.

Landrine, H. (1985). Race x class stereotypes of women. *Sex Roles, 13*, 65–75.

Landy, F. J. (2008). Stereotypes, bias, and personnel decisions: Strange and stranger. *Industrial and Organizational Psychology, 1*, 379–392.

Lane, K. A., Goh, J. X., & Driver-Linn, E. (2012). Implicit science stereotypes mediate the relationship between gender and academic participation. *Sex Roles, 66*, 220–234.

Leaper, C., & Friedman, C. K. (2007). The socialization of gender. In J. E. Grusec & P. D. Hastings (Eds.), *Handbook of socialization. Theory and research* (pp. 561–587). New York, NY: Guilford.

Lips, H. M. (2013). The gender pay gap: Challenging the rationalizations. Perceived equity, discrimination, and the limits of human capital models. *Sex Roles, 68*, 169–185.

Liss, M., Crawford, M., & Popp, D. (2004). Predictors and correlates of collective action. *Sex Roles, 50*, 771–779.

Livingston, R. W., Rosette, A. S., & Washington, E. F. (2012). Can an angry black woman get ahead? The impact of race and dominance on perceptions of female leaders. *Psychological Science, 23*, 354–358.

Locksley, A., Borgida, E., Brekke, N., & Hepburn, C. (1980). Sex stereotypes and social judgment. *Journal of Personality and Social Psychology, 39*, 821–831.

London, B., Downey, G., Romero-Canyas, R., Rattan, A., & Tyson, D. (2012). Gender-based rejection sensitivity and academic self-silencing in women. *Journal of Personality and Social Psychology, 102*, 961–979.

Lubinski, D., & Benbow, C. P. (2006). Study of mathematically precocious youth after 35 years: Uncovering antecedents for the development of math-science expertise. *Perspectives on Psychological Science, 1*, 316–345.

Lubinski, D. S., & Benbow, C. P. (2007). Sex differences in personal attributes for the development of scientific enterprise. In S. J. Ceci & M. Williams (Eds.), *Why aren't more women in science? Top researchers debate the evidence* (pp. 79–100). Washington, DC: American Psychological Association.

Lyness, K. S., & Thompson, D. E. (2000). Climbing the corporate ladder: Do female and male executives follow the same route? *Journal of Applied Psychology, 85*, 86–101.

Lytton, H., & Romney, D. M. (1991). Parents' differential socialization of boys and girls: A meta-analysis. *Psychological Bulletin, 109*, 267–296.

Maass, A., & Cadinu, M. (2003). Stereotype threat: When minority members underperform. In W. Stroebe & M. Hewstone (Eds.), *European Review of Social Psychology, 14*, 243–275.

Maass, A., Cadinu, M., Guarnieri, G., & Grasselli, A. (2003). Sexual harassment under social identity threat: The computer harassment paradigm. *Journal of Personality and Social Psychology, 85*, 853–870.

Maass, A. & Cadinu, M. (2006). Protecting a threatened identity through sexual harassment: A social identity interpretation. In R. Brown & D. Capozza (Eds.), *Social Identities: Motivational, Emotional and Cultural Influences* (pp. 109–131). London, UK: Psychology Press.

Machunsky, M., Meiser, T., & Mummendey, A. (2009). On the crucial role of the mental ingroup representation for ingroup bias and the ingroup prototypicality–ingroup bias link. *Experimental Psychology, 56*, 156–164.

Macke, A. S. (1981). Token men and women: A note on the salience of sex and occupation among professionals and semiprofessionals. *Sociology of Work and Occupations, 8*, 25–38.

Macrae, C. N., Bodenhausen, G. V., & Milne, A. B. (1995). The dissection of selection in person perception: Inhibitory processes in social stereotyping. *Journal of Personality and Social Psychology, 69*, 397–407.

Madera, J. M., King, E. B., & Hebl, M. R. (2012). Bringing social identity to work: The influence of manifestation and suppression on perceived discrimination, job satisfaction, and turnover intentions. *Cultural Diversity & Ethnic Minority Psychology, 18*, 165–170.

Maio, G. R., Haddock, G., Manstead, A. S. R., & Spears, R. (2010). Attitudes and intergroup relations. In J. F. Dovidio, M. Hewstone, P. Glick, & V. M. Esses (Eds.), *Handbook of prejudice, stereotyping and discrimination* (pp. 261–275). London, UK: Sage.

Major, B., Quinton, W. J., & Schmader, T. (2003). Attributions to discrimination and self-esteem: Impact of social identification and group ambiguity. *Journal of Experimental Social Psychology, 39*, 220–231.

Major, B., Sawyer, P., & Kunstman, J. W. (2013). Minority perceptions of Whites' motives for responding without prejudice: The perceived internal and external motivation to avoid prejudice scales. *Personality and Social Psychology Bulletin, 39,* 401–414.

Manuel, T., Shefte, S., & Swiss, D. J. (1999). *Suiting themselves: Women's leadership styles in today's workplace. Public Policy Institute and The Boston Club.* Cambridge, MA: Radcliffe Public Policy Institute.

Marsh, H. W. (1989). Age and sex effects in multiple dimensions of self-concept: Preadolescence to early adulthood. *Journal of Educational Psychology, 81,* 417–430.

Marsh, H. W., & Yeung, A. S. (1997). Causal effects of academic self-concept on academic achievement: Structural equation models of longitudinal data. *Journal of Educational Psychology, 89,* 41–54.

Martell, R. F. (1996). What mediates gender bias in work behavior ratings? *Sex Roles, 35,* 153–169.

Martell, R. F., Emrich, C. G., & Robison-Cox, J. (2012). From bias to exclusion: A multilevel emergent theory of gender segregation in organizations. *Research in Organizational Behavior: An Annual Series of Analytical Essays and Critical Reviews, 32,* 137–162.

Martell, R. F., Lane, D. M., & Emrich, C. (1996). Male-female differences: A computer simulation. *American Psychologist, 51,* 157–158.

Martins, L. L., & Parsons, C. K. (2007). Effects of gender diversity management on perceptions of organizational attractiveness: The role of individual differences in attitudes and beliefs. *Journal of Applied Psychology, 92,* 865–875.

Martiny, S. E., & Götz, T. (2011). Stereotype threat in Lern- und Leistungssituationen: Theoretische Ansätze, empirische Befunde und praktische Implikationen [Stereotype threat in study and performance situations: Theoretical perspectives, empirical findings, and practical implications]. In M. Dresel & L. Lämmle (Eds.), *Motivation, Selbstregulation und Leistungsexzellenz [Motivation, self regulation, and performance excellence]* (pp. 153–177). Münster, Germany: Lit.

Martiny, S. E., Roth, J., Jelenec, P., Steffens, M. C., & Croizet, J.-C. (2012). When a new group identity does harm on the spot: Stereotype threat in newly created groups. *European Journal of Social Psychology, 42,* 65–71.

Marx, D. M., & Roman, J. S. (2002). Female role models: Protecting women's math test performance. *Personality and Social Psychology Bulletin, 28,* 1183–1193.

Matsa, D. A., & Miller, A. R. (2013). A female style in corporate leadership? Evidence from quotas. *American Economic Journal: Applied Economics, 5,* 136–169.

Maynard, D. C., & Brooks, M. E. (2008). The persistence of stereotypes in the context of familiarity. *Industrial and Organizational Psychology, 1,* 417–419.

McGarty, C., Haslam, S. A., Hutchinson, K. J., & Turner, J. C. (1994). The effects of salient group memberships on persuasion. *Small Group Research, 25*(2), 267–293.

McHugh, M. C., & Frieze, I. H. (1997). The measurement of gender-role attitudes. *Psychology of Women Quarterly, 21,* 1–16.

McIlwee, J., & Robinson, G. (1992). *Women in engineering: Gender, power and workplace culture.* Albany: State University of New York Press.

McIntyre, R. B., Paulson, R. M., Taylor, C. A., Morin, A. L., & Lord, C. G. (2011). Effects of role model deservingness on overcoming performance deficits induced by stereotype threat. *European Journal of Social Psychology, 41,* 301–311.

McKay, P. F., Avery, D. R., & Morris, M. A. (2008). Mean racial-ethnic differences in employee sales performance: The moderating role of diversity climate. *Personnel Psychology, 61*, 349–374.

Meier-Pesti, K., & Penz, E. (2008). Sex or gender? Expanding the sex-based view by introducing masculinity and femininity as predictors of financial risk taking. *Journal of Economic Psychology, 29*, 180–196.

Meyer, I. H. (2003). Prejudice, social stress, and mental health in lesbian, gay, and bisexual populations: Conceptual issues and research evidence. *Psychological Bulletin, 129*, 674–697.

Mikula, G. (2012). Perceived justice in the division of family labor: Antecedents and consequences. In E. Kals & J. Maes (Eds.), *Justice and Conflicts* (pp. 153–167): Berlin, Germany: Springer-Verlag.

Mikula, G. (2013). Gerechtigkeitspsychologische Aspekte der Aufteilung von Familienarbeit zwischen Frauen und Männern [Aspects of justice psychology in the distribution of family work between women and men]. In M. Gollwitzer, S. Lotz, T. Schlösser, & B. Streicher (Eds.), *Soziale Gerechtigkeit: Was unsere Gesellschaft aus den Erkenntnissen der Gerechtigkeitspsychologie lernen kann* [Psychology of justice: What our society can learn from justice psychology] (pp. 55–75): Göttingen, Germany: Hogrefe Verlag.

Mishra, S. (2014). Decision-making under risk: Integrating perspectives from biology, economics, and psychology. *Personality and Social Psychology Review, 18*, 1–28.

Mölders, C., & Van Quaquebeke, N. (2011). Frauen in Führungspositionen: Prototypen von Führung hinterfragen [Women in leadership positions: Questioning leader prototypes]. *Personalführung, 7*, 42–47.

Moreschi, R. W. (2005). An analysis of the ability of individuals to predict their own risk tolerance. *Journal of Business & Economics Research, 3*, 39–48.

Morrison, K. R., Plaut, V. C., & Ybarra, O. (2010). Predicting whether multiculturalism positively or negatively influences White Americans' intergroup attitudes: The role of ethnic identification. *Personality and Social Psychology Bulletin, 36*, 1648–1661.

Morton, T. A., Postmes, T., & Jetten, J. (2007). Playing the game: When group success is more important than downgrading deviants. *European Journal of Social Psychology, 37*, 599–616.

Morton, T. A., Wright, R. G., Peters, K., Reynolds, K. J., & Haslam, S. A. (2012). Social identity and the dynamics of organizational communication. In H. Giles & C. Gallois (Eds.), *The handbook of intergroup communication* (pp. 319–330). New York, NY: Routledge.

Moss-Racusin, C. A., Dovidio, J. F., Brescoll, V. L., Graham, M. J., & Handelsman, J. (2012). Science faculty's subtle gender biases favor male students. *Proceedings of the National Academy of Sciences of the United States of America, 109*, 16474–16479.

Moya, M., Glick, P., Expósito, F., de Lemus, S., & Hart, J. (2007). It's for your own good: Benevolent sexism and women's reactions to protectively justified restrictions. *Personality and Social Psychology Bulletin, 33*, 1421–1434.

Mulac, A., Giles, H., Bradac, J. J., & Palomares, N. A. (2013). The gender-linked language effect: An empirical test of a general process model. *Language Sciences, 38*, 22–31.

Mulligan-Ferry, L., Bartkiewicz, M. J., Soares, R., Singh, A., & Winkleman, I. (2014). *2013 Catalyst census: Financial post 500 women board directors*. New York, NY: Catalyst.

Mummendey, A., & Wenzel, M. (1999). Social discrimination and tolerance in intergroup relations: Reactions to intergroup difference. *Personality and Social Psychology Review, 3,* 158–174.

Muñoz, K. (2011). *How did I get talked into this?* Barcelona, Spain: Aresta.

Murphy, M. C., Steele, C. M., & Gross, J. J. (2007). Signaling threat: How situational cues affect women in math, science, and engineering settings. *Psychological Science, 18,* 879–885.

Muzzatti, B., & Agnoli, F. (2007). Gender and mathematics: Attitudes and stereotype threat susceptibility in Italian children. *Developmental Psychology, 43,* 747–759.

National Science Foundation. (2006). Women, minorities, and persons with disabilities in science and engineering. Retrieved from http://www.nsf.gov/statistics/wmpd/sex.htm

Neely, J. H. (1976). Semantic priming and retrieval from lexical memory: Evidence for facilitatory and inhibitory processes. *Memory and Cognition, 4,* 648–654.

Nelson, T. D. (2009). *Handbook of prejudice, stereotyping, and discrimination.* New York, NY: Psychology Press.

Nen (nens) and *nena (nenes)* are Catalan for boy(s) and girl(s).

Newcombe, N. S. (2007). Taking science seriously: Straight thinking about spatial sex differences. In S. J. Ceci & M. Williams (Eds.), *Why aren't more women in science? Top researchers debate the evidence* (pp. 69–77). Washington, DC: American Psychological Association.

Newport, F. (2008). Wives still do laundry, men do yard work. Retrieved from http://www.gallup.com/poll/106249/Wives-Still-Laundry-Men-Yard-Work.aspx

Ng, T. W. H., Eby, L. T., Sorensen, K. L., & Feldman, D. C. (2005). Predictors of objective and subjective career success: A meta-analysis. *Personnel Psychology, 58,* 367–408.

Niederle, M., & Vesterlund, L. (2007). Do women shy away from competition? Do men compete too much? *Quarterly Journal of Economics, 122,* 1067–1101.

Niederle, M., & Yestrumskas, A. H. (2008). *Gender differences in seeking challenges: The role of institutions* (NBER Working Paper No. 13922). Retrieved from http://www.nber.org/papers/w13922

Niedlich, C., Steffens, M. C., Krause, J., Settke, E., & Ebert, I. D. (2014). Ironic effects of sexual minority group membership: Are lesbians less susceptible to invoking negative female stereotypes than heterosexual women? *Archives of Sexual Behavior.* Doi: 10.1007/s10508-014-0412-1.

Nisbett, R. E., & Wilson, T. D. (1977). Telling more than we can know: Verbal reports on mental processes. *Psychological Review, 84,* 231–259.

Nosek, B. A., & Banaji, M. R. (2001). The Go/No-Go Association Task. *Social Cognition, 19,* 625–666.

Nosek, B. A., Banaji, M. R., & Greenwald, A. G. (2002a). Harvesting implicit group attitudes and beliefs from a demonstration web site. *Group Dynamics, 6,* 101–115.

Nosek, B. A., Banaji, M. R., & Greenwald, A. G. (2002b). Math = male, me = female, therefore math not = me. *Journal of Personality and Social Psychology, 83,* 44–59.

Nosek, B. A., Smyth, F. L., Sriram, N., Lindner, N. M., Devos, T., Ayala, A.,... Greenwald, A. G. (2009). National differences in gender-science stereotypes predict national sex differences in science and math achievement. *Proceedings of the National Academy of Sciences, 106,* 10593–10597.

O'Brien, L. T., & Crandall, C. S. (2003). Stereotype threat and arousal: Effects on women's math performance. *Personality and Social Psychology Bulletin, 29*, 782–789.

O'Leary, B. J., & Turillo, C. J. (2008). Focusing on the goal of research. *Industrial and Organizational Psychology, 1*, 420–422.

Okimoto, T. G., & Heilman, M. E. (2012). The "bad parent" assumption: How gender stereotypes affect reactions to working mothers. *Journal of Social Issues, 68*, 704–724.

Olson, J. M., & Zanna, M. P. (1993). Attitudes and attitude change. *Annual Review of Psychology, 44*, 117–154.

Operario, D., & Fiske, S. T. (2001). Causes and consequences of stereotypes in organizations. In M. London (Ed.), *How people evaluate others in organizations: perception and interpersonal judgment in industrial-organizational psychology* (pp. 45–62). Mahwah, NJ: Lawrence Erlbaum.

Ostrom, T. M., & Sedikides, C. (1992). Out-group homogeneity effects in natural and minimal groups. *Psychological Bulletin, 112*, 536–552.

Padgett, M., Harland, L., & Moser, S. B. (2009). The bad news and the good news: The long-term consequences of having used an alternative work schedule. *Scholarship and Professional Work-Business*. Retrieved from http://digitalcommons.butler.edu/cob_papers/70

Palomares, N. A. (2012). Gender and intergroup communication. In H. Giles & C. Gallois (Eds.), *The handbook of intergroup communication* (pp. 197–210). New York, NY: Routledge.

Paluck, E. L., & Green, D. P. (2009). Prejudice reduction: What works? A review and assessment of research and practice. *Annual Review of Psychology, 60*, 339–367.

Park, B., Smith, J. A., & Correll, J. (2008). "Having it all" or "doing it all"? Perceived trait attributes and behavioral obligations as a function of workload, parenthood, and gender. *European Journal of Social Psychology, 38*, 1156–1164.

Parks-Stamm, E. J., Heilman, M. E., & Hearns, K. A. (2008). Motivated to penalize: Women's strategic rejection of successful women. *Personality and Social Psychology Bulletin, 34*, 237–247.

Paulsen, N., Jones, E. L., Graham, P. W., Callan, V. J., & Gallois, C. (2005). Organizations as intergroup contexts: Communication, discourse, and identification. In J. Harwood & H. Giles (Eds.), *Intergroup communication: Multiple perspectives* (pp. 165–188). New York, NY: Peter Lang.

PayScale (2014). PayScale's Salary Negotiation Guide. http://www.payscale.com/salary-negotiation-guide

Pearce, J. A., II, & Robinson, R. B. (2011). *Strategic management: Formulation, implementation, and control* (11th ed.). Boston, MA: McGraw-Hill.

Pendry, L. F., Driscoll, D. M., & Field, S. C. T. (2007). Diversity training: Putting theory into practice. *Journal of Occupational and Organizational Psychology, 80*, 27–50.

Peplau, L. A., & Fingerhut, A. (2004). The paradox of the lesbian worker. *Journal of Social Issues, 60*, 719–735.

Pernas, B., Román, M., Olza, J., & Naredo, M. (2000). *La dignidad quebrada. Las raíces del acoso sexual en el trabajo* [The broken dignity. The roots of sexual harassment at work]. Madrid, Spain: Ediciones La Catarata.

Pettigrew, T. F., & Tropp, L. R. (2006). A meta-analytical test of intergroup contact theory. *Journal of Personality and Social Psychology, 90*, 751–783.

Pettigrew, T. F., & Tropp, L. R. (2011). *When groups meet* (p. 309). New York, NY: Psychology Press.

Pierce, L., Dahl, M. S., & Nielsen, J. (2013). In sickness and in wealth: Psychological and sexual costs of income comparison in marriage. *Personality and Social Psychology Bulletin, 39*, 359–374.

Piñuel, I., & Oñate, A. (2002). La incidencia del mobbing o acoso psicológico en el trabajo en España [The incidence of bullying or mobbing at work in Spain]. *Lan Harremanak, 7*, 35–62.

Plaut, V. C., Garnett, F. G., Buffardi, L. E., & Sanches-Burks, J. (2011). "What about me?" Perceptions of exclusion and Whites' reactions to multiculturalism. *Journal of Personality and Social Psychology, 101*, 337–353.

Plaut, V. C., Thomas, K. M., & Goren, M. J. (2009). Is multiculturalism or color blindness better for minorities? *Psychological Science, 20*, 444–446.

Popovich, P. M., & Warren, M. A. (2010). The role of power in sexual harassment as a counterproductive behavior in organizations. *Human Resource Management Review, 20*, 45–53.

Pörhölä, M., & Kinney, T.A. (2009). *Bullying contexts, consequences, and control.* Barcelona, Spain: Aresta.

Powell, M., & Ansic, D. (1997). Gender differences in risk behaviour in financial decision-making: An experimental analysis. *Journal of Economic Psychology, 18*, 605–628.

Powell, P. L., & Johnson, J. E. V. (1995). Gender and DSS design: The research implications. *Decision Support Systems, 14*, 27–58.

Pratto, F., & Bargh, J. A. (1991). Stereotyping based on apparently individuating information: Trait and global components of sex stereotypes under attention overload. *Journal of Experimental Social Psychology, 27*, 26–47.

Pratto, F., Sidanius, J., Stallworth, L. M., & Malle, B. F. (1994). Social dominance orientation: A personality variable predicting social and political attitudes. *Journal of Personality and Social Psychology, 67*, 741–763.

Pratto, F., Stallworth, L. M., Sidanius, J., & Siers, B. (1997). The gender gap in occupational role attainment: A social dominance approach. *Journal of Personality and Social Psychology, 72*, 37–53.

Prentice, D. A., & Carranza, E. (2002). What women should be, shouldn't be, are allowed to be, and don't have to be: The contents of prescriptive gender stereotypes. *Psychology of Women Quarterly, 26*, 269–281.

Pronin, E., Steele, C. M., & Ross, L. (2004). Identity bifurcation in response to stereotype threat: Women and mathematics. *Journal of Experimental Social Psychology, 40*, 152–168.

Prothro, E. T., & Melikian, L. H. (1955). Studies in stereotypes: V. Familiarity and the kernel of truth hypothesis. *Journal of Social Psychology, 41*, 3–10.

Pryor, J. (1995). Gender issues in groupwork—A case study involving work with computers. *British Educational Research Journal, 21*, 277–288.

Pryor, J. B., LaVite, M., & Stoller, L. M. (1993). A social psychological analysis of sexual harassment: The person situation interaction. *Journal of Vocational Behavior, 42,* 68–83.

Quaiser-Pohl, C., Geiser, C., & Lehmann, W. (2006). The relationship between computer-game preference, gender, and mental-rotation ability. *Personality and Individual Differences, 40,* 609–619.

Quaiser-Pohl, C., & Reichle, B. (2007). *Kinder, Küche, Konferenzen oder Die Kunst des Jonglierens* [Kids, kitchen, conferences or the art of juggling]. Munich, Germany: Beck.

Quinn, D. M., Kallen, R. W., & Spencer, S. J. (2010). Stereotype threat. In J. F. Dovidio, M. Hewstone, P. Glick, & V. M. Esses (Eds.), *The Sage handbook of prejudice, stereotyping, and discrimination* (pp. 379–394). Thousand Oaks, CA: Sage.

Rai, T. S., & Fiske, A. P. (2011). Moral psychology is relationship regulation: Moral motives for unity, hierarchy, equality, and proportionality. *Psychological Review, 118,* 57–75.

Rakić, T. (2008). *Who said what... and how? On the influence of pronunciation on social categorization* (Unpublished doctoral dissertation). Friedrich Schiller University, Jena, Germany.

Reese, G., Berthold, A., & Steffens, M. C. (2012). We are the world—And they are not: Prototypicality for the world community, legitimacy, and responses to global inequality. *Political Psychology, 33,* 683–700.

Reid, S. A., Giles, H., & Harwood, J. (2005). A self-categorization perspective on communication and intergroup relations. In J. Harwood & H. Giles (Eds.), *Intergroup communication: Multiples perspectives* (pp. 241–263). New York, NY: Peter Lang.

Reilly, D., & Neumann, D. L. (2013). Gender-role differences in spatial ability: A meta-analytic review. *Sex Roles, 68,* 521–535.

Reinhard, M.-A., Stahlberg, D., & Messner, M. (2009). When failing feels good–relative prototypicality for a high-status group can counteract ego-threat after individual failure. *Journal of Experimental Social Psychology, 45,* 788–795.

Reskin, B. F., & Bielby, D. D. (2005). A sociological perspective on gender and career outcomes. *Journal of Economic Perspectives, 19,* 71–86.

Rhoads, S. E., & Rhoads, C. H. (2012). Gender roles and infant/toddler care: Male and female professors on the tenure track. *Journal of Social, Evolutionary, and Cultural Psychology, 6,* 13–31.

Rhode, D. L., & Williams, J. C. (2007). Legal perspectives on employment discrimination. In F. J. Crosby, M. S. Stockdale, & S. A. Ropp (Eds.), *Sex discrimination in the workplace: Multidisciplinary perspectives* (pp. 235–270). Malden, MA: Blackwell.

Richard, F. D., Bond, C. F., & Stokes-Zoota, J. J. (2003). One hundred years of social psychology quantitatively described. *Review of General Psychology, 7,* 331–363.

Richeson, J. A., & Ambady, N. (2001). Who's in charge? Effects of situational roles on automatic gender bias. *Sex Roles, 44,* 493–512.

Riggs, J. M. (1997). Mandates for mothers and fathers: Perceptions of breadwinners and care givers. *Sex Roles, 37,* 565–580.

Roberts, T. A., & Nolen-Hoeksema, S. (1994). Gender comparisons in responsiveness to others' evaluations in achievement settings. *Psychology of Women Quarterly, 18,* 221–240.

Roccas, S., & Amit, A. (2011). Group heterogeneity and tolerance: The moderating role of conservation values. *Journal of Experimental Social Psychology, 47,* 898–907.

Rodler, C., Kirchler, E., & Hölzl, E. (2001). Gender stereotypes of leaders: An analysis of the contents of obituaries from 1974 to 1998. *Sex Roles, 45,* 827–843.

Rosette, A. S., & Tost, L. P. (2010). Agentic women and communal leadership: How role prescriptions confer advantage to top women leaders. *Journal of Applied Psychology, 95,* 221–235.

Roth, L. M. (2007). Women on Wall Street: Despite diversity measures, Wall Street remains vulnerable to sex discrimination charges. *Academy of Management Perspectives, 21,* 24–35.

Roth, L. M. (2009). Gendered jobs: Negotiating opportunity and recognition. *Negotiation and Conflict Management Research, 2,* 17–30.

Roth, P. L., Purvis, K. L., & Bobko, P. (2012). A meta-analysis of gender group differences for measures of job performance in field studies. *Journal of Management, 38,* 719–739.

Rudman, L. A. (1998). Self-promotion as a risk factor for women: The costs and benefits of counterstereotypical impression management. *Journal of Personality and Social Psychology, 74,* 629–645.

Rudman, L. A., & Fairchild, K. (2004). Reactions to counterstereotypic behavior: The role of backlash in cultural stereotype maintenance. *Journal of Personality and Social Psychology, 87,* 157–176.

Rudman, L. A., & Glick, P. (1999). Feminized management and backlash toward agentic women: The hidden costs to women of a kinder, gentler image of middle managers. *Journal of Personality and Social Psychology, 77,* 1004–1010.

Rudman, L. A., & Glick, P. (2001). Prescriptive gender stereotypes and backlash toward agentic women. *Journal of Social Issues, 57,* 743–762.

Rudman, L. A., & Glick, P. (2008). *The social psychology of gender.* New York, NY: Guilford.

Rudman, L. A., & Goodwin, S. A. (2004). Gender differences in automatic in-group bias: Why do women like women more than men like men? *Journal of Personality and Social Psychology, 87,* 494–509.

Rudman, L. A., Greenwald, A. G., & McGhee, D. E. (2001). Implicit self-concept and evaluative implicit gender stereotypes: Self and ingroup share desirable traits. *Personality and Social Psychology Bulletin, 27,* 1164–1178.

Rudman, L. A., & Heppen, J. B. (2003). Implicit romantic fantasies and women's interest in personal power: A glass slipper effect? *Personality and Social Psychology Bulletin, 29,* 1357–1370.

Rudman, L. A., & Kilianski, S. E. (2000). Implicit and explicit attitudes toward female authority. *Personality and Social Psychology Bulletin, 26,* 1315–1328.

Rudman, L. A., & Mescher, K. (2013). Penalizing men who request a family leave: Is flexibility stigma a femininity stigma? *Journal of Social Issues, 69,* 322–340.

Rudman, L. A., Moss-Racusin, C. A., Phelan, J. E., & Nauts, S. (2012). Status incongruity and backlash effects: Defending the gender hierarchy motivates prejudice against female leaders. *Journal of Experimental Social Psychology, 48,* 165–179.

Rudman, L. A., & Phelan, J. E. (2010). The effect of priming gender roles on women's implicit gender beliefs and career aspirations. *Social Psychology, 41,* 192–202.

Rudolph, U., Böhm, R., & Lummer, M. (2007). Ein Vorname sagt mehr als 1000 Worte: Zur sozialen Wahrnehmung von Vornamen [A first name says more than 1000 words: On the social perception of first names]. *Zeitschrift für Sozialpsychologie, 38,* 17–31.

Ryan, E. B., & Bannister, K. A. (2009). *Ability speaks: Talking with a person with disability.* Barcelona, Spain: Aresta.

Ryan, M. K., & Haslam, S. A. (2005). The glass cliff: Evidence that women are over-represented in precarious leadership positions. *British Journal of Management, 16,* 81–90.

Rydell, R. J., Loo, K. J., & Boucher, K. L. (2014). Stereotype threat and executive functions: Which functions mediate different threat-related outcomes? *Personality and Social Psychology Bulletin, 40,* 377–390.

Sabattini, L., & Crosby, F. J. (2009). Ceilings and walls: Work-life and "family-friendly" policies. In M. Barreto, M. K. Ryan, & M. T. Schmitt (Eds.), *The glass ceiling in the 21st century: Understanding barriers to gender equality* (pp. 201–223). Washington, DC: American Psychological Association.

Sachdev, I., & Bourhis, R. Y. (2005). Multilingual communication and social identification. In J. Harwood & H. Giles (Eds.), *Intergroup communication: Multiple perspectives* (pp. 65–92). New York, NY: Peter Lang.

Sandberg, S. (2013). *Lean in.* New York, NY: Alfred A. Knopf.

Sandfort, T. G. M., de Graaf, R., Bijl, R. V., & Schnabel, P. (2001). Same-sex sexual behavior and psychiatric disorders: Findings from the Netherlands mental health survey and incidence study (NEMESIS). *Archives of General Psychiatry, 58,* 85–91.

Schein, V. E. (2001). A global look at psychological barriers to women's progress in management. *Journal of Social Issues, 57,* 675–688.

Schein, V. E., Mueller, R., & Jacobson, C. (1989). The relationship between sex role stereotypes and requisite management characteristics among college students. *Sex Roles, 20,* 103–110.

Schmader, T. (2010). Stereotype threat deconstructed. *Current Directions in Psychological Science, 19,* 14–18.

Schmader, T., & Johns, M. (2003). Converging evidence that stereotype threat reduces working memory capacity. *Journal of Personality and Social Psychology, 85,* 440–452.

Schmader, T., Johns, M., & Forbes, C. (2008). An integrated process model of stereotype threat effects on performance. *Psychological Review, 115,* 336–356.

Schmitt, M. T., Branscombe, N. R., Kobrynowicz, D., & Owen, S. (2002). Perceiving discrimination against one's gender group has different implications for well-being in women and men. *Personality and Social Psychology Bulletin, 28,* 197–210.

Schmitt, M. T., Branscombe, N. R., & Postmes, T. (2003). Women's emotional responses to the pervasiveness of gender discrimination. *European Journal of Social Psychology, 33,* 297–312.

Schmitt, M. T., Ellemers, N., & Branscombe, N. R. (2003). Perceiving and responding to gender discrimination at work. In S. A. Haslam, D. Van Knippenberg, M. J. Platow, & N. Ellemers (Eds.), *Social identity at work: Developing theory for organizational practice* (pp. 277–292). Philadelphia, PA: Psychology Press.

Schmitt, M. T., Spoor, J. R., Danaher, K., & Branscombe, N. R. (2009). Rose-colored glasses: How tokenism and comparisons with the past reduce the visibility of gender inequality.

In M. Barreto, M. K. Ryan, & M. T. Schmitt (Eds.), *The glass ceiling in the 21st century: Understanding barriers to gender equality* (pp. 49–71). Washington, DC: American Psychological Association.

Schneeweis, N., & Zweimüller, M. (2012). Girls, girls, girls: Gender composition and female school choice. *Economics of Education Review, 31,* 482–500.

Schneider, D. J. (2004). *The psychology of stereotyping.* New York, NY: Guilford.

Schubert, R., Brown, M., Gysler, M., & Brachinger, H. W. (1999). Financial decision-making: Are women really more risk-averse? *American Economic Review, 89,* 381–385.

Sczesny, S. (2003). A closer look beneath the surface: Various facets of the think-manager-think-male stereotype. *Sex Roles, 49,* 353–363.

Sczesny, S., Bosak, J., Diekman, A. B., & Twenge, J. M. (2007). Dynamics of sex-role stereotypes. In Y. Kashima, K. Fiedler & P. Freytag (Eds.), *Stereotype dynamics: Language-based approaches to the formation, maintenance, and transformation of stereotypes* (pp. 135–161). Mahwah, NJ: Lawrence Erlbaum.

Sczesny, S., Bosak, J., Neff, D., & Schyns, B. (2004). Gender stereotypes and the attribution of leadership traits: A cross-cultural comparison. *Sex Roles, 51,* 631–645.

Sczesny, S., & Stahlberg, D. (2002). The influence of gender-stereotyped perfumes on leadership attribution. *European Journal of Social Psychology, 32,* 815–828.

Sechrist, G. B., & Stangor, C. (2001). Perceived consensus influences intergroup behavior and stereotype accessibility. *Journal of Personality and Social Psychology, 80,* 645–654.

Sekaquaptewa, D., & Thompson, M. (2003). Solo status, stereotype threat, and performance expectancies: Their effects on women's performance. *Journal of Experimental Social Psychology, 39,* 68–74.

Settles, I. H., Cortina, L. M., Buchanan, N. T., & Miner, K. N. (2012). Derogation, discrimination, and (dis)satisfaction with jobs in science: A gendered analysis. *Psychology of Women Quarterly, 37,* 179–191.

Shelton, B. A. (1992). *Women, men and time: Gender differences in paid work, housework, and leisure.* New York, NY: Greenwood.

Shepard, C. A., Giles, H., & Le Poire, B. A. (2001). Communication accommodation theory. In W. P. Robinson & H. Giles (Eds.), *The new handbook of language and social psychology* (pp. 33–52). Chichester, UK: John Wiley & Sons.

Shields, S. A. (2008). Gender: An intersectionality perspective. *Sex Roles, 59,* 301–311.

Sidanius, J., & Pratto, F. (1999). *Social dominance: An intergroup theory of social hierarchy and oppression.* New York, NY: Cambridge University Press.

Sidanius, J., Pratto, F., & Bobo, L. (1994). Social dominance orientation and the political psychology of gender: A case of invariance? *Journal of Personality and Social Psychology, 67,* 998–1011.

Sieverding, M. (2003). Frauen unterschätzen sich: Selbstbeurteilungs-Biases in einer simulierten Bewerbungssituation [Women underestimate themselves: Self-judgment biases in a simulated job search situation]. *Zeitschrift für Sozialpsychologie, 34,* 147–160.

Sieverding, M. (2009). "Be cool!": Emotional costs of hiding feelings in a job interview. *International Journal of Selection and Assessment, 17,* 391–401.

Simon, B., & Klandermans, B. (2001). Politicized collective identity: A social psychology analysis. *American Psychologist, 56*, 319–331.

Simon, S., & Hoyt, C. (2008). Exploring the gender gap in support for a woman for president. *Analyses of Social Issues and Public Policy, 8*, 157–181.

Sinclair, S., & Huntsinger, J. R. (2006). The interpersonal basis of self-stereotyping. In S. Levin & C. van Laar (Eds.), *Claremont Symposium on Applied Social Psychology: Stigma and Group Inequality: Social Psychological Approaches* (pp. 235–260). Mahwah, NJ: Lawrence Erlbaum.

Skowronski, J. J., & Lawrence, M. A. (2001). A comparative study of the implicit and explicit gender attitudes of children and college students. *Psychology of Women Quarterly, 25*, 155–165.

Smith, F. L., Tabak, F., Showail, S., Parks, J. M., & Kleist, J. S. (2005). The name game: Employability evaluations of prototypical applicants with stereotypical feminine and masculine first names. *Sex Roles, 52*, 63–82.

Smith, J. L., Karyn, L. L., Hawthorne, L., & Hodges, S. D. (2012). When trying hard isn't natural: Women's belonging with and motivation for male-dominated STEM fields as a function of effort expenditure concerns. *Personality and Social Psychology Bulletin, 39*, 131–143.

Soliz, J., & Harwood, J. (2006). Shared family identity, age salience, and intergroup contact: Investigation of the grandparent-grandchild relationship. *Communication Monographs, 73*, 87–107.

Spelke, E. S., & Grace, A. D. (2007). Sex, math, and science. In S. J. Ceci & W. M. Williams (Eds.), *Why aren't more women in science? Top researchers debate the evidence* (pp. 57–67). Washington, DC: American Psychological Association.

Spence, J. T., & Buckner, C. E. (2000). Instrumental and expressive traits, trait stereotypes, and sexist attitudes: What do they signify? *Psychology of Women Quarterly, 24*, 44–62.

Spencer, S. J., Steele, C. M., & Quinn, D. (1999). Stereotype threat and women's math performance. *Journal of Experimental Social Psychology, 35*, 4–28.

Stangor, C., Lynch, L., Duan, C. M., & Glass, B. (1992). Categorization of individuals on the basis of multiple social features. *Journal of Personality and Social Psychology, 62*, 207–218.

Steele, C. M. (1997). A threat in the air: How stereotypes shape intellectual identity and performance. *American Psychologist, 52*, 613–629.

Steele, C. M., & Aronson, J. (1995). Stereotype threat and the intellectual test performance of African-Americans. *Journal of Personality and Social Psychology, 69*, 797–811.

Steele, C. M., Spencer, S. J., & Aronson, J. (2002). Contending with group image: The psychology of stereotype and social identity threat. In M. Zanna (Ed.), *Advances in experimental social psychology* (pp. 379–440). New York, NY: Academic Press.

Steele, J. R., & Ambady, N. (2006). "Math is hard!" The effect of gender priming on women's attitudes. *Journal of Experimental Social Psychology, 42*, 428–436.

Steffens, M. C., & Jelenec, P. (2011). Separating implicit gender stereotypes regarding math and language: Implicit ability stereotypes are self-serving for boys and men, but not for girls and women. *Sex Roles, 64*, 324–335.

Steffens, M. C., Jelenec, P., & Noack, P. (2010). On the leaky math pipeline: Comparing implicit math-gender stereotypes and math withdrawal in female and male children and adolescents. *Journal of Educational Psychology, 102*, 947–963.

Steffens, M. C., & Mehl, B. (2003). Erscheinen "Karrierefrauen" weniger sozial kompetent als "Karrieremänner"? Geschlechterstereotype und Kompetenzzuschreibung [Do "career women" appear less socially competent than "career men"? Gender stereotypes and competence ascription]. *Zeitschrift für Sozialpsychologie, 34*, 173–185.

Steffens, M. C., & Plewe, I. (2001). Items' cross-category associations as a confounding factor in the Implicit Association Test. *Zeitschrift für Experimentelle Psychologie, 48*, 123–134.

Steffens, M. C., Reese, G., Ehrke, F., & Jonas, K. J. (2015). *When does activating diversity improve, when does it impair intergroup bias? An ingroup projection perspective.* Manuscript submitted for publication.

Steffens, M. C., Schult, J. C., & Ebert, I. D. (2009). Feminization of management leads to backlash against agentic applicants: Lack of social skills, not gender, determines low hireability judgments in student samples. *Psychology Science Quarterly, 51*, 16–46.

Steffens, N. K., Haslam, S. A., Stephen, D. R., Platow, M. J., Fransen, K., Yang. J.,... Boen, F. (2014). Leadership as social identity management: Introducing the identity leadership inventory (ILI) to assess and validate a four-dimensional model. *The Leadership Quarterly, 25*, 1001–1024.

Stephan, W. G., & Renfro, C. L. (2003). The role of threats in intergroup relations. In D. M. Mackie & E. R. Smith (Eds.), *From prejudice to intergroup emotions* (pp. 191–208). New York, NY: Psychology Press.

Stephan, W. G., & Stephan, C. W. (2000). An integrated threat theory of prejudice. In S. Oskamp (Ed.), *Reducing prejudice and discrimination* (pp. 23–46). Mahwah, NJ: Lawrence Erlbaum.

Stern, M., & Karraker, K. H. (1989). Sex stereotyping infants: A review of gender labeling studies. *Sex Roles, 20*, 501–522.

Stevens, F. G., Plaut, V. C., & Sanchez-Burks, J. (2008). Unlocking the benefits of diversity: All-inclusive multiculturalism and positive organizational change. *The Journal of Applied Behavioral Science, 44*, 116–133.

Stout, J. G., Dasgupta, N., Hunsinger, M., & McManus, M. A. (2011). STEMing the tide: Using ingroup experts to inoculate women's self-concept in science, technology, engineering, and mathematics (STEM). *Journal of Personality and Social Psychology, 100*, 255–270.

Stroebe, K., Dovidio, J. F., Barreto, M., Ellemers, N., & John, M. S. (2011). Is the world a just place? Countering the negative consequences of pervasive discrimination by reaffirming the world as just. *British Journal of Social Psychology, 50*, 484–500.

Swim, J., Borgida, E., Maruyama, G., & Myers, D. G. (1989). Joan McKay versus John McKay: Do gender stereotypes bias evaluations? *Psychological Bulletin, 105*, 409–429.

Swim, J. K. (1994). Perceived versus meta-analytic effect sizes: An assessment of the accuracy of gender stereotypes. *Journal of Personality and Social Psychology, 66*, 21–36.

Swim, J. K., Aikin, K. J., Hall, W. S., & Hunter, B. A. (1995). Sexism and racism: Old-fashioned and modern prejudices. *Journal of Personality and Social Psychology, 68*, 199–214.

Swim, J. K., & Cohen, L. L. (1997). Overt, covert, and subtle sexism: A comparison between the attitudes toward women and modern sexism scales. *Psychology of Women Quarterly, 21*, 103–118.

Swim, J. K., & Sanna, L. J. (1996). He's skilled, she's lucky: A meta-analysis of obersver's attributions for women's and men's successes and failures. *Personality and Social Psychology Bulletin, 22*, 507–519.

Taasoobshirazi, G., & Carr, M. (2009). A structural equation model of expertise in college physics. *Journal of Educational Psychology, 101*, 630–643.

Tajfel, H. (1982). Social psychology of intergroup relations. *Annual Review of Psychology, 33*, 1–39.

Talley, A. E., & Bettencourt, B. A. (2008). Evaluations and aggression directed at a gay male target: The role of threat and antigay prejudice. *Journal of Applied Social Psychology, 38*, 647–683.

Tetlock, P. E., Mitchell, G., & Murray, T. L. (2008). The challenge of debiasing personnel decisions: Avoiding both under- and overcorrection. *Industrial and Organizational Psychology, 1*, 439–443.

Torres, J. B., Solberg, V. S. H., & Carlstrom, A. H. (2002). The myth of sameness among Latino men and their machismo. *American Journal of Orthopsychiatry, 72*, 163–181.

Tropp, L. R. (2006). Stigma and intergroup contact among members of minority and majority status groups. In S. Levin & C. Van Laar (Eds.), *Stigma and group inequality: Social psychological perspectives* (pp. 171–219). Mahwah, NJ: Lawrence Erlbaum.

Tropp, L. R., & Pettigrew, T. F. (2004). Intergroup contact and the central role of affect in intergroup prejudice. In C. W. Leach & L. Z. Tiedens (Eds.), *The social life of emotions* (pp. 246–269). Cambridge, UK: Cambridge University Press.

Tropp, L. R., & Pettigrew, T. F. (2005). Relationships between intergroup contact and prejudice among minority and majority status groups. *Psychological Science, 16*, 951–957.

Turner, J. C., & Haslam, S. A. (2001). Social identity, organizations and leadership. In M. E. Turner (Ed.), *Groups at work: Advances in theory and research* (pp. 25–65). Mahwah, NJ: Lawrence Erlbaum.

Turner, J. C., Hogg, M., Oakes, P., Reicher, S., & Wetherell, M. (1987). *Rediscovering the social group: A self-categorization theory.* Oxford, UK: Blackwell.

Turner, R. N., Hewstone, M., & Voci, A. (2007). Reducing explicit and implicit outgroup prejudice via direct and extended contact: The mediating role of self-disclosure and intergroup anxiety. *Journal of Personality and Social Psychology, 93*, 369–388.

Turner, R. N., Hewstone, M., Voci, A., & Vonofakou, C. (2008). A test of the extended contact hypothesis: The mediating role of intergroup anxiety, perceived ingroup and outgroup norms, and inclusion of the outgroup in the self. *Journal of Personality and Social Psychology, 95*, 843–860.

Twenge, J. M. (1997). Attitudes toward women, 1970–1995: A meta-analysis. *Psychology of Women Quarterly, 21*, 35–51.

Twenge, J. M. (2001). Changes in women's assertiveness in response to status and roles: A cross-temporal meta-analysis, 1931–1993. *Journal of Personality and Social Psychology, 81*, 133–145.

Uhlmann, E. L., & Cohen, G. L. (2005). Constructed criteria: Redefining merit to justify discrimination. *Psychological Science, 16*, 474–480.

Unger, R. K. (1979). Toward a redefinition of sex and gender. *American Psychologist, 34*, 1085–1094.

United Nations Development Program Human Development Report. (2014). Gender inequality index. Retrieved from http://hdr.undp.org/en/content/table-4-gender-inequality-index

U.S. Department of Education. (2000). *Educational equity for girls and women* (NCES 2000–030). Washington, DC: U.S. Government Printing Office.

U.S. Department of Labor. (2005). Labor force statistics from the current population survey. Retrieved from Bureau of Labor Statistics website: http://www.bls.gov/cps/wlf-databook-2005.pdf

Valian, V. (1997). *Why so slow? The advancement of women.* Cambridge, MA: The MIT Press.

Valian, V. (2007). Women at the top in science—And elsewhere. In S. J. Ceci & W. M. Williams (Eds.), *Why aren't more women in science? Top researchers debate the evidence* (pp. 27–37). Washington, DC: American Psychological Association.

Valian, V. (2014). Interests, gender, and science. *Perspectives on Psychological Science, 9,* 225–230.

van Knippenberg, D., Haslam, S. A., & Platow, M. J. (2007). Unity through diversity: Value-in-diversity beliefs, work group diversity, and group identification. *Group Dynamics: Theory, Research, and Practice, 11,* 207–222.

van Knippenberg, D., & Schippers, M. C. (2007). Work group diversity. *Annual Review of Psychology, 58,* 515–541.

van Laar, C. (2000). Declining optimism in ethnic minority students: The role of attributions and self-esteem. In F. Salili, C. Y. Chiu, & Y. Y. Hong (Eds.), *Student motivation: The culture and context of learning* (pp. 1–40). New York, NY: Plenum Press.

van Laar, C., & Derks, B. (2003). Managing stigma: Disidentification from the academic domain among members of stigmatized groups. In F. Salili & R. Hoosain (Eds.), *Teaching, learning, and motivation in a multicultural context* (pp. 345–393). Greenwich, CT: Information Age Publishing.

van Laar, C., Levin, S., & Sidanius, J. (2008). Ingroup and outgroup contact: A longitudinal study of the effects of cross-ethnic friendships, dates, roommate relationships and participation in segregated organizations. In U. Wagner, L. R. Tropp, G. Finchilescu, & C. Tredoux (Eds.)., *Improving intergroup relations: The legacy of Thomas F. Pettigrew* (pp. 127–142). Malden, MA: Blackwell.

van Quaquebeke, N., & Schmerling, A. (2010). Kognitive Gleichstellung—Wie die bloße Abbildung bekannter weiblicher und männlicher Führungskräfte unser implizites Denken zu Führung beeinflusst [Cognitive gender equality—How merely depicting known female and male leaders influences our implicit thinking about leadership]. *Zeitschrift für Arbeits- und Organisationspsychologie, 54,* 91–104.

van Vianen, A. E. M., & Fischer, A. H. (2002). Illuminating the glass ceiling: The role of organizational culture preferences. *Journal of Occupational and Organizational Psychology, 75,* 315–337.

Vandello, J. A., Bosson, J. K., Cohen, D., Burnaford, R. M., & Weaver, J. R. (2008). Precarious manhood. *Journal of Personality and Social Psychology, 95,* 1325–1339.

Vandello, J. A., Hettinger, V. E., Bosson, J. K., & Siddiqi, J. (2013). When equal isn't really equal: The masculine dilemma of seeking work flexibility. *Journal of Social Issues, 69,* 303–321.

Verkuyten, M. (2011). Assimilation ideology and outgroup attitudes among ethnic majority members. *Group Processes & Intergroup Relations, 14,* 1–18.

Vescio, T. K., Gervais, S., Snyder, M., & Hoover, A. (2005). Power and the creation of patronizing environments: The stereotype-based behaviors of the powerful and their effects on female performance in masculine domains. *Journal of Personality and Social Psychology, 88,* 658–672.

Vescio, T. K., Sechrist, G. B., & Paolucci, M. P. (2003). Perspective taking and prejudice reduction: The mediational role of empathy arousal and situational attributions. *European Journal of Social Psychology, 33,* 455–472.

Viladot, M. À., & Esteban-Guitart, M., (2011). Un estudio transversal sobre la percepción de la vitalidad etnolingüística en jóvenes y adultos de Cataluña [A cross-sectional study on perceptions of ethnolinguistic vitality in youth and adults in Catalonia]. *Revista Internacional de Sociología, 69,* 229–252.

Viladot, M. À., Esteban-Guitart, M., Nadal, J. M., & Giles, H. (2007). Identidad, percepción de vitalidad etnolingüística y comunicación intergrupal en Cataluña (España) [Identity perceptions of ethnolinguistic vitality and intergroup communication in Catalonia (Spain)]. *Revista de Psicología Social Aplicada, 17,* 223–247.

Viladot, M. À., & Giles, H. (1998). Habla condescendiente y ancianidad: Evaluaciones intergeneracionales en Cataluña [Patronizing talk and aging: Intergenerational assessment in Catalonia]. *Revista de Psicología Social Aplicada, 8,* 29–60.

Viladot, M. À., Giles, H., Bolaños, J. L., & Esteban-Guitart, M. (2013). Identidad nacional, vitalidad etnolingüística e indigenismo en Chiapas (Mexico) [National identity, ethnolinguistic vitality and indigenismo in Chiapas (Mexico)]. *Estudios de Psicología, 34,* 89–93.

Viladot, M. À., Giles, H., Gasiorek, J., & Esteban-Guitart, M. (2012). Vitalidad etnolingüística, medios de comunicación e identidad étnica: Un estudio con grupos indígenas de Chiapas (México) [Ethnolinguistic vitality, media and ethnicity: A study with indigenous groups in Chiapas (Mexico)]. *Sociolinguistic Studies, 6,* 82–101.

Vinkenburg, C. J., van Engen, M. L., Coffeng, J., & Dikkers, J. S. E. (2012). Bias in employment decisions about mothers and fathers: The (dis)advantages of sharing care responsibilities. *Journal of Social Issues, 68,* 725–741.

Vogt, A.-C., & Pull, K. (2010). Warum Väter ihre Erwerbstätigkeit (nicht) unterbrechen: Mikroökonomische versus in der Persönlichkeit des Vaters begründete Determinanten der Inanspruchnahme von Elternzeit durch Väter [Why fathers (don't) take parental leave. Microeconomic vs. personality based determinants]. *Zeitschrift für Personalforschung (ZfP), 24,* 48–68.

von Hippel, C. V., Issa, M., Ma, R., & Stokes, A. (2011). Stereotype threat: Antecedents and consequences for working women. *European Journal of Social Psychology, 41,* 151–161.

Vonk, R., & Ashmore, R. D. (2003). Thinking about gender types: Cognitive organization of female and male types. *British Journal of Social Psychology, 42,* 257–280.

Waldzus, S., Mummendey, A., Wenzel, M., & Boettcher, F. (2004). Of bikers, teachers and Germans: Groups' diverging views about their prototypicality. *British Journal of Social Psychology, 43,* 385–400.

Waldzus, S., Mummendey, A., Wenzel, M., & Weber, U. (2003). Towards tolerance: Representations of superordinate categories and perceived ingroup prototypicality. *Journal of Experimental Social Psychology, 39*, 31–47.

Wang, M. T., Eccles, J. S., & Kenny, S. (2013). Not lack of ability but more choice: Individual and gender differences in choice of careers in science, technology, engineering, and mathematics. *Psychological Science, 24*, 770–775.

Wayne, J. H., & Cordeiro, B. L. (2003). Who is a good organizational citizen? Social perception of male and female employees who use family leave. *Sex Roles, 49*, 233–246.

Weatherall, A., & Gallois, C. (2005). Gender and identity: Representation and social action. In J. Holmes & M. Meyerhoff (Eds.), *The handbook of language and gender* (pp. 487–508). Malden, MA: Blackwell.

Wennerås, C., & Wold, A. (1997). Nepotism and sexism in peer review. *Nature, 387*, 341–343.

Wenzel, M., Mummendey, A., & Waldzus, S. (2007). Superordinate identities and intergroup conflict: The ingroup projection model. *European Review of Social Psychology, 18*, 331–372.

Wenzel, M., Mummendey, A., Weber, U., & Waldzus, S. (2003). The ingroup as pars pro toto: Projection from the ingroup onto the inclusive category as a precursor to social discrimination. *Personality and Social Psychology Bulletin, 29*, 461–473.

Wessel, J. L., & Ryan, A. M. (2008). Past the first encounter: The role of stereotypes. *Industrial and Organizational Psychology, 1*, 409–411.

Wharton, A. S. (2008). *The sociology of gender. An introduction to theory and research.* Malden, MA: Blackwell.

Wheeler, S. C., & Petty, R. E. (2001). The effects of stereotype activation on behavior: A review of possible mechanisms. *Psychological Bulletin, 127*, 797–826.

Wiemann, M. (2009). *Love you/hate you. Negotiating intimate relationships.* Barcelona, Spain: Aresta.

Wilde, A., & Diekman, A. B. (2005). Cross-cultural similarities and differences in dynamic stereotypes: A comparison between Germany and the United States. *Psychology of Women Quarterly, 29*, 188–196.

Williams, A., & Giles, H. (1978). The changing status of women in society: An intergroup perspective. In H. Tajfel (Ed.), *Differentiation between social groups: Studies in the social psychology of intergroup behavior* (pp. 431–446). London, UK: Academic Press.

Williams, A., & Giles, H. (1998). Communication of ageism. In M. L. Hecht & L. Michael (Eds.), *Communicating prejudice* (pp. 136–160). Thousand Oaks, CA: Sage.

Williams, A., & Nussbaum, J. F. (2001). *Intergenerational communication across the life span.* Mahwah, NJ: Lawrence Erlbaum.

Williams, C. L. (1992). The Glass escalator: Hidden advantages for men in the "female" professions. *Social Problems, 39*, 253–267.

Williams, J. E., & Best, D. L. (1990). *Measuring sex stereotypes: A multination study* (rev. ed.). Thousand Oaks, CA: Sage.

Williams, R. J. (2003). Women on corporate boards of directors and their influence on corporate philanthropy. *Journal of Business Ethics, 42*, 1–10.

Williams, W. M., & Ceci, S. J. (2007). Introduction: Striving for perspective in the debate on women in science. In S. J. Ceci & W. M. Williams (Eds.), *Why aren't more women in science? Top researchers debate the evidence* (pp. 3–23). Washington, DC: American Psychological Association.

Williams, Z. (2014). Freezing women's eggs? The tech industry isn't modern, it's Neanderthal. *The Guardian*, Wednesday 15 October. Retrieved from http://www.theguardian.com/commentisfree/2014/oct/15/freezing-eggs-tech-industry-neanderthal?CMP=twt_gu

Word, C. O., Zanna, M. P., & Cooper, J. (1974). The nonverbal mediation of self-fulfilling prophecies in interracial interaction. *Journal of Experimental Social Psychology, 10*, 109–120.

Wright, R. G., Reynolds, K. J., Haslam, S. A., & Willingham, J. (2011). *Overcoming the perils of intergroup communication and realising the benefits for the group*. Canberra: Australian National University.

Wright, S. C. (2010). Collective action and social change. In J. F. Dovidio, M. Hewstone, P. Glick, & V. M. Esses (Eds.), *Handbook of prejudice, stereotyping and discrimination* (pp. 577–596). Thousand Oaks, CA: Sage.

Wright, S. C., Aron, A., & Tropp, L. R. (2002). Including others (and their groups) in the self: Self-expansion theory and intergroup relations. In J. P. Forgas & K. D. Williams (Eds.), *The social self: Cognitive, interpersonal, and intergroup perspectives* (pp. 343–363). Philadelphia, PA: Psychology Press.

Young, D. M., Rudman, L. A., Buettner, H. M., & McLean, M. C. (2013). The influence of female role models on women's implicit science cognitions. *Psychology of Women Quarterly, 37*, 283–292.

Ytsma, J., & Giles, H. (1997). Reactions to patronizing talk: Some Dutch data. *Journal of Sociolinguistics, 1*, 259–268.

Zuckerman, M. (2007). *Sensation seeking and risky behavior*. Washington, DC: American Psychological Association.

INDEX

A

Accent, 19
Accommodation. *See* Communication accommodation theory, **203ff**, 218, 219, 224, 227, 229, 231, 232
Affirmative action(s), 174, 216, 237
Agency. *See* Assertiveness/competence
Age pyramid, 238, 239
Aggression, 56, 57, 73, 77, 78, 166, 181, 187, 198, 209, 210, 211
Ambiguous information, 40, 46, 140
Ambivalent behavior, 209
Anxiety, 57, 176, 177, 215, 216, 222, 243–245
Appreciative, 210
Assertiveness, 20–22, 25, 26, 34, 40–42, 49, 74, **78ff**, 88, 89, 93–95, 106, 111, 112, 121, 125, 137, 138, 140, 141, 144, 146, 150, 160, 173, 210, 238, 242
Assimilation, 178, 219, 220, 228

Attitude(s), 7–9, 11, 14, 25, 54, 55, **63ff**, 90, 111, 112, 130–132, 134, 157, 161, 177, 182, 187, 192, 194, 210, 215–222, 226, 228, 229, 232, 243, 244, 245

B

Backlash effect, **40ff**
Belief system, 30, 65, 165, 172
Bias, 2, 6, 13, 34, 36, 47, 49, 50, 51, 125, 150, 180, 187, 192, 229
  Gender, 18, 29, 38, 44–47, 50, 120, 140, 150, 192
  Hiring, 38
  Language selection, 236
  Motherhood, 143
  Profemale, 64
  Promale, 38
  Structural, 235
Biological characteristics, 185

Biological determinism, 185
Birth rate, 245, 246
Black(s), 6, 18, 22, 36, 59, 105, 106, 128, 144
Blue collar work, 140, 141
Boss(es), 5, 33, 42, 77, 78, 84, 150, 204
  Female, 42, 191, 216
  Male, 42, 191, 216
Boundary (ies), 15, 28, 99, 165, 166, 168–170, 193, 199, **203ff**, 221, 226–228, 230, 245
Boys' club, old boys' club, 194, 206, 213, 225, 227
Businesswoman, businesswomen, 21, 22, 40, 41, 206

C

Career choice, 101, **113ff**, 182
Causal attribution, 49, 55
Childcare, 86, 94, 98, 103, 122, 139, 141, 143, 151, 153, 238, 239
Coed, coeducation, 30, 59, 86, 115, 116
Collective action, 165, 166, 168
Communication accommodation theory (CAT), **203ff**
Communication process, Communicative process, 5, 153, 180, 189, 213, 217, 224, 230, 233, 242
Communicative divergence, 217
Communion/communality. *See* Warmth
Competence, Incompetence, 20–22, 24–27, 34–36, 38, 40–51, 65, 68, 69, 74, **78ff**, 88, 89, 91, 93–97, 106, 111, 123, 117, 127, 134, 137, 138, 140, 141, 143, 144, 146, 148, 150, 152, 168, 177, 187, 208, 209, 210, 237, 238
Competition, competitive, 15, 20, 26, 34, 67, 95, 128, 165–167, 171, 182–184, 206, 208, 213, 220, 225
Computer science, 114, 117–119, 135
Confidence, 30, 85, 212, 235
Conservative(s), conservative, 78, 81, 110, **191ff**, 205, 228, 242

Control, 23, 62, 68, 172, 184, 196, 199, 212
  Control condition, example, 19, 28, 29, 30, 55, 57, 132, 143, 200
Convergence, divergence, **204ff**
Cooperation, cooperative, 77, 182–184, 213, 216, 220, 225, 227, 231, 244
  Cooperative activity, 216
Counterstereotype, counterstereotypic(al), 21, 29, 30, 40, 55, 62, 88, 109, 114, 116, 133–136, 148, 149, 152, 186, 241
Creative identity management, 229
Culture(s), 6, 8, 13, 15, 42, 66–68, 73, 75, 94, 117, **123ff**, 150, 156, 157, 162, 169, 181, 194, 196, 198, 213, 223, 233, 244

D

Decision making, 3, 44, 80, 81, 84–86, 171, 186, 212, 227, 228
Depression, 101, 244
Dignity, 209
Dirty jokes, 206
Discrimination, 4, 5, 14, 16, 27, 36, 40, 41, 49, 62, 66, 67, 69, 105, 107, 108, 112, 124, 129, 130, 140, 141, 144, 146, 147, 150, 166, 171, 172, **174ff**, 177, 178, **179ff**, 192–194, 197, 209, 212, 213, 215–221, 229, 231, 236–238, 241–244
  Covert discrimination, 209
  Discriminatory action, 172, 175
  Discriminatory practices, 244
  Gender discrimination, 175, 179, 193, 194, 213, 244
  Self-discrimination, 175, **179ff**, 194, 231
  Subtle discrimination, 156, **174ff**, 209, 236
Disidentification, 108, 175, 178, 186
Distinctiveness, 230
Diversification, 220
Diversity, 72, 123, **127ff**, 150, 174, 185, 220, 227–229, 231, 244
  Diversity training, 29 Intergender, 220
Domestic responsibilities, 186

Dominance, domination, 41–44, 66, 107, 112, 160, 163, 197, 199, 209, 220, 245
Double-bind, 181
Double standard(s), 43, 46, 65

E

Effect of the extension of contact, 218
Effects of contact, 221, 222, 244
Emotion(s), emotional, 6, 14, 87, 88, 112, 126, 127, 131, 174, 177, 204, 243
Empathy, empathic, 87, 107, 162, 232
Entrepreneurship, entrepreneur(s), 7, 79, 80, 83, 84, 113, **121ff**
Equality, 1, 78, 87, 105, 108, 114, 179, 180, 188, 232, 233, 244
   Economic equality, 149
   Gender (in)equality, 1, 65, 66, 68, 69, 99, 102, 107, 110, 130, 136, 156, 163, 168, 191, 193, 194, 206, 209, 236, 241, 245
   Group (in)equality, 236, 244
   Inequality, 1, 67, 68, 106, 166, 193, 195, 196, 236
   Role equality, 95
   Status equality, 216
Equal opportunities, 6, 98, 152, 201, 216, 237
Ethnicity, 19, 22, 36, 107, 195
Executive, 23, 65, 128, 129, 171, 172, 174, 175, 183, 208

F

Family(ies), 25, 26, 31, 74, 80, 97, 98, 99, 100–104, 114, 122, 136, 137, 141, 144, 147, 149, 151–153, 157, 158, 184, 186, 193, 207, 212, 221, 237, 242, 245
Feedback, 46, 61, 62, 87, 212
Female behavior, 143, 160, 187
Female candidate(s), 28, 36, 192, 236
Female dominated work, 193
Female manager(s), 5, 25, 26, 37, 68, 84, 85, 208
Female professions, 194
Female schema. *See* Gender schema
Female talent, 181, 237
Femininity, 22, 38, 144, 183, 200, 205
Feminism, feminist, 22, 68, 107, 108, 110, 116, 160, 161, 168, 180, 200, 209

G

Gambling, 14, 82, 84–86
Gay (man, men), 17, 57, 128, 201
Gender (a)typicality, 28, 43, 54–57, 73, 77, 93, 95, 115, 116, 142
Gender categorization(s), **18ff**, 53, 158
Gender differences, 4, 6, **7ff**, 8, 11, 14, 15, 25, 34, 42, 54, 60, 61, **71ff**, 95, 97, 107, 119–122, 125, 140, 160, 182, 183, 185, 193, 194, 196, 201, 205
Gender group, 7, 8, 72, 86, 163, 166, 167, 170, 171, 173–178, 195, 200, 224, 225, 230, 231, 233, 243
Gender identity, 57, 64, 117, 158, 163, **168ff**, **170ff**, 178, 179, 186, 194, 209, **223ff**, 243
Gender pay gap, 114, **145ff**
Gender-power relations, 199
Gender salience, 18, 53, **159ff**, 162, 181, 229
Gender schema, 53, 159, 160, 187, 205
Gender segregation, 5, 71, 76, 106, 107, 114, 116, 223
Gender status, 200
Gender stereotypes, 5, 6, 8, 9, 11, **13ff**, **23ff**, **33ff**, **53ff**, 73–75, 77, 79, 81, 84–88, 90, 91, 93–96, 98, 101, 102, 104, 110, 111, 113, 115, 117, 120, 121, 124, 126, 129, 133–135, 139–142, 147, 148, 150, 152, 153, 159, 160, 162, 172, 173, 176, 177, 180–183, 185, 186–188, 192, 193, 194, 197, 205, 224, 229, 230, 238, 241–243, 245
   Activation, 19, 24, 27, 28, 50, 59–61, 125

Descriptive stereotypes, 17, 18, 186
Envious stereotypes, 22, 112
Implicit stereotypes, **23ff**, 96, 114, 120, 125, 134, 136
Malleability of implicit stereotypes, **27ff**, 37
Paternalistic stereotypes, 22, 112, 148
Prescriptive stereotypes, 17, 18, 44, 50, 65, 126, 150, 186, 238, 242
Gender subtypes, **21ff**, 152
Generosity, 182, 184, 218, 219
Glass ceiling, 147, 148, 165, 180, 224, 232
Glass escalator, 193
Goldberg paradigm, 120, 137
Group entitativity, 161
Group, group membership, 14, 15, 50, 60, 159, 193, 205, 225, 226, 231, 233, 237
Group of men, 167, 170, 177, 178, 232
Group salience, 204, 205, 226

H

Health, 1, 82, 102, 104, 212, 219
Heterosexual(s), 38, 56, 57, 64, 66, 67, 97, 99, 100, 104, 106, 146, 149, 153, 209, 242
Hierarchy, hierarchies, 34, 83, 89, 102, 114, 125
   Gender, 11, 99
   Occupational, 93
   Organizational, 2, 34, 180, 191
   Power, 6, 17
   Social, 44, 67, 78, **105ff**, 135, 153, 200
High-status group, 43, 56, 64, 158, 166–168, 170, 174, 176, 193, 206, 224
Hormone
   Female hormone, 184
   Male sex hormone, 185
Household, housework, 39, 74, 94, 98, 99, 100, 103, 104, 141, 146, 194, 238, 239
Housewife, Housewives, 68, 158, 165, 197, 238
Humanities, 36, 53, 119
Human rights, 196, 231

I

Identity, identification, 76, 116, 117, 129, 134, 141, 158, **165ff**, 183, 186, 187, 200, 218, 220, 226, 227, 230, 231, 233, 243
   Construction of identity, 167, 223
   Cultural, 231
   Feminist, 107, 168
   Group, 6, 158, 167, 186, 205, 218, 219
   Intersection(s), 6, 123
   Level of, 216
   Men, 97, 158, 167, 200, 201, 209
   Occupational, 186
   Organizational, **223ff**
   Professional, 186, 187
   Shared, 224, 226–228, 230, 231
   Women, 97, 167, **186ff**, 187, 209, 210
   Work, **186ff**
Ideology, 110, 129, 167, 194, 221
Illusory correlation(s), 16
Image, imagery, 29, 37, 107, 119, 121, 122, 151, 153, 158, 168, 187, 200, 218, 245
Impermeability: *See* Permeability
Implementation intention(s), 27, 28
Implicit association test, 25
Implicit measures, 23–25, 64, 95, 111
Impression formation, 35, 38, 39, 228
Income(s), 3, 6, 37, 48, 76, 81, 100–102, 114, 122, 133, 141, 146, 147, 153
Individual merit(s), 129, 171, 176, 237
Individual mobility, 165–167, 170–172, 174, 177
Individuating information, 15, 16, 39, 40, 44, 94, 150
Inequality, 1, 20, 65, 67, 68, 105–107, 110, 130, 166, 168, 188, 193–196, 206, 209, 212, 236, 244, 245
Informal network(s), 128, 150, 206, 207
In-group(s), 21, 64, 96, 129, 131, 132, 158, 159, 161, 166, 168, 169, 170, 175, 205–207, 216, 217, 221, 225–227, 236, 237
Integration, 4, 185, 221, 228, 231, 233, 244
Intergender, 196, **203ff**, 219, 220, 245

Intergroup attitudes, 64, 216–219, 221, 222, 243, 244
Intergroup behavior, 159
Intergroup communication, 156, 157, 159, 189, 213, 226, 233, 242, 243
Intergroup conflict, 105, 220
Intergroup contact, **215ff**, 244, 245
Intergroup differences, 161, 231
Intergroup friendship, 218, 222
Intergroup harmony, 189, 222
Intergroup hostility, 231
Intergroup interaction, 243
Intergroup problems, 231
Intergroup relation(ship), 64, 78, 105, 165, 170, 217, 220, 222, 244, 245
Intergroup strategies, 217
Interpersonal contact, 218, 244

J

Job
    Female-typed job, 37, 146
    Gender-typed job, 44, 138
    Job search, 23, **123ff**
    Job success, 80, 123, **124ff**, 206
    Male-typed job, 38, 40, 42
Justice, Injustice, 3, 100, 105, 106

L

Labyrinth(s), 148
Lack of fit model, 36, 38, 114, 138
Language(s), 8, 14, 18, 26, 31, 48, 54, 74, 150, 195, 196, 205, 236, 244
Leadership, 3, 24, 26, 29–30, 36, 37, 65, 72, 134, 135, 148–150, 151, 162, 170, 177, 180–183, 185, 192, 206, **215ff, 223ff,** 235, 236
    Leadership behavior, 181
    Leadership job, 109
    Leadership position, 2, 26, 28, 40, 50, 51, 109, 114, 136, 138, 144, 151, 193, 241

Leadership qualities, 17, 24, 75, 136
Leadership role, 41, 186, 187, 192, 242
Leadership style, 13, 34, 129
Legitimacy, 165, 168, 200
Lesbian(s), 6, 17, 22, 38, 106, 141, 146, 180
Liberal(s), liberal, 47, **191ff**, 228, 238
Likelihood to Sexually Harass (LHS), 198
Long hours, 33, 79, 151
Low-status group, 43, 64, 110, 158, 174, 193

M

Maintenance, 210, 211
Male group, 167, 169, 171, 176, 177, 184, 200, 201
Male schema. *See* Gender schema
Management, 2, 3, 20, 23, 24, 37, 40, 41, 80, 84, 98, 128–130, 139, 150, **165ff**, 183, 197, 198, 206, 207, 212, 213, 221, 224, 229, 231, 233
Masculinity, 38, 57, 103, 144, 173, 181, 200
Maternal wall, 138
Math, 13, 14, 25, 26, 31, 48, 54, 55, 59–61, 72, 74, 75, 82, 90, 103, 114–120, 134, 177, 238, 241
Medicine, 3, 6, 7, 37, 79, 80, 115, 133, 146
Melting pot, 219
Memory, 61, 72, 75
Mental rotation, 75
Mentor(s), 133, 206
Mentoring relationship, 206, 207
Merit(s), 124, 125, 129, 166, 169, 171, 174, 176, 237
Meritocracy, 106, 166, 171–174, 176, 180
Meta-analysis(es), 15, 35, 36, 38, 40, 46, 73, 75, 78, 82, 87, 88, 95, 125, 197, 216
Minority stress, 62
Mobility, 98, 99, 128, 150–152, 165–167, 170–172, 174, 177, 242
Motherhood, 38, 101, 143, 152, 237, 239
    Motherhood penalty, 138, 139, 141
    Working mothers, 94, 138, 140, 141, 238

Motivation, 3, 27, 50, 55, 58, 64, 76, 79, 110, 112, 117, 118, 120, 122, 139, 153, 159, 176, 185, 189, 204, 225, 226, 230–232, 237, 238
  Work motivation, 176
Myth(s), 13, 106, 109, 112, 198

N

Negative Consequences, 41, 67, 82, 89, 102, 120, 129, 131, 141, 144, 175, 215
Negotiation(s), negotiate, 43, 62, 72, 78, 89, 90, 116, 123, **125ff**, 147, 150, 152, 153, 209, 233
Networking, 79, 124, 125, 128, 148, 206
Neurobiological research, 184
Nontraditional women, 65, 112, 197
Nonverbal information, 88
Norm(s), 41, 54, 65, 115, 127, 161, 183, 188, 198, 216, 223, 225, 228, 229, 242, 244

O

Organization, 41, 80, 102, 107, 108, 141, 150–152, 171, 172, 175, 178, 181, 183, 186, 188, 192, 197, 198, 206–208, 212, 213, 220, **223ff**, 236–239, 244
  Organizational citizenship, 143, 144
  Organizational climate, 199
  Organizational commitment, 142, 151
  Organizational communication, 213
  Organizational context, 41, 167, 210, 219, 229
  Organizational cultures, **123ff**, 194, 198
  Organizational hierarchy, 2, 34, 162, 180, 191
  Organizational level, 98, 211
  Organizational management, 213
  Organizational programs, 156
  Organizational setting, 218
  Organizational structure, 151

Out-group(s), 16, 64, 96, 131, 132, 159, 161, 163, 166–170, 177, 188, 201, 205–207, 215–221, 225–227, 231, 243
Overprotection, overprotective, 208, 209, 228

P

Parenthood, parenting, 97, 100, **137ff**, 147, 242
  Parental leave, 89, 94, 137, 141–143
Paternalism, paternalistic, 22, 67, 112, 148, 151, 208, 209, 218, 231, 232, 242
Patron, patronizing, patronage, 43, 206, 208, 228
Perceptual speed, 72, 75
Performance, 23, 28, 35, 42, 44, 46–50, 54, 55, 58–62, 74, 75, 78, 81, 85, 93, 108, 120, 124, 125, 129, 130, 139, 142, 143, 148, 150, 152, 162, 176, 185, 187, 209, 212, 231, 232, 237, 242
Permeability, 165, 166, 168, 238
Personal identity, 158, 159, 225
Perspective of the other, **218ff**, 232
Persuasion, Persuasive, 33, 186, 226
Physics, 31, 55, 59, 62, 114–117, 119, 148, 211
Potency, 26
Power, 6, 26, 29, 31, 37, 66, 78, 90, 99, 105, 106, 109, 110, 112, 162, 192, **195ff**, 204, 208, 212, 215, 228, 230, 232, 243
  And sex, 198, 199
  Group in, 232
  Hierarchies, 6
  Position(s), 45, 78, 187, 216, 219
Powerful structural factors, 236
Precarious manhood, **55ff**, 102, 201
Prejudice, 14, 16, 27, 31, 35, 36, 64, 67, 138, 166, 173–177, 183, 192, 197, 216, 219, 221, 243
Priming, 25, 135
Professional career, 180, 237

INDEX

Professional development, 233
Professional role, 186
Professional women, 163, 171, 172, 174, 175, 177, 192, 201, 208, 211, 217, 223, 226, 227, 242, 244
Promotion, 24, 34, 38, 42, 48, 125, 127, 133, 139, 140–143, 150, 156, 169, 182, 184, 196, 208
Prototype, 119–122, 131, 135, 150, 160, **161ff**, 192, 229
Punishment(s), 4, 56, 169, 187, 196

Q

Quality of contact, 221
Quality of experiences, 221

R

Rape
   Myth(s), 198
   Proclivity, 198
Rationalization, 17, 111
Representation, Underrepresentation, 2, 3, 20, 67, 75, 86, 97, 106, 132, 134, 161, 174, 209, 225, 228, 232, 235
Risk aversion, 81, 83, 84, 179, 182, 183
Risk behavior, 185
Risk rejection, 187
Risk taking, risk propensity, 7, 14, **80ff**, 114, 122, 183, 184
Role
   Congruence, 192
   Gender role(s), 4, 11, 26, 35, 54, 58, 65, 66, 68, 75, 85, 86, 89, 90, **94ff**, 98, 101–103, 115, 121, 132, 133, 136, 138, 141–143, 146, 149, 183, 192, 197, 224, 242, 245
   Model, 29, 30, 61, 122, **133ff**, 150, 151, 245
   Social role(s), 5, 8, 20, 78, 80, 93, 94, 95, **96ff**, 104, 106, 136, 137, 141, 144, 146–148, 153, 183, 242, 245

S

Salience, salient, 16, 18, 53, **159ff**, 162, 174, 184, 205, 225, 226, 230
Schema. *See* Gender schema
Science(s), 2, 3, 8, 36, 45, 46, 53, 55, 72, 73, 79, 86, 89, 114, 115, 117–120, 134, 135, 145, 194, 211, 236, 238
Second shift, 97, 99, 104, 148
Segregation, desegregation, 59, 90, 173
Selection, 38, 42, 54, 118, 119, 124, 150, 151, 236, 244
Self-categorization theory, 131, 157
Self-concept(s), 54, 59, 61, 74, 77, 78, 104, 114–116, 120, 148, 158, 186, 225, 241
Self-confidence, 7, 175, 199
Self-definition, 87, 226
Self-disclosure, 67, 77, 217
Self-esteem, 57, 78, 143, 158, 160, 163, 169, 171, 172, 177, 180, 184, 186, 209, 210, 243, 244
Self-fulfilling prophecy, 77, 109, 187, 242
Self-promotion, 41, 42, 123, 152
Self-stereotype(s), 133, 136, 231
Self-uncertainty, 228
Sensation seeking, 185
Sense of belonging, 118, 168, 169, 170, 175
Sexism, 11, **65ff**, 129, 132, 208, 221
   Ambivalent sexism, 66–68
   Benevolent sexism, 43, 106, 110, 208, 209
   Hostile sexism, 67–69, 209
   Modern sexism, 46, 66, 67
   Old-fashioned sexism, 65, 66
Sexual harassment, 168, 194, **195ff**
Sexual innuendo, 206
Sexual orientation, 17, 39, 130
Sexy women, 197
Shared objectives, 216
Shifting standards, **47ff**, 139, 148
Social behavior, 93, 173, 182, 196
Social change, 110, 112, 133, 135, 165, 167, 168, 170, 171, 217, 229
Social competition, 165–167
Social context, 46, 98, 149, 155, 156

Social creativity, 165–167, 169, 170
Social desirability, 24, 63, 95, 112
Social distance, 205
Social dominance orientation, 107, 108, 111, 112, 148
Social dominance theory, 105–110, 112
Social harmony, 220, 230
Social hierarchies. *See* Hierarchies
Social identity, 6, 9, 96, 119, 131, 153, 156–159, 161, 165, 167, 168, 170, 171, 174, 186, 210, 211, 222–225, 227, 229, 231–233, 244, 245
Social identity leadership theory, 228
Social identity perspective, 9, 156, **157ff**, 167, 177, 188, 189, 199, 203, 227, 230, 242
Social interaction, 27, 155, 159, 196, 242
Socialization, 54, 73, 74, 76, 86, 89, 121, 185, 244
Social mobility, 165, 170
Social position, 171, 184
Social relation(s), 58, 96, 102, 118, 126, 160, 189, 227
Social role theory, 34, 78, **93ff**, 142
Social skill(s), 17, 35, 36, 41, 42, 73, 96, 118
Social status, 95, 168, 171, 193, 207, 211
Sociostructural factor(s), 100, 224
Spatial ability(ies), 75
Speech divergence, 205
Status of women, 66, 167, 178, 224
Status quo, 22, 109–112, 158, 167, 168, 178, 192, 194, 209, 213, 236
STEM fields, 55, 59, 61, 62, 72, 75, 113, **114ff**, 122, 133–135, 238
Stereotype, (in)consistent, 192, 193
Stereotype content model, 20, 22, 68, 91
Stereotype inoculation, 61
Stereotype threat, **58ff**, 74, 86, 88, 114, 117, 120, 125, 134, 148, 176, 186, 231, 241
Stereotype(s), **14ff**, **17ff**, 39, 48–51, 74, 90, 106, 109, 110, 112, 114, 118, 121, 123, 125, 131, 135, 142, 161, 162, 166, 172, 173, 175, 176, 177, 180, 181, 186, 188, 192, 193, 197, 207, 216, 217, 222, 238, 241–243

Stigma, stigmatized, 105, 165, 170, 175, 176, 177, 219, 232
Stress in the workplace, 212
Structural policy, 185
Subordinate(s), 4, 24, 37, 42, 44, 77, 78, 108, 181, 196, 197, 223
Subtyping, 217
Superordinate goal(s), 220, 221, 230
System justification theory, 109–112, 146

T

Think manager, think male, 37, 121, 180
Threat, 30, 57, 97, 108, 111, 112, 117, 177, 178, 186, 198, 200, 213, 215, 216, 220, 228, 230, 232. *See also* Stereotype threat
Token(s), 30, 109, 110, 112, 135, 173
Top positions, 30, 44, 73, 75, 83, 96, 100, 110, 112, 115, **147ff**, 224, 235, 237, 245
Traditionally male work, 160, 177, 224–226, 231
Transgression(s), 58

V

Value(s), 76, 77, 87, 89, 99, 107, 130, 147, 162, 166, 167, 169, 170, 171, 174, 176, 177, 184, 192, 215, 225, 228, 229, 231, 242, 243
Vanguards, 61, 136
Verbal ability/abilities, 7, 13, 72, 75, 120
Vitality, 178, 195, 219
Voice, 31, 36, 38, 39, 41, 89

W

Warmth, 17, 20–22, 25, 26, 31, 34, 44, 63, 68, 74, 87–89, 91, 93, 96, 107, 110, 112, 140, 150
Welfare of women, 184

Well-being, 100, 105, 167, 171, 175, 176, 178, 181, 215, 219, 228, 231, 244
White(s), 16, 18, 19, 22, 59, 105, 127, 129, 131, 144, 235
Who said what paradigm, 19
Women are wonderful effect, 63, 64
Women at work, 49, 108, **179ff**, 233, 244
Women leaders, Women leadership, 24, 44, 177, 180, 192, 194, 212, 213, 228–230, 233, 245
Women managers, 183, 211
Work flexibility, 97, 98
Work life balance, 97–99, 212
Workplace discrimination, 36, 215, 219

AUTHOR INDEX

A

Abele, A. E. 3, 72, 75, 76, 78, 79, 85, 88, 89, 100, 150, 152
Abrams, D. 157, 159
Abrams, J. R. 158
Agnoli, F. 120
Agthe, M. 49
Aguiar, F. 182
Aikin, K. J. 66
Akerlof, G. A. 229, 232
Alicke, M. A. 26
Allen, T. D. 137, 142
Allport, G. W. 15, 17, 216, 244, 245
Alter, A. L. 61
Altés-Tárrega, J. A. 199, 201
Amanatullah, E. T. 126, 127, 147, 150, 153
Ambady, N. 26, 55, 64, 88, 129
Amit, A. 131
Amo, R. 176
Anderson, M. C. 203
Andrade, C. 97
Andreoni, J. 182
Ansic, D. 7, 81, 83–85
Apfelbaum, E. P. 129
Apicella, C. L. 185
Appel, M. 61
Aranda, B. 141
Aron, A. 218
Aronson, J. 59, 61, 175, 176, 180
Asgari, S. 29, 30, 37, 134, 136
Ashburn-Nardo, L. 45
Ashmore, R. D. 20, 21
Ashton, M. C. 88
Asmundson, G. J. G. 88
Athenstaedt, U. 14
Atkinson, S. M. 183
Avery, D. R. 129

B

Babcock, L. 126
Bache, L. M. 61

Bailey-Werner, B. 66
Bakan, D. 20
Banaji, M. R. 17, 23–25, 28, 29, 64, 109
Bandura, A. 134
Bannister, K. A. 208, 209, 232
Barbato, R. 79
Bargh, J. A. 23, 39, 47, 199
Barnes-Farrell, J. 137
Barnett, S. M. 45
Baron, A. S. 136, 194
Baron, R. A. 40, 121, 136
Barreto, M. 166, 172, 174, 176, 184, 187, 208, 228, 237
Bartkiewicz, M. J. 2
Bathmann, N. 97–100, 151, 153
Baumert, J. 54
Baumgarten, P. 231
Bavishi, A. 36
Bear, J. B. 126
Becker, J. C. 68, 110, 168, 209
Beilock, S. L. 54
Bem, S. L. 159, 205
Benard, S. 40, 100, 138–140, 151
Benbow, C. P. 79, 87, 120
Benito, J. M. 182
Bennett-AbuAyyash, C. 168
Benschop, Y. 174, 175, 229
Ben-Zeev, T. 176
Berthold, A. 132
Best, D. L. 15
Bettencourt, B. A. 57, 170, 174
Betz, D. E. 135
Bhawe, N. M. 121
Bianchi, M. 132
Bielby, D. D. 46, 103, 124, 128, 146
Biernat, M. 36, 38, 47, 48, 140
Bijl, R. V. 62
Bird, S. R. 174, 205, 206, 208, 212
Blair, I. V. 27–29
Blanco, K. 26
Blass, F. R. 42
Blau, F. D. 2
Bless, H. 59
Blickle, G. 42, 133
Block, K. 136, 194

Bobko, P. 46
Bobo, L. 20
Bodenhausen, G. V. 28, 29
Bodi, O. 100
Boettcher, F. 131
Boggs, C. 156
Böhm, R. 35
Bolaños, J. L. 195
Bolen, L. M. 74
Bollier, T. 209
Bond, C. F. 78
Bonnot, V. 118
Bonvini, A. 140
Booth, A. L. 81, 86
Borgida, E. 36, 39
Bosak, J. 37, 95, 181, 212
Bosch-Doménech, A. 184
Bosson, J. K. 55, 57, 97
Boucher, K. L. 83
Boulouta, I. 229, 231–233
Bourhis, R. Y. 210, 220
Bowles, H. R. 128
Boyce Baird, S. 183
Brachinger, H. W. 85
Bradac, J. J. 225
Brañas-Garza, P. 183, 185
Brandt, M. J. 65
Branscombe, N. R. 166, 169, 171, 172, 175, 176, 194, 237
Brauer, M. 16, 131
Brekke, N. 39
Brescoll, V. L. 42, 46, 47, 138
Brewer, M. B. 39
Bridges, J. S. 137
Brisswalter, J. 185
Brooks, M. E. 45
Brown, B. L. 208
Brown, E. R. 109, 118, 135
Brown, M. 85
Brown, R. J. 216, 217
Brown, R. P. 61
Bruckmüller, S. 85, 147, 193, 194
Brunet, I. 181
Buchanan, N. T. 129
Buckner, C. E. 65

AUTHOR INDEX

Buettner, H. M. 134
Buffardi, L. E. 131
Bukowski, M. 175
Bundesministerium für Familie, Senioren, Frauen und Jugend 100
Burke, M. J. 38, 40
Burke, R. J. 231
Burnaford, R. M. 57
Burnette, J. L. 171, 192, 205, 217, 228
Butler, A. B. 143
Byrnes, J. P. 82

C

Cable, D. M. 108, 111
Cadinu, M. 59–61, 176, 199, 201
Callan, V. J. 166
Cameron, J. E. 232
Campbell, B. 185
Cantisano, G. T. 197
Cárdenas, M. C. 207
Carleton, R. N. 88
Carli, L. L. vii, 2, 87, 148, 171, 174, 207, 208, 211, 226
Carlstrom, A. H. 66
Carnes, M. 37
Carr, M. 114
Carranza, E. 18
Carter, N. M. 232, 237
Carton, A. M. 180
Castaño, C. 177, 194, 223
Catalyst 171, 180
Ceci, S. J. 3, 45, 72, 73, 75, 86, 101, 103, 115, 119–121, 181
Cejka, M. A. 93
Chalabaev, A. 185
Charlton, K. 170
Cheryan, S. 117, 119, 134, 135, 151
Chia, R. 74
CIA 238
Cialdini, R. B. 41–43
Cihangir, S. 172
Cikara, M. 187
Clark, E. K. 118

Clément, R. 180, 196
Clément-Guillotin, C. 185
Cleveland, J. N. 171, 206, 212, 229, 230, 237
Coates, L. 155, 193, 233
Coffeng, J. 138
Cogliser, C. C. 230
Cohen, D. 57
Cohen, G. L. 118, 124, 150
Cohen, L. L. 66
Cole, E. R. 6
Coleman, J. M. 143, 144
Collimore, K. C. 88
Collins, K. A. 180, 196
Cook, A. 180
Coombes, S. A. 185
Cooper, J. 187
Cordeiro, B. L. 143
Cornelißen, W. 97
Correll, J. 137
Correll, S. J. 40, 100, 138–140, 151
Cortina, L. M. 129, 196–198, 199
Cosmides, L. 18
Costea, B. 231, 232
Coupland, J. 196, 204, 207
Coupland, N. 155, 196, 203, 204, 207
Crandall, C. S. 60
Crawford, M. 168
Crisp, R. J. 61
Croft, A. 136, 194
Croizet, J.-C. 60
Crosby, F. J. 172, 186, 237
Croson, R. 182
Cross, S. E. 87
Cuddy, A. J. C. 20, 22, 36, 40, 138, 140
Cunningham, G. B. 129
Cvencek, D. 54, 120

D

Dahl, M. S. 98
Danaher, K. 171
Daniels, Z. 54
Dardenne, B. 209

Darley, J. M. 61
Dasgupta, N. 29, 30, 37, 61, 134
Davidson, M. J. 231
Davies, P. G. 59, 60, 117
Davis, K. M. 230
Davis, N. B. 74
Davis, S. 208
Davison, H. K. 38, 40
Dawson, E. 47
Deaux, K. 8, 9, 14, 20, 36, 39, 49, 53, 54, 65, 71, 73, 76, 77, 88, 90
de Gilder, D. 140
de Graaf, R. 62
De Houwer, J. 24
Del Boca, F. K. 20
de Lemus, S. 175, 209
DeMartino, R. 79, 121, 122
Depolo, M. 197
Derks, B. 128, 168, 172, 177, 184, 232
Desvaux, G. 231
DeVaro, J. 2
Devillard-Hoellinger, S. 231
Devine, P. G. 24
Devos, T. 26, 79, 97
De Vries, R. E. 88
Dezsö, C. L. 230
Dickens, M. P. 230
Diebold, J. 66
Diekman, A. B. 20, 93, 95, 109, 118, 135
Dikkers, J. S. E. 138
Diversity Inc. 231
Domenico, M. E. 184
Domínguez, J. F. M. 197
Dorr, N. 170
Douglas, K. 236
Dovidio, J. 180
Dovidio, J. F. 29, 47, 174, 180, 219, 220, 225, 226, 228, 230
Downey, G. 128
Dreber, A. 185
Driscoll, D. M. 131
Driver-Linn, E. 53
Drury, B. J. 134, 135
Duan, C. M. 18

Dumont, M. 209
Dunn, R. 26
Dunning, D. 39
Dunning, D. A. 26
Dweck, C. S. 192

E

Eagly, A. H. vii, 2–4, 14, 20, 36–38, 40, 43, 45, 46, 63, 64, 68, 87, 88, 93–95, 107, 127, 128, 148, 149, 171, 173, 174, 180, 183, 185, 187, 192, 193, 207, 208, 211, 226, 237
Easthope, C. 185
Eaton, A. 107
Ebert, I. D. 25, 27, 38, 64, 96
Eby, L. T. 124
Eccles, J. S. 54, 118, 120
Eckel, C. C. 80, 81, 84, 85, 183
Eckes, T. 17, 40, 66, 112
Ehrenberg, K. 19, 160
Ehrke, F. 129–132
Eisenberg, N. 87, 88
Ellemers, N. 128, 129, 140, 166–168, 170, 171–174, 176, 180, 181, 184, 187, 224, 226, 228, 232, 236, 237
Ellis, A. B. 54
Elsbach, K. D. 209
Emrich, C. 34
Emrich, C. G. 34
Endicott, N. F. 138, 141
England, P. 95
Erdley, C. A. 192
Ergun, S. 182
Er-rafiy, A. 16, 131
Espín, A. M. 185
Espinosa, M. P. 182
Esses, V. 180
Esses, V. M. 168
Esteban-Guitart, M. 184, 195
Etaugh, C. 100, 137, 138, 140
Evers, A. 3, 7, 79, 146, 147
Expósito, F. 209

F

Fairchild, K. 56, 58
Falomir-Pichastor, J. M. 57
Faludi, S. 168, 180
Fazio, R. H. 24
Federico, C. M. 237
Feldman, D. C. 124
Fernández, J. L. 23
Ferreira, M. C. 95
Ferris, G. R. 42
Field, S. C. T. 131
Figner, B. 81
Fingerhut, A. 99, 141, 146
Fischer, A. H. 232
Fiske, A. P. 18, 229
Fiske, S. T. 7, 18, 20, 36, 39, 66–68, 91, 181, 183, 187, 195, 228
Fitzgerald, L. P. 199
Folger, D. 100, 138, 140
Forbes, C. 59
Formanowicz 236
Foschi, M. 44, 47
Foss, K. A. 184
Foss, S. K. 184
Franiuk, R. 143, 144
Fransen, K. 226
Franzway, S. 181
Friedman, C. K. 54, 74
Friesen, J. 236
Frieze, I. H. 65, 66
Frigerio, S. 61
Frye, M. B. 183
Fuchs, D. 42
Fuegen, K. 36, 137, 138, 141

G

Gaertner, S. L. 219, 220, 225, 226, 230
Gal, D. 15, 57
Galinsky, A. 125
Galinsky, A. D. 22
Gallois, C. 166, 203–205, 227

Gallup Poll Survey 191
Garcia, D. M. 176
Garcia, J. 118
García-Izquierdo, M. 196
García-Muñoz, T. 182
Gardner, W. L. 230
Garnett, F. G. 131
Gartzia, L. 187
Gasiorek, J. 195, 196, 203–205, 207, 208, 210, 211, 217, 224, 227, 229, 231
Gaucher, D. 236
Geiser, C. 75
Gelfand, M. J. 126
Gerhardstein, R. 59
German Federal Office of Statistics 2, 94
Gerstenberg, F. X. R. 61
Gervais, S. 208
Gesn, P. R. 88
Gifford, R. K. 16
Gilbert, D. T. 29
Giles, H. 155, 156, 158, 159, 161, 167, 168, 170, 171, 180, 184, 193, 195, 196, 203–208, 210, 211, 217, 220, 224, 225, 227, 228, 231
Giles, J. 208
Gill, J. 181
Glaser, D. 80
Glass, B. 18
Glass, C. 180
Glick, P. 20, 25, 36, 39, 41, 42, 44, 58, 66–68, 90, 96, 141, 168, 180, 197, 209
Gneezy, U. 182
Goh, J. X. 53
Goldberg, P. A. 35
Gollwitzer, P. M. 17, 27, 28
Good, C. 61
Goodwin, S. A. 26, 64
Goren, M. J. 129
Götz, T. 60
Grace, A. D. 74, 87, 100
Grace, P. E. 209, 230
Graham, M. J. 46
Graham, P. W. 166

Grasselli, A. 199
Gray, P. B. 185
Green, D. P. 131
Greenwald, A. G. 23–26, 54
Gregor, A. 8
Gross, J. J. 118
Grossman, P. J. 80, 81, 84, 85, 183
Guadagno, R. E. 41–43
Guarnieri, G. 199
Gunderson, E. A. 54
Güngör, G. 38, 140
Gupta, V. K. 121
Gysler, M. 85

H

Haddock, G. 68, 159
Haines, E. 36
Hajek, C. 180, 208
Hall, C. W. 74
Hall, E. V. 22
Hall, J. A. 88
Hall, W. S. 66
Hallahan, M. 88
Halpern, D. F. 100
Hamilton, D. L. 16, 17
Handelsman, J. 46
Hanges, P. J. 45
Hannover, B. 55, 116, 117, 119
Hardin, C. D. 24
Harland, L. 151
Harris, C. R. 80, 82, 85
Hart, J. 209
Harwood, J. 155, 158, 159, 161, 210, 217, 219, 221
Haselhuhn, M. P. 89
Haslam, N. 18
Haslam, S. A. vii, 2, 130, 147, 166, 168, 180, 193, 223–232
Hatzenbuehler, M. L. 62
Hawthorne, L. 55
Haynes, E. L. 14
Hearns, K. A. 136
Heatherton, T. F. 60

Hebl, M. R. 36, 130
Hegarty, P. 6, 56, 85, 194
Heilman, M. E. 17, 18, 23, 27, 36–38, 41, 42, 44–46, 50, 124, 136–138, 140, 180, 187, 229, 237
Henwood, K. 204
Hepburn, C. 39
Heppen, J. B. 110
Hermsen, S. 29
Hernández, P. 182
Hettinger, V. E. 97
Hewstone, M. 180, 215–217
Heyder, A. 54
Hirigoyen, M. 156, 196, 197, 199, 201, 207
Hirsa, A. 40
Hixon, J. G. 29
Hodges, S. D. 55
Hoffman, C. 17, 20
Hoffman, M. 185
Hogg, M. 157
Hogg, M. A. 157, 159, 162, 175, 220, 225–228, 230
Holleran, S. E. 117
Holoien, D. S. 129
Hölzl, E. 34
Hoover, A. 208
Hornsey, M. J. 220, 230
Horstman Reser, A. 176
Hoyt, C. 192
Hoyt, C. L. 2, 167, 171, 180, 192, 205, 217, 228
Huffman, M. L. 136
Huguet, P. 59
Hume, D. L. 170
Hummert, M. L. 208
Hunsinger, M. 61
Hunter, B. A. 66
Huntsinger, J. R. 177
Hunyady, O. 109, 146
Hurst, N. 17, 20
Hutchinson, K. J. 225
Hyde, J. S. 54, 73–75
Hyrsky, K. 7, 80, 85, 86, 121, 122

I

Ibañez, M. 196, 197, 199
Ickes, W. 88
Idescat 238
I+DTinfo 239
Imhoff, R. 61
Impagliazzo, L. 61
Inesi, M. E. 108, 111
Inzlicht, M. 61, 62, 176
Isaac, C. 37, 38, 150, 152
Issa, M. 186

J

Jackson, L. M. 168
Jacobs, J. E. 54
Jacobson, C. 37
Jacques, P. H. 79
Jelenec, P. 26, 54, 60
Jenkins, M. 80
Jetten, J. 169, 171, 226
John, M. S. 228
Johns, M. 59, 61
Johnson, J. E. V. 7, 80, 82–86, 127, 183
Johnson, T. 155, 193, 233
Johnston, A. M. 118
Jonas, K. J. 131
Jones, E. L. 166
Jost, J. T. 17, 109–111, 118, 146, 209
Joy, L. 232
Joyce, N. 217, 219
Judd, C. M. 38

K

Kabat-Farr, D. 196–199
Kahn, L. M. 2
Kaiser, C. R. 176
Kalbfleisch, P. 168
Kallen, R. W. 167
Kang, S. K. 61, 62
Kanter, R. 160
Karau, S. J. 4, 36–38, 40, 43, 45, 127, 128, 173, 183, 187, 192, 193
Kardes, F. R. 24
Karraker, K. H. 73
Karyn, L. L. 55
Kasof, J. 35
Katz, D. 14
Katz, I. 59
Kaufman, E. K. 209, 230
Kawakami, K. 29
Kay, A. C. 109, 110, 236
Keller, J. 59, 60
Kellerman, B. 170, 171, 212
Kelley, W. M. 60
Kennedy, J. A. 89, 90
Kenny, S. 120
Kessels, U. 54, 55, 116, 117, 119
Kessler, T. 132
Kiefer, A. K. 55
Kiesner, J. 59
Kilianski, S. E. 25, 26, 192
Kim, S. 134
King, E. B. 79, 98, 130, 139
Kinney, T. A. 196
Kirchler, E. 34
Kite, M. E. 14, 17, 21, 66, 149
Klandermans, B. 168
Klauer, K. C. 19, 160
Kleist, J. S. 43
Kling, K. C. 75
Ko, S. J. 38
Kobrynowicz, D. 47, 48, 171
Koenig, A. M. 88
Köller, O. 54
Krause, J. 38
Kray, L. J. 43, 89, 90, 125, 126
Krendl, A. C. 60
Kronberger, N. 61
Kroth, A. 27
Krueger, J. I. 26
Kuenzler, J. 94
Kulich, C. 2, 180
Kunda, Z. 36, 39, 40
Kunstman, J. W. 204
Kurzban, R. 18

L

LaFrance, M. 20
Lakoff, R. 187
Lalonde, R. N. 232
Landrine, H. 22
Landy, F. J. 44, 45
Lane, D. M. 34
Lane, K. A. 53
Latinotti, S. 61
LaVite, M. 198
Lawrence, M. A. 64
Leaper, C. 54, 74
Lee, B. 37
Lee, K. 88
Lehmann, W. 75
Lemieux, A. F. 6, 56
Lennon, R. 87, 88
Lenton, A. P. 29
Le Poire, B. A. 203, 205
Levin, S. 215, 237
Levine, S. C. 54
Lewis, L. L. 14, 39
Lezaún, Z. 196
Lindberg, S. M. 54
Linn, M. C. 54
Lips, H. M. 2, 118, 146
Liss, M. 168
Little, A. 185
Livingston, R. W. 180
Locke, C. C. 43
Locksley, A. 39
London, B. 128
Loo, K. J. 83
Lord, C. G. 61
Lubinski, D. 120
Lubinski, D. S. 79, 87
Luecke, B. 132
Lummer, M. 35
Lupiáñez, J. 175
Lynch, L. 18
Lyness, K. S. 127, 128, 133, 150
Lytton, H. 73

M

Ma, J. E. 29
Ma, R. 186
Maass, A. 59–61, 140, 199–201
Machunsky, M. 132
Macke, A. S. 160
Macrae, C. N. 28
Madera, J. M. 36, 130, 173
Madson, L. 87
Maio, G. R. 159
Maitner, A. T. 61
Major, B. 49, 53, 73, 76, 77, 175, 204, 232
Malle, B. F. 105
Maner, J. K. 49
Manstead, A. S. R. 159
Manuel, T. 206
Markman, G. D. 40
Marsh, H. W. 54
Martell, R. F. 34, 47, 83, 125, 128, 150
Martens, A. 61
Martins, L. L. 129
Martiny, S. E. 60
Maruyama, G. 36
Marx, D. M. 61, 134
Matsa, D. A. 236
Matsumoto, D. 88
Maynard, D. C. 45
McGarty, C. 225
McGhee, D. E. 26
McHugh, M. C. 65, 66, 107
McIlwee, J. 181
McIntyre, R. B. 61, 134
McKay, P. F. 129
McKimmie, B. M. 169
McLean, M. C. 134
McManus, M. A. 61
McWueen, G. 6
Mehl, B. 26, 36, 45
Mehl, M. R. 117
Meier-Pesti, K. 183
Meiser, T. 132
Melikian, L. H. 15

Meltzoff, A. N. 54
Mescher, K. 143, 144
Meseguer, M. 196
Messner, M. 57
Meyer, I. H. 62
Mikula, G. 97–100
Miller, A. R. 236
Miller, C. T. 176
Miller, D. C. 82
Miller, L. 182
Mills, J. E. 181
Milne, A. B. 28
Miner, K. N. 129
Mishra, S. 80, 81, 84
Mitchell, G. 45
Mladinic, A. 14, 63, 68, 95
Mölders, C. 37, 41, 79, 100, 128, 129
Molix, L. 60
Moll, J. 29
Moors, A. 24
Moreschi, R. W. 81, 83
Morin, A. L. 61
Morris, M. A. 129
Morris, M. W. 126
Morrison, K. R. 131
Morton, T. A. 223, 224, 226, 227
Moser, S. B. 151
Moss, C. 137
Moss-Racusin, C. A. 42, 46, 120
Moya, M. 175, 209
Mueller, R. 37
Mugny, G. 57
Mulac, A. 225, 236
Müller, D. 97
Mulligan-Ferry, L. 2
Mummendey, A. 131, 132
Muñoz, K. 226
Murphy, K. R. 171, 206, 229, 237
Murphy, M. C. 118
Murray, T. L. 45
Muzzatti, B. 120
Myers, D. G. 36

N

Nadal, J. M. 195
Narayanan, S. 232
Naredo, M. 201
National Science Foundation 114
Nauts, S. 42
Neely, J. H. 25
Neff, D. 37
Nelson, C. 39
Nelson, T. D. 180
Neuberg, S. L. 39
Neumann, D. L. 7, 75
Newcombe, N. S. 75, 86
Newport, F. 94
Ng, T. W. H. 124
Niederle, M. 182, 183
Niedlich, C. 38
Nielsen, J. 98
Nisbett, R. E. 24
Noack, P. 54
Noftle, E. E. 75
Nolen, P. 81, 86
Nolen-Hoeksema, S. 78, 87
Nosek, B. A. 25, 26, 64, 109, 117, 120
Nussbaum, J. F. 211

O

Oakes, P. 157
O'Brien, L. T. 60
Ogay, T. 196, 203
Okimoto, T. G. 36, 45, 137, 138, 180, 229
O'Leary, B. J. 45
Olson, J. M. 14
Olza, J. 201
Oñate, A. 196
Operario, D. 187
Ostrom, T. M. 16
Otto, S. 63
Owen, S. 171

P

Padgett, M. 151
Paik, I. 40
Palacios, M. S. 172
Palomares, N. A. 159, 160, 224, 225
Paluck, E. L. 131
Paolucci, M. P. 218
Parapar, C. 238
Park, B. 137, 143
Parks, J. M. 43
Parks-Stamm, E. J. 18, 37, 38, 41, 42, 44, 50, 124, 136, 140
Parsons, C. K. 129
Pauker, K. 129
Paulsen, N. 166
Paulson, R. M. 61
PayScale 191
Pearce, J. A., II 201
Pendry, L. F. 131
Penz, E. 183
Peplau, L. A. 99, 141, 146
Pernas, B. 201
Perrewé, P. L. 42
Peters, K. 147, 193, 223
Pettigrew, T. F. 215, 216, 218, 222, 232
Petty, R. E. 175
Pfister, G. 94
Phelan, J. E. 42, 135
Pierce, L. 98, 101, 102
Pinel, E. C. 61
Piñuel, I. 196
Platow, M. J. 130, 223, 226
Plaut, V. C. 117, 119, 129, 131
Plewe, I. 64
Poehlman, T. A. 24
Popovich, P. M. 199, 201, 206, 208
Popp, D. 168
Pörhölä, M. 196
Postmes, T. 171, 172, 175, 224, 226
Powell, M. 7, 81, 83–85
Powell, M. C. 24
Powell, P. L. 7, 80, 82–86, 127, 183

Pratto, F. 5, 6, 17, 20, 39, 47, 56, 76, 87, 105–107, 109, 194
Prentice, D. A. 18
Prewitt-Freilino, J. L. 57
Pronin, E. 186
Prothro, E. T. 15
Pryor, J. 197–199
Pryor, J. B. 198
Pull, K. 141
Purvis, K. L. 46

Q

Quaiser-Pohl, C. 75, 97, 99
Quinn, D. 59
Quinn, D. M. 59, 167
Quinton, W. J. 175, 180

R

Radel, R. 185
Rai, T. S. 229
Rakić, T. 19
Ramirez, G. 54
Rattan, A. 128
Rau, M. 55
Raymond, P. 199
Redersdoff, S. 176
Reese, G. 131, 132
Regner, I. 59
Reichart, E. 94
Reicher, S. D. 157, 223, 226
Reichle, B. 97, 99
Reid, S. A. 155, 158, 161, 210
Reilly, D. 7, 75
Reinhard, M.-A. 57
Renfro, C. L. 167
Renneboog, L. D. R. 2, 180
Reskin, B. F. 46, 103, 124, 128, 145
Rey-Biel, P. 182
Reynolds, K. J. 223, 226
Rhoads, S. E. 100

Rhode, D. L. 170, 171, 206, 212
Rhoton, L. A. 174, 208, 212
Richard, F. D. 78, 88
Richeson, J. A. 26, 60, 64
Rico, F. 26
Riederer, B. 100
Riger, S. 107
Riggs, J. M. 140, 141
Rink, F. 128, 172
Rivas, M. F. 182
Roberts, T. A. 78, 87
Robins, R. W. 75
Robinson, G. 181
Robinson, R. B. 201
Robison-Cox, J. 34
Roccas, S. 131
Rodler, C. 34
Rodriguez, C. 61
Rodríguez Soler, J. 181
Roman, J. S. 61, 134
Román, M. 201
Romero-Canyas, R. 128
Romney, D. M. 73
Ropp, S. A. 172
Rosabianca, A. 59
Rose, S. M. 107
Rosenthal, R. 88
Rosette, A. S. 40, 44, 180
Ross, D. G. 230
Ross, L. 186
Roth, J. 60
Roth, L. M. 180, 206
Roth, P. L. 46, 48
Rothman, A. J. 24
Ruble, D. N. 61
Rudman, L. A. 25, 26, 36, 41–44, 56, 58, 64, 90, 96, 110, 111, 134, 135, 143, 144, 168, 192, 197, 209
Rudolph, U. 35
Ruíz, M. 238
Rush, M. C. 137
Russell, J. E. A. 137, 142
Russin, A. 29

Rustichini, A. 182
Ryan, A. M. 45
Ryan, E. B. 208, 209, 232
Ryan, M. 2, 180
Ryan, M. K. vii, 128, 147, 172, 193, 232
Rydell, R. J. 83, 86

S

Sabattini, L. 186
Sachdev, I. 210, 220
Sáez, Mª C. 196
Sanbonmatsu, D. M. 24
Sanchez-Burks, J. 131
Sanchis, J. A. 182
Sandberg, S. viii
Sandfort, T. G. M. 62
Sanna, L. J. 49, 91
Sawyer, P. 204
Schaal, B. 17, 27, 28
Schafer, W. D. 82
Scheepers, D. 184
Schein, V. E. 37, 121, 167
Schippers, M. C. 233
Schmader, T. 59, 61, 117, 136, 175, 180, 194
Schmerling, A. 2, 37
Schmitt, M. 61
Schmitt, M. T. 166, 167, 169, 171, 172, 175, 176, 237
Schnabel, K. 54
Schnabel, P. 62
Schneeweis, N. 114–116, 145
Schneider, D. J. 15
Schneider, P. B. 42
Schubert, R. 85
Schubert, T. 132
Schult, J. C. 25
Schyns, B. 37
Sczesny, S. 28, 37, 38, 79, 95, 180, 181, 183, 193, 212, 236
Sechrist, G. B. 28, 218
Sedikides, C. 16

Sekaquaptewa, D. 55, 60, 135
Serrano, M. 196
Settke, E. 38
Settles, I. H. 129
Sharp, R. 181
Shefte, S. 206
Shelton, B. A. 94
Shelton, J. N. 129
Shepard, C. A. 203, 205
Sherman, D. A. 39
Sherman, J. W. 17
Shields, S. A. 6
Showail, S. 43
Sidanius, J. 5, 17, 20, 73, 78, 105–107, 215, 237
Siddiqi, J. 97
Siers, B. 5
Sieverding, M. 3, 7, 78, 79, 127, 146, 147
Silva, C. 237
Simon, B. 168
Simon, S. 192
Sinclair, S. 177
Singh, A. 2
Six-Materna, I. 66
Siy, J. O. 134
Skattebo, A. 143
Skowronski, J. J. 64
Smith, F. L. 43, 142, 144, 147
Smith, J. A. 137
Smith, J. L. 55
Smith, P. 205
Snyder, M. 208
Soares, R. 2
Solberg, V. S. H. 66
Soler, Mª I. 196
Soliz, J. 217
Sommers, S. R. 129
Sorensen, K. L. 124
Spears, R. 159, 171
Spelke, E. S. 74, 87, 100
Spence, J. T. 65
Spencer, S. J. 59, 61, 167, 175, 180
Spoor, J. R. 171
Spörrle, M. 49

Spruyt, A. 24
Spurk, D. 100, 152
Stahlberg, D. 28, 38, 57
Stallworth, L. M. 5, 105
Stangor, C. 18, 19, 28
Stapel, D. A. 38
Steele, C. M. 59, 61, 117, 118, 175–177, 180, 186
Steele, J. R. 55
Steffen, V. J. 20, 93–95
Steffens, M. C. 8, 25–27, 36, 38, 42, 44, 45, 54, 60, 64, 74, 120, 129–132
Steffens, N. K. 226
Steinberg, M. 118
Stephan, C. W. 167, 177, 215
Stephan, W. G. 167, 177, 215
Stephen, D. R. 226
Stern, M. 73
Stevens, F. G. 131
Stockdale, M. 171, 206, 229, 237
Stockdale, M. S. 172
Stokes, A. 186
Stokes-Zoota, J. J. 78
Stoller, L. M. 198
Stotland, E. 14
Stout, J. G. 61, 134
Strack, F. 199
Stroebe, K. 172, 228
Sutton, R. M. 236
Swim, J. 36, 124
Swim, J. K. 15, 49, 66, 68, 91
Swiss, D. J. 206

T

Taasoobshirazi, G. 114
Tabak, F. 43
Tajfel, H. 155, 157, 159, 161, 165, 169, 225
Talley, A. E. 57
Tamkins, M. M. 42
Taylor, C. A. 61
Taylor, J. N. 57

Taylor, S. E. 228
Teige-Mocigemba, S. 24
Tetlock, P. E. 45
Thagard, P. 36, 39, 40
Thakerar, J. N. 208
Thomas, K. M. 129
Thompson, D. E. 127, 128, 133, 150
Thompson, L. 125
Thompson, M. 60
Tomás, G. 196
Tooby, J. 18
Torres, J. B. 66
Tost, L. P. 44
Trojanowski, G. 2, 180
Tropp, L. R. 177, 215–218, 221, 222, 232
Turban, D. B. 121
Turillo, C. J. 45
Turner, J. C. 157, 161, 168, 225
Turner, R. N. 215, 216
Tuunanen, M. 7, 80, 85, 86, 121, 122
Twenge, J. M. 79, 95
Tyson, D. 128

U

Uhlmann, E. L. 24, 42, 47, 124, 138, 150
Unger, R. K. 7
United Nations Development Program Human Development Report 1
U.S. Department of Education 1
U.S. Department of Labor 2

V

Valian, V. vii, 35, 118, 124
Vandello, J. A. 55, 57, 97, 143, 144
van den Heuvel, H. 140
van Engen, M. 187
van Engen, M. L. 138
van Kamp, S. 29
van Knippenberg, D. 130, 233
van Laar, C. 166, 168, 171, 173, 174, 176, 177, 180, 215, 232, 237
van Quaquebeke, N. 2, 37, 41, 79, 100, 128, 129
van Vianen, A. E. M. 232
Van Zant, A. B. 43
Verkuyten, M. 131
Verloo, M. 174, 175, 229
Vescio, T. K. 208, 209, 218
Vesterlund, L. 182
Vichayapai, M. 134, 135
Viladot, M. À. 9, 168, 170, 184, 195, 208, 228
Vinkenburg, C. J. 138
Voci, A. 215
Vogt, A.-C. 141
von Hippel, C. V. 186
Vonk, R. 21
Vonofakou, C. 215

W

Wagner, H. M. 232
Waldzus, S. 131, 132
Wallen, A. S. 42
Walter, W. 94
Wang, M. T. 120
Warren, M. A. 199, 201, 206, 208
Washington, E. F. 180
Wayne, J. H. 143
Weatherall, A. 166, 205
Weaver, J. R. 57
Weber, E. U. 81
Weber, U. 131, 132
Webster, J. 177, 194, 223
Wegener, I. 19, 160
Wennerås, C. 45
Wenzel, M. 131, 132
Wessel, J. L. 45
Wetherell, M. 157
Wharton, A. S. 20
Wheeler, S. C. 175
Whitehead, J. 117

Whitley, B. E., Jr. 17
Wiemann, J. 155, 203
Wiemann, M. 196
Wiese, B. S. 150
Wilde, A. 95
Wilkie, J. 15, 57
Willemyns, M. 203
Williams, A. 156, 158, 167, 168, 171, 180, 193, 206, 208, 211
Williams, C. C. 54
Williams, C. L. 193
Williams, J. C. 206
Williams, J. E. 15
Williams, R. J. 229
Williams, W. M. 3, 45, 72, 181
Williams, Z. 238
Willingham, J. 226
Wilson, T. D. 24
Winkleman, I. 2
Wold, A. 45
Wood, W. 3, 93, 185
Word, C. O. 187
Wright, R. G. 223, 226, 231
Wright, S. C. 110, 166, 168, 209, 218, 231

X

Xu, J. 20

Y

Yang, J. 226
Ybarra, O. 131
Yestrumskas, A. H. 182, 183
Yeung, A. S. 54
Young, D. M. 134
Ytsma, J. 208
Yzerbyt, V. 132

Z

Zanna, M. P. 14, 68, 187
Zhu, L. 66
Ziegert, J. C. 45
Zion, C. 39
Zuckerman, M. 185
Zwang-Weissman, Y. 208
Zweimüller, M. 114–116, 145

Howard Giles
GENERAL EDITOR

This series explores new and exciting advances in the ways in which language both reflects and fashions social reality—and thereby constitutes critical means of social action. As well as these being central foci in face-to-face interactions across different cultures, they also assume significance in the ways that language functions in the mass media, new technologies, organizations, and social institutions. Language as Social Action does not uphold apartheid against any particular methodological and/or ideological position, but, rather, promotes (wherever possible) cross-fertilization of ideas and empirical data across the many, all-too-contrastive, social scientific approaches to language and communication. Contributors to the series will also accord due attention to the historical, political, and economic forces that contextually bound the ways in which language patterns are analyzed, produced, and received. The series will also provide an important platform for theory-driven works that have profound, and often times provocative, implications for social policy.

For further information about the series and submitting manuscripts, please contact:

>   Howard Giles
>   Department of Communication
>   University of California at Santa Barbara
>   Santa Barbara, CA 93106-4020
>   HowieGiles@cox.net

To order other books in this series, please contact our Customer Service Department at:

>   (800) 770-LANG (within the U.S.)
>   (212) 647-7706 (outside the U.S.)
>   (212) 647-7707 FAX

Or browse online by series at:

>   www.peterlang.com